The Author

Arthur W. Pink was born in Nottingham, England, and died in Stornway, Scotland, in 1952. His widespread ministry included pastorates in Australia and the United States. He originated *Studies in the Scriptures,* a monthly magazine concerned solely with the exposition of Scripture.

Mr. Pink's view of the Scriptures, of doctrine, and of Christian practice was not the view of the twentieth century, nor even of many of his contemporary evangelicals. Few men have traveled so widely and yet remained so uninfluenced by prevailing opinions and accepted customs. Independent Bible study convinced him that much of modern evangelism was defective at its very foundations; when Puritan and Reformed books were being thrown out, he advanced the majority of their principles with untiring zeal. He was, in some ways, a Puritan born out of time.

Events have justified his outlook. Two world wars have substantiated his view on human depravity; the progressive decline of his nation (Britain) was to him the inevitable consequence of the prevalence of a gospel which is able neither to wound nor heal.

Familiar with the whole range of revelation, Mr. Pink could divide the truth with due weight, emphasis, and proportion. He is rarely sidetracked from the great themes of Scripture—grace, justification, and sanctification. One looks in vain for any quaint theories on prophecy and kindred subjects. The works of God the Father, the Son, and the Holy Spirit receive their true emphasis. There is balanced presentation of Christian graces. Mr. Pink rivals the Puritans in his ability to distinguish true conversion experience, detect false peace, and give consolation and exhortation to meet the believer's needs.

GLEANINGS
in
GENESIS

GLEANINGS
in
GENESIS

By
ARTHUR W. PINK

MOODY PRESS · CHICAGO

ISBN: 0-8024-2968-8

Fourteenth Printing, 1978

Printed in the United States of America

CONTENTS

INTRODUCTION

Appropriately has Genesis been termed "the seed plot of the Bible," for in it we have, in germ form, almost all of the great doctrines which are afterwards fully developed in the books of Scripture which follow.

In Genesis *God is revealed* as the Creator-God, as the Covenant-God, as the Almighty-God, as well as "the Most High, Possessor of heaven and earth."

In Genesis we have the first hint of *the Blessed Trinity*, of a plurality of Persons in the Godhead—"Let *us* make man in *our* image" (1:26).

In Genesis *man* is exhibited. First as the creature of God's hands, then as a fallen and sinful being, and later as one who is brought back to God, finding grace in His sight (6:8), walking with God (6:9), made "the friend of God" (James 2:23).

In Genesis the *wiles of Satan* are exposed. We "are not ignorant of his devices," for here the Holy Spirit has fully uncovered them. The realm in which the arch-enemy works is not the moral but the spiritual. He calls into question the Word of God, casts doubt on its integrity, denies its veracity.

In Genesis the truth of *sovereign election* is first exhibited. God singles out Abraham from an idolatrous people, and makes him the father of the chosen Nation. God passes by Ishmael and calls Isaac.

In Genesis the truth of *salvation* is typically displayed. Our fallen first parents are clothed by God Himself, clothed with skins: to procure those skins death had to come in, blood must be shed, the innocent was slain in the stead of the guilty. Only *thus* could man's shame be covered, and only *thus* could the sinner be fitted to stand before the thrice holy God.

In Genesis the truth of *justification by faith* is first made known: "And he believed in the Lord; and He counted it to him for righteousness" (15:6). Abraham believed God: not Abraham obeyed God, or loved God, or served God; but Abraham *believed* God. And it was counted unto him for (not instead of, but *unto*) righteousness. Then, if righteousness was "counted" unto Abraham, he had *none of his own.* Believing God, righteousness was reckoned to Abraham's account.

In Genesis *the believer's security* is strikingly illustrated. The flood of Divine judgment descends on the earth, and swallows up all its guilty inhabitants. But Noah, who had found grace in the eyes of the Lord, was safely preserved in the ark, into which God had shut him.

In Genesis the truth of *separation* is clearly inculcated. Enoch's lot was cast in days wherein evil abounded, but he lived apart from the world, walking with God. Abraham was called upon to separate himself from idolatrous Chaldea, and to step out upon the promises of God. Lot is held up before us as a solemn example of the direful consequences of being unequally yoked with unbelievers, and of having fellowship with the unfruitful works of darkness.

In Genesis God's *disciplinary chastisements* upon an erring believer are portrayed. Jacob is the standing example of what happens to a child of God who walks after the flesh, instead of after the spirit. But in the end we are shown how Divine grace triumphs over human frailty.

In Genesis we are shown the importance and value of *prayer.* Abraham prayed unto God and Abimelech's life was spared (20:17). Abraham's servant cries to the Lord that God would prosper his efforts to secure a wife for Isaac, and God answered his petition (chap. 24). Jacob, too, prays, and God hearkened.

In Genesis *the saint's rapture to heaven* is vividly portrayed. Enoch, the man who walked with God, "was not," for God had translated him. He did not pass through the portals of death. He was suddenly removed from these scenes of sin and suffering and transported into the realm of glory without seeing death.

In Genesis the *divine incarnation* is first declared. The Coming One was to be supernaturally begotten. He was to enter this world as none other ever did. He was to be the Son of Man, and yet have no human father. The One who should bruise the serpent's head was to be the *woman's* "Seed."

In Genesis the *death and resurrection* of the Saviour are strikingly foreshadowed. The ark, in which were preserved Noah and his family, were brought safely through the deluge of death on to the new earth. Isaac, the beloved son of Abraham, at the bidding of his father, is laid, unresistingly, on the altar, and from it Abraham "received him back as in a figure from the dead."

In Genesis we also learn of the *Saviour's coming exaltation.* This is strikingly typified in the history of Joseph—the most complete of all the personal types of Christ—who, after a period of humiliation and suffering was exalted to be the governor over all Egypt. Jacob, too, on his deathbed, also declares of Shiloh that "unto him shall the gathering of the peoples be" (49:10).

In Genesis the *priesthood* of Christ is anticipated. The Lord Jesus is a Priest not of the Aaronic system, but "after the order of Melchzedek." And it is in Genesis that this mysterious character, who received tithes from and blessed Abraham, is brought before our view.

In Genesis the coming *Antichrist* is announced, announced as "the seed of the serpent" (3:15). He is seen, too, foreshadowed in the person and history of Nimrod, the rebel against the Lord, the man who headed the first great federation in open opposition to the Most High.

In Genesis we first read of God *giving Palestine* to Abraham and to his seed: "And the Lord appeared unto Abraham, and said, Unto thy seed will I give this land" (12:7). And again, "For all the land which thou seest, to thee will I give it, and to thy seed forever" (13:15).

In Genesis *the wondrous future of Israel* is made known. "And I will make thy seed as the dust of the earth: so that if a man can number the dust of the earth, then shall thy seed also be numbered" (13:16). "And in thy seed shall all the nations of the earth be blessed" (22:18).

In Genesis the *judgment of God on the wicked* is solemnly exhibited. Cain confesses his punishment is greater than he can bear. The flood comes on the world of the ungodly and sweeps them all away. Fire and brimstone descend on Sodom and Gomorrah, till naught but their ashes remain. Lot's wife, for one act of disobedience, is turned into a pillar of salt.

What a marvelous proof is all this of the Divine Authorship! Who but the One who knows the end from the beginning, could have embodied, in germ form, what is afterwards expanded and amplified in the rest of the Bible? What unequivocal demonstration that there was One superintending *mind,* directing the pens of all who wrote the later books of Holy Scripture! May the blessing of God rest upon us as we seek to enjoy some of the inexhaustible riches of this book of beginnings.

ARTHUR W. PINK.

Swengel, Pa.

1. CREATION AND RESTORATION

Genesis 1

The manner in which the Holy Scriptures open is worthy of their Divine Author. "In the beginning God created the heaven and the earth," and that is *all* that is here recorded concerning the original creation. Nothing is said which enables us to fix the date of their creation; nothing is revealed concerning their appearance or inhabitants; nothing is told us about the modus operandi of their Divine Architect. We do not know whether the primitive heaven and earth were created a few thousands, or many millions of years ago. We are not informed as to whether they were called into existence in a moment of time, or whether the process of their formation covered an interval of long ages. The bare fact is stated: "In the beginning God created," and nothing is added to gratify the curious. The opening sentence of Holy Writ is not to be philosophized about, but is presented as a statement of truth to be received with unquestioning faith.

"In the beginning God created." No argument is entered into to *prove* the existence of God: instead, His existence is affirmed as a fact to be believed. And yet, sufficient is expressed in this one brief sentence to expose every fallacy which man has invented concerning the Deity. This opening sentence of the Bible repudiates *atheism,* for it postulates the *existence* of God. It refutes *materialism,* for it *distinguishes between* God and His material creation. It abolishes *pantheism,* for it predicates that which necessitates a *personal* God. *"In the beginning* God created," tells us that He was Himself *before* the beginning, and hence, Eternal. "In the beginning God *created,"* and that informs us He is a *personal being,* for an abstraction, an impersonal "first cause," could not create. "In the beginning God created *the heaven and the earth,"* and that argues He is *infinite* and *omnipotent,* for no finite being possesses the power to "create," and none but an Omnipotent Being could create "the heaven and the earth."

"In the beginning God." *This is the foundation truth of all real theology.* God is the great Originator and Initiator. It is the ignoring of this which is the basic error in all human schemes. False systems of theology and philosophy begin with man, and seek to work up to God. But this is a turning of things upside down. We must, in all our thinking, begin with God, and work down to man. Again, this is true of *the Divine inspiration of the Scriptures.* The Bible is couched in human language, it is addressed to human ears, it was written by human hands, but, in the beginning *God*—"holy men of God spake, moved by the Holy Spirit" (2 Pet. 1:21). This is also true of *salvation.* In Eden, Adam sinned, and brought in death; but his Maker was not taken by surprise: in the beginning God had provided for just such an emergency, for, "the Lamb" was "foreordained before the foundation of the world" (1 Pet. 1:20). This is also true of *the new creation.* The soul that is saved, repents, believes, and serves the Lord; but, in the beginning, God chose us in Christ (Eph. 1:4), and now, "we love Him, because He *first* loved us."

"In the beginning God created the heaven and the earth," and we cannot but believe that these creations were worthy of Himself, that they reflected the perfections of their Maker, that they were exceedingly fair in their pristine beauty. Certainly, the earth, on the morning of its creation, must have been vastly different from its chaotic state as described in Genesis 1:2. "And the earth was *without form and void*" must refer to a condition of the earth much later than what is before us in the preceding verse. It is now over a hundred years ago since Dr. Chalmers called attention to the fact that the word "was" in Genesis 1:2 should be translated "became," and that between the first two verses of Genesis 1 some terrible catastrophe must have intervened. That this catastrophe may have been connected with the apostasy of Satan, seems more than likely; that some catastrophe *did* occur is certain from Isa. 45:18, which expressly declares that the earth was not *created* in the condition in which Genesis 1:2 views it.

What is found in the remainder of Genesis 1 refers not to the primitive creation but to the *restoration* of that which had fallen into ruins. Genesis 1:1 speaks of the original creation; Genesis 1:2 describes the then condition of the earth six days before Adam was called into existence. To what remote point in time Genesis 1:1 conducts us, or as to how long an interval passed before the earth *"became"* a ruin, we have no means of knowing; but if the surmises of geologists could be conclusively established there would be no conflict at all between the findings of science and the teaching of Scripture. The unknown interval between the first two verses of Genesis 1, is wide enough to embrace all the prehistoric ages which may have elapsed; but all that took place from Genesis 1:3 onwards transpired less than six thousand years ago.

"In six days the Lord *made* heaven and earth, the sea, and all that in them is" (Ex. 20:11). There is a wide difference between *"creating"* and *"making":* to "create" is to call into existence something out of nothing; to "make" is to form or fashion something out of materials *already* existing. A carpenter can "make" a chair out of wood, but he is quite unable to "create" the wood itself. "In the beginning (whenever that was) God *created* the heaven and the earth"; subsequently (after the primitive creation had become a ruin) "the Lord *made* heaven and earth, the sea, and all that in them is." This Exodus scripture settles the controversy which has been raised as to what kind of "days" are meant in Genesis 1, whether days of 24 hours, or protracted periods of time. In "six days," that is, literal days of twenty-four hours duration, the Lord completed the work of restoring and re-fashioning that which some terrible catastrophe had blasted and plunged into chaos.

What follows in the remainder of Genesis 1 is to be regarded not as a poem, still less as an allegory, but as a *literal,* historical statement of Divine revelation. We have little patience with those who labor to show that the teaching of this chapter is in harmony with modern science—as well ask whether the celestial chronometer is in keeping with the timepiece at Greenwich. Rather must it be the part of scientists to bring their declarations into accord with the teaching of Genesis 1, if they are to receive the respect of the children of God. The faith of the Christian rests not in the wisdom of man, nor does it stand in any need of buttressing from scientific *savants.* The faith of the Christian rests upon the impregnable rock of Holy Scripture, and we need nothing more. Too often have Christian apologists deserted their proper ground. For instance: one of the ancient tablets of Assyria is deciphered, and then it is triumphantly announced that some statements found in the historical portions of the Old Testament have been *confirmed*. But that is only a turning of things upside down again. The Word of God needs no "confirming." If the writing upon an Assyrian tablet agrees with what is recorded in Scripture, *that* confirms the historical accuracy of the Assyrian tablet; if it disagrees, that is proof positive that the Assyrian writer was at fault. In like manner, if the teachings of science square with Scripture, that goes to show the former are correct; if they conflict, that proves the postulates of science are false. The man of the world, and the pseudo-scientist may sneer at our logic, but that only demonstrates the truth of God's Word, which declares, "but the natural man receiveth not the things of the Spirit of God: for they are *foolishness unto him:* neither can he know them, because they are spiritually discerned" (1 Cor. 2:14).

Marvelouslyconcise is what is found in Genesis 1. A single verse suffices to speak of the original creation of the heaven and the earth. Another verse is all that is needed to describe the awful chaos into which the ruined earth was plunged. And less than thirty verses more tell of the six days' work, during which the Lord "made heaven and earth, the sea, and all that in them is." Not all the combined skill of the greatest literary genuii, historians, poets, or philosophers this world has ever produced, could design a composition which began to equal Genesis 1. For reconditeness of theme, and yet simplicity of language; for comprehensiveness of scope, and yet terseness of expression; for scientific exactitude, and yet the avoidance of all technical terms; it is unrivalled, and nothing can be found in the whole realm of literature which can be compared with it for a moment. It stands in a class all by itself. If "brevity is the soul of wit" (i. e. wisdom) then the brevity of what is recorded in this opening chapter of the Bible evidences the *divine* wisdom of Him who inspired it. Contrast the labored formulæ of the scientists, contrast the verbose writings of the poets, contrast the meaningless cosmogonies of the ancients and the foolish mythologies of the heathen, and the uniqueness of this Divine account of Creation and Restoration will at once appear. Every line of this opening chapter of Holy Writ has stamped across it the autograph of Deity.

Concerning the details of the six days' work we cannot now say very much. The orderly manner in which God proceeded, the ease with which He accomplished His work, the excellency of that which was produced, and the simplicity of the narrative, at once impress the reader. Out of the chaos was brought the "cosmos," which signifies order, arrangement, beauty; out of the waters emerged the earth; a scene of desolation, darkness and death, was transformed into one of light, life, and fertility, so that at the end all was pronounced "very good." Observe that here is to be found the first Divine Decalogue: ten times we read, "and God said, *let there be,*" etc. (vv. 3, 6, 9, 11, 14, 14, 20, 24, 26, 30), which may be termed the Ten Commandments of Creation.

In the Hebrew there are just *seven* words in the opening verse of Genesis 1, and these are composed of twenty-eight letters, which is 7 multiplied by 4. Seven is the number of perfection, and four of creation, hence, we learn that the primary creation was *perfect* as it left its Maker's hands. It is equally significant that there were *seven* distinct stages in God's work of restoring the earth: first, there was the activity of the Holy Spirit (1:2); second, the calling of light into existence (1:3); third, the making of the firmament (1:6-9); fourth, the clothing of the earth with vegetation (1:11); fifth, the making and arranging of the heavenly bodies (1:14-18); sixth, the storing of the waters (1:20-21); seventh, the stocking of the earth (1:24). The perfection of God's handiwork is further made to appear in the *seven* times the word "good" occurs here —vv. 4, 10, 12, 18, 21, 25, 31—also the word "made" is found *seven* times in this section—1:7, 16, 25, 26, 31; 2:2, 3. *Seven* times "heaven" is mentioned in this chapter—vv. 1, 8, 9, 14, 15, 17, 20. And, it may be added, that "God" Himself is referred to in this opening section (1:1-2:4) thirty-five times, which is 7 multiplied by 5. Thus the seal of *perfection* is stamped upon everything God here did and made.

Turning from the literal meaning of what is before us in this opening chapter of Holy Writ, we would dwell now upon that which has often been pointed out by others, namely, the *typical significance* of these verses. The order followed by God in re-constructing the old creation is the same which obtains in connection with the new creation, and in a remarkable manner the one is here made to foreshadow the other. The early history of this earth corresponds with the spiritual history of the believer in Christ. What occurred in connection with the world of old, finds its counterpart in the regenerated man. It is this line of truth which will now engage our attention.

1. *"In the beginning God created the heaven and the earth."* As we have already observed, the original condition of this primary creation was vastly different from the state in which we view it in the next verse. Coming fresh from the hands of their Creator, the heaven and the earth must have presented a scene of unequalled freshness and beauty. No groans of suffering were heard to mar the harmony of the song of "the morning stars" as they sang together (Job 38:7). No worm of corruption was there to defile the perfections of the Creator's handiwork. No iniquitous rebel was there to challenge the supremacy of God. And no death shades were there to spread the spirit of gloom. God reigned supreme, without a rival, and everything was very good.

So, too, in the beginning of this world's history, God also created man, and vastly different was his original state from that into which he subsequently fell. Made in the image and likeness of God, provided with a helpmate, placed in a small garden of delights, given dominion over all the lower orders of creation, "blessed" by His Maker, bidden to be fruitful and multiply and replenish the earth, and included in that which God pronounced "very good," Adam had all that heart could desire. Behind him was no sinful heredity, within him was no deceitful and wicked heart, upon him were no marks of corruption, and around him were no signs of death. Together with his helpmate, in fellowship with his Maker, there was everything to make him happy and contented.

2. *"And the earth became without form and void; and darkness was upon the face of the deep."* Some fearful catastrophe must have occurred. Sin had dared to raise its horrid head against God, and with sin came death and all its attendant evils. The fair handiwork of the Creator was blasted. That which at first was so fair was now marred, and what was very good became very evil. The

light was quenched, and the earth was submerged beneath the waters of judgment. That which was perfect in the beginning became a ruin, and darkness abode upon the face of the deep. Profoundly mysterious is this, and unspeakably tragic. A greater contrast than what is presented in the first two verses of Genesis 1 can hardly be conceived. Yet there it is: the primitive earth, created by God "in the beginning," had become a ruin.

No less tragic was that which befell the first man. Like the original earth before him, Adam remained not in his primitive state. A dreadful catastrophe occurred. Description of this is given in Genesis 3. By one man *sin entered the world,* and death by sin. The spirit of insubordination possessed him; he rebelled against his Maker; he ate of the forbidden fruit; and terrible were the consequences which followed. The fair handiwork of the Creator was blasted. Where before there was blessing, there now descended the curse. Into a scene of life and joy, entered death and sorrow. That which at the first was "very good," became very evil. Just as the primitive earth before him, so man became a wreck and a ruin. He was submerged in evil and enveloped in darkness. Unspeakably tragic was this, but the truth of it is verified in the heart of every descendant of Adam.

"There was, then, a primary creation, afterward a fall; first, 'heaven and earth,' in due order, then earth without a heaven—in darkness, and buried under a 'deep' of salt and barren and restless waters. What a picture of man's condition, as fallen away from God! How complete the confusion! How profound the darkness! How deep the restless waves of passion roll over the wreck of what was once so fair! 'The wicked are like the troubled sea, when it cannot rest, whose waters cast up mire and dirt' " (F. W. Grant).

Here, then, is the key to human destiny. Here is the cause of all the suffering and sorrow which is in the world. Here is the explanation of human depravity. Man is not now as God created him. God made man "upright" (Eccl. 7:9), but he continued not thus. God faithfully warned man that if he ate of the forbidden fruit he should surely die. And die he did, spiritually. Man is, henceforth, a fallen creature. He is born into this world "alienated from the life of God" (Eph. 4:18). He was born into this world with a heart that is "deceitful above all things, and desperately wicked" (Jer. 17:9). This is the heritage of The Fall. This is the entail of Adam's transgression. Man is a ruined creature, and "darkness," moral and spiritual, rents upon the face of his understanding. (Eph. 4:18).

3. *"And the spirit of God moved upon the face of the waters."* Here is where hope begins to dawn. God did not abandon the primitive earth, which had become a ruin. It would not have been surprising, though, if He had. Why should God trouble any further about that which lay under His righteous judgment? Why should He condescend to notice that which was now a desolate waste? Why, indeed. But here was where sovereign mercy intervened. He had gracious designs toward that formless void. He purposed to resurrect it, restore it, refructify it. And the first thing we read of in bringing about this desired end was, "the Spirit of God moved upon the face of the waters." There was *Divine activity*. There was a movement on the part of the Holy Spirit. *And this was a prime necessity.* How could the earth resurrect itself? How could that which lay under the righteous judgment of God bring itself into the place of blessing? How could darkness transform itself into life? In the very nature of the case it could not. The ruined creation was helpless. If there was to be restoration, and a new creation, Divine power must intervene, the Spirit of God must "move."

The analogy holds good in the spiritual realm. Fallen man had no more claim upon God's notice than had the desolated primitive earth. When Adam rebelled against his Maker, he merited naught but unsparing judgment at His hands, and if God was inclined to have any further regard for him, it was due alone to sovereign mercy. What wonder if God had left man to the doom he so richly deserved! But no. God had designs of grace toward him. From the wreck and ruin of fallen humanity, God purposed to bring forth a "new creation." Out of the death of sin, God is now bringing on to resurrection ground all who are united to Christ His Son. And the first thing in bringing this about is *the activity of the Holy Spirit.* And this, again, is *a prime necessity.* Fallen man, in himself, is as helpless as was the fallen earth. The sinner can no more regenerate himself than could the ruined earth lift itself out of the deep which rested upon it. The new creation, like the restoration of the material creation, must be accomplished by God Himself.

4. *"And God said, let there be light, and there was light."* First the activity of the Holy Spirit and now the spoken Word. No less than ten times in this chapter do we read "and God said." God might have refashioned and refurnished the earth without speaking at all, but He did not. Instead, He plainly intimated from the beginning, that His purpose was to be worked out and His counsels accomplished by the Word. The first thing God said was, "Let there be light," and we read, "There was light." Light, then, came in, was produced by, the Word. And then we are told, "God saw the light, that it was good."

It is so in the work of the new creation. These two are inseparably joined together—the activity of the Spirit and the ministry of the Word of God. It is by these the man in Christ became a new creation. And the initial step toward this was the entrance of light into the darkness. The entrance of sin has blinded the eyes of man's heart and has darkened his understanding. So much so that, left to himself, man is unable to perceive the awfulness of his condition, the condemnation which rests upon him, or the peril in which he stands. Unable to see his urgent need of a Saviour, he is, spiritually, in total darkness. And neither the affections of his heart, the reasonings of his mind, nor the power of his will, can dissipate this awful darkness. Light comes to the sinner *through the Word applied by the Spirit.* As it is written, "the entrance of Thy words giveth light" (Psa. 119:130). This marks the initial step of God's work in the soul. Just as the shining of the light in Genesis 1 made manifest the desolation upon which it shone, so the entrance of God's Word into the human heart reveals the awful ruin which sin has wrought.

5. *"And God divided the light from the darkness."* Heb. 4:12 tells us, the Word of God is quick, and powerful, and sharper than any two-edged sword, piercing even to the *dividing asunder of soul and spirit,* and of the joints and marrow, and is a discerner of the thoughts and intents of the heart." This is not a figurative expression but, we believe, a statement of literal fact. Man is a tripartite being, made up of "spirit and soul and body" (1 Thess. 5:23). The late Dr. Pierson distinguished between them thus: "The spirit is capable of God-consciousness; the soul is

the seat of self-consciousness; the body of sense-consciousness." In the day that Adam sinned, he died spiritually. Physical death is the separation of the spirit from the body; spiritual death is the separation of the spirit from God. When Adam died, his spirit was not annihilated, but it was "alienated" from God. There was a *fall.* The spirit, the highest part of Adam's complex being, no longer dominated; instead, it was degraded, it fell to the level of the soul, and ceased to function separately. Hence, today, the unregenerate man is dominated by his soul, which is the seat of lust, passion, emotion. But in the work of regeneration, the Word of God "pierces even to the *dividing asunder* of soul and spirit," and the spirit is rescued from the lower level to which it has fallen, being brought back again into communion with God. The "spirit" being that part of man which is capable of communion with God, is *light;* the "soul" when it is not dominated and regulated by the spirit is in *darkness,* hence, in that part of the six days' work of restoration which adumbrated the dividing asunder of soul and spirit, we read, "And God divided the light from the darkness."

6. *"And God said, let there be a firmament in the midst of the waters, and let it divide the waters from the waters ....and God called the firmament heaven"* (Gen. 1:6, 8). This brings us to the second days work, and here, for the first time, we read that "God made" something (1:7). This was the formation of the atmospheric heaven, the "firmament," named by God "heaven." That which corresponds to this in the new creation, is the impartation of a new nature. The one who is "born of the Spirit" becomes a "partaker of the Divine nature" (2 Pet. 1:4). Regeneration is not the improvement of the flesh, or the cultivation of the old nature; it is the reception of an altogether new and heavenly nature. It is important to note that the "firmament" was produced by the Word, for, again we read, "And God said." So it is by the written Word of God that the new birth is produced, "Of His own will begat He us *with the Word of truth"* (James 1:18). And again, "being born again, not of corruptible seed, but of incorruptible, *by the Word of God"* (1 Pet. 1:23).

7. *"And God said, Let the waters under the heaven be gathered together unto one place, and let the dry land appear: and it was so. And God said. Let the earth bring*

forth grass, the herb yielding seed, and the fruit tree yielding fruit after his kind, whose seed is in itself" (Gen. 1: 9-11). These verses bring before us God's work on the third day, and in harmony with the meaning of this numeral we find that which clearly speaks of *resurrection.* The earth was raised out of the waters which had submerged it, and then it was clothed with vegetation. Where before there was only desolation and death, life and fertility now appeared. So it is in regeneration. The one who was dead in trespasses and sins, has been raised to walk in newness of life. The one who was by the old creation "in Adam," is now by new creation "in Christ." The one who before produced nothing but dead works, is now fitted to bring forth fruit to the glory of God.

And here we must conclude. Much has been left untouched, but sufficient has been said, we trust, to show that the order followed by God in the six days' work of restoration, foreshadowed His work of grace in the new creation: that which He did of old in the material world, typified His present work in the spiritual realm. Every stage was accomplished by the putting forth of Divine power, and everything was produced by the operation of His Word. May writer and reader be more and more subject to that Word, and then shall we be pleasing to Him and fruitful in His service.

2. CHRIST IN GENESIS 1

In our first meditation upon this wonderful book of beginnings we pointed out some of the striking analogies which exist between the order followed by God in His work of creation and His method of procedure in the "new creation," the spiritual creation in the believer. First, there was darkness, then the action of the Holy Spirit, then the word of power going forth, and then light as the result, and later resurrection and fruit. There is also a striking foreshadowment of God's great dispensational dealings with our race, in this record of His work in the six days, but as this has already received attention from more capable pens than ours, we pass on to still another application of this scripture. There is much concerning *Christ* in this first chapter of Genesis if only we have eyes to see, and it is the typical application of Genesis 1 to Christ and His work we would here direct attention.

Christ is the key which unlocks the golden doors into the temple of Divine truth. "Search the Scriptures," is His command, "for they are they which testify of *Me.*" And again, He declares, "In the volume of the Book it is written of Me." In every section of the written Word the Personal Word is enshrined—in Genesis as much as in Matthew. And we would now submit that on the frontispiece of Divine Revelation we have *a typical programme of the entire Work of Redemption.*

In the opening statements of this chapter we discover, in type, the great *need* of Redemption. "In the beginning God created the heavens and the earth." This carries us back to the primal creation which, like everything else that comes from the hand of God, must have been perfect, beautiful, glorious. Such also was the original condition of man. Made in the image of his Creator, endowed with the breath of Elohim, he was pronounced "very good."

But the next words present a very different picture—"And the earth was without form and void," or, as the original Hebrew might be more literally translated, "The earth *became* a ruin." Between the first two verses in Genesis 1 a terrible calamity occurred. Sin entered the universe. The heart of the mightiest of all God's creatures was filled with pride—Satan had dared to oppose the will of the Almighty. The dire effects of his fall reached to our earth, and what was originally created by God fair and beautiful, became a ruin. Again we see in this a striking analogy to the history of man. He too fell. He also became a ruin. The effects of his sin likewise reached beyond himself—the generations of an unborn humanity being curst as the result of the sin of our first parents.

"And darkness was upon the face of the deep." Darkness is the opposite of light. God is light. Darkness is the emblem of Satan. Well do these words describe the natural condition of our fallen race. Judicially separated from God, morally and spiritually blind, experimentally the slaves of Satan, an awful pall of darkness rests upon the entire mass of an unregenerate humanity. But this only furnishes a black background upon which can be displayed the glories of Divine Grace. "Where sin abounded grace did much more abound." The *method* of this "abounding of grace" is, in type, outlined in God's work during the six days. In the work of the first four days we have a most remarkable foreshadowment of the four great stages in the Work of Redemption. We cannot now do much more than call attention to the outlines of this marvellous primitive picture. But as we approach it, to gaze upon it in awe and wonderment, may the Spirit of God take of the things of Christ and show them unto us.

I. In the first day's work the Divine Incarnation is typically set forth.

If fallen and sinful men are to be reconciled to the thrice holy God what must be done? How can the infinite chasm separating Deity from humanity be bridged? What ladder shall be able to rest here upon earth and yet reach right into heaven itself? Only one answer is possible to these questions. The initial step in the work of human redemption must be the Incarnation of Deity. Of necessity this must be the starting point. The Word must become flesh. God Himself must come right down to the very pit where a ruined humanity helplessly lies, if it is ever to be lifted out of the miry clay and transported to heavenly places. The Son of God must take upon Himself the form of a servant and be made in the likeness of men.

This is precisely what the first day's work typifies in its foreshadowment of the initial step in the Work of Redemption, namely, the Incarnation of the Divine Redeemer. Notice here five things.

First, there is the work of *the Holy Spirit.* "And the Spirit of God moved (Heb. 'brooded') upon the face of the waters" (v. 2). So also was this the order in the Divine Incarnation. Concerning the mother of the Saviour we read, "And the angel answered and said unto her, The Holy Ghost shall come upon thee and the power of the Highest shall *overshadow* thee: therefore also that holy thing which shall be born of thee shall be called the Son of God" (Luke 1:35).

Second, *the word* issues forth *as light.* "And God *said* (the word) let there be light and there was light" (v. 3). So also as soon as Mary brings forth the Holy Child "The glory of the Lord *shone* round about" the shepherds on Bethlehem's plains (Luke 2:9). And when He is presented in the temple, Simeon was moved by the Holy Spirit to say, "For mine eyes have seen Thy salvation, which Thou hast prepared before the face of all people: *a light to lighten* the Gentiles, and the glory of Thy people Israel."

Third, the light is *approved* by God. "And God saw the light, that it was *good"* (v. 4). We cannot now enlarge much upon the deep typical import of this statement, but would remark in passing that the Hebrew word here translated "good" is also in (Eccl. 3:11) rendered "beautiful"—"He hath made everything *beautiful* in his time." God *saw* that the light was good, beautiful! How obvious is the application to our incarnate Lord! After His advent into this world we are told that "Jesus increased in wisdom and stature and *in favor with God* and man" (Luke 2:52), and the first words of the Father concerning Him were, "This is My beloved Son in whom *I am well pleased."* Yes, good and beautiful was the light in the sight of the Father. How blind was man that he should see in Him no beauty that he should desire Him!

Fourth, the light was *separated* from the darkness. "And God divided the light from the darkness" (v. 4). How jealously did the Holy Spirit guard the types! How careful is He to call our attention to the immeasurable difference between the Son of Man and the sons of men! Though in His infinite condescension He saw fit to share our humanity, yet He shared not our depravity. The light of Christ was *divided* from the darkness (fallen humanity). "For such a high priest became us, who is holy, harmless, undefiled, *separate from sinners*" (Heb. 7:26).

Fifth, the light was *named by God.* "And God called the light Day" (v. 5). So also was it with Him who is the Light of the world. It was not left to Joseph and Mary to select the name for the Holy Child. Of old the prophet had declared, "Listen, O isles unto me; and hearken, ye people, from far; the Lord hath called Me from the womb; *from the bowels of My mother hath He made mention of My name*" (Isa. 49:1). And in fulfilment thereof, while yet in His mother's womb, an angel is sent by God to Joseph, saying, "And she shall bring forth a son, and thou shalt call His name Jesus."

II. In the second day's work the Cross of Christ is typically set forth.

What was the next thing necessary in the accomplishment of the Work of Redemption? The Incarnation by itself would not meet our need. "Except a corn of wheat fall into the ground *and die,* it abideth alone: but if it die, it bringeth forth much fruit" (John 12:24). The Incarnate Christ reveals the spotless and perfect life which alone meets the Divine mind, but it helps not to bridge the awful gulf between a holy God and a ruined sinner. For this, sin must put away, and that cannot be done except death comes in. "For without shedding of blood is no remission." The Lamb of God must be slain. The Holy One must lay down His life. The Cross is the only place where the righteous claims of God's throne can be met.

And in the second day's work this second step in the acplishment of human redemption is typically set forth. The prominent thing in this second day's work is *division, separation, isolation.* "And God said, Let there be a firmament in the midst of the waters, and let it *divide* the waters from the waters. And God made the firmament, and *divided* the waters which were under the firmament from the waters which were above the firmament: and it was so" (vs. 6-7). It is striking to note here that there is a *twofold* division. First there is a firmament in the midst of the waters and this firmament divides the waters from the waters, and secondly, the firmament divided the waters which were under it from those which were above it. We believe that the "firmament" here typifies *the Cross,* and sets forth its *twofold* aspect. There our blessed Lord was divided or *separated* from God Himself—"My God, My God, why hast Thou *forsaken* Me?"; and there also He was separated from man—"*Cut off* out of the land of the living."

That the "firmament" here *does* foreshadow the Cross seems to be clearly borne out by the marvellous analogy between what is here told us concerning it and its typical agreement with the Cross of Christ. Observe four things.

First, the firmament was *purposed* by God *before* it was actually made. In verse 6 it reads, "And God said *let there be* a firmament," and in verse 7, "And God *made* the firmament." How perfect is the agreement between type and antitype! Long, long before the Cross was erected on Golgotha's heights, it was purposed by God. Christ was "The Lamb slain from the foundation of the world" (Rev. 13:8).

Second, the firmament was set *in the midst* of the waters. It is well known to Bible students that in Scripture "waters" symbolize *peoples,* nations (cf. Rev. 17:15). In its typical application then, these words would seem to signify, "Let there be a Cross in the midst of the peoples." Manifold are the applications suggested by these words. Accurate beyond degree is the type. Our minds immediately turn to the words, "They crucified Him, and two others with Him, on either side one, and Jesus *in the midst*" (John 19:18). The geographical situation of Calvary is likewise a fulfilment: Palestine being practically the centre or midst of the earth.

Third, the firmament *divided* the waters. So the Cross has divided the "peoples." The Cross of Christ is the great divider of mankind. So it was historically, for it divided the believing thief from the impotent thief. So it has been ever since, and so it is today. On the one hand, "The preaching of the Cross is to them that perish, foolishness," but on the other, "unto us which are saved, it is the power of God" (1 Cor. 1:18).

Fourth, the firmament was *designed by God.* "And God made the firmament." So was it announced on the Day of Pentecost concerning the Lord Jesus Christ. "Him, being delivered by the determinate counsel and foreknowledge of God" (Acts 2:23). So was it declared of old, "It pleased *the Lord* to bruise Him; *He* hath put Him to grief." The Cross was of Divine design and appointment.

Is it not also deeply significant that the words, "And God saw that it was good" are omitted at the close of this *second* day's work? Had they been included here the type would have been marred. The second day's work pointed forward to the Cross, and at the Cross God was dealing with *sin.* There His wrath was being expended on the Just One who was dying for the unjust. Though He was without any sin, yet was He "made sin for us" and dealt with accordingly. Does not then the *omission* here of the usual expression "God saw that it was *good*" assume a deeper significance than has been hitherto allowed.

III. In the third day's work our Lord's Resurrection is typically set forth.

Our article has already exceeded the limits we originally designed, so perforce, we must abbreviate.

The third thing necessary in the accomplishment of the Work of Redemption was the Resurrection of the Crucified One. A dead Saviour could not save anyone. "Wherefore He is able also to save them to the uttermost that come unto God by Him"; Why? *"Seeing He ever liveth"* (Heb. 7:25).

Thus it is in our type. Beyond doubt, that which is foreshadowed on the third day's work is *resurrection.* It is in the record concerning this third day that we read "Let the dry land *appear*" (v. 9). Previously the earth had been submerged, buried beneath the waters. But now the land is raised above the level of the seas; there is resurrection, the earth appears. But this is not all. In verse 11 we read, "And let the earth bring forth grass, etc." Hitherto death had reigned supreme. No life appeared upon the surface of the ruined earth. But on the third day the earth is commanded to "bring forth." Not on the second, not on the fourth, but on *the third day* was life seen upon the barren earth! Perfect is the type for all who have eyes to see. Wonderfully pregnant are the words, "Let the earth *bring forth*" to all who have ears to hear. It was on the *third* day that our Lord rose again from the dead "according to the Scriptures." According to *what* Scriptures? Do we not have in these 9th and 11th verses of Genesis 1 *the first* of these scriptures, as well as the primitive picture of our Lord's Resurrection!

IV. In the fourth day's work our Lord's Ascension is typically suggested.

The Resurrection did not complete our Lord's redemption work. In order for that He must enter the Heavenly Place not made with hands. He must take His seat on the right hand of the Majesty on high. He must go "into heaven itself now to appear in the presence of God for us" (Heb. 9:24).

Once more we find the type corresponds with the Antitype. In the fourth day's work our eyes are removed from the earth and all its affairs and are turned *to the heavens!* (See vs. 14-19). As we read these verses and gather something of their typical import, do we not hear the Holy Spirit saying, "Seek those things which are above, where Christ sitteth on the right hand of God. Set your affection on things above, not on things on the earth" (Col. 3:1, 2).

And as we lift our eyes heavenwards what do we see? *"Two great lights"*—typically, Christ and His people. The sun which speaks to us of "the Sun of Righteousness" (Malachi 4:2), and the moon which tells of Israel and the Church (Rev. 12:1), borrowing its light from, and reflecting the light of, the sun. And observe their functions. First, they are "to give light upon the earth (v. 17), and secondly, they are "to rule over the day and over the night" (v. 18). So it is with Christ and His people. During the present interval of darkness, the world's night, Christ and His people are "the light of the world," but during the Millennium they shall *rule and reign* over the earth.

Thus in the first four days' work in Genesis 1, we have foreshadowed the four great stages or crises in the accomplishment of the Work of Redemption. The Incarnation, the Death, the Resurrection, and the Ascension of our blessed Lord are respectively typified. In the light of this how precious are those words at the close of the six days' work: "Thus the heavens and the earth were *finished,* and all the host of them. And on the seventh day God ended His work which He had made; and He *rested* on the seventh day from all His work which He had made" (Gen. 2:1, 2). The work of Redemption is *completed,* and in that work God finds *His rest!*

As we continue our meditations on the book of Genesis may God in His condescending grace reveal unto us "wondrous things out of His Law."

3. TWO TREES

GENESIS 2

It is not our purpose to give a detailed and exhaustive exposition of Genesis, rather shall we attempt to single out some of the less obvious treasures from this wonderful mine, in which are stored inexhaustible supplies of spiritual riches. This first book in the Word of God is full of typical pictures, prophetic foreshadowings, and dispensational adumbrations, as well as important practical lessons, and it will be our delight to call attention to a few of these as we pass from chapter to chapter.

In studying the typical teaching of the Old Testament Scriptures we learn from them sometimes by way of contrast and sometimes by way of comparison. A striking illustration of this double fact is found in the second chapter of Genesis. In the ninth verse we read of "The tree of knowledge of good and evil." In Acts 5:30 we read, "The God of our fathers raised up Jesus, whom ye slew and hanged on a *tree";* and again in 1 Peter 2:24, "Who His own self bare our sins in His own body *on the tree."* Now the thoughtful reader will naturally inquire, Why should the Cross of our blessed Lord be spoken of as a "tree"? Surely there must be some deeper meaning than that which appears on the surface. Was it not intended by the Holy Spirit that we should refer back to Gen. 2:9 and compare and contrast these two trees? We believe so, and a quiet meditation thereon reveals some remarkable points both of comparison and contrast between the tree of knowledge of good and evil and the tree on which our Lord was crucified. Let us consider some of the points of contrast first.

1. The first tree was planted by *God.* "And out of the ground made *the Lord God* to grow every tree that is pleasant to the sight and good for food; the tree of life also in the midst of the garden and the Tree of Knowledge of good and evil" (Gen. 2:9). This tree then was planted not by Adam, but by Adam's Maker—God. But the second tree, the tree to which our Lord was nailed, was planted by *man.* "And *they* crucified Him" (Mat. 27:35) is the brief but terrible record. It was human hands which devised, provided and erected that cruel tree on the hill of Calvary.

In marked contrast from the first tree, it was the hands of the creature and not the Creator which planted the second tree.

2. The first tree was *pleasant to the eyes.* "And when the woman saw that the tree was good for food, and that it was pleasant to the eyes, and a tree to be desired to make one wise, she took of the fruit thereof, and did eat" (Gen. 3:6). Exactly in what this "pleasantness" consisted we do not know, but the Divine record seems to indicate that this tree was an object of beauty and delight. What a contrast from the second Tree! Here everything was hideous and repellant. The suffering Saviour, the vulgar crowd, the taunting priests, the two thieves, the flowing blood, the three hours darkness—nothing was there to please the outward eye. The first tree was "pleasant to the eyes," but concerning the One on the second tree it is written, "They saw in Him *no beauty* that they should desire Him."

3. God *forbade* man to eat of the first tree. "But of the tree of the knowledge of good and evil, thou shalt *not* eat of it" (Gen. 2:17). A divine prohibition was placed upon the fruit of this tree. But again, how different from the second tree! How startling the contrast! There is no restriction here. In this case man is freely *invited* to draw near and eat of the fruit of this tree. The sinner is bidden to "Taste and see that the Lord is good." "All things are ready, Come." The position is exactly reversed. Just as man was commanded *not* to eat of the fruit of the first tree, he is now *commanded* to eat of the second.

4. Because God forbade man to eat of the first tree, Satan used every artifice to get man *to eat of it.* Contrariwise, because God now invites men to eat of the second tree, Satan uses all his powers *to prevent men eating of it.* Is not this another designed contrast marked out for us by the Holy Spirit? Humanly speaking it was solely due to the cunning and malice of the great enemy of God and man that our first parents ate of the forbidden fruit, and can we not also say, that it is now primarily due to the subtle devices of the old serpent the Devil that sinners are kept from eating the fruit of that second tree?

5. The eating of the first tree *brought sin and death* "For in the day that thou eatest thereof thou shalt surely die" (Gen. 2:17). It was through eating of the fruit of

this tree that the Curse descended upon our race with all its attendant miseries. By eating of the second Tree *comes life and salvation.* "Verily, verily, I say unto you, Except ye *eat* the flesh of the Son of Man, and drink His blood, ye have no life in you. Whoso *eateth* my flesh, and drinketh my blood, hath eternal life" (John 6:53, 54). Is there not in these words of our Lord a latent reference to the history of man's fall, and a designed contrast from the first tree? Just as by the act of "eating" man lost his spiritual life, so by an act of "eating" man now obtains spiritual and eternal life!

6. Adam, the thief, through eating of the first tree, was *turned* out *of Paradise,* while the repentant thief, through eating of the second Tree, *entered Paradise.* We doubt not that once again there is a designed antithesis in these two things. A thief is connected with both trees, for in eating of the forbidden fruit our first parents committed an act of theft. Is it not then something more than a coincidence that we find a "thief" (yea, *two* thieves) connected with the second Tree also? And when we note the widely different experiences of the two thieves the point is even more striking. As we have said one was cast out of Paradise (the garden), the other was admitted into Paradise, and to say the least, it is remarkable that our Lord should employ the word "Paradise" in this connection—the only time He ever did use it!

Now, briefly, let us consider some of the points of resemblance:

1. Both trees were planted in *a garden.* The first in the Garden of Eden, the second in a garden which is unnamed. "Now in the place where He was crucified there was *a garden*" (John 19:41). Are we not told this, for one reason, in order that we should connect the two trees? Is it not a striking point of analogy, that both the first Adam and the last Adam *died* in a "garden"!

2. In connection with both trees we find the words "in the midst." "The tree of life also in the midst of the garden, and the tree of knowledge of good and evil" (Gen. 2:9). The word "and" connecting the two trees together and intimating their juxtaposition in the midst of the garden. In like manner we also read concerning our Saviour, "They crucified Him, and two others with Him on either side one, and Jesus *in the midst.*"

3. Both are trees of *the Knowledge of Good and Evil.*

Where in all the world, or in all the Scriptures, do we learn the knowledge of good and evil as we do at the second Tree—the Cross? There we see Goodness incarnate. There we behold the Holiness of God displayed as nowhere else. There we discover the unfathomable love and matchless grace of Deity unveiled as never before or since. But there, too, we also see Evil—see it in all its native hideousness. There we witness the consummation and climax of the creature's wickedness. There we behold as nowhere else the vileness, the heinousness, the awfulness of sin as it appears in the sight of the thrice holy God. Yes, there is a designed resemblance as well as a contrast between the two trees. The Cross also is the tree of *the knowledge of* good and evil.

4. Finally, there is another tree beside the one that was planted in Eden, of which Genesis 3:6 is true, "And when the woman saw that the tree was good for food, and that it was pleasant to the eyes, and a tree to be desired to make one wise, she took of the fruit thereof, and did eat." Ah! that second Tree is surely "good for food," too. The Cross of Christ and all that it stands for, is the very meat and marrow of the believer's life. It is "good" as "food" for the soul! And how "pleasant" it is "to the eyes" of faith! There we see all our sins blotted out. There we see our old man crucified. There we see the ground upon which a holy God can meet a guilty sinner. There we see the Finished Work of our adorable Redeemer. Truly, it is "pleasant to the eyes." And is not this second Tree also "a tree to be desired to make one wise"? Yes; the preaching of the Cross is not only the power of God, but "the *wisdom* of God" as well. The knowledge of this second Tree makes the sinner "wise" unto salvation.

In closing this little meditation we would call attention to one or two other scriptures in which a "tree" figures prominently. First, from Genesis 3:17 we learn that the "tree" is linked directly with the Curse: "Because thou hast hearkened unto the voice of thy wife, and hast eaten of *the tree,* of which I commanded thee, saying, Thou shalt not eat of it: *cursed* is the ground for thy sake; in sorrow shalt thou eat of it all the days of thy life." In the light of this how significant are the following passages: In Genesis 40 we have recorded the dreams of the two men who were in prison with Joseph. When interpreting the baker's dream, Joseph said, "Within three days shall Pharaoh lift up thy head from off thee, and shalt hang thee on *a tree*" (Gen. 40:19). Again, in Joshua 8:29 we are told, "And the king of Ai was hanged on *a tree* until eventide: and as soon as the sun was down, Joshua commanded that they should take his carcass down from the tree." Once more, in Esther 2:23 we read, "And when inquisition was made of the matter, it was found out; therefore they were both hanged on *a tree:* and it was written in the book of the chronicles before the king." What striking illustrations are these of what we find in Gal. 3:13, "Christ hath redeemed us from the curse of the law, being made a curse for us: for it is written, *cursed* is every one that hangeth on *a tree"!*

"And the Lord appeared unto him in the plains of Mamre: and he sat in the tent door in the heat of the day; And he lifted up his eyes and looked, and, lo, three men stood by him: when he saw them, he ran to meet them from the tent door, and bowed himself toward the ground, And said, My lord, if now I have found favor in thy sight, pass not away, I pray thee, from thy servant: Let a little water, I pray thee, be fetched, and wash your feet, and *rest yourselves under the tree"* (Gen. 18:1-4). How suggestive are the last words of this quotation. *Why* should we be told that Abraham invited his three visitors to rest "under the tree," unless there is some *typical* meaning to his words? The "tree," as we have seen, speaks of the *Cross of Christ,* and it is *there* that "rest" is to be found. An additional point is brought out in the eighth verse of Genesis 18: "And he took butter, and milk, and the calf which he had dressed, and set it before them; and he stood by them *under the tree,* and they did *eat."* Eating is the symbol of *communion,* and it was under the *tree* these three men ate: so, it is the Cross of Christ which is the basis and ground of our *fellowship* with God. How striking, too, the order here: first, *rest* under the "tree," and then *eating,* or fellowship!

Finally, how meaningful is Exodus 15:23-25. When Israel, at the commencement of their wilderness journey reached Marah, "they could not drink of the waters of Marah, for they were bitter." And Moses "cried unto the Lord, and the Lord showed him *a tree,* which when he had cast into the waters, the waters were made sweet." Comment is almost needless, the type is so apparent. Here again, the "tree" typifies the Cross of Christ and the Christ of the Cross. It was our blessed Lord Who, by going down into the place of death, sweetened the bitter waters for us. Furthermore, it is only as the believer applies, practically, the principle of the Cross to his daily life, that the Marahs of our wilderness experiences are transmuted into "waters that are made sweet." To enter into "the fellowship of His sufferings," and to be "made conformable unto His death," is the highest Christian privilege.

How remarkable is the order, the progressive order, of these passages! First, the "tree" is seen as the place of the *curse.* Second, the "tree" is seen as the place where *rest* is found. Third, the "tree" is seen as the ground of *communion.* Fourth, the "tree" is seen as *the principle* of action to the daily life of the believer.

4. THE FALL

Genesis 3

The third chapter in Genesis is one of the most important in all the Word of God. What has often been said of Genesis as a whole is peculiarly true of this chapter: it is the "seed-plot of the Bible." Here are the foundations upon which rest many of the cardinal doctrines of our faith. Here we trace back to their source many of the rivers of divine truth. Here commences the great drama which is being enacted on the stage of human history, and which well-nigh six thousand years has not yet completed. Here we find the Divine explanation of the present fallen and ruined condition of our race. Here we learn of the subtle devices of our enemy, the Devil. Here we behold the utter powerlessness of man to walk in the path of righteousness when divine grace is withheld from him. Here we discover the spiritual effects of sin—man seeking to flee from God. Here we discern the attitude of God toward the guilty sinner Here we mark the universal tendency of human nature to cover its own moral shame by a device of man's own handiwork. Here we are taught of the gracious provision which God has made to meet our great need. Here begins that marvellous stream of prophecy which runs all through the Holy Scriptures. Here we learn that man cannot approach God except through a mediator. To some of these deeply important subjects we shall now give our attention.

I. The Fall Itself

The divine record of the Fall of man is an unequivocal refutation of the Darwinian hypothesis of evolution. Instead of teaching that man began at the bottom of the moral ladder and is now slowly but surely climbing heavenwards, it declares that man began at the top and fell to the bottom. Moreover, it emphatically repudiates the modern theory about Heredity and Environment. During the last fifty years socialistic philosophers have taught that all the ills to which man is heir are solely attributable to heredity and environment. This conception is an attempt to deny that man is a fallen creature and at heart desperately wicked.

We are told that if legislators will only make possible a perfect environment, man will then be able to realize his ideals and heredity will be purified. But man has already been tested under the most favorable conditions and was found wanting. With no evil heredity behind them, our first parents were placed in the fairest imaginable environment, an environment which God Himself pronounced "very good." Only a single restriction was placed upon their liberty, but they failed and fell. The trouble with man is not external but internal. What he needs most is not a new berth, but a new birth.

A single restriction was placed upon man's liberty, and this from the necessity and nature of the case. Man is a responsible being, responsible to serve, obey and glorify his Maker. Man is not an independent creature, for he did not make himself. Having been created by God he owes a debt to his Creator. We repeat, man is a responsible creature, and as such, subject to the Divine government. This is the great fact which God would impress upon us from the commencement of human history. "But of the tree of the knowledge of good and evil, *thou shalt not eat of it*" (Gen. 2:17). There was no other reason why the fruit of this tree should not be eaten save the plain command of God. And, as we have sought to show, this command was not given arbitrarily in the real meaning of that word, but gave emphasis to the relationship in which man stood to God. As an intelligent, responsible creature, man is subject to the Divine government. But the creature became self-seeking, self-centred, self-willed, and as the result he disobeyed, sinned, fell.

The record of the Fall deserves the closest study. Abler pens than ours have called attention to the different steps which led up to the overt act. First, the voice of the tempter was heeded. Instead of saying, "Get thee behind me, Satan," Eve quietly listened to the Evil One challenging the word of Jehovah. Not only so, but she proceeds to parley with him. Next there is a tampering with God's Word. Eve begins by *adding* to what God has said—always a fatal course to pursue. "Ye shall not eat of it, *neither shall ye touch it*." This last clause was her own addition, and Proverbs 30:6 received its first exemplification, "Add thou not unto his words, lest He reprove thee, and thou be found a liar." Next she proceeded to *alter*

God's Word, "*lest* ye die." The sharp point of the Spirit's Sword was blunted. Finally, she altogether *omits* God's solemn threat, "Thou shalt surely die." How true it is that "History repeats itself." God's enemies today are treading the same path: His Word is either added to, altered, or flatly denied. Having forsaken the only source of light, the act of transgression became the natural consequence. The forbidden fruit is now looked upon, desired, taken, eaten, and given to her husband. This is ever the logical order. Such, in brief, is the Divine account of the entry of sin into our world. The *will* of God was resisted, the *word* of God was rejected, the *way* of God was deserted.

The Divine record of the Fall is the only possible explanation of the present condition of the human race. It alone accounts for the presence of evil in a world made by a beneficent and perfect Creator. It affords the only adequate explanation for the universality of sin. Why is it that the king's son in the palace, and the saint's daughter in the cottage, in spite of every safeguard which human love and watchfulness can devise, manifest from their earliest days an unmistakable bias toward evil and tendency to sin? Why is it that sin is universal, that there is no empire, no nation, no family free from this awful disease? Reject the Divine explanation and no satisfactory answer is possible to these questions. Accept it, and we see that sin is universal because all share a common ancestry, all spring from a common stock, "In Adam *all* die." The Divine record of the Fall alone explains the mystery of death. Man possesses an imperishable soul, why then should he die? He had breathed into him the breath of the Eternal One, why then should he not live on in this world for ever? Reject the Divine explanation and we face an insoluble enigma. Accept it, receive the fact that, "*By one man* sin entered into the world, and death by sin, and so death passed upon all men, for that all have sinned" (Rom. 5: 12), and we have an explanation which meets all the facts of the case.

II. Satan and the Fall

Here for the first time in Scripture we meet with that mysterious personage the Devil. He is introduced without any word of explanation concerning his previous history. For our knowledge of his creation, his pre-Adamic existence, the exalted position which he occupied, and his terrible fall from it, we are dependent upon other passages, notably Isaiah 14:12-15, and Ezekiel 28:12-19. In the chapter now before us we are taught several important lessons respecting our great Adversary. We learn what is the sphere of his activities, what the method of his approach and what the form of his temptations. And here also we learn of the certainty of his ultimate overthrow and destruction.

Contrary to the popular conception, which makes Satan the author of the grosser sins of the flesh, and which attributes to him that which our Lord plainly declared issues out of the human heart, we are here informed that the sphere of his operations is *the religious or spiritual realm.* His chief aim is to get between the soul and God, to estrange *man's* heart from his Maker and inspire confidence instead, in himself. He seeks to usurp the place of the Most High to make His creatures his own willing subjects and children. His work consists of substituting his own lies in the place of divine truth. Genesis 3 gives us a sample of his operations and the method he employs. These things are written for our learning, for his activities, and the realm in which he works are the same today as they were in the Garden of Eden.

The method of Satan's approach was the same then as it is now. "Yea hath God said?" He begins by throwing doubt on the Divine Word! He questions its veracity. He suggests that God did not mean what He had said. So it is today. Every effort that is being made to deny the Divine inspiration of the Scriptures, every attempt put forward to set aside their absolute authority, every attack on the Bible which we now witness in the name of scholarship, is only a repetition of this ancient question, "Yea, *hath* God said?" Next, he substitutes his own word for God's, "Ye shall *not* surely die." We see the same principle illustrated in the first two parables in Matthew 13. The Lord Jesus goes forth sowing the seed which is the Word of God, and then the Evil One immediately follows and sows his tares. And the sad thing is that while men refuse to believe the Word of the living God, yet they are sufficiently credulous to accept Satan's lies. So it was at the beginning, and so it has been ever since. Finally, he dares to cast reflection upon God's goodness, and to call in question His perfections. "For God doth know that in the day ye eat thereof, then your eyes shall be opened, and ye shall be as gods, knowing good and evil." In other words, the Devil here suggests, that God was despotically withholding from man something which would be advantageous to him, and he presents as his bait the promise that, if only Eve will believe his lie rather than God's Word she shall be the gainer, and the obtainer of a knowledge and wisdom previously denied her. The same attraction is being dangled by him before the eyes of the devotees of Spiritism and Theosophy, but into this we cannot now enter.

It is to be noted that in the temptation a threefold appeal was made to Eve corresponding with the tripartite nature of the human constitution. "The woman saw that the tree was good for *food*"—appealing to the bodily senses; "and that it was *pleasant* to the eyes"—appealing to the desire nature, the emotions, which have their seat in the soul; "and a tree to be desired to make one *wise*"—appealing to the intelligence, which has its centre in the spirit (Cf. 1 Cor. 2:11). Thus we learn here a deeply important fact, namely, that Satan *works from without to within,* which is the very reverse of the Divine operations. God begins His work in man's heart, and the change wrought there reacts and transforms the outward life. But Satan begins with the external and through the bodily senses and emotions of the soul works back to the spirit—the reason for this being, that normally he has not direct access to man's spirit as God has. This same line was followed in reference to our blessed Lord. "Command that these stones be made bread"—appealing to the bodily senses; "Cast Thyself down"—a challenge to His courage or an appeal to the emotional nature of the soul. "Fall down and worship me"—an appeal to the spirit, for we worship the Father "in *spirit* and in truth."

III. The Fall and Man

The first effect of the Fall upon Adam and Eve was a realization of their shame. "And the eyes of them both were opened, and they knew that they were naked." Through sin man obtained that which he did not have before (at least, in operation), namely, *a conscience*—a knowledge of both good and evil. This was something which unfallen man did not possess, for man was created in a state of innocency, and innocence is ignorance of evil. But as soon as man partook of the forbidden fruit he became conscious of his wrongdoing, and his eyes were opened to see his fallen condition. And conscience, the moral instinct, is something which is now common to human nature. Man has that within him which witnesses to his fallen and sinful condition! But not only does conscience bear witness to man's depravity, it is also one of the marks of a personal Creator's handiwork. The conscience cannot be of man's making. He would not voluntarily have set up an accuser, a judge, a tormentor, in his own breast. From whence then does it proceed? It is no more the result of education than is reason or memory, though like both it may be cultivated. Conscience is the still small voice of God within the soul, testifying to the fact that man is not his own master but responsible to a moral law which either approves or reproves.

Having become conscious of their shame Adam and Eve at once endeavored to hide it by making unto themselves aprons of fig leaves. This action of theirs was highly significant. Instead of seeking God and openly confessing their guilt, they attempted to conceal it both from Him and from themselves. Such has ever been the way of the natural man. The very last thing he will do is to own before God his lost and undone condition. Conscious that something is wrong with him, he seeks shelter behind his own self-righteousness and trusts that his good works will more than counter-balance his evil ones. Church-going, religious exercises, attention to ordinances, philanthropy and altruism are the fig leaves which many today are weaving into aprons to cover their spiritual shame. But like those which our first parents sewed together they will not endure the test of eternity. At best they are but things of time which will speedily crumble away to dust.

A passage in the Gospels throws light on the one we are now considering—we refer to another fig tree, the one on which our Lord found no fruit. How striking is the lesson taught us by comparing these two Scriptures! Why are we told that Adam and Eve sewed *fig* leaves together? And why are we informed that it was a *fig* tree which our Lord cursed? Was it not in order that we should connect them together? The fig tree was the *only* thing which our

Lord cursed while He was here upon earth, and are we not intended to learn from that action of His that that which man employs to hide his spiritual shame is directly *under the curse of Christ,* bears no fruit, and is doomed to quickly wither away!

But these self-manufactured aprons did not remove from Adam and Eve the sense of their shame, for when they heard the voice of the Lord God they "hid themselves" from Him. Man's conscience then did not bring him to God—for that there must be the work of the Holy Spirit—rather did it terrify him and drive him away from God. Our first parents sought to hide themselves. Again we note how characteristic and representative was their action. They had some faint conception at least of the moral distance that there was between themselves and their Creator. He was holy, they were sinful, consequently they were afraid of Him and sought to flee from His presence. So it is with the unregenerate today. In spite of all their proud boastings, religious exercises, and self-manufactured coverings, men are uneasy and fearful. Why is it that the Bible is so much neglected? It is because it brings man nearer to God than any other book, and men are uneasy in the presence of God and wish to hide from Him. Why is it that the public ministry of the Word is so sparsely attended? People will proffer many excuses, but the real reason is because that these services bring God near to them and this makes them uncomfortable in their sin, so they seek to flee from Him. How evident it is then that we all shared in the first sin and died in Adam. The position in which the first man stood was a federal one; and that he acted in a representative capacity is seen by the fact that all his children share his nature and perpetuate his transgression.

When God sought out Adam and brought him face to face with his guilt, he was given fair and full opportunity to confess his sin. "Hast thou eaten of the tree, whereof I commanded thee that thou shouldest not eat?" And what was the reply? How did Adam avail himself of this opportunity? Instead of a broken-hearted confession of his sin he *excused* himself—"And the man said, The woman whom thou gavest to be with me, she gave me of the tree, and I did eat." It was the same with Eve: "And the Lord God said unto the woman, What is this that thou hast done? And the woman said, The serpent beguiled me, and I did eat.'' Attempt was thus made to palliate the sin by shifting the responsibility upon others. How marvellously true to life in this twentieth century! What undesigned proofs are these of Divine inspiration! But the very excuse man makes is the ground of his condemnation. We have another illustration of this principle in the parable of the marriage supper. ''I have bought a piece of ground and must *needs* go to see it. I pray thee have me *excused.*'' Where was the ''needs'' be? Just this, that he preferred his own gratification rather than to accept God's invitation. So it was with Adam—''the woman whom thou gavest to be with me''—the excuse he furnishes is the very ground of his condemnation. ''Because thou hast hearkened unto the voice of thy wife, and hast eaten of the tree, of which I commanded thee, saying, thou shalt not eat of it; cursed is the ground for thy sake; in sorrow shalt thou eat of it all the days of thy life.'' All these subterfuges were unavailing and man stood face to face with a holy God and was convicted of his guilt and unspeakable shame. Thus will it be at the great white throne.

We find then that the effects of the Fall (so far as we have yet considered it) upon man himself were fourfold: the discovery that something was wrong with himself; the effort to hide his shame by a self-provided covering; fear of God and an attempt to hide from His presence; and instead of confessing his sin, seeking to excuse it. The same effects are observable today the world over.

5. THE FALL, CONTINUED

IV. The Fall and God

"And the Lord God called unto Adam, and said unto him, Where art thou?" Beautiful indeed is this record of Divine grace. This was not the voice of the policeman, but the call of a yearning love. Dark as is the background here, it only serves more clearly to reveal the riches of God's grace. Highly favored as our first parents were, blest with everything the heart could desire, only a single restriction placed upon their liberty in order to test their loyalty and fidelity to their Maker—how fearful then their fall, how terrible, their sin! What wonder if God had consigned them to "everlasting chains under darkness," as He did the angels when they sinned? What wonder if His wrath had instantly consumed them? Such would have been no undue severity. It would simply have been bare justice. It was all they deserved. But no. In His infinite condescension and abundant mercy, God deigned to be the Seeker, and came down to Eden crying, Where art thou?

W. Griffith Thomas has forcibly summed up the significance of this question in the following words: "God's question to Adam still sounds in the ear of every sinner: 'Where art thou?' It is the call of Divine *justice,* which cannot overlook sin. It is the call of Divine *sorrow,* which grieves over the sinner. It is the call of Divine *love.* which offers redemption from sin. To each and to every one of us the call is reiterated, 'Where art thou?' "

Everything recorded in Genesis 3 has far more than a local significance. God's attitude and action there were typical and characteristic. It was not Adam who sought God, but God that sought Adam. And this has been the order ever since. "There is none that seeketh after God" (Rom. 3:11). It was God who sought out and called Abram while yet an idolater. It was God who sought Jacob at Bethel when he was fleeing from the consequences of his wrong doing. It was God who sought out Moses while a fugitive in Midian. It was Christ who sought out the apostles whilst they were engaged in fishing, so that He could say, "Ye have not chosen Me, but I have chosen you."

It was Christ who, in His ineffable love, came to seek and to save that which was lost. It is the Shepherd who seeks the sheep, and not the sheep that seek the Shepherd. How true it is that "We love Him because He first loved us." O, that we might appreciate more deeply the marvellous condescension of Deity in stooping so low as to care for and seek out such poor worms of the dust.

"And I will put enmity between thee and the woman, and between thy seed and her seed; it shall bruise thy head, and thou shalt bruise his heel" (Gen. 3:15). Here again we behold the exceeding riches of God's grace. Before He acted in judgment He displayed His mercy; before He banished the guilty ones from Eden, He gave them a blessed promise and hope. Though Satan had encompassed the downfall of man, it is announced that One shall come and bruise his head. By woman had come sin, by woman should come the Saviour. By woman had come the curse, by woman should come Him who would bear and remove the curse. By woman Paradise was lost, yet by woman should be born the One who should regain it. O what grace —the Lord of glory was to be *the woman's* Seed!

Here we have the beginning and germ of all prophecy. It would be outside our province now to attempt anything more than a bare outline of the contents of this wonderful verse. But three things should be carefully noted. First, it is announced that there should be enmity between Satan and the woman. This part of the verse is invariably passed over by commentators. Yet it is of profound importance. The "woman" here typifies *Israel*—the woman from whom the promised Seed came—the woman of Revelation 12. The children of Israel being the appointed channel through which the Messiah was to come, became the object of Satan's continued enmity and assault. How marvellously this prediction has already been fulfilled all students of Scripture know full well. The "famines" mentioned in Genesis were the first efforts of the enemy to destroy the fathers of the chosen race. The edict of Pharaoh to destroy all the male children; the Egyptian attack at the Red Sea; the assaults of the Canaanites when in the land; the plot of Haman, are all so many examples of this enmity between Satan and "the woman," while the continued persecution of the Jew by the Gentiles and the yet future opposition by the Beast witness to the same truth.

Second, two "seeds" are here referred to—another item which is generally overlooked—"thy seed" and "her seed" —Satan's seed and the woman's Seed—the Antichrist and the Christ. In these two persons all prophecy converges. In the former of these expressions—"thy seed" (Satan's seed) we have more than a hint of the supernatural and satanic nature and character of the Antichrist. From the beginning the Devil has been an imitator, and the climax will not be reached until he daringly travesties the hypostatic union of the two natures in our blessed Lord—His humanity and His Deity. The Antichrist will be the Man of Sin and yet the Son of Perdition—literally the "seed" of the serpent—just as our Lord was the Son of Man and the Son of God in one person. This is the only logical conclusion. If "her seed" ultimates in a single personality—the Christ—then by every principle of sound interpretation "thy seed" must also ultimate in a single person—the Antichrist.

"Her seed"—the woman's Seed. Here we have the first announcement concerning the supernatural birth of our Saviour. It was prophetically foretold that He should enter this world in an unique manner. "*Her* seed—the woman's seed, not the man's! How literally this was fulfilled we learn from the two inspired records given us in the New Testament of the miraculous conception. A "*virgin*" was with child and four thousand years after this initial prediction "God sent forth His Son, *made of a woman*" (Gal. 4:4).

In the third item of this marvelous prophecy reference is made to a double "bruising"—the woman's Seed shall bruise the Serpent's head, and the Serpent should bruise His heel. The last clause in this prediction has already become history. The "bruising" of the heel of the woman's Seed is a symbolical reference to the sufferings and death of our Saviour, who was "wounded for our transgressions and *bruised* for our iniquities." The first of these clauses yet awaits fulfilment. The bruising of the Serpent's head will take place when our Lord returns to the earth in person and in power, and when "the dragon, that old *serpent*, which is the Devil and Satan shall be bound for a thousand years (the Millennium) and cast into the bottomelss pit (Rev. 20:2, 3). Again, we say, what a remarkable *proof* this verse furnishes us of the Divine Inspiration of the

Scriptures! Who but He who knoweth the end from the beginning could have given such an accurate outline of subsequent history, and packed it within the limits of this one verse?

"Unto Adam also and to his wife did the Lord God make coats of skins, and clothed them" (Gen. 3:21). In order to adequately explain and expound this verse many pages might well be written, but perforce, we must content ourselves with a few lines. This verse gives us a typical picture of a sinner's salvation. It was the first Gospel sermon, preached by God Himself, not in words but in symbol and action. It was a setting forth of the way by which a sinful creature could return unto and approach his holy Creator. It was the initial declaration of the fundamental fact that "without shedding of blood is no remission." It was a blessed illustration of *substitution*—the innocent dying in the stead of the guilty.

Before the Fall, God had defined the wages of sin: "In the day thou eatest thereof thou shalt surely *die.*" God is righteous, and as Judge of all the earth He must do right. His law had been broken and justice cried aloud for the enforcing of its penalty. But is justice to override mercy? Is there no way by which grace can reign through righteousness? Blessed be God there is, there was. Mercy desired to spare the offender and because justice demands death, another shall be slain in his place. The Lord God clothed Adam and Eve with *skins,* and in order to procure these skins animals must have been slain, life must have been taken, blood must have been shed! And *in this way* was a covering provided for the fallen and ruined sinner. The application of the type is obvious. The Death of the Son of God was shadowed forth. Because the Lord Jesus laid down His life for the sheep God can now be *just* and the justifier of him which believeth in Jesus.

How beautiful and perfect is the type! It was the Lord God who furnished the skins, made them into coats and clothed our first parents. They did nothing. God did it all. They were entirely passive. The same blessed truth is illustrated in the parable of the prodigal son. When the wanderer had taken the place of a lost and undone creature and had owned his sin, the grace of the father's heart was displayed. "But the father said to his servants, Bring forth the best robe, and *put it on him*" (Luke 15:22). The prodigal did not have to furnish the robe, nor did he have put it on himself, *all was done for him.* And so it is with every sinner. "For by grace are ye saved through faith, *and that not of yourselves:* it is the gift of God" (Eph. 2:8). Well may we sing, "I will greatly rejoice in the Lord, my soul shall be joyful in my God; for *He hath clothed me with the garments of salvation, He hath covered me with the robe of righteousness*" (Isa. 61:10).

"So He drove out the man; and He placed at the east of the Garden of Eden cherubim and a flaming sword which turned every way to keep the way of the tree of life" (Gen. 3:24). This was the immediate climax in the Divine condemnation of the first sin. After sentence of judgment had been passed first upon the serpent, then upon the woman, and finally upon the man, and after God had acted in mercy by giving them a precious promise to stay their hearts and by providing a covering for their shame, Adam and Eve were driven out of Paradise. The moral significance of this is plain. It was impossible for them to remain in the garden and continue in fellowship with the Lord. He is holy, and that which defileth cannot enter His presence. Sin always results in separation. "But your iniquities have separated between you and your God, and your sins have hid His face from you" (Isa. 59:2).

Here we see the fulfilment of God's threat. He had announced, "In the day thou eatest thereof thou shalt surely *die.*" Die, not only physically—there is something infinitely worse than that—but die spiritually. Just as physical death is the separation of the soul from the body, so spiritual death is the separation of the soul from God.—"This my son was *dead* (separated from me) and is alive again—restored to me. When it is said that we are by nature "dead in trespasses and sins," it is because men are "*alienated from the life of God* through the ignorance that is in them, because of the blindness of their heart" (Eph. 4:18). In like manner, that judicial death which awaits all who die in their sins—the "Second Death"—is not annihilation as so many are now falsely teaching,* but eternal separation from God and everlasting punishment in the lake of fire. And so here in Genesis 3 we have God's own definition of

(*Note in Rev. 20 after the unsaved are resurrected, they are still termed "dead"—dead for ever, dead to God even while they live).

death—separation from Him, evidenced by the expulsion of man from Eden.

The barring of the way to the tree of life illustrated an important spiritual truth. In some peculiar way this tree seems to have been a symbol of the Divine presence (see Prov. 3:18), and the fact that fallen man had no right of access to it further emphasized the moral distance at which he stood from God. The sinner, as such, had no access to God, for the sword of justice barred his way, just as the veil in the Tabernacle and Temple shut man out from the Divine presence. But blessed be God, we read of One who has opened for us a "new and living way" to God, yea, who is Himself the Way (John 14:6). And how has that been accomplished? Did justice withdraw her sword? Nay, it sheathed it in the side of our adorable Saviour. Doubtless that solemn but precious word in Zechariah 13:7, "Awake, *O sword,* against My Shepherd," looks back to Genesis 3:24. And because the Shepherd was smitten the sheep are spared, and in the Paradise of God we shall eat of the fruit of that tree from which Adam was barred (see Rev. 2:7).

Summing up, then, this important division of our subject—God and the Fall—we discover here: An exhibition of His condescension in seeking man; an evidence of His mercy in giving a blessed prophecy and promise to sustain and cheer the heart of man; a demonstration of His grace in providing a covering for the shame of man; a display of His holiness in punishing the sin of man; and a typical foreshadowment of the urgent need of a Mediator between God and man.

6. THE FALL, CONCLUDED

The philosophy of life as interpreted by the Darwinian school, affirms that sin is merely a present imperfection and limitation which will gradually disappear as the human race ascends the hill of life. The evolutionary hypothesis, therefore, not only denies the teaching of Genesis one, but it also repudiates the facts recorded in Genesis three. And here is the real point and purpose of Satan's attack. The specious reasoning of our modern theologians has not only attempted to undermine the authenticity of the account of Creation, but it has also succeeded in blunting the point of the Gospel's appeal.

By denying the Fall, the imperative need of the new birth has been concealed. For, if man began at the *bottom* of the moral ladder—as evolutionists ask us to believe—and is now slowly but surely climbing heavenwards, then all he needs is education and cultivation. On the other hand, if man commenced at the top of the ladder *but through sin fell to the bottom*—as the Bible declares—then he is in urgent need of regeneration and justification. The issue thus raised is vital and fundamental.

V. The Fall and Human History

While we are entirely dependent upon the revelation which God has given us in His Word for our knowledge of the beginnings of human history, and while His Word is absolutely authoritative and to be received with unquestioning faith, and while the Holy Scriptures need no buttressing with human logic and argument, yet an appeal to history and experience is not without interest and value. This is the case in respect to the "Fall." And we would now submit that the teaching of Genesis three is substantiated and vindicated by the great facts of human history and experience.

1. *The Teaching of Human Experience*

Read the annals of history, examine the reports of our police courts, study life in the slums of our large cities, and then ask, How comes it that man, the king of creation, designed and fitted to be its leader and lord, should have sunken lower than the animals? Illustrations are scarcely necessary to show *how* low man *has* sunk, for all who know vice as it really exists beneath the thin covering provided by the conventionalities of modern civilization, are only too painfully aware of the degradation and desolation which exist on all sides. A beast will not abandon its young as is now so frequently the case with the parents of illegitimate children. The beasts of the field put multitudes of human beings to shame, for in the breeding season *they* confine themselves to their own mates—exceptions being found only among those animals which *man* has partially domesticated! No animal will drink foul and poisoned water, yet thousands of well educated men and women are annually poisoned with alcohol.

But what is the cause of these effects. What is the true explanation of these sad facts? How comes it that the king of creation has sunken lower than the beasts of the field? Only one answer is possible—*SIN*, the *FALL*. Sin has entered the human constitution; man is a fallen creature, and as such, capable of any vileness and wickedness.

2. *The Discords of Human Nature*

Man, the unregenerate man, is a composite being. Two principles are at work within him. He is a self-contradiction. One moment he does that which is noble and praiseworthy, but the next that which is base and vile. Sometimes he is amenable to that which is good and elevating, but more often he abandons himself to the pleasures of sin. In some moods he seems closely akin to God, in others he is clearly a child of the devil.

Whence comes this conflict between good and evil? Why this perplexing duality in our common make-up? Only one explanation meets all the facts of the case. On the one hand, man is "the offspring of God"; but, on the other, sin has come in through the Fall and marred the Creator's handiwork.

3. *The Universality of Sin*

Why is it that the king's son in the palace and the saint's daughter in the cottage, in spite of every safeguard which love and watchfulness can devise, manifest an unmistakable bias towards evil and tendency to sin? Why is it that heredity and environment, education and civilization are powerless to change this order? Why are *all* sinful? Why is it that there is no nation, no tribe, no family, free from the taint of sin? Only the Word of God solves this problem. All have a common origin (Adam); all share a common heritage (the Fall); all enter into a common legacy (Sin).

4. *The Existence of Death*

"There is one event that happeneth to all," but why should it? We have been created by the Eternal God, we possess a never-dying soul; why, then, should not men continue to live on this earth for ever? Why should there be such things as decay and destruction? Why should man die? Science can furnish no answer to these questions, and philosophy offers no explanation. Again we are shut up to the Word of God. Death is the wages of sin, and death is universal because sin is universal. If any inquire, Why are sin and death universal, the answer is, "By one man sin entered the world, and death by sin; and so death passed upon all men, for all have sinned."

5. *The Present Paralysis of the Human Race*

Every being and organism is subject to a necessity of becoming other than it is—in a single word, it must *grow.* Not only the animal and the plant, but the crystal, too, obeys this law, and it is difficult to see why humanity which, as history shows, forms an organic whole, alone does not follow it. The only solution of this problem is, that man is not now in his original and normal state: he is no longer as God created him. He who denies the Fall has no light upon this profound mystery. It is beyond doubt that had man never fallen, he would have continued to grow in knowledge, goodness and happiness: in fact, would have become more and more like to God. Enoch, the man who walked with God, and whom He took to Himself after he had lived the great cycle of three hundred and sixty-five years—a year for a day—is an example of a human being who had fulfilled his destiny, and most probably a type of what the destiny of all men might have been. But alas! man fell, hence progress and advancement in the final sense became impossible.

The fact that man has *not* progressed, or rather, is not now progressing, may be seen by comparing the products from the various fields of human enterprise of today with those of two or three thousand years ago. In literature, nothing has appeared which equals the Book of Job, or which rivals the Psalms. In Philology—which is a sure test of the intellectual development and mental life of a people—there is no modern language which matches the Sanskrit. In Art, all that is best we borrow from the ancient Greeks. In Science, we are still far behind the designers and builders of the Pyramids—a recent examination of some mummies has revealed the fact that the Egyptians were ahead of us even in dentistry. In Ethics, the marvellous system formulated by Confucius is superior to anything we have today outside of the Bible. In gigantic civilizations, none have outstripped those of the Babylonians and Phœnicians, which flourished hundreds of years before the Christian era commenced. In legislation, forensic and organizing ability, the Romans have never been surpassed. While physically, we compare unfavorably with the ancients.

Here then is a fact fully demonstrated, that as an organic whole, our race is making no real progress and evidencing no signs of growth. And we repeat, it is the only one among all living organisms which is not growing—growing, not evolving. What, then, is the cause of this mysterious paralysis? How can we account for it except by the explanation furnished in the Word of God, namely, that *this* organism has had a terrible fall, is marred and broken, is not now in its normal and original state!

If then the Fall is a historical fact and the only adequate explanation of human history, what follows? First, man is a fallen creature; second, he is a sinner; third, he needs a Saviour. This then is the foundation of the Gospel appeal. By nature, man is alienated from God, under condemnation, lost. What then is the remedy? The answer is, A new creation. "If any man be in Christ he is a new creation" (2 Cor. 5:17). It is not the cultivation of the old nature which is needed, for that is ruined by the Fall, but the reception of an entirely new nature which is begotten by the Holy Spirit. "Ye *must* be born again." Anything short of this is worthless and useless.

VI. The Fall and Christ

No study of Genesis 3 would be complete without meditating upon it with the Lord Jesus before the heart.

Several passages in the Word link together Adam and Christ, and therefore it behooves us to carefully compare and contrast them. In thinking of Christ and the Fall a threefold line of thought may be developed. First, a contrast between the first man and the second man in their characters and conduct. Second, Christ Himself bearing the Curse of the Fall. Third, Christ reversing the effects of the Fall and bringing in the "better thing." Let us take up these thoughts in this order.

It has been suggested by another, that in eating of the forbidden fruit Adam cast reproach upon God's love, God's truth and God's majesty. Created in the image of his Maker: vitalized by the very breath of Deity: placed in a perfect environment: surrounded by every blessing the heart could desire: put in complete authority over the works of God's hands: provided with a suitable companion and helpmeet: made an example to all the universe of Jehovah's goodness and love, and given one single command that he might have opportunity to show his appreciation by an easy observance of it—yet, he gives ear to the voice of the tempter and believes the Devil's lie.

"And the serpent said unto the woman, Ye shall not surely die: For God doth know that in the day ye eat thereof then your eyes shall be opened, and ye shall be as God, knowing good and evil." What did Satan wish these words to imply? They were as though he said: Did God tell you not to eat of this tree? How unkind! He is withholding from you the very best thing in the garden. He knows full well that if you partake of this fruit your eyes will be opened, and you yourselves will become as God. In other words, it was an appeal for them to distrust God, to doubt His grace, and to question His goodness. Thus in eating of the forbidden fruit, Adam repudiated and dishonored God's *love.*

Moreover, he questioned and dishonored God's veracity. God had plainly warned him. In unequivocal language He had threatened, "In the day thou eatest thereof thou shalt *surely* die." Adam knew nothing of death. He was surrounded only by living creatures. Reason might have argued that it was impossible for *death* to enter such a fair land as Paradise. But there rang the Word of Him who cannot lie, "Thou *shalt* surely die." The serpent, however, boldly denies Jehovah's Word—"Ye shall *not* surely die," he declares. Which would Adam believe—God or Satan. He had more confidence in the latter: he dared to doubt the former, and the fell deed was done. Thus, in eating of the forbidden fruit, Adam repudiated and dishonored God's *Truth*.

Further: he rejected God's authority. As the Creator, God possesses the inherent right to issue commands, and to demand from His creatures implicit obedience. It is His prerogative to act as Law-giver, Controller, Governor, and to define the limits of His subjects' freedom. And in Eden He exercised His prerogative and exprest His will. But Adam imagined he had a better friend than God. He regarded Him as austere and despotic, as One who begrudged him that which would promote his best interests. He felt that in being denied the fruit of this tree which was pleasant to the eyes and capable of making one wise God was acting arbitrarily, cruelly, so he determined to assert himself, claim his rights and throw off the restraint of the Divine government. He substitutes the Devil's word for God's law: he puts his own desire before Jehovah's command. Thus, in eating of the forbidden fruit, Adam repudiated and dishonored God's *Majesty*. So much then for the character and conduct of the first Adam.

In turning to the last Adam we shall find that everything is in direct antithesis. In thought, word and deed, the Christ of God completely vindicated the love, truth, and majesty of Deity which the first man had so grievously and deliberately dishonored. How He vindicated the *love* of God! Adam harbored the wicked thought that God begrudged him that which was beneficial, and thereby questioned His goodness. But how the Lord Jesus has reversed that decision! In coming down to this earth to seek and to save that which was lost, He fully revealed the compassion of Deity for humanity. In His sympathy for the afflicted, in His miracles of healing, in His tears over Jerusalem, in His unselfish and unwearied works of mercy, He has openly displayed the beneficence and benevolence of God. And what shall we say of His sufferings and death on the cruel tree? In laying down His life for us, in dying upon the cross He unveiled the heart of the Father as nothing else could. "God commendeth His *love* toward us, in that, while we were yet sinners, CHRIST *died* for us." In the light of Calvary we can never more doubt the goodness and grace of God.

How Christ vindicated the *truth* of God! When tempted by Satan to doubt God's goodness, question His truth and repudiate His majesty, He answered each time, "It is *written.*" When He entered the synagogue on the Sabbath day it was to read out of the Holy Oracles. When selecting the twelve apostles He designedly chose Judas in order that the Scriptures "might be fulfilled." When censuring His critics, He declared that by their traditions they made void "the Word of God." In His last moments upon the Cross, knowing that all things had been accomplished, in order that the Scriptures might be fulfilled He said, "I thirst." After He had risen from the dead and was journeying with the two disciples to Emmaus, He "expounded unto them in all the Scriptures the things concerning Himself." At every point, and in every detail of His life He honored and magnified God's truth.

Finally, Christ completely vindicated the *majesty* of God. The creature had aspired to be equal with the Creator. Adam chafed against the governmental restraint which Jehovah had placed upon him. He despised God's law, insulted His majesty, defied His authority. How different with our blessed Saviour! Though He was the Lord of Glory and equal with God, yet He made Himself of no reputation, and took upon the form of a *servant.* O matchless grace! He condescended to be "made under the law," and during the whole of His stay here upon earth He refused to assert His rights, and was ever subject to the Father. "Not My will" was His holy cry. Nay, more: "He became *obedient* unto death, *even* the death of the cross." Never was God's law so magnified, never was God's authority so honored, never were God's government claims so illustriously upheld, as during the thirty-three years when His own Son tabernacled among men. Thus in His own Person Christ vindicated the outraged majesty of God.

We turn now to contemplate Christ Himself *bearing* the Curse of the Fall. What was the punishment which followed the first Adam's sin? In answering this question we confine ourselves to the chapter now before us. Beginning at the seventeenth verse of Genesis 3 we may trace a sevenfold consequence upon the entrance of sin into this world. First, the ground was *cursed.* Second, in *sorrow* man was to eat of it all the days of his life. Third, *thorns* and thistles it was to bring forth. Fourth, in the *sweat* of his face man was to eat his bread. Fifth, unto *dust* man was to return. Sixth, a flaming *sword* barred his way to the tree of life. Seventh, there was the execution of God's threat that in the day man partook of the forbidden fruit he should surely *die.* Such was the curse which fell upon Adam as the result of the Fall.

Observe now how completely the Lord Jesus bore the full consequences of man's sin. First, Christ was "made a *curse* for us" (Gal. 3:13). Second, so thoroughly was He acquainted with grief, He was denominated "the man of *sorrows*" (Isa. 53:3). Third, in order that we might know how literally the Holy One bore in His own body the consequences of Adam's sin, we read "Then came Jesus forth wearing the crown of *thorns*" (John 18:8). Fourth, corresponding with the sweat of his face in which the first man was to eat his bread, we learn concerning the second man, "And His *sweat* was as it were great drops of blood falling down to the ground" (Luke 22:44). Fifth, just as the first Adam was to return unto the dust, so the cry of the last Adam, in that wonderful prophetic Psalm, was "Thou hast brought Me into the *dust* of death" (Psalm 22:15). Sixth, the sword of justice which barred the way to the tree of life was sheathed in the side of God's Son, for of old, Jehovah had said, "Awake, O *sword,* against My shepherd, and against the man that is My Fellow" (Zech. 13:7). Seventh, the counterpart of God's original threat to Adam, namely, spiritual death (for he did not die physically that same day), which is the separation of the soul from God, is witnessed in that most solemn of all cries, "My God, My God, Why hast Thou *forsaken* Me?" (Mat. 27:46). How absolutely did our blessed Saviour identify Himself with those which were lost, took their place and suffered the Just for the unjust! How apparent it is, that Christ in His own body, *did* bear the Curse entailed by the Fall.

In conclusion we shall now consider Christ *reversing* the effects of the Fall. God alone is able to bring good out of evil and make even the wrath of man to praise Him. The Fall has afforded Him an opportunity to exhibit His wisdom and display the riches of His grace to an extent which, so far as we can see. He never could have done, had not sin entered the world. In the sphere of redemption Christ has not only reversed the effects of the Fall, but because of it has brought in a better thing. If God could have found a way, consistently with His own character, to restore man to the position which he occupied before he became a transgressor, it would have been a remarkable triumph, but that through Christ man should actually be the *gainer* is a transcendent miracle of Divine wisdom and grace. Yet such is the case. The redeemed have gained more through the last Adam than they lost through the first Adam. They occupy a more exalted position. Before the Fall Adam dwelt in an earthly Paradise, but the redeemed have been made to sit with Christ in heavenly places. Through redemption they have been blest with a nobler nature. Before the Fall man possessed a natural life, but now, all in Christ have been made partakers of the Divine nature. They have obtained a new standing before God. Adam was merely innocent, which is a negative condition, but believers in Christ are righteous, which is a positive state. We share a better inheritance. Adam was lord of Eden, but believers are "heirs of all things," "heirs of God and joint heirs with Christ." Through grace we have been made capable of a deeper joy than unfallen spirits have known: the bliss of pardoned sin, the heaven of deep conscious obligation to Divine mercy. In Christ believers enjoy a closer relationship to God than was possible before the Fall. Adam was merely a creature, but we are members of the body of Christ—"members of His body, of His flesh and of His bones." How marvellous! We have been taken into union with Deity itself, so that the Son of God is not ashamed to call us *brethren.* The Fall provided the need of Redemption, and through the redeeming work of the Cross, believers have a portion which unfallen Adam could never have attained unto. Truly, "where sin abounded, grace did *much more* abound."

7. CAIN AND ABEL

GENESIS 4

There is a very close connection between Genesis 3 and 4. In the former we see the beginning of sin in man, in the latter we read of its progress and fruits; in the one it was sin in the individual, in the other, sin in the family. Like leprosy, sin contaminates, spreads and issues in death. In Genesis 3 the sin was against God, in Genesis 4 it is against a fellow-man. The order here is ever the same; the one who has no fear of God before his eyes, has no genuine respect for the rights of his neighbor. Again, in Genesis 4 we see the *local* fulfilment of Genesis 3:15—the *enmity* between the two seeds—the wicked and the righteous, Cain and Abel. Further; we are shown, even more clearly than by the coats of skins in the previous chapter, that the guilty sinner can only approach God by means of a sacrifice. We propose now to study briefly the contents of Genesis 4 from three viewpoints, namely; the historical, the typical and the dispensational.

I. Cain and Abel Considered Historically

The record of Genesis 4 is exceedingly terse and much is gathered up which scarcely appears on the surface. The central truth of the chapter is that God is to be worshipped, that He is to be worshipped through sacrifice, that He is to be worshipped by means of a sacrifice which is appropriated by faith (cf. Heb. 11:4). Three things are to be carefully noted in regard to the worship of Cain and Abel. First, that there was a place where God was to be worshipped. This is indicated in the third verse: "Cain brought of the fruit of the ground an offering unto the Lord." That is, he *brought* his offering to some particular place. This supposition seems to be supported by the language of verse 16—"And Cain *went out from* the presence of the Lord." A further corroboration may be discovered in the mention of "the fat" which Abel brought (verse 4). "The firstlings of his flock and the fat thereof" suggests an *altar* upon which the victim should be offered and upon which the fat should be burned. Where this place of worship was located perhaps we cannot say for certain, but there is ground for believing that it was at the east of the Garden of Eden. Jamieson, Fausset and Brown, in their commentary on Genesis, translate the last verse of Genesis 3 as follows: "And He (God) dwelt at the east of the Garden of Eden between the Cherubim, as a Shekinah (a fire-tongue or fire-sword) to keep open the way to the tree of life."* The same thought is presented in the Jerusalem Targum. If the grammatical construction of the Hebrew will warrant this translation, then Genesis 3:24 would seem to signify that, having expelled man from the garden, God established a mercy-seat protected by the Cherubim, the fire-tongue or sword being the symbol of the Divine presence, and whoever would worship God must approach this mercy-seat by way of sacrifice. We commend this suggestion to the prayerful consideration of our readers. To say the least, Genesis 4 seems to imply that there was some definite place to which Cain and Abel brought their offerings, a place which they entered and from which they went out.

Second: Not only does there appear to have been a definite place of worship, but there seems also to have been an appointed *time* for worship. The marginal reading of Genesis 4:3 gives, "And at the end of days it came to pass, that Cain brought of the fruit of the ground an offering unto the Lord." May not this signify, at the end of the week? In other words, does not this expression appear to point to *the Sabbath day* as the time when God was to be formally worshipped? A third thing implied is a prescribed *means* of worship. God could be approached and worshipped only by means of sacrifice. This incident then seems to intimate that the children of Adam and Eve had been definitely instructed that there was a place where God could be found, that there was a time in which to come before Him, and that appointed means of approach had been established. Neither Cain nor Abel would have known anything about sacrifices unless sacrifices had been definitely appointed. From Hebrews 11:4 we learn that it was "By faith Abel offered" his sacrifice, and in Romans 10:17 we are told that "Faith cometh by hearing." It was by faith and not by fancy that Abel brought his offering to God.

---

*We may say that the Hebrew word *shaken*, which in Genesis 3:24 is translated "placed" is defined in Young's Concordance "to tabernacle," etc. Nowhere else in the Old Testament is *shaken* translated "placed," but eighty-three times it is rendered "to dwell." It is the same Hebrew word which is given as "to dwell" in Exodus 25:8.

He had *heard* that God required a sacrifice, he believed, and he evidenced his faith by a compliance with God s revealed will.

The *nature* of the offerings which Cain and Abel brought unto the Lord, and God's rejection of the one and acceptance of the other, point us to the most important truth in the chapter. Attention should be fixed not so much on the two men themselves, as upon the difference between their offerings. So far as the record goes there is nothing to intimate that up to this time Cain was the worst man of the two, that is, considered from a natural and moral standpoint. Cain was no infidel or atheist. He was ready to acknowledge the existence of God, he was prepared to worship Him after his own fashion. He "brought of the fruit of the ground an offering unto the Lord." But mark three things. First, his offering was a bloodless one, and "without shedding of blood is no remission" (Heb. 9:22). Second, his offering consisted of the fruit of his own toil, it was the product of his own labors, in a word, it was the works of his own hands. Third, he brought of "the fruit of the ground," thus ignoring the Divine sentence recorded in Genesis 3:17, "Cursed is the ground." Abel "brought of the firstlings of his flock and the fat thereof," and to secure this, sacrifice had to be made, life had to be taken, blood had to be shed. The comment of the Holy Spirit upon this incident is, that "By faith Abel offered unto God *a more excellent sacrifice* than Cain" (Heb. 11:4). He does not state that Abel was more excellent, but that the offering which he presented was more pleasing and acceptable to his Maker.

Next we learn that "The Lord had respect unto Abel and to his offering," or, as Hebrews 11:4 expresses it, "God *testifying* of his gifts." By comparing later Scriptures we may justly infer that the manner in which Jehovah showed His acceptance of the offering was by fire coming down from heaven and consuming the sacrifice (see Lev. 9:24; Judges 6:21; 1 Kings 18:38; 1 Chron. 21:26; 2 Chron. 7:1). "But unto Cain and his offering He had not respect." No doubt Cain's offering was a very beautiful one. No doubt he selected the very choicest fruits that could be found. No doubt his offering cost him considerable toil and labor, and probably it was with no little self-satisfaction that he came before the Lord. But Jehovah had no respect unto his gift; there was no visible token of the Divine approval; no fire came down from heaven to consume it in proof of God's acceptance. And Cain's countenance fell. He was furious that all his labors should stand for nothing. He was angry at the thought that he could not approach and worship God according to the dictates of his own mind. And, as we shall see later, he was filled with wrath as he contemplated the exaltation of Abel above him. So it is today. Unless the darkened understanding of man be illumined by the Holy Spirit and the enmity of the carnal mind be subdued, the human heart rebels against the idea of the impossibility of approaching God save through a bloody sacrifice. The natural man in his pride and self-righteousness hates the truths of substitution and expiation worse than he hates the Devil.

"And the Lord said unto Cain, Why art thou wroth? and why is thy countenance fallen?" The condition of Cain's heart was clearly revealed by his anger at God's refusal to receive his offering. His worship, like that of multitudes in our day, was merely "a form of godliness, but denying the power thereof" (2 Tim. 3:5), that is, destitute of any genuineness or reality. Had Cain's offering been presented in the right spirit there would have been no "wroth" when Jehovah refused to accept it, but instead, a humble desire to learn God's will.

"If thou doest well, shalt thou not be accepted? And if thou doest not well, sin lieth at the door; and unto thee shall be his desire, and thou shalt rule over him" (Gen. 4:7). This verse has always been a difficult one to expositors and commentators, and we have never yet seen any explanation of it that fully satisfied us. The interpretation most widely received is as follows: Why art thou wroth, Cain? If thou doest well—if you will present the proper and specified offering it will be accepted; and if thou doest not well—if the offering you brought has been rejected the remedy is simple—"sin lieth at the door," *i. e.*, a suitable and meet offering, a sin offering is right to your hand, and if you present this you shall "have the excellency" (margin), that is, you shall retain the right of the firstborn and have the precedence over Abel your younger brother. The Hebrew word here translated sin, is in other passages sometimes rendered sin-offering—the one Hebrew word doing duty for our two English expressions. Though many of the ablest Bible students have accepted this translation and interpretation, we feel obliged to humbly dissent from it. And for this reason. Apart from this one doubtful case (Gen. 4:7), doubtful, as to whether or not the Hebrew word should be translated sin or sin-offering—there is no other reference in Scripture of any Sin offering before the giving of the Law at Sinai. We do read of the patriarch's presenting burnt and meat offerings, but never of sin offerings. In the light of Romans 3:20 we firmly believe that there was *no sin offering before Moses.* "By the Law is the knowledge of sin." The Law was given in order that sin might be recognized as sin. It was the Law which convicted men of sin and of their need of a sin offering. Hence we submit that there was no sin offering before the Law was given. Job 1:5 supports this contention, "And it was so, when the days of their feasting were gone about, that Job sent and sanctified them, and rose up early in the morning, and *offered burnt offerings* according to the number of them all, for Job said, It may be that my sons have sinned and cursed God in their hearts"—had they sinned after the Law was given a sin offering, not a burnt offering, would have been needed. What then is the significance of Genesis 4:7?

Undoubtedly the words "If thou doest well" have reference to the bringing of a proper offering to the Lord. In case Cain was willing to do this Jehovah asks, "Shalt thou not have the excellency" (margin), which means, Shalt thou not retain the right of primogeniture over Abel? "And if thou doest not well sin lieth at the door," which we understand to mean, If you refuse to bring the required offering, sin lieth (Hebrew, is crouching) at the door, and like a wild beast is ready to spring upon you and devour you. The remainder of the verse referring back to the matter of Cain's rights by virtue of his seniority.

The use of the word "And" all through the passage and the word "Also" in verse 4 seem to show that Cain and Abel came together to present their offerings unto the Lord. Abel's offering was accepted, Cain's was rejected. Probably, Cain reasoned from this that there would likely be a change in the order of primogeniture and that his younger brother should become his ruler. Hence his "wroth" and readiness to kill Abel rather than submit to him. In a word Cain intended to be first at all costs. Believing that he had lost the place and privilege of the firstborn—for only upon his bringing of the stipulated offering could he continue to rule over his brother—and refusing to sacrifice according to God's requirements, and fearing that Abel would now be his ruler, he decided that rather than submit to this, he would kill his brother. Such we believe to be the real explanation, the motive, the cause of the first murder. The first word of verse 8 which recounts the deed bears this out, linking it as it does with the previous verse.

To summarize our suggested interpretation of verse 7: Cain's offering having been refused, anger filled his heart. Jehovah asks him why he is wroth, and tells him there is no just cause for his displeasure, and that if he will bring the required offering it would be accepted and Cain would then retain the rights of the firstborn. At the same time God faithfully and solemnly warns him of the consequences which will follow his refusal to bring the specified sacrifice. If his sin is not removed by an expiatory offering, it will spring upon and devour him. Cain refused to comply with Jehovah's demands and the Divine threat was carried out. What an illustration of James 1:15! "When lust (desire, passion) hath conceived, it bringeth forth sin: and sin when it is finished (consummated), bringeth forth death." This was the precise order in Cain's case: first—lust, anger—then, sin—lying at the door,—then, death—Abel murdered.

"And the Lord said unto Cain, Where is Abel thy brother? And he said, I know not. Am I my brother's keeper? And He said, What hast thou done? the voice of thy brother's blood crieth unto me from the ground." Sin cannot be hid. There may have been no human witness to Cain's crime, but the eye of God had seen it. Solemn is the lesson taught here. "Be not deceived, God is not mocked." "Be sure your sin will find you out." "For there is nothing covered, that shall not be revealed; neither hid, that shall not be known," are only so many ways of stating the same truth. To Jehovah's pointed inquiry, Cain replied, "I know not." How this brings out the inveterate evil of the human heart! There was no contrition, no confessing of sin, but instead, a repudiation and covering of it. So it was with our first parents in Eden, and so it ever is with all their descendants until God's grace works effectually in us. It is to be noted that we have here the first mention of "blood" in Scripture, and like all first mentionings therein, it expresses what is primary and fundamental, hinting also at the amplifications of subsequent teaching. The blood here was innocent blood, blood shed by wicked hands, blood which cried aloud to God. How deeply significant! How it speaks to us of the precious blood of Christ!

After the Divine inquisition comes the Divine sentence upon the guilty one telling of God's holiness and righteousness which will not for an instant tolerate sin, "And now art thou cursed from the earth, which hath opened her mouth to receive thy brother's blood from thy hand. When thou tillest the ground, it shall not henceforth yield unto thee her strength; a fugitive and a vagabond shalt thou be in the earth." No matter where he should go in the world the ground should be against him, the ground that held the blood of his brother, the blood of his victim. The remembrance of his murder should pursue him, so that he would not be able to content himself long in any one place.

"And Cain said unto the Lord, My punishment is greater than I can bear." Cain now realizes something of what he has done, though his mind is occupied more with his punishment than with the sin which had caused it. "My punishment is greater than I can bear" will be the language of the lost in the Lake of Fire. The awful lot of the unsaved will be unbearable, and yet it will have to be endured and endured for ever. "From Thy face shall I be hid" cried Cain. Though the sinner knows it not, this will be the most terrible feature of his punishment—eternally banished from God. "Depart from Me ye cursed" will be the fearful sentence passed upon the wicked in the day of judgment. "And Cain went out from the presence of the Lord, and dwelt in the land of Nod." Nod means "wandering"—there is no peace or rest for the wicked: in this world they are like the troubled waves of the sea; in the world to come, they shall be like wandering stars, lost in the blackness of darkness for ever. My reader, if you reject the Sacrifice of the Lord Jesus Christ, Cain's doom shall be your doom. "He that believeth on the Son hath everlasting life: and he that believeth not the Son shall not see life; but the wrath of God abideth on him."

8. CAIN AND ABEL, CONTINUED

II. Cain and Abel Considered Typically or Representatively

Cain and Abel stand as the representatives of two great classes of people. They typify respectively the lost and the saved; the self-righteous and the broken-spirited; the formal professor and the genuine believer; those who rely upon their own works, and those who rest upon the finished work of Christ; those who insist upon salvation by human merits, and those who are willing to be saved by Divine grace; those who are rejected and cursed by God, and those who are accepted and blessed. Both Cain and Abel were the children of fallen parents, and both of them were born outside of Eden. Both were, therefore, by nature "children of wrath," and as such judicially alienated from God. Both had been shapen in iniquity and conceived in sin, and hence both stood in need of a Saviour. But, as we shall show, Cain denied his ruined and fallen condition and refused to accept the Remedy God provided; while Abel acknowledged his sinnership, believed the Divine testimony, put his faith in a sacrificial substitute, and was accounted righteous before God.

In our study of Genesis 3, we saw that before God banished our first parents from Eden, He revealed to them the way of salvation: "Unto Adam also and to his wife did the Lord God make coats of skins and clothed them (Gen. 3: 21). This was the first Gospel sermon ever preached on this earth, preached not by word but by symbol. By clothing Adam and Eve with these skins God taught them four lessons. First, that in order for a guilty sinner to approach a holy God he needed a suitable covering. Second, that the aprons of fig leaves which their own hands had made were not acceptable to Him. Third, that God Himself must provide the covering. Fourth, that the necessary covering could only be obtained through death. Death is the wages of sin. Adam and Eve had broken God's command, and justice clamored for the execution of law's penalty. Either they must die or another must die in their place. Mercy can only come in after justice has been satisfied. Grace reigns "through righteousness," and never at the expense of it. God dealt with Adam and Eve in mercy, but in doing so He first met the claims of His broken law. In clothing them with *skins* God showed them by forceful symbol that sin could only be covered—atoned for, for the Hebrew word for atone means "to cover"—at the cost of sacrifice, by life being taken, by blood being shed. And so in Eden itself we find the first type and foreshadowment of the Cross of Christ. To Adam and Eve, God preached the blessed and basic truth of *substitution*—the just dying for the unjust, the innocent suffering for the guilty. Adam and Eve were guilty and merited destruction, but these animals died in their stead, and by their death a covering was provided to hide their sin and shame. So it is with Christ and the believer. In Him I am provided with a robe of righteousness—"the best robe"—which perfectly satisfies the eye of the thrice holy God.

In Eden then we hear the first Gospel message. But not only so, in Eden God showed man plainly and unmistakably *what He required of him.* In the slaying of those animals from whose bodies the skins were taken to clothe our first parents, God revealed the condition upon which alone the sinner can approach his Maker, namely, blood-shedding. *Man must put a substitute between himself and God's wrath.* In the slaying of the animal, the offerer identified himself with his offering and acknowledged that he was a sinner, that he deserved naught but judgment at God's hands, that death was his legitimate due. In the slaying of the offering with which the offerer had identified himself, he saw the death of his *substitute,* the meeting of God's claims, the satisfying of Divine justice, and that, because his substitute had died in his stead, he went free.

We have again commented somewhat freely upon Genesis 3:21 because our understanding of this important verse is necessary in order to intelligently apprehend the contents of Genesis 4. As we have seen, Adam and Eve were clearly and definitely instructed by God Himself concerning the terms of approach to their Maker. To them He explicitly revealed His requirements, *and these requirements were made known by Adam and Eve to their children.* It is beyond question that Cain and Abel knew that in order to come before Jehovah with acceptance they must bring with them a bloody offering. Heb. 11:4 makes that fact abundantly clear. It was "by faith" that Abel presented his sacrifice to God, and Romans 10:17 tells us "Faith cometh *by hearing* and hearing by the Word of God," hence it is evident that he and his brother had "heard" of God's requirements.

"And in process of time it came to pass, that Cain brought of the fruit of the ground an offering unto the Lord." In bringing such an offering Cain deliberately turned his back on God's revealed will and dared to set up his own will in defiance. In bringing the offering he did, Cain denied that he was a fallen creature—the fallen child of fallen parents—and as such under the sentence of Divine condemnation. He denied that he was a guilty sinner, morally and penally separated from God. He deliberately ignored God's demand for expiation by the death of a sacrificial substitute. He insisted upon approaching God on the ground of personal worthiness. Instead of accepting God's way, he audaciously went his own way and selected an offering which commended itself to his own tastes. He offered to God the fruits of the ground which God had cursed. He presented the product of his own toil, the work of his own hands, and God refused to receive it.

Cain represents the *natural* man. He represents those who turn their back upon the blood of the Cross and who speak of the Atonement as "a doctrine of the shambles." He represents that large class of people who reject the finished Work of the Lord Jesus Christ, and who think to obtain salvation by works of righteousness which they have done. Cain is the father of the Pharisee, who prides himself that he is the superior of the contritious Publican, and who boasts loudly of his morality and religiousness. He is the representative of all who pride themselves that they can in their own strength live a life which is pleasing to God and who can by their own efforts produce that which shall merit Divine esteem.

Jude, verse 11, pronounces a solemn woe upon those who have "gone in the way of Cain." To whom does he refer? They are those who deny that the whole human race sinned and fell in Adam and who are therefore by nature children of wrath. They are those who deny that man has been driven out of God's presence and that a great gulf is now fixed between them. They deny that that gulf can only be bridged by the Cross of Christ and that through Him and

His redemption lies the sole way back to the Father. They deny that human nature is essentially evil, incurably wicked, and under the curse of God. They deny that it is absolutely impossible for a clean thing to come out of an unclean, and that unless a man be born again he cannot see the Kingdom of God. On the contrary, they declare that human nature is essentially good, and that by a process of development and culture it can bring forth good fruit —fruit which is acceptable to God. They offer this fruit unto God in the form of moral character, unselfish deeds and charitable works. Their language is, Something in my hands I bring, to my goodness I do cling. *This* is the way of Cain. Cain brought of the fruits of the ground which God had cursed, and God had no respect unto such an offering. Human nature is under God's curse, and as like can only produce like, it follows that human works—the best of them—are only the fruits of a cursed ground; as it is written, "All our righteousnesses are as filthy rags," *i. e.,* obnoxious to God. As it was in the beginning, so it is now. God has no respect for such offerers and offerings. He will not accept them. The only offering that God will receive is that which is presented to Him on the ground of the merits of His blessed Son.

"And Abel, he also brought of the firstlings of his flock and of the fat thereof. And the Lord had respect unto Abel and to his offering" (Gen. 4:4). Abel presents a sharp antithesis to Cain. In bringing the offering which he did Abel confessed that he was a fallen creature, a guilty sinner, one at a moral and penal distance from God. He bowed to the Divine sentence of condemnation resting upon him and owned its justice. He acknowledged that he was worthy of death. By offering a lamb he testified that his only hope before God lay in a substitute taking his place and bearing the penalty which was his due. He presented his offering "by faith." That is to say, he believed that God would accept this slain lamb, that its shed blood would meet all His requirements and satisfy His justice. He had heard from the lips of his parents that the only way back to God was through sacrifice—through an innocent life being offered up on the behalf of the guilty, and having heard this he believed it, and believing it he acted upon it. This is precisely what constitutes saving faith: It is believing God's Word *and acting on it.* Consider an illustration in proof: "He said unto Simon, Launch out into the deep, and let down your nets for a draught. And Simon answering said unto Him, Master, we have toiled all the night, and have taken nothing: *nevertheless at Thy Word* I will let down the net" (Luke 5:4, 5). Faith is more than an intellectual assent. Faith is the committal of ourselves to God's Word. Faith necessarily involves volition, "*I will let* down the net." Faith flies in the face of all carnal reasonings, feelings and experience and says, "*Nevertheless at* Thy Word I will." Abel then took God at His Word, offered his sacrifice by faith and was accepted and pronounced righteous.

As Cain represents the natural man so Abel typifies the spiritual man, the man born from above, the man created anew in Christ Jesus. Abel is the representative of those who take God's side against themselves; who accept the character which God has given them in His Word; who own that they are lost, undone, helpless; who realize their only hope lies outside of themselves in Another, and who realizing this, cast themselves upon God's grace, crying, "God be merciful to me a sinner." Abel represents those who pin their faith to the atoning sacrifice of Calvary, who rest their all both for time and eternity on the redemptive work of the Cross, who sing from their hearts, "My hope is built on nothing less than Jesus' blood and righteousness." In short, Abel stands as a lasting type of all who receive as their substitute and Saviour the Lamb of God which taketh away the sin of the world.

The ultimate difference, then, between Cain and Abel was not in their characters, but in their offerings. In one word, it was a difference of blood. Abel was accepted because he offered to God a bleeding lamb. Cain was rejected because he refused to offer such. Here, then, we have traced back to their fountain head the two streams which empty themselves in Heaven and Hell, namely, the saved and the lost, and the dividing line between them in a line of blood. That was the difference between the Israelites and the Egyptians. On the night when God's avenging angel passed through the land of Pharaoh and found a house upon whose door blood was sprinkled—the blood of a lamb, he passed over. But, when he found a house without blood upon it, he entered and slew the firstborn, from the king upon his throne to the prisoner in the dungeon.

This will be the test in the day of judgment—all whose names are not found written in *the Lamb's* book of life shall be cast into the lake of fire. Redemption is to be obtained only through Jesus Christ. "Whom God hath set forth to be a propitiation *through faith in His blood*" (Rom. 3:26). Reader, on what is your hope based? If you are relying upon your efforts and works, if you are trusting to your own goodness and morality to carry you through, you are building your house upon a foundation of sand and great will be the fall of it. But, if you are trusting in and relying upon the merits of the precious blood of Christ, then are you building upon the rock, and in that Rock shall you find shelter from the wrath to come. And now in conclusion:

III. Cain and Abel Considered Dispensationally

"Now all these things happened unto them *for types* (margin); and they are written for our admonition" (1 Cor. 10:11). Abel is a striking type of Christ, and his murder by Cain was a remarkable foreshadowment of our Lord's rejection and crucifixion by the Jews. At least thirty-five points of resemblance can be traced here between type and antitype. In considering Abel as a type of our Lord, it is to be noted that, like Isaac, offered up on the altar and the ram caught in a thicket, which afterwards took his place in death, we have here a double type also. Both Abel and the offering which he brought pointed to the Lord Jesus. To make it easier for our readers to follow us, we have numbered the different points of agreement in type and antitype.

(1) Abel was a shepherd (Gen. 4:2) and (2) it was *as* a shepherd that he presented his offering unto God. (3) Though giving no cause for it, he was hated by his brother. As we have shown in the last chapter, Cain was jealous of his brother and (4) it was out of "envy" that he slew him. (5) Abel then did not die a natural death, but (6) met with a violent end at the hand of his own brother. (7) After his death God declared that Abel's blood "cried" unto Him, and severe punishment was meted out upon his murderer.

Turning from Abel himself to his offering, we note: (8) Abel presented an offering "unto God" (Heb. 11:4). (9) That the offering which he presented was "the firstlings of his flock": in other words, a "lamb." (10) In bringing his offering "by faith," he honored and magnified the Will and Word of the Lord. (11) The offering which Abel presented is described as an "excellent" one (Heb. 11:4). (12) God had "respect unto Abel and to his offering": in other words, He accepted them. (13) In the presentation of his offering Abel "obtained witness that he was righteous" (Heb. 11:4). (14) After he had presented his offering, God publicly "testified" His acceptance of it. (15) Finally, Abel's offering still "speaks" to God —"*By it* he being dead *yet speaketh.*"

The type is perfect at every point. (1) Our Lord is a "shepherd"—the Good Shepherd—and (2) it was *as* the Shepherd He presented His offering to God (John 10:11). (3) Though giving no cause for it, He was hated by His brethren according to the flesh (John 15:25). (4) It was through "envy" that He was delivered up to be crucified (Matt. 27:18). (5) Our Lord did not die a natural death. He was "slain" by wicked hands (Acts 2:23). (6) He was crucified by "The House of Israel" (Acts 2:36), His own brethren according to the flesh. (7) After His death our Lord's murderers were severely punished by God (Mark 12:9).

Turning from Himself to His offering we note: (8) The Lord Jesus presented an offering "to God" (Eph. 5:2). (9) The offering He presented was Himself—a "Lamb" (1 Peter 1:19). (10) In presenting Himself as an offering He honored and magnified the Will and Word of God (Heb. 10:7-9). (11) The offering Christ presented was an "excellent" one—it was a "sweet smelling savor" (Eph. 5:2). (12) God accepted His offering: the proof of this is seen in the fact that He is now seated at God's right hand (Heb. 10:12). (13) While presenting Himself on the Cross as an offering to God, He "obtained witness that He was righteous"—the centurion crying, "Certainly this was a *righteous* man" (Luke 23:47). (14) God publicly testified His acceptance of Christ's offering by raising Him from the dead (Acts 2:32). (15) Christ's offering now "speaks" to God (Heb. 12:24).

Just as Abel and his offering are, at every point, a wonderful type of Christ and His offering, so Cain, who slew Abel, prefigures the Jews, who crucified their Messiah. (16) Cain was "a tiller of the ground" (Gen. 4:2). Thus the first thing told us about him connects him with *the land.*

(17) In refusing to bring the required lamb, Cain rejected the offering which God's grace had provided. (18) In his self-righteousness Cain brought an offering of his own choosing. (19) The offering he brought was the product of his own labors. (20) This offering was rejected by God. (21) It was Cain's God-given privilege to rule over his brother (Gen. 4:7). (22) This privilege he forfeited. (23) Being envious of Abel, he wickedly slew him. (24) God charged him with his crime. (25) God told him that Abel's blood cried for vengeance. (26) Because of the shedding of his brother's blood, God's curse fell upon Cain. (27) Part of his punishment consisted in the ground becoming barren to him (Gen. 4:12). (28) Further, he was to be a fugitive and vagabond in the earth. (29) Cain acknowledged that his punishment was greater than he could bear. (30) Because of his sin, he was "driven out" (Gen. 4:14). (31) Because of his sin, he was hidden from God's face. (32) Every man's hand was now against him (Gen. 4:14). (33) God set a mark upon him (Gen. 4:15). (34) God declared that He would visit with a sevenfold vengeance those who slew Cain. (35) Cain left the land and went and dwelt in a city (Gen. 4:17).

Turning once more to the antitype, let us note how accurately Cain foreshadowed the history of Israel. (16) The first thing which is conspicuous about the Jews was that they were the people of a land—the promised land, the Holy Land (Gen. 13:15). (17) In refusing the Lamb of God (John 1:11) the Jews rejected the offering which God's grace had provided. (18) The apostle Paul declares that the Jews were "ignorant of God's righteousness and going about to establish *their own* righteousness" (Rom. 10:3). (19) The Jews rested upon their own obedience to God's Law (Rom. 9:21). (20) But God had no respect to their works (Acts 13:39). (21) Had Israel walked in God's statutes they would have been the head of the nations (Deut. 28:13). (22) But through sin they forfeited the place and privilege (Isa. 9:14). (23) It was the Jews who crucified the Christ of God (Acts 5:30). (24) God charged them with their crime (Acts 2:22, 23). (25) Christ's blood is now judicially resting "upon" the Jews (Matt. 27:25). (26) Because of the crucifixion of their Messiah, God's curse fell upon Israel (Jer. 24:9). (27) Part of the curse which God threatened of old to bring upon Israel was the barrenness of their land—"desolate" (Lev. 26:34, 35). (28) The Jew has been an age-long wanderer in the earth (Deut. 28:65). (29) Israel will yet acknowledge their punishment is greater than they can bear (Zech. 12:10). (30) Forty years after the Crucifixion, Israel was driven out of Palestine. (31) Since then God's face has been hid from them (Hos. 1:9). (32) For nigh 2,000 years, almost every man's hand has been against the Jew (Deut. 28:66). (33) A mark of identification has been placed upon the Jew so that he can be recognized anywhere. (34) God's special curse has always rested on those who have cursed Israel (Gen. 12:3). (35) For the most part, even to this day, the Jews continue to congregate in large cities.

Upon what ground can we account for this remarkable agreement between type and antitype? The only possible explanation lies in the supernatural inspiration of the Old Testament Scriptures. The Holy Spirit "moved" the writer of Genesis. Only He who knew the end from the beginning could have foreshadowed so accurately and minutely that which came to pass thousands of years afterwards. Prophecy, either in direct utterance or in symbolic type, is the Divine autograph upon the sacred page. May God continue to strengthen our faith in the divinity, the authority and the absolute sufficiency of the Holy Oracles.

9. ENOCH

GENESIS 5

In our comments upon the fourth chapter of Genesis, we noted how that the descendants of Adam followed two distinct lines of worship through Cain and Abel, Abel worshipping God by faith and bringing a bleeding sacrifice as the ground of his approach; Cain, ignoring the double fact that he was *depraved* by nature because descended from fallen parents, and a *sinner* by choice and deed and, therefore, rejecting the vicarious expiation prescribed by grace, tendered only the product of his own labors, which was promptly refused by his Maker. The remainder of the chapter traces the godless line of Cain down to the seventh generation, and then closes with an account of the birth of Seth—the appointed successor of Abel and the one from whom the chosen race and the Messiah should come.

Genesis 5 begins a new section and traces for us the line of Seth. The opening words of this chapter are worthy of close attention. No less than ten times we find in Genesis this phrase, "These are the generations of," (see 2:4; 6:9; 10:1; 11:10; 11:27; 25:12; 25:19; 36:1; 36:9; 37:2); but here in Genesis 5:1 there is an important addition —"*This is the book* of the generations of Adam." Nowhere else in Genesis, nor, indeed, in the Old Testament (compare Num. 3:1 and Ruth 4:18), does *this* form of expression recur. But we *do* find it once more when we open the New Testament, and there it meets us in the very first verse! "*The book* of the generation of Jesus Christ."* This is deeply significant and a remarkable proof of *verbal* inspiration.

Why, then, should there be these two different forms of expression, and only these two—Genesis 5:1 and Matthew 1:1—exceptions to the usual form? Surely the answer is not far to seek. Are not these the two books of Federal Headship? In the first book—"The *book* of the generations

*Students of Scripture Numerics will observe above that there are just *thirteen* of these "generations" recorded in the Old Testament—the number of rebellion and apostasy (see Gen. 14:4). It is man's ruin fully told out! Thirteen was all that the law could reveal! But grace and truth came by Jesus Christ, hence, *He* added (Matt. 1:1) to the Old Testament. Fourteen gives us double perfection—perfect God and perfect Man. Or, taking the multiples separately, we have division or difference (the significance of two) and completeness (seven). What a *complete difference* the fourteenth—"The generation of Jesus Christ"—has made!

of Adam"—are enrolled the names of the fallen descendants of the first man; in the second—"The *book* of the generation of Jesus Christ"—are inscribed the names of all who have been redeemed by sovereign grace. One is the Book of Death; the other is the Lamb's Book of Life.

"The book of the generations of Adam,"	"The book of the generation of Jesus Christ,"

and do we not see the marvelous *unity* of the two Testaments? The whole of the Bible centers around these two books—the book of the generations of Adam, and the book of the generation of Jesus Christ.

But what is the force of this word "generations"? Here the law of First Mention will help us. The initial occurrence of this expression defines its scope. When we read in Genesis 2:4 "These are the generations of the heavens and of the earth" the reference is not to origin but to development. Had Genesis 2:4 been intended to supply information as to how the heavens and the earth were produced, this expression would have occurred at the commencement of Genesis 1, which treats of that subject. Again, when we read of "The generations of Noah" (Gen. 6:9) it is *not* to give us the *ancestry* of this patriarch—that is found in Genesis 5—but to tell us who were his *descendants,* as the very next verse goes on to show. "Generations," then, means *history, development,* and not origin. Try this key in each lock and you will find it fits perfectly. "The generations (or history) of the heavens and of the earth." So here in Genesis 5:1. From this point onwards we have the history and development of Adam's progeny. So, too, of Matthew 1:1. What is the New Testament but the history and development of Jesus Christ and His "brethren"?

As we have stated, chapter five opens a new section of Genesis. Righteous Abel has been slain, and all the descendants of Cain are doomed to destruction by the Flood. It is from *Seth* that there shall issue Noah, whose children, coming out of the Ark, shall replenish the earth. Hence it is that we are here taken back once more *to the beginning.* Adam is again brought before us—fallen Adam—to show us the source from which Seth sprang.

Two sentences in the opening verses of this chapter (Gen. 5) need to be carefully compared and contrasted.

"In the day that God created man, *in the likeness of God made He him,*" Gen. 5:1. "And Adam...begat a son *in his own likeness, after his image,*" Gen. 5:3. By sin Adam lost the image of God and became corrupt in his nature and a fallen parent could do no more than beget a fallen child. Seth was begotten in the likeness of a sinful father! Since Noah was the direct descendant of Seth and is the father of us all, and since he was able to transmit to us only that which he had, himself, received from Seth, we have here the doctrine of *universal depravity.* Every man living in the world today is, through Noah and his three sons, a descendant of Seth, hence it is that care is here taken at the beginning of this new section to trace the spring back to its fountain head, and show how all are, by nature, the fallen offspring of a fallen parent—that we have all been begotten in the image and likeness of a corrupt and sinful father.

Until we reach the twenty-first verse of Genesis 5, there is little else in the chapter which calls for comment. The intervening verses trace for us the line of Seth's seed, and death is writ large across the record. Eight times we read, "And he died." But in verses 21 to 24 we have a notable exception. Enoch, the seventh from Adam, died not. He was translated without seeing death. And to the consideration of this remarkable man we shall now direct our attention.

Enoch is a striking character. He is one of but two men of whom it is said in Scripture that he "walked with God." He is one of but two men who lived on this earth and went to heaven without passing through the portals of death. And he is the only one, except our blessed Lord, of whom it is written, "He pleased God."* He is one of the very few who lived before the Flood of whom we know anything at all. The days when Enoch lived on the earth were flagrantly wicked, as the Epistle of Jude plainly shows. He seems to have stood quite alone in his fearless denunciation of the ungodly and in his faithful testimony for God. Very little is recorded of him, which is another proof of the Divine inspiration of the Scriptures—a truth which cannot be overemphasized. Had the Bible been a human production, much would have been written about Enoch and an attempt

*In this, as in everything, our Lord has the preëminence. He alone could say, "I do *always* those things that please Him!"

made to show the cause and explain the method of his mysterious exit from this world. The silence of Holy Scripture attest their Divine origin! But though little is told us about Enoch, a careful examination of what is recorded suggests and supplies a wonderfully complete biography.

"And Enoch lived sixty and five years, and begat Methuselah: And Enoch walked with God after he begat Methuselah three hundred years, and begat sons and daughters: And all the days of Enoch were three hundred sixty and five years. And Enoch walked with God: and he was not; for God took him." (Gen. 5:21-24).

The first thing implied in Enoch's walk with God is *reconciliation.* A pertinent question is asked in Amos 3:3, "How can two walk together except they be *agreed?*" Thus two walking together supposes agreement, sympathy, harmony. From the nature of the case, it is implied that one of the two had been at enmity with the other and that there had been a reconciliation. So that when we say of any man that he walks with God, it implies that he has been reconciled to God. God has not conformed to him, but he has conformed to God.

To walk with God implies *a correspondency of nature.* Light hath no communion with darkness. No sinner can walk with God for he has nothing in common with Him, and more, his mind is at enmity against Him. It is sin which separates from God. The day that Adam sinned he fled from his Maker and hid himself among the trees of the garden. A walk with God then supposes the judicial putting away of sin and the impartation of the Divine nature to the one who walked with Him.

To walk with God implies *a moral fitness.* God does not walk out of the way of holiness. Before God would walk through Israel's camp everything which defiled had to be put away. Before Christ commences His millennial reign all things that offend must be gathered out of His Kingdom. The thrice holy God keeps no company with the unclean. "If we say that we have fellowship with Him, and walk in darkness, we lie, and do not the truth: But, if we walk in the light, as He is in the light, we have fellowship one with another, and the blood of Jesus Christ His Son cleanseth us from all sin." 1 John 1:6, 7. In a sentence, then, walking with God means that we cease taking our own way, that we abandon the world's way, that we follow the Divine way.

To walk with God implies *a surrendered will.* God does not force His company upon any. "How can two walk together except *they* be agreed?" The supreme example and illustration is the Lord Jesus. None enjoyed such perfect and intimate communication with the Father as He. And what was the secret of it all? "I delight to do *Thy will,* O God," supplies the explanation. If, then, we would walk with the Lord, there must be a willingness and readiness on our part. "*Take* My yoke upon you." He does not force it on any!

To walk with God implies *spiritual communion.* "How can two *walk together* except they be agreed?" The word "walk" suggests steady progress. It has been quaintly but well said, Enoch "did not take a turn or two with God and then leave His company, but he walked with God for hundreds of years. What a splendid walk! A walk of three hundred years! It was not a run, a leap, a spurt, but a steady walk."

"And Enoch *walked* with God." What light that one word casts on the life and character of this man! How much it reveals to us. Like every other descendant of Adam, Enoch was by nature a child of wrath, alienated from the life of God. But a day came when he was reconciled to his Maker. If it be asked, What was the cause of this reconciliation? Hebrews 11:5 supplies the answer—Enoch "had this testimony, that he *pleased* God." If it be further asked, *How* did he please God? the very next verse informs us, "Without *faith* it is impossible to please Him." Faith then was the instrumental cause of his reconciliation. Again we say, how much that one sentence tells us about this "seventh from Adam"! Born into this world a lost sinner, he is saved by grace through faith. He is born again and thus made a partaker of the Divine nature. He is brought into agreement with the Most High and fitted to have fellowship with the Holy One.

But from the analogy of other Scriptures, by comparing text with text we may learn still more about this man who "pleased God." What would be *the result* of his walk with God? Would not the first consequence of such a walk be *a growth in grace?* Walking implies progress, and that in a *forward* direction. Enoch's life must have been progressive. At the close of three hundred years of communion with God, Enoch could not be morally and spiritually where he was at the beginning. He would have a deeper abhorrence of sin and a humbler estimate of himself. He would be more conscious of his own helplessness and would feel more and more his need of absolute dependency on God. There would be a larger capacity to enjoy God. There would be a going on from strength to strength and from glory to glory.

There would also be *a growth in the knowledge of the Lord.* It is one thing to talk about God, to reason and speculate about Him, to hear and read about Him, it is quite another to *know* Him. This is the practical and experimental side of the Christian life. If we would know God we must walk with Him: we must come into living contact with Him, have personal dealings with Him, commune with Him. After such a walk of three hundred years Enoch would have a deeper appreciation of God's excellency, a greater enjoyment of His perfections and would manifest a more earnest concern for His glory.

Another consequence of Enoch's walk with God would be *a deep settled joy and peace.* Enoch's life must have been supremely happy. How could he be miserable with such a Companion! He could not be gloomy in such company. "Yea, though I walk through the valley of the shadow of death I will fear no evil: *for Thou art with me.*" Walking with God ensures protection. He that dwelleth in the secret place of the Most High shall abide under the shadow of the Almighty. Nothing can harm the man who has the Lord God at his right hand.

A further consequence of Enoch's walk was *his witness for God*—see Jude 14 and 15. This is something which needs to be stressed. This order cannot be reversed, it is of Divine appointment. Before we can witness *for* God, we must walk *with* God. It is greatly to be feared that much of what passes for "Christian service" in our day is not the product of such a walk, and that it will prove but "wood, hay and stubble" in the day of testing. There is something which must precede service, "Thou shalt *worship* the Lord thy God *and* Him only shalt thou *serve.*"

Having considered at some length the character of Enoch's walk, let us in closing note two other things, *the commencement and the culmination* of this walk.

"And Enoch lived sixty and five years and begat Methuselah: And Enoch walked with God" (Gen. 5:21, 22). It is not said that Enoch walked with God before his son was born, and the inference seems to be that the coming into his life of this little one—God's gift—may have been the means of leading him into this close fellowship. Such ought ever to be the case. The responsibilities of parenthood should cast us more and more upon God.

The name of his son strongly implies that Enoch had received a revelation from God. Methuselah signifies, *"When he is dead it shall be sent," i. e., the Deluge* (Newberry). In all probability then, a Divine revelation is memorialized in this name. It was as though God had said to Enoch, "Do you see that baby? The world will last as long as he lives and no longer! When that child dies, I shall deal with the world in judgment. The windows of heaven will be opened. The fountains of the great deep will be broken up, and all humanity will perish." What would be the effect of such a communication upon Enoch? Imagine for a moment a parallel case today. Suppose God should make known to you, in such a way that you could not question His veracity, that this world would last only as long as the life of some little one in your home. Suppose God should say to you, "The life of that little one is to be the life of the world. When that child dies the world will be destroyed." What would be the effect upon you? Not knowing how soon that child might die, there would come before you the possibility that the world might perish at any time. Every time that child fell sick the world's doom would stare you in the face! Suppose further, that you were unsaved. Would you not be deeply exercised? Would you not realize as never before your urgent need of preparing to meet God? Would you not at once begin to occupy yourself with spiritual things? May not some such effects have been produced upon Enoch? Be this as it may —and it is difficult to escape such a conclusion—it is certainly implied that from the time Methuselah was born, the world lost all its attractiveness for Enoch and from that time on, if never before, he walked with God.

"By faith Enoch was translated that he should not see death and was not found, because God had translated him: for before his translation he had this testimony, that he pleased God" (Heb. 11:5). God had translated him.* After Enoch had lived on earth the great cycle—a year for a day—of three hundred and sixty-five years, God took him to Himself, as if to show that he was an example of a human being, who had fulfilled his destiny, and a type of what the destiny of all mankind might have been had sin never entered the world (Bettex).

God had translated him. We cannot do better than quote here from Dr. B. H. Carroll's exposition of Genesis—a work from which many original and excellent suggestions may be gathered: "God translated him. This is an old Latin word, an irregular verb, and it simply means carried over or carried across. God carried him across. Across what? Across death. Death is the river that divides this world from the world to come, and here was a man that never did go through that river at all. When he got there God carried him across. God transferred him; translated him; God picked him up and carried him over and put him on the other shore. And walking along here in time and communing with God by faith, in an instant he was communing with God by sight in another world. Faith, Oh, precious faith! Faith had turned to sight, and hope had turned to fruition in a single moment. The life of faith was thus crowned by entrance into the life of perfect fellowship above, "And they shall walk with Me in white" (Rev. 3:4).

In conclusion, we would point out the fact that Enoch is a *type* of those believers who shall be alive on the earth when our Lord shall descend into the air to catch up to Himself His blood bought people "Behold, I show you a mystery; *We shall not all sleep* (*die*), but we shall be all changed, in a moment, in the twinkling of an eye (1 Cor. 15:51, 52). Just as Enoch was translated to heaven without seeing death, so also will those of the Lord's people who remain on the earth till the time of His return. May it be ours to "walk with God" during the short interval that now intervenes, and, if it pleaseth Him, may we be among that number which shall be raptured to glory without having to first pass through the portals of the grave.

*"God had *translated* him." Here again, by contrast we see the uniqueness of our blessed Lord. He alone *ascended* to heaven (John 3:13)—this by virtue of His own rights and by the exercise of His own power. Of Enoch it is said, "God *took* him." Of Elijah it is written, "Elijah went up by a whirlwind into heaven." At the second coming of Christ the saints will be "caught up."

10. NOAH

GENESIS 6

Little is told us of the *parentage* of Noah, yet sufficient is revealed to indicate that he was the descendant of believing ancestors and the child of a God-fearing father. Noah was the grandson of Methuselah, and the great grandson of Enoch who was translated to heaven. The name of his father was Lamech, and on the birth of his son we are told that "he called his name Noah, saying, This same shall comfort us concerning our work and toil of our hands, because of the ground which the Lord hath cursed" (Gen. 5:29). That Lamech was a man of faith appears from the fact that he attributed his "toil" and the condition of the ground to the Lord's "curse." Further, it seems as though God had revealed to him something of His future purposes in connection with Noah in that he looked on him as one that was to bring "comfort" or "rest."

The *times* in which Noah lived and the condition of the world then serve as a dark background to bring out in vivid relief the faith and righteousness of the one who was "perfect in his generations" and "walked with God." "And God saw that the wickedness of man was great in the earth, and that every imagination of the thoughts of his heart was only evil continually. And it repented the Lord that He had made man on the earth, and it grieved Him at His heart. And the Lord said, I will destroy man whom I have created from the face of the earth; both man, and beast, and the creeping thing, and the fowls of the air; for it repenteth Me that I have made man" (Gen. 6:5-7). What a terrible scene was here spread before the all-seeing eye of God, and how startling the contrast between it and the one on which He had looked at the close of the six days' work! There we are told, "God saw everything that He had made, and, behold, it was *very good*" (Gen. 1:31). But here, the next time we read that "God saw" we are told that "the wickedness of man was great in the earth." How awful is sin, and how fearful its course when unrestrained by God!

But there is another, and a blessed contrast here, too. After we read of the greatness of man's wickedness and the consequent grief of God's heart, we are told, "But Noah found grace in *the eyes* of the Lord" (Gen. 6:8). There was an oasis in the midst of the dreary desert, an oasis which the *grace* of God had prepared, and on which His eyes dwelt. When beholding the wicked we read only that God "saw,' but when Noah is in view the "eyes of the Lord" are mentioned. A look at the former was sufficient; but something more definite and protracted greeted the latter. Before we study the Character of Noah, a word first on the one following the last quoted.

"These are the generations of Noah" (Gen. 6:9). Here a new section of Genesis commences. The Chronology of Genesis having been brought up to Noah's day in Genesis 5, the opening verses of Genesis 6 look backward not forward, giving us the history of the world and describing the character of mankind in the days which preceded the Flood Verses 5 to 8 of Genesis 6 close the second main division of the book. Each new division opens with the words "These are the generations of," see 2:4; 5:1; 6:9, etc. The thought to which we would now call attention is that each of these divisions *ends* (we use the word relatively) with a picture that portrays *the effects and results of sin.* The first division (the concluding verses of Genesis 4, closes with the record of Abel's murder by Cain, and of Lamech's glorying over a young man whom he had slain. The second division closes (Gen. 6:1-8) with God looking down on the wickedness of the Antediluvians. The third division closes (Gen. 9:20-29) with the sad scene of Noah's drunkenness, the curse pronounced on a part of his descendants, and the patriarch's death. The fourth division closes (Gen. 11:1-9) by bringing before us the overthrow of the Tower of Babel. The fifth division closes (Gen. 11:10-26) with the births, ages, and *deaths* of Shem's descendants. The sixth division closes (Gen. 11:31, 32) with the death of Terah. The seventh division closes (Gen. 25:10, 11) with the burial of Abraham. The eighth division closes (Gen. 25:18) with the death of Ishmael. The ninth division closes (Gen. 35:29) with the death of Isaac. The tenth division closes (Gen. 36:8) with the *departure* of Esau from the promised land, the birthright to which he had sold for a mess of pottage. The eleventh division closes (Gen. 36) with a list of the descendants of Esau, and significantly ends with the words, "He is Esau the father of *the Edomites.*" While the last division closes (Gen. 1:26) with the death of Joseph.

"But Noah found grace in the eyes of the Lord" (Gen. 6:8). This is the first thing that is told us about Noah. Grace is the foundation of every life that is well-pleasing to God. Grace is the source from which issues every blessing we receive. It was the grace of God and not the graces of Noah which preserved him from a watery grave. Is it not beautiful to note that it is here this precious word "grace" is seen for the first time in God's Word! It was when the sin of the creature had reached its climax that Grace was exercised and displayed, as if to teach us from the onset, that it is nothing within man which calls forth the bestowment of Divine favors.

When God said, "I will destroy man whom I have created from the face of the earth; both man, and beast, and the creeping thing, and the fowls of the air," it seemed as if He was about to make an end of the entire race. But Noah found grace in the eyes of the Lord. He was as a lily among the thorns, whose godly walk would appear the lovelier from contrast with that of the world about him. Humanly speaking it has never been an easy matter for the believer to live that life that brings glory to God, not even when he receives encouragement from fellow-saints. But here was a man living in a world of wickedness, where "*all flesh* had corrupted his way on the earth." Here was a man who was compelled to set his face against the whole current of public opinion and conduct. What a testimony to the sufficiency and keeping power of Divine grace!

The *character* of Noah is described in Genesis 6:9 where three things are told us about him: "Noah was a just man and perfect in his generations, and Noah walked with God." first, he was "just." He is the first man so called, though not the first man who was so. The *meritorious* ground of justification is the Blood of Christ (Rom. 5:9); the *instrumental* cause is faith (Rom. 5:1). The just shall live by faith, hence we find Noah among the fifteen believers mentioned in the great faith chapter (Heb. 11). The faith by which Noah was justified before God was evidenced by him being "moved with fear" and in his obedience to the Divine command to build the ark. Second, he was "perfect in his generations." Here the reference seems to point to Noah and his family having kept themselves separate from the moral evil around them and preserved themselves from contact with the Nephilim. The Hebrew word is "tamim" and is elsewhere translated in the Old Testament "without blemish" forty-four times. It is probably the word from which our English "contaminated" springs. Noah was uncontaminated in his generations. Third, he "walked with God." It is only as we walk with Him that we are kept from the evil around us.

The *faith* of Noah is described in Hebrews 11:7: "By faith Noah, being warned of God of things not seen as yet, moved with fear, prepared an ark to the saving of his house; by which he condemned the world, and became heir of the righteousness which is by faith." In this remarkable verse, remarkable for its fulness and terseness, seven things are told us about Noah's faith, each of which we do well to ponder. The first thing we learn here of Noah's faith is *its ground,* namely, God's Word—"being warned of God." The ground of all faith which is acceptable to God is that which rests neither on feelings nor fancy, but on the naked Word. "Faith cometh by hearing, and hearing by the Word of God" (Rom. 10:17). Simon and his partners had fished from sunset to sunrise and their labors had been in vain. The Lord entered their ship and said, "Launch out into the deep and let down your nets for a draught," and Simon replied, "Master, we have toiled all the night, and have taken nothing: *nevertheless, at Thy word* I will let down the net" (Luke 5:4, 5). Once again: for many days the ship in which the apostle was journeying to Italy battled with stormy seas, until all hope that he and his fellow passengers should be saved had disappeared. Then it was, when everything to the outward eye seemed to contradict, that Paul stood forth and said, "Sirs, be of good cheer: for I believe God, that it shall be *even as it was told me*" (Acts 27:25). A faith that does not rest upon the written word is mere credulity.

The second thing mentioned in connection with Noah's faith is *its sphere.* His faith laid hold of things "not seen as yet," that is, of things which pertained to the realm of the unseen. Believers walk by faith and not by sight (2 Cor. 5:7). As Noah labored at the building of the ark, doubtless, the world looked upon him as an enthusiastic fanatic, as one who was putting himself to a great deal of needless trouble. What was there to portend such a calamity as the Deluge? Nothing at all. All things continued as they were from the beginning of creation. History furnished no analogy whatever. Not only had there never been any previous flood, but even rain was then unknown. What then could induce Noah to act in the way he did? Nothing but *the testimony of God.* Here then is an exemplification and demonstration of the nature of faith. Faith is the eye of the spirit. It is that which visualizes the unseen; it is that which gives tangibility to the invisible; it is that which makes substantial the things hoped for.

In the third place we learn here of *the character* of Noah's faith—it was "moved with *fear.*" Faith not only relies upon the precious promises of God, but it also believes His solemn threatenings. As the beloved Spurgeon said, "He who does not believe that God will punish sin, will not believe that He will pardon it through the atoning blood. He who does not believe that God will cast unbelievers into hell, will not be sure that He will take believers to heaven. If we doubt God's Word about one thing, we shall have small confidence in it upon another thing. Since faith in God must treat all God's Word alike; for the faith which accepts one word of God, and rejects another, is evidently not faith in God, but faith in our own judgment, faith in our own taste." Noah had received from God a gracious promise, but he had also been warned of a coming judgment which should destroy all living things with a flood, and his faith believed both the promise and the warning. Again, we need the admonition of Mr. Spurgeon—"I charge you who profess to be the Lord's, not to be unbelieving with regard to the terrible threatenings of God to the ungodly. Believe the threat, even though it should chill your blood; believe, though nature shrinks from the overwhelming doom, for, if you do not believe, the act of disbelieving God about one point will drive you to disbelieve Him upon the other parts of revealed truth, and you will never come to that true, childlike faith which God will accept and honor."

Fourth, we see *the evidence* of Noah's faith—he "prepared an ark." "Faith, if it hath not works is dead, being by itself" (Jas. 2:17), which means, it is a lifeless faith, a merely nominal faith, and not the "faith of God's elect" (Titus 1:1). To the same effect: "What doth it profit, my brethren, though a man *say* he hath faith, and have not works" (Jas. 2:14). The Apostle Paul writes of the justification of believing sinners; James writes of the justification of faith itself, or rather, the claim to be in possession of faith. I profess to be a believer, how shall I justify my claim? By my works, my walk, my witness for God. Read through Hebrews 11 and it will be seen that in every case recorded there, faith was evidenced by works. Abel had faith. How did he display it? By presenting to God the Divinely preserved sacrifice. Enoch had faith. How did he manifest it? By walking with God. Noah had faith. How did he evidence it? By preparing the ark. And mark this also—faith expresses itself in that which costs its possessor something! The preparing of the ark was no small undertaking. It was not only a very laborious and protracted task, but it must have been a very expensive one, too. It has ever been thus; Abraham was the father of the faithful, and his faith found expression and resulted in that which meant personal sacrifice. To Abraham it meant leaving home, kindred and country, and subsequently the offering up of his well beloved son on the altar of sacrifice. What is it *costing you* to express your faith? A faith that does not issue in that which is costly is not worth much.

Fifth, we see *the issue* of Noah's faith—Noah "prepared an ark to the saving of his house." God always honors real faith in Him. The particular issue of Noah's faith deserves prayerful consideration. While it is true that there is no such thing as salvation by proxy, that no parent can believe to the saving of his child's soul, yet, Scripture furnishes many examples of God's blessings coming upon those who exercised no faith themselves on account of the faith of others. Because Abraham exercised faith, God gave to his seed the land of Palestine. Because Rahab believed the report of the spies, her whole household was preserved from destruction. Coming to the New Testament, we remember such cases as the man sick of the palsy, who was brought to the Lord Jesus by others—"And Jesus *seeing their faith* said unto the sick of the palsy: Son, be of good cheer; thy sins be forgiven thee" (Matt. 8:2). Because of the nobleman's faith, his servant was healed. Because of the Canaanitish woman's faith, her daughter was made whole. Noah's faith then issued in the temporal salvation of "his house." Is not this written for our learning? Is there no word of encouragement here for believing parents today who have unsaved children? Do we remember the word spoken to the Philippian jailor—"Believe on the Lord Jesus Christ, and thou shalt be saved, *and thy house*"—do we appropriate it and plead it before God?

Sixth, we learn of *the witness* of Noah's faith—"by which he condemned the world." In considering this clause we would first inquire into the *nature* of faith. What is faith? In Rom. 14:23, we read, "Whatsoever is not of faith is sin." *Faith is the opposite of sin.* What then is sin? The divinely inspired answer is found in 1 John 3:4—"Sin is *lawlessness*" (R. V.). Sin is more than an act, it is an attitude. Sin is rebellion against God's government, a defiance of His authority. Sin is spiritual anarchy. Sin is the exercise of self-will, self-assertion, self-independency. God says, "Thou shalt," and I don't; what is that but me saying "I won't!" God says "Thou shalt not," and I do; what is that but me saying, "I will!" But faith is in every respect the antithesis of sin. Faith is also more than an act, it is an attitude. Faith is submission to God's government, a yielding to His authority, a compliance with His revealed will. Faith in God is a coming to the end of myself. Faith is the spirit of entire dependency on God. There is a great gulf then separating between those who are members of the household of faith and those who are the children of the wicked one. We walk by faith, they by sight; we live for God's glory, they for self-gratification; we live for eternity, they for time. And every Christian who is walking by faith, necessarily condemns the world. His conduct is a silent rebuke upon the course followed by the ungodly. His life is a witness against their sin.

Finally, we learn here *the reward* of Noah's faith—he "became heir of the righteousness which is by faith." Faith brings a present blessing: it wins God's smile of approval, fills the heart with peace, oils the machinery of life, and makes "all things" possible. But the grand reward of faith is not received in this life. The inheritance into which faith conducts us is not possessed here and now. Abraham, Isaac, and Jacob never did anything more than "*sojourn* in the land of promise." The children of God are "heirs of God and joint heirs with Christ," but the entering into their inheritance is yet future—we do not say the *enjoy-*

ment of it, for *faith* appropriates it and revels in it even now. The Son Himself has been "appointed heir of all things" (Heb. 1:2), and it is not until *He* enters into His possessions that we shall share them with Him. Meanwhile, we are, with Noah, "*heirs* of the righteousness which is by faith."

11. THE FLOOD

Genesis 6

In our article on "Enoch" it was pointed out that the name of his child intimated that God had given warning to him of the coming of the Deluge—"And Enoch lived sixty and five years, and begat Methuselah" (Gen. 5:21). The signification of Methuselah is, "*When he is dead it shall be sent,*" *i. e., the Deluge* (Newberry). A divine revelation then was memorialized in this name. The world was to last only as long as this son of Enoch lived. If 1 Peter 3:20 be linked to Genesis 5:21 an interesting and precious thought is brought before us: "Which (the antediluvians now in 'prison') some time were disobedient, when once the long-suffering of God waited in the days of Noah." To what does this "long-suffering" refer which "waited" while the ark was a preparing? How long had God's patience been exercised? Nine hundred and sixty-nine years seems to be the answer—the span of Methuselah's life. As long as Enoch's son lived the world was safe; but when he died, then should it (the Deluge) be sent. Is it not a most impressive demonstration of God's "long-suffering" that the man whose life was to measure the breath of a world's probation, was permitted to live *longer than any one else ever did live!* Nine hundred and sixty-nine years—what an exhibition of God's mercy! How wondrous are the ways of Jehovah! As that child was to live until the time came for mankind to be swept away by the flood; and, as during this interval God's servants were to warn men from the coming wrath, shall not the mercy of God prolong that day? Shall not this man live longer than any other man ever did live? Shall not his age be unique, standing out from the ages of all others?—because that from the hour of his birth the Divine decree had gone forth, "When the breath leaves his body the throes of dissolution shall commence; when he departs the thunder clouds of God's anger shall burst, the windows of heaven shall be opened, the foundations of the great deeps shall give way, and every living thing shall be swept from this earth by the besom of Divine destruction." And so it was. Methuselah outlived all his contemporaries and remained on earth almost a thousand years.

Having viewed the *postponement* of the flood through the long-suffering of God, let us next consider the *provocation* of it. We have already dwelt upon the fact that the New Testament Scriptures call our attention to the "long-suffering of God (which) waited in the days of Noah" (1 Pet. 3:20). These words intimate that God's long-suffering had *already been exercised* and that it continued to "wait" even in the days of Noah. This causes us to inquire *how* and *when* had God's "long-suffering" been manifested *previously* to Noah?

The word "long-suffering" implies that God had dealt in mercy, that His mercy had been slighted, and that His patience (humanly speaking) had been sorely tried. And this leads us to ask another question—a deeply interesting and important one: What Divine light did the antediluvians enjoy? What knowledge of God, of His character and of His ways, did they possess? What was the measure of their responsibility? To answer these questions is to discover the enormity of their sin, is to measure the extent of their wickedness, is to determine the degree of their aggravation of God; and, consequently, is to demonstrate the magnitude of His long-suffering in bearing with them for so long.

While the record is exceedingly brief, sufficient is revealed to show that men in general possessed no small amount of light even in days before the flood. Not only had they, in common with all generations the "light of Nature," or as Romans 1:19, 20 expresses it, "Because that which may be known of God is manifest in them; for God hath shewed it unto them. For the invisible things of Him from the creation of the world are clearly seen, being understood by the things that are made, even His eternal power and Godhead"—which rendered them *"without excuse"*; not only had they the testimony of conscience (Rom. 2:14, 15), but, in addition, they possessed the light of Divine revelation. In what this latter consisted we shall now endeavor to show.

First, man had the Promise of a Redeemer. Before our first parents were banished from Eden, God declared that the woman's Seed should bruise the serpent's head, and for His appearing believers looked and longed (see Gen. 49:

18). Second: There was the institution of expiatory sacrifices as the one means of approach to Jehovah. This was made known by God to Adam and Eve by means of the coats of skins which He provided as a covering for their nakedness. The meaning of His gracious condescension was clearly understood by them, and the significance of it and need of such sacrifice was communicated to their children, as is clear from the acts of Cain and Abel. That such knowledge was handed down from father to son is also seen in the fact that as soon as Noah came out of the ark he "built an altar unto the Lord...and offered burnt offerings on the altar" (Gen. 8:20).

Third: There was the "mark" which God set upon Cain (Gen. 4:15), which was a reminder of his disapprobation, a visible memorial of his own sin, and a solemn warning unto those among whom his lot was subsequently cast. Fourth: As we indicated in our comments on Genesis 4, the institution of the Sabbath was even then established, as may be seen from the fact that there was a set time for worship (Gen. 4:3, margin). Fifth: The longevity of the patriarchs must be borne in mind. But two lives spanned the interval from the beginning of human history to the Deluge itself, namely Adam's and Methuselah's. For nine hundred and thirty years the first man lived to tell of his original creation and condition, of his wicked disobedience against God, and of the fearful consequences which followed his sin. A striking illustration of the communication of this knowledge from one generation to another may be seen in the words of Lamech, who lived to within a few years of the flood itself—words recorded in Genesis 5:29, where it will be found he makes reference to "the ground which the Lord God hath *cursed.*" Sixth: There was the preaching of Enoch through whom God warned the world of its approaching doom (Jude 14, 15). Seventh: The mysterious and supernatural translation of Enoch, which must have made a profound impression upon those among whom his lot was cast. Eighth: The preaching of Noah (2 Pet. 2:25), followed by his building of the ark, by which he condemned the world. Ninth: The ministry of the Holy Spirit (Gen. 6:3; 1 Pet. 3:19), striving with men and, as the record implies, this for some considerable time. From these things then it is abundantly clear that the antediluvians fell not through ignorance but by wilfully rejecting a Divine revelation, and from deliberately persisting in their wickedness.

Having considered the Provocation of the Flood, let us now examine *the cause* of it. Stated in a sentence, this was the awful depravity and wickedness of mankind, or to quote the language of our chapter, "And God looked upon the earth, and, behold, it was corrupt; for all flesh had corrupted his way upon the earth. And God said unto Noah, The end of all flesh is come before me; for the earth is filled with violence through them; and, behold, I will destroy them with the earth" (Gen. 6:12, 13).

God's saints are the salt of the earth (Matt. 5:13), and little as the world realizes or appreciates it, the fact remains that it is the presence of God's people here which prevents the mystery of iniquity coming to a head and preserves mankind from an outpouring of God's wrath. Ten righteous men in Sodom would have stayed the Divine judgment, but only one could be found.

The *salt* character of God's people is due to the Holy Spirit dwelling within and working through them. Let *His* gracious manifestations be resisted and despised and they will be withdrawn, then the measure of man's iniquity will be quickly filled up. These two preserving and restraining factors are brought together in 2 Thessalonians 2. Before our Lord shall return to the earth itself, accompanied by the saints (previously translated), there shall come one who is denominated, "the man of sin, the son of perdition." This superman shall oppose God and blasphemously exalt himself above all that has any reference to God, so that he shall sit in God's temple (at Jerusalem) claiming to be God, and demanding Divine homage. His coming will be "after the working of Satan, with all power and signs and lying wonders, and with all receivableness of unrighteousness." But though this "mystery of iniquity" was at work, even in the days of the apostles, two things have prevented it coming to full fruition. The Man of Sin cannot be "revealed" till "his time" because of "*what* withholdeth" and "*he* who now letteth (hindereth) *until* he be taken out of the way" (2 Thess. 6:7). Undoubtedly the neuter pronoun here has reference to the Church of God, and the masculine one to the Holy Spirit Himself. While they are upon earth Satan's work is held in check; but let them—the Holy Spirit and the Church—be removed, let *the salt* be taken away and the One who gives it pungency, and the restraining and preserving influences are gone, and then nothing remains to stay corruption or hinder the outworking of Satan's plans.

From the above premises, established by the analogies furnished in Scripture, we have no difficulty in discovering the immediate cause of the Flood. A Divine revelation had been despised and rejected. Repeated warnings had been flouted. Atonement for sin by an expiatory sacrifice had been spurned. Men loved darkness rather than light, because their deeds were evil. The number of God's saints had been diminished to such an extent that there was but one family left who feared the Lord and walked by faith. There was not sufficient "salt" left to preserve the carcass. God had forewarned the race that His Spirit would not always strive with man, and now His long-suffering was ended; therefore, His Spirit would be withdrawn, and naught then remained but summary judgment. Though the faithful remnant should be sheltered, yet, the storm of Divine wrath must now burst upon a world filled with iniquity.

We turn now to consider *the occasion* of the Flood. "And it came to pass, when men began to multiply on the face of the earth, and daughters were born unto them, that the sons of God saw the daughters of men that they were fair; and they took them wives of all which they chose" (Gen. 6:1, 2). There has been considerable difference of opinion among commentators and expositors in respect to the identity of these "sons of God." The view which has been most widely promulgated and accepted is, that these marriages between the sons of God and the daughters of men refer to unions between believers and unbelievers. It is supposed that the "sons of God" were the descendants of Seth, while the "daughters of men" are regarded as the offspring of Cain, and that these two lines gradually amalgamated, until the line of distinction between God's people and the world was obliterated. It is further supposed that the Deluge was a visitation of God's judgment, resulting from His peoples' failure to maintain their place of separation. But, it seems to us, there are a number of insuperable objections to this interpretation.

If the above theory were true, then, it would follow that at the time this amalgamation took place God's people were *limited* to the *male* sex, for the "sons of God" were the ones who "married" the "*daughters* of men." Again; if the popular theory were true, if these "sons of God" were *believers,* then they *perished* at the Flood, but 2 Peter 2:5 states otherwise—"Bringing in the flood upon the world of *the ungodly.*" Once more; there is no hint in the Divine record (so far as we can discover) that God had yet given any specific command *forbidding* His people to marry unbelievers. In view of this silence it seems exceedingly strange that this sin should have been visited with such a fearful judgment. In all ages there have been many of God's people who have united with worldlings, who have been "unequally yoked together," yet no calamity in anywise comparable with the Deluge has followed. Finally; one wonders why the union of believers with unbelievers should result in "giants"—"there were *giants* in the earth *in those days*" (Gen. 6:4).

If, then, the words "sons of God" *do not* signify the saints of that age, to whom do they refer? In Job 1:6, 2:1, 38:7, the same expression is found, and in these passages the reference is clearly to *angels.* It is a significant fact that some versions of the Septuagint contain the word "angels" in Genesis 6:2, 4. That the "sons of God," who are here represented as cohabiting with the daughters of men *were* angels—fallen angels—seems to be taught in Jude 6: "And the angels which *kept not their principality* but *left their own habitation,* He hath reserved in everlasting chains under darkness, unto the judgment of the great day."

These "sons of God," then, appear to be *angels* who left their own habitation, came down to earth, and cohabited with the daughters of men. Before we consider the outcome of this illicit intercourse, let us first enquire into the *cause* of it. *Why* did these angels thus "sin" (2 Pet. 2:4)? The answer to this question leads us into a mysterious subject which we cannot now treat at length: the "why" finds its answer in *Satan.*

Immediately after that old serpent, the Devil, had brought about the downfall of our first parents, God passed sentence on the "serpent" and declared that the woman's "Seed" should "bruise his head" (Gen. 3:15). Hence, in due course, Satan sought to *frustrate* this purpose of God. His first effort was an endeavor to prevent his

Bruiser entering this world. This effort is plainly to be seen in his attempts to *destroy the channel* through which the Lord Jesus was to come.

First, God revealed the fact that the Coming One was to be of human kind, the woman's Seed, hence, as we shall seek to show, Satan attempted to destroy the human race. Next, God made known to Abraham that the Coming One was to be a descendant of his (Gen. 12:3; Gal. 3:18; Matt. 1:1); hence, four hundred years later, when the descendants of Abraham became numerous in Egypt Satan sought to destroy the Abrahamic stock, by moving Pharaoh to seek the destruction of all the *male children* (Ex. 1:15, 16). Later, God made known the fact that the Coming One was to be of the offspring of David (2 Sam. 7:12, 13); hence, the subsequent attack made upon David through *Absalom* (2 Sam. 15). As, then, the Coming One was to be of the seed of David, He must spring from the tribe of Judah, and hence the significance of the *divided* Kingdom, and the attacks of the Ten Tribes upon the Tribe of Judah!

The reference in Jude 6 to the angels leaving their own habitation, appears to point to and correspond with these "sons of God" (angels) coming in unto the daughters of men. Apparently, by this means, Satan hoped to *destroy* the human race (the channel through which the woman's Seed was to come) *by producing a race of monstrosities.* How nearly he succeeded is evident from the fact, that with the exception of one family, "all flesh had *corrupted* his way upon the earth" (Gen. 6:12). That monstrosities *were* produced as the result of this unnatural union between the "sons of God" (angels) and the daughters of men, is evident from the words of Genesis 6:4: "There were *giants* in the earth in those days." The Hebrew word for "giants" here is nephilim, which means *fallen ones,* from "naphal" to fall. The term "men of renoun" in Genesis 6:4 probably finds its historical equivalent in the "heroes" of Grecian mythology. Satan's special object in seeking to prevent the advent of the woman's "Seed" by destroying the human race was evidently an attempt to avert his threatened doom!

Against the view that "the sons of God" refer to fallen angels Matt. 22:30 is often cited. But when the contents of this verse are closely studied it will be found there is, really, nothing in it which conflicts with what we have said above. Had our Lord said, "in the resurrection they neither marry, nor are given in marriage, but are as the angels of God" *and stopped there,* the objection would have real force. But the Lord did not stop there. He added a *qualifying* clause about the angels: He said "as the angels of God *in heaven.*" The last two words make all the difference. The angels *in heaven* neither marry nor are they given in marriage. But the angels referred to in Genesis 6 as the "sons of God" were *no longer in heaven:* as Jude 6 expressly informs us "they *left* their own principality." They fell from their celestial position and came down to earth, entering into unlawful alliance with the daughters of men. This, we are assured, is the reason why Christ modified and qualified His assertion in Matt. 22:30. The angels of God *in heaven* do not marry, but those who *left* their own principality did.

Ere we close, there is one other passage of Scripture which ought to be considered in this connection, namely, Matt. 24:37—"But as the days of Noah were, so shall also the coming of the Son of Man be." History is to repeat itself. Ere the Lord returns to this earth, the condition which prevailed in the world before the Flood are to be reproduced. The characteristic of the days of Noah may be summarized in the following ten items:

1. Multiplication of mankind (Gen. 6:1)—note the great increase of earth's population during the past century. 2. God dealing in long-suffering with a wicked world. 3. God sending His messengers to warn sinners of coming judgment. 4. God's Spirit striving with men, and the threat that He would not always do so—cf 2 Thessalonians 2, which tells of His Spirit being taken away once more. 5. God's overtures toward men despised and rejected—such is the condition of the world today. 6. A small remnant who find grace in the sight of the Lord and walk with Him. 7. Enoch miraculously translated—typifying the removal of the saints from the earth caught up to meet the Lord in the air. 8. Descent to the earth of the fallen angels and their union with the daughters of men: how near we have already approached to a repetition of this may be discovered in the demoniacal activities among Spiritists, Theosophists and Christian Scientists. 9. God's judgments poured forth on the ungodly—cf Revelation 6 to 19. 10. Noah and his family miraculously preserved—type of the Jewish remnant preserved through the Tribulation, see Revelation 12.

12. NOAH A TYPE OF CHRIST

GENESIS 6

No study of the person and character of Noah would be complete without viewing him as a type of the Lord Jesus. With one or two notable exceptions it will be beside our purpose to do more than call attention to some of the most striking points of correspondency between the type and the antitype, leaving our readers to develop at greater length these seed thoughts.

1. To begin at the beginning, Noah's very *name* foreshadowed the Coming One. In Genesis 5:28, 29 we read, "And Lamech lived a hundred eighty and two years, and begat a son; and he called his name Noah." Noah means *"rest."* His father regarded him as the one who should be the rest-giver, and as one who should provide comfort from the toil incurred by the Curse. "He called his name Noah, saying, This same shall *comfort us* concerning our work and toil of our hands, *because of* the ground which the Lord hath cursed." Lamech looked upon his son as one who should bring deliverance from the Curse, as one who should provide comfort and rest from the weariness of toil. Our readers will readily see how this ancient prophecy (for prophecy it undoubtedly was) receives its fulfilment in the One of whom it was also written, "And His *rest* shall be glorious" (Isaiah 11:10), and who when on earth said, "Come unto Me, all ye that labor and are heavy laden, and I will give you *rest"* (Matt. 11:28). But further than this, Noah's name, and the prophecy of his father on the occasion of the bestowment of it upon his son, also looks forward to the time of our Lord's Second Advent when He shall deliver the earth from its Curse—See Isaiah 9; 35, etc.

2. The *first* thing which is told us in connection with Noah is that he "found grace in the eyes of the Lord" (Gen. 6:8). In a previous article we have commented upon the setting of these words and have pointed out the contrast which they are designed to emphasize. "All flesh had corrupted his way upon the earth." The ruinous and ravaging effects of sin were universal. But as God looked down upon the creatures of His hand, now fallen and depraved, there was one who stood out by himself, one who

was just and perfect in his generation, one upon whom God's eye delighted to rest. It is very significant that nothing at all is said about Noah's family—his "sons and their wives"—in this connection; Noah only is mentioned, as if to show he is the one on whom our attention should be fixed. When we note what a striking type of our Lord Jesus Noah is, the reason for this is obvious; He is the one in whom the heart of the Father delighted, and just as the *first* thing told us in connection with Noah is that he "found grace in the eyes of the Lord," so the *first* words of the Father after the Lord Jesus had commenced His public ministry were, "This is My beloved Son, *in whom I am well pleased*" (Matt. 3:17).

3. The next thing told us about Noah is that he "was a just man" (Gen. 6:9). As is well known, the word just means "righteous." Like all other sinners who find acceptance with God, Noah was "justified by faith." He possessed no inherent righteousness of his own. Righteousness is *imputed,* imputed to those that believe (Rom. 4:6, 22-25). There was only one man who has ever walked our earth who was inherently and intrinsically righteous and that was He whom Noah foreshadowed, He of whom the centurion testified, "Certainly this was a *righteous man*" (Luke 23:47).

4. Next we read that Noah was "perfect in his generations" (Gen. 6:9). In a previous article we have seen that this expression has reference to the body and not to perfection of character. Noah and his family had not been defiled by contact with the Nephilim. "Perfect in his generations" signifies that Noah was uncontaminated physically. "Perfect in his generations" is predicated of Noah alone; of none other is this said. How plain and perfect the type! Does it not point to the immaculate humanity of our Lord? When the Eternal Word was "made flesh" He did not contract the corruptions of our fallen nature. Unlike all of human kind, *He was not* "shapen in iniquity and conceived in sin." On the contrary His mother was told, "That *holy* thing which shall be born of thee shall be called the Son of God" (Luke 1:35). In His humanity our Lord was "separate from sinners" (Heb. 7:26). He was *uncontaminated* by the virus of sin; He was "perfect in His generation."

5. Next we read of Noah that he "walked with God" (Gen. 6:9). In this also he was a type of Him who for thirty-three years lived here in unbroken communion with the Father. All through those years, however varied His circumstances, we find Him enjoying holy and blessed fellowship with the Father. During His early life, in the seclusion of Nazareth we learn that "Jesus increased in wisdom and stature, and *in favor with God* and man" (Luke 2:52). During the long season of fasting and temptation in the wilderness, we find Him living by "every word of *God*" (Luke 4:4). While His disciples slept, our blessed Lord retired to the solitudes of the mountain, there to pour out His soul to God and enjoy fellowship with His Father (Luke 6:12). At the close of His sufferings on the Cross we hear Him cry, "Father, *into Thy hands* I commend My spirit" (Luke 23:46). Truly *His* walk was ever "with God."

6. God Gave Noah an Honorous Work to Do

"Make thee an ark of gopher wood; rooms shalt thou make in the ark, and shalt pitch it within and without with pitch. With thee will I establish My covenant; and thou shalt come into the ark, thou, and thy sons, and thy wife, and thy sons' wives with thee. And of every living thing of all flesh, two of every sort shalt thou bring in the ark, to keep them alive with thee" (Gen. 6:14, 18, 19). Here we find a work is entrusted to Noah by God, a highly important work, a momentous and stupendous work. Never before or since has such a task been allotted to a single man. The task of *preserving from God's judgment representatives of all creation* was committed to Noah! The type is so clear and plain that comment is almost needless. To the Lord Jesus Christ, God's beloved Son, was entrusted the task of effecting the salvation of lost and ruined sinners. It is to this He refers when He says, "I have finished the work *which Thou gavest Me to do*" (John 17:4)—speaking here as though in Glory, where He now is as our great High Priest.

7. Noah, Alone, Did the Work

We shall consider separately the typical significance of the ark; for the moment we would direct attention upon Noah and his work. Is it not striking that there is no reference here to any *help* that Noah received in the executing of his God-given task? There is no hint whatever that any *assisted* him in the work of building the ark. The record reads as though Noah *alone* provided the necessary means for securing the lives of those that God had entrusted to his care! Surely the reason is obvious. The truth which is foreshadowed here is parallel with the typology of Leviticus 16:17—"And *there shall be no man* in the tabernacle of the congregation when he goeth in *to make an atonement* in the holy place, until he come out"—when atonement was being made the High Priest must be *alone.* So it was in the antitype. The work of redemption was accomplished by our Lord Jesus Christ, "Who His own self bare our sins in His own body on the tree" (1 Pet. 2:24), and He *needed no assistance* in this work, for God had "laid help upon One that is *mighty*" (Ps. 89:19, R. V.). In full harmony then with the Leviticus 16 type, and in perfect accord with its fulfilment in our gracious Saviour, we find that the record in Genesis reads as though Noah was alone in his task and received no assistance in the work of providing a refuge from the coming storm of Divine wrath.

8. Moreover, is not the perfection of the type further to be seen in the fact that the inspired record passes over the interval of time necessary for Noah to have performed his task? This is very striking, for many months, and probably years, would be required to build an ark of the dimensions given us in Genesis. But not a word is said about this. After God gave instructions to Noah to build the ark, the *next* thing we read is, "Thus did Noah according to all that God commanded him, so did he. And the Lord said unto Noah, Come thou and all thy house into the ark" (Gen. 6:22; 7:1)—as though to show that when he began, his work was *speedily accomplished!* How much we may learn from the silences of Scripture! Again we call attention to the parallel type in Leviticus 16—"For *on that day* shall the priest make an atonement for you to cleanse you, that you may be clean from all your sins before the Lord" (v. 30). In Leviticus 23 the Day of Atonement is classed among Israel's great feasts, and by noting this the point we are now making comes out more clearly by way of contrast. Others of these feasts, e. g., Unleavened Bread, Tabernacles, etc., extended over a period of several days, but Atonement was *accomplished in one day.* Nothing was left over to be *completed* on the next day; which reminds us of the blessed

words of our triumphant Saviour—"It is finished." There is nothing now for us to do but rest on *His* Finished Work. In one day, yes, in three hours, on the Cross, our Lord put away sin by the sacrifice of Himself. As we have said, this was anticipated in the typical significance of Noah's work by the silence of Scripture upon the length of time he was engaged in the performance of his task, the record reading as though it was *speedily executed.*

9. The successful issue of Noah's work, seen in "the saving of *his house*" (Heb. 11:7) reminds us of the language of Hebrews 3:6, "But Christ as a son over his own house" (Heb. 3:6). But the type goes further: Noah's work brings blessing to all creation as is seen from the fact that the animals and birds were also preserved in the ark. Observe how beautifully this is brought out in Genesis 8:1—"And God remembered Noah, *and every living thing, and all the cattle* that was with him in the ark." So, too, the work of Christ shall yet bring blessing to the beasts of the field. At His return to the earth "the creation itself also shall be delivered from the bondage of corruption into the glorious liberty of the children of God" (Rom. 8:21).

10. In Genesis 6:19 we have a hint of the animal creation being *subject* to Noah—"And of every living thing of all flesh, two of every sort *shalt thou bring* into the ark, to keep them alive *with thee.*" We have a passing glimpse of the yet future fulfilment of this part of the type in Mark 1:13—"And He was there in the wilderness forty days tempted of Satan; and *was with* the wild beasts." Noah's *headship* over all creatures comes out even more clearly in Genesis 9:2—"And the fear of you and the dread of you shall be upon every beast of the earth, and upon every fowl of the air, upon all that moveth upon earth, and upon all the fishes of the sea; *into your hand are they delivered.*" How this reminds us of Psalm 8, which speaks of the future dominion of the Son of Man. "For Thou hast made Him a little lower than the angels, and hast crowned Him with glory and honor. For thou madest Him to have dominion over the works of Thy hands; Thou hast put all things under His feet (compare Heb. 2:8), "But now we see not *yet* all things put under Him, all sheep and oxen, yea, and the beasts of the field; the fowl of the air and the fish of the sea!" This same thought is repeated in the Genesis narrative again and again as if with deliberate empha-

sis. When we read of the animals entering the Ark we are told "They went in *unto Noah* (not unto Noah and his family) into the Ark," and then we are told "And the Lord shut *him* (not 'them') in" (Gen. 7:15, 16). And again, on leaving the ark we read that God said unto Noah, "Every moving thing that liveth shall be meat for you; even as the green herb have I *given you all things*" (Gen. 9:3). So Christ is "the Heir of all things" (Heb. 1:2).

11. In Genesis 6:21 we find Noah presented as the great food-provider: "And take thou unto thee of all food that is eaten, and thou shalt gather it to thee; and it shall be for food for thee, and for them." We need hardly say that this finds its complement in Christ the Bread of Life. He is God's Manna for our souls. He is the Shewbread which was eaten by Aaron and his sons (Lev. 24:9). He is the Old Corn of the land (Joshua 5:11). In short, it is only as we feed upon Christ as He is presented unto us in the written Word that our spiritual life is quickened and nourished.

12. In Genesis 6:22 we learn of Noah's implicit and complete *obedience*—"Thus did Noah according to *all* that God commanded him, so did he." And again, "And Noah did according unto all that the Lord commanded him" (Gen. 7:5). So, too, we read of the perfect obedience of Him whom Noah foreshadowed: "If ye keep My commandments, ye shall abide in My love; even so I have *kept My Father's commandments,* and abide in His love" (John 15:10). Only, be it noted, the obedience of our blessed Lord went farther than that of Noah, for He "became *obedient unto death,* even the death of the cross" (Phil. 2:8)—in all things He has the preëminence.

13. "And Noah went forth, and his sons, and his wife, and his sons' wives with him; every beast, every creeping thing, and every fowl, and whatsoever creepeth upon the earth, after their kinds went forth out of the ark" (Gen. 8:18, 19). In these verses we see Noah bringing *all* whom God had committed to his care on to the new earth, which reminds us of our Lord's words, "Of them which Thou gavest Me have I *lost none*" (John 18:9). However, the fact that the animal creation is here specifically mentioned as sharing in this blessing seems to point to a *milennial* scene when all creation shall enjoy the benefit of Christ's reign (cf. Isaiah 11).

14. "And Noah builded an altar unto the Lord; and took of every clean beast, and of every clean fowl, and offered burnt offerings on the altar (Gen. 8:20). Here we see Noah offering a burnt offering unto the Lord: the antitypical parallel is found in Ephesians 5:2—"Christ also hath loved us, and hath given Himself for us an *offering and a sacrifice to God* for a sweet smelling savor."

15. "And God *blessed* Noah *and his sons*" (Gen. 9:1). It is beautiful to see Noah and his sons here linked together in the enjoyment of God's blessing, as though to foreshadow the blessed fact that every mercy we now enjoy is ours for Christ's sake." "Blessed be the God and Father of our Lord Jesus Christ who hath *blessed us* with all spiritual blessings in heavenly places *in Christ*" (Eph. 1:3).

16. With Noah and his sons God established *His Covenant*, "And God spake unto Noah, and to his sons with him, saying, And I, behold, I establish My covenant with you, and with your seed after you" (Gen. 9:8, 9). The word "covenant" occurs just seven times in this passage, namely, in verses 9, 11, 12, 13, 15, 16, 17. Note, the covenant that God made with Noah was "an *everlasting* covenant" (Gen. 9:16), and so we read concerning the antitype—"Now the God of peace, that brought again from the dead our Lord Jesus, that great shepherd of the sheep, through the blood of *the everlasting covenant*" (Heb. 13:20).

13. THE TYPOLOGY OF THE ARK

Genesis 7

The ark which was built by Noah according to divine directions, in which he and his house, together with representatives from the lower creation, found shelter from the storm of God's wrath, is one of the clearest and most comprehensive types of the believer's salvation in Christ which is to be found in all the Scriptures. So important do we deem it, we have decided to devote a separate article to its prayerful and careful consideration.

1. The first thing to be noted in connection with the ark is that it was *a Divine provision.* This is very clear from the words of Genesis 6:13, 14—"And God said unto Noah, the end of all flesh is come before Me....make thee an ark." *Before* the flood came and before the ark was made, a means of escape for His own people existed in the mind of God. The ark was not provided by Him after the waters had begun to descend. Noah was commanded to construct it before a drop had fallen. So, too, the Saviourship of Christ was no afterthought of God when sin had come in and blighted His creation; from all eternity He had purposed to redeem a people unto Himself, and in consequence, Christ, in the counsels of the Godhead, was "a lamb slain from the foundation of the world" (Rev. 13:8). The ark was God's provision for Noah as Christ is God's provision for sinners.

2. Observe now that God *revealed* to Noah His own designs and ordered him to build a place of refuge into which he could flee from the impending storm of judgment. The ark was no invention of Noah's; had not God revealed His thoughts to him, he would have perished along with his fellow creatures. In like manner, God has to *reveal* by His Spirit His thoughts of mercy and grace toward us; otherwise, in our blindness and ignorance we should be eternally lost. "For God, who commanded the light to shine out of darkness, hath shined in our hearts, *to give the light of the knowledge of the* glory of God in the face of Jesus Christ" (2 Cor. 4:6).

3. In the next place, we note that Noah was commanded to make an ark of gopher-wood (Gen. 6:14). *The material*

out of which the ark was built teaches an important lesson. The ark was made, not of steel like our modern "dreadnoughts," but out of *wood.* The typical truth which this fact is designed to teach us lies not on the surface, yet is one that is brought before us again and again both in the Word and in Nature; the truth, that life comes out of death, that life can be secured only by sacrifice. Before the ark could be made, trees must be *cut down.* That which secured the life of Noah and his house was obtained by *the death* of the trees. We have a hint here, too, of our Lord's *humanity.* The trees from which the wood of the ark was taken were a thing of the earth, reminding us of Isaiah's description of Christ—"a root out of a dry ground" (Isa. 53:2). So Christ, who was the eternal Son of God must become the Son of man—part of that which, originally, was made out of the dust of the earth—and as such be cut down, or, in the language of prophecy, be "cut off" (Dan. 9:26), before a refuge could be provided for us.

4. The ark was *a refuge from Divine judgment.* There are three arks mentioned in Scripture and each of them was a shelter and place of safety. The ark of Noah secured those within it from the outpoured wrath of God. The ark of bulrushes (Ex. 2:3) protected the young child Moses from the murderous designs of Pharaoh, who was a type of Satan. The ark of the covenant sheltered the two tables of stone on which were inscribed the holy law of God. Each ark speaks of Christ, and putting the three together, we learn that the believer is sheltered from God's wrath, Satan's assaults and the condemnation of the law—the only three things in all the universe which can threaten or harm us. The ark of Noah was a place of safety. It was provided by God when death threatened *all.* It was the *only* place of deliverance from the wrath to come, and as such it speaks of our Lord Jesus Christ, the *only* Saviour of lost sinners—"Neither is there salvation in any other; for there is none other name under heaven given among men, whereby we must be saved" (Acts 4:12).

5. Into this ark man was *invited to come.* He was invited by God Himself, "And the Lord said unto Noah, Come thou and all thy house into the ark" (Gen. 7:1). This is the first time the word "come" is found in the Scriptures, and it recurs over five hundred times in the remainder of the

Bible. Is it not highly significant that we meet with it *here* as its *first* occurrence! A number of thoughts are suggested by this connection, for several of which we are indebted to Dr. Thomas' work on Genesis. Observe that the Lord does not say "*Go* into the ark," but "Come." "Go" would have been a command, "Come" was a gracious invitation; "Go" would have implied that the Lord was bidding Noah *depart* from Him, "Come" intimated that in the ark the Lord would be present with him. Is it not the same thought as we have in the Gospel—"Come *unto Me* and I will give you rest!" Observe further that the invitation was a personal one—"Come *thou";* God always addresses Himself to the heart and conscience of the individual. Yet, the invitation went further—"Come thou *and all thy house* into the ark," and again we find a parallel in the Gospel of grace in our day: "Believe on the Lord Jesus Christ, and thou shalt be saved, *and thy house"* (Acts 16:31).

6. The ark was a place of *absolute security.* This truth is seen from several particulars. First, the ark itself was pitched "within and without with pitch" (Gen. 6:14), hence it would be thoroughly watertight, and as such, a perfect shelter. No matter how hard it rained or how high the waters rose, all inside the ark were secure. The ark was in this respect also, a type of our salvation in Christ. Speaking to the saints, the apostle said, "Your life *is hid* (like Noah in the ark) with Christ in God" (Col. 3:3). In the next place, we read concerning Noah after he had entered the ark, "And the Lord *shut him in"* (Gen. 7:16). What a blessed word is this! Noah did not have to take care of himself; having entered the ark, God was then responsible for his preservation. So it is with those who have fled to Christ for refuge, they are "*kept by the power of God* through faith unto salvation ready to be revealed in the last time" (1 Pet. 1:5). Finally, the security of *all* in the ark is seen in the issuing of them forth one year later on to the destruction-swept earth—"And Noah went forth, and his sons and his wife and his sons' wives with him: *every* beast, *every* creeping thing, and *every* fowl, and whatsoever creepeth upon the earth, after their kinds, went forth out of the ark" (Gen. 8:18, 19). All who had entered that ark had been preserved, none had perished by the flood, and none had died a natural death, so perfect is the type.

How this reminds us of our Lord's words, "Of them which thou gavest Me *have I lost none*" (John 18:9).

7. Next we would note what has often been pointed out by others, that the ark had *only one door* to it. There was not one entrance for Noah and his family, another for the animals, and yet another for the birds. *One* door was all it had. The same was true later of the tabernacle; it, too, had but a single entrance. The spiritual application is apparent. There is only one way of escape from eternal death. There is only one way of deliverance from the wrath to come. There is only one Saviour from the Lake of Fire, and that is the Lord Jesus Christ—"I am the way, the truth, and the life, no man cometh unto the Father *but by Me*" (John 14:6). The language of our type is directly employed by Christ in John 10:9, where we hear Him say, "I am *the door.*" It is also worthy of attention to note that Noah was ordered by God to set the door "in the *side*" of the ark (Gen. 6:16). Surely this pointed forward to the piercing of our Lord's "side" (John 19:34) which was the intimation that the way to *the heart of God* is now open to guilty and ruined sinners.

8. The ark had *three stories in it,* "with lower, second, and third stories shalt thou make it" (Gen. 6:16). Why are we told this? What difference does it make to God's saints living four thousand years afterwards how many stories the ark had, whether it had one or a dozen? Every devout student of the Word has learned that everything in the Holy Scriptures has some significance and spiritual value. Necessarily so, for *every* word of God is pure. When the Holy Spirit "moved" Moses to write the book of Genesis, He knew that a book was being written which should be read by the Lord's people thousands of years later, therefore, what He caused to be written must have in every instance, something more than a merely local application. "*Whatsoever* was written aforetime was written for our learning." What then are we to "learn" from the fact that in the ark there were *three* stories, no less and no more?

We have already seen that the ark itself unmistakably foreshadowed the Lord Jesus. Passing through the waters of judgment, being itself submerged by them; grounding on the seventeenth day of the month—as we shall see, the day of our Lord's Resurrection; and affording a shelter to all who were within it, the ark was a very clear type of Christ. Therefore *the inside* of the ark must speak to us of what we have *in Christ.* Is it not clear then that the ark divided into three stories more than hints at our *threefold salvation in Christ?* The salvation which we have in Christ *is* a threefold one, and that in a double sense. It is a salvation which embraces each part of our threefold constitution, making provision for the redemption of our spirit, and soul, and body (1 Thess. 5:23); and further, our salvation is a *three tense* salvation—we *have been* saved from the penalty of sin, *are being* saved from the power of sin, we *shall yet be* saved from the presence of sin.

9. Next, we observe that the ark was furnished with *a window* and this was placed "above"—"A window shalt thou make to the ark and in a cubit shalt thou finish it *above*" (Gen. 6:16). The spiritual application is patent. Noah and his companions were not to be looking down on the scene of destruction beneath and around them, but up toward the living God. The same lesson was taught to Jehovah's people in the Wilderness. The pillar of cloud to guide them by day and the pillar of fire to protect them by night was provided not only for their guidance, but was furnished for their instruction as well. Israel must *look up* to the great Jehovah and not be occupied with the difficulties and dangers of the wilderness. So, we, called upon to walk by faith, are to journey with our eyes turned heavenward. Our affection must be set upon "things *above,* not on things on the earth" (Col. 3:2).

10. The ark was furnished with *"rooms"* or *"nests"*—"Make thee an ark of gopher wood; rooms (margin "nests") shalt thou make in the ark" (Gen. 6:14). In every other passage in the Old Testament where the Hebrew word "gen" occurs, it is translated "nest." We hesitate to press the spiritual signification here; yet, we have seen that the ark is such a striking and comprehensive type of our salvation in Christ we must believe that *this* detail in the picture has some meaning, whether we are able to discern it or no. The thought which is suggested to us is, that in Christ we have something more than a refuge, we have a *resting place;* we are like birds in their nests, the objects of Another's loving care. Oh, is it that the "nests" in the ark look forward to the "many mansions" in the Father's House? which our Lord has gone to prepare for us. It is

rather curious that there is some uncertainty about the precise meaning of the Greek word here translated "mansions." Weymouth renders it, "In My Father's house are many *resting places!*"

11. In connection with the ark the great truth of *Atonement* is typically presented. This comes out in several particulars: "Make thee an ark of gopher wood; rooms shalt thou make in the ark, and shalt *pitch* it within and without with pitch" (Gen. 6:14). The Hebrew word here is not the common one for "pitch" which is "zetteth," but is "kapher," which is translated seventy times in the Old Testament "to make atonement." The simple meaning of "kapher" is *"to cover"* and nowhere else is it rendered "pitch." Atonement was made by the blood which provided a *covering* for sin. Our readers being familiar with this thought, there is no need for us to develop it. God is holy, and as such He is "of purer eyes than to behold evil, and canst not look on iniquity" (Hab. 1:13), hence sin must be *covered*—covered by blood. It is therefore remarkable that this word "kapher" should be employed (for the first time in Scripture) in connection with the ark, as though to teach us that a shelter from God's wrath can be found only beneath the atoning blood! Again we notice that the storm *fell upon the ark* which provided shelter for Noah and those that were with him. So, too, the clouds of Divine judgment burst upon our adorable Redeemer as He suffered in our stead: "All Thy waves and thy billows are gone over Me" (Ps. 42:7) was His cry; and may not His words here be language pointing back to the very type we are now considering?

12. As others have pointed out, the typical teaching of the ark reaches beyond the truth of atonement to *resurrection* itself. We quote here from the writings of the late Mr. William Lincoln: "There seems no reason to doubt that the day the ark rested on the mountain of Ararat is identical with the day on which the Lord rose from the dead. It rested "on *the seventeenth day* of the seventh month." But by the commandment of the Lord, given at the time of the institution of the feast of the Passover, the seventh month was changed into the first month. Then three days after the Passover, which was on the *fourteenth* day of the month, the Lord, having passed quite through the waters of judgment, stood in resurrection in the midst

of His disciples, saying, "Peace be unto you." They, as well as Himself, had reached the haven of everlasting rest." But not only does our type prefigure our Lord's resurrection from the dead, it also suggests the truth of His *ascension,* for we read "And the ark rested in the seventh month, on the seventeenth day of the month *upon the mountains of Ararat*" (Gen. 8:4). The final resting place of the ark was upon the mountain top, speaking of the place "on high" where our Saviour is now seated at the right hand of God.

We lay our pen down with a strengthened conviction that the Holy Scriptures are no mere "cunningly devised fables," but that they are indeed the inspired Word of the living God.

14. GOD'S COVENANT WITH NOAH

GENESIS 8

The covenants referred to therein constitute one of the principal keys to the interpretation of the Old Testament, denoting, as they do, the dividing lines between the different Dispensations, and indicating the several changes of procedure in God's dealings with the earth. At various times God condescended to enter into a compact with man, and failure to observe the terms and scope of these compacts necessarily leads to the utmost confusion. The Word of truth can only be rightly divided as due attention is paid to the different covenants recorded therein. The covenants varied in their requirements, in their scope, in their promises and in the seals or signs connected with them. The inspired history growing out of the covenants furnishes a signal demonstration of God's faithfulness and of man's faithlessness and failure.

There are exactly *seven* covenants made by *God* referred to in Scripture, neither more nor less. First, the *Adamic* which concerned man's continued enjoyment of Eden on the condition that he refrained from eating the fruit of the forbidden tree. But Adam failed to keep his part of the agreement, see Hosea 6:7 margin. Second, the *Noahic* which concerned the earth and its seasons, see Genesis 9. Third, the *Abrahamic* which concerned Israel's occupancy of Palestine, see Genesis 15:18, etc. Fourth, the *Mosaic* which concerned Israel's continued enjoyment of God's favors, conditioned by their obedience to His law, see Exodus 24:7, 8; 34:27. Fifth, the *Levitic* which concerned the priesthood, promising that it should remain in this tribe, see Numbers 25:12, 13; Malachi 2:4, 5; Ezekiel 44:15, which proves God's faithfulness in respect to this covenant in the Millennium. Sixth, the *Davidic* which concerns the Kingdom and particularly the throne, see 2 Samuel 23:5; 2 Chronicles 13:5. Seventh, the *Messianic* or New Covenant which concerns the Millennium, see Isaiah 42:6; Jeremiah 31:31-34. Much might be written concerning these different covenants, but we limit ourselves to the second, the Noahic. We wish to say, however, that a careful study of the above references will richly repay every diligent and prayerful reader.

1. Coming now to the second of these great covenants let us notice the *occasion* of it. It was as it were the beginning of a new world. There was to be a fresh start. With the exception of those who found shelter in the ark, the flood had completely destroyed both the human family and the lower orders of creation. On to the destruction-swept earth came Noah and his family. Noah's first act was to build, not a house for himself, but an altar "unto the Lord," on which he presented burnt offerings. These were, unto the Lord, a "sweet savor," and after declaring that He would not curse the ground any more for man's sake, and after promising that while the earth remained its seasons should not cease, we are told "God *blessed* Noah and his sons" (9:1). This is the first time that we read of God blessing any since He had blessed unfallen man in Eden (Gen. 1:28). The *basis* of this "blessing" was the burnt offerings; the *design* of it to show that the same Divine favor that was extended to Adam and Eve should now rest upon the new progenitors of the human race.

Here then we have the second "beginning" of Genesis, a beginning which, in several respects, resembled the first, particularly in the command to be fruitful and multiply, and in the subjection of the irrational creature to man's dominion. But there is one difference here which it is important to notice: all now rests upon *a covenant of grace based upon shed blood.* Man had forfeited the "blessing" of God and his position as lord of creation, but grace restores and reinstates him. God makes a covenant with Noah which in its *scope* included the beasts of the field (9:2) who are made to be at peace with him and subject to his authority; and which in its *duration* would last while the earth remained. Let us now note:

2. The *source* of this covenant. At least two of the seven covenants referred to above (the first and the fourth) were mutual agreements between God and man, but in the one now before us, God Himself was the initiator and sole compacter. The whole passage emphasizes the fact that it was a covenant of God with Noah, and not of Noah with God. God was the giver, man the receiver. Note—"I will establish *My covenant* with you" (v. 11); "This is the token of the covenant which *I make*" (v. 12); "And I will remember *My covenant*" (v. 15). That this was *God's covenant with Noah,* and that man had no part in the mak-

ing or keeping of it is further seen from the following language: "I do set My bow in the cloud, and it shall be for a token of a covenant *between Me and the earth*" (v. 13), and, "I will remember My covenant, which is between *Me* and you *and every living creature of all flesh*" (v. 15).

It is further to be noted that God said to Noah "with *thee* will I establish My covenant" (Gen. 6:18). The benefits of it have been enjoyed by Noah's posterity, yet the covenant was not made with them. Favor has been shown to his descendants for *Noah's* sake. Similarly, God made a covenant with Abraham in which He promised to bless his offspring. Thus, at this early period in human history God was revealing the great principle by which redemption should afterwards be effected by His Son, namely, that of *representation,* the one acting for the many, the many receiving blessing through the one.

3. The *basis* of this covenant is seen in the closing verses of Genesis 8. The chapter division here is most unfortunate. Genesis 8 ought to terminate with the nineteenth verse, the remaining three forming the proper commencement of the ninth chapter. "And Noah builded an altar unto the Lord; and took of every clean beast, and of every clean fowl, and offered burnt offerings on the altar" (Gen. 8:20)—the next two verses, and the whole of chapter nine down to the seventeenth verse, contain *Jehovah's response* to Noah's offering. It is in these verses we learn God's *answer* to the "sweet savor" that ascended from the altar. This covenant, then, was based upon *sacrifice,* and being made by God with Noah, and not by Noah with God, is therefore unconditionable and inviolable. How blessed to learn from this type that every temporal blessing which the earth enjoys as well as every spiritual blessing which is the portion of the saints, accrues to us from the Sacrifice of the Lord Jesus Christ of whom Noah's burnt offerings spoke.

4. The *contents* of this covenant call for careful consideration. A part of these has already engaged our attention. "While the earth remaineth, seedtime and harvest, and cold and heat, and summer and winter, and day and night, shall not cease" (8:20); "And I will establish My covenant with you; neither shall all flesh be cut off any more by the waters of a flood; neither shall there any more be a flood to destroy the earth" (9:11). These promises were given more than four thousand years ago, and the

unfailing annual fulfilment of them all through the centuries forms a striking demonstration of the faithfulness of God. The terms of this covenant refer us to that which is almost universally lost sight of in these days, namely, the fact that behind Nature's "laws" is Nature's Lord. Men now seek to shut God out of His own creation. We hear so much of the science of farming and the laws of diet that our daily bread and the health of the body are regarded as something that man produces and controls. Our daily bread is a *gift*, for without the recurring seasons and God's "renewal of the face of the earth" (Ps. 104:30) man could produce no grain at all, and the recurring of the seasons and the renewal of the earth are *the fulfilment* of the covenant that God made with Noah. A casual observation of Nature's "laws" reveals the fact that they are not uniform in their operation, hence if a Divine Revelation be eliminated man possesses no guarantee that the seasons may not radically change or that the earth shall not be destroyed again by a flood. Nature's "laws" did not prevent the Deluge in Noah's day, why should they prevent a recurrence of it in ours? How blessed for the child of God to turn to the inerrant Word and hear his Father say, "And I will establish My covenant with you; neither shall all flesh be cut off any more by the waters of a flood; neither shall there any more be a flood to destroy the earth!"

5. The *design* of the covenant is hinted at in the scripture just quoted. The timeliness and blessedness of such a revelation are apparent. Such an awful catastrophe as the Flood would shake violently the confidence of men in the established order of Nature, and distressing apprehensions were likely to obsess their minds for generations to come. They would be filled with terror as they feared a repetition of it. It was therefore a merciful act on the part of God to set their minds at rest and assure His creatures that He would no more destroy the earth with a flood. It was a wondrous display of His grace, for man had fully shown that he was utterly unworthy of the least of heaven's mercies, yet, despite the fact that "the imagination of man's heart is evil from his youth," the Lord said in His heart, "Neither will I again smite any more every thing living, as I have done" (8:21). It was also an affirmation of His Creatorship—the varying seasons, the planets that rule them, the influences of climatic conditions, were all beneath

the control of Him who upholds "all things by the word of His power" (Heb. 1:3).

6. The *requirements* of the covenant are of deep interest. Though the word itself does not occur till the eleventh verse of the ninth chapter, a careful study of the context makes it clear that the covenant itself is expressed in 8:22, and that from there on the "covenant" is the one theme of the entire passage. Three things are included among the Divine requirements: first, blood must not be eaten; second, the principle of retributive judgment is clearly enunciated for the first time, capital punishment as the penalty of murder being now commanded; the human race was to multiply and people the earth which had been depopulated by the flood. Let us take a brief look at each of these things.

"But flesh with the life thereof, which is the blood thereof, shall ye not eat" (9:4). This is the second passage in Scripture in which the word *blood* occurs. Here, as everywhere in the Word, the earliest references forecast in outline all that is subsequently said upon the subject. The first seven passages in which the word blood is found contain a complete summary of the teaching of God's Word upon this fundamental theme. (1) Genesis 4:10, 11, gives us the first mention of blood, and here we learn that *the blood cries unto God.* (2) Genesis 9:4-6, here we learn that *the blood is the life,* and that *blood must be held sacred.* (3) Genesis 37:22, 26, 31, Joseph's coat is dipped in blood and is brought to Jacob: here we learn, in type, that *the blood of the Son is presented to the Father.* (4) Genesis 42:22, here we learn that *blood is required at the hand of those who shed it.* (5) Genesis 49:11, here, in poetic and prophetic language, Judah's clothes are said to be *washed in the blood* of grapes." (6) Exodus 4:9, the waters of the Nile are turned into blood, teaching us that *blood is the symbol and expression of God's judgment upon sin.* (7) Exodus 12:13, *the blood provides a covering and shelter* for Israel from the avenging angel. We say again, that in these passages which are *the first seven* in the Scriptures in which *blood* is referred to, we discover a marvellously complete summary of all that is subsequently said about the precious blood. It is deeply significant, then, that in the first requirement in this covenant, which God made with Noah, man should be taught to regard the blood as *sacred.*

We turn now to the second of God's requirements mentioned here in connection with His covenant with Noah—"Whoso sheddeth man's blood, by man shall his blood be shed: for in the image of God made He man" (9:6). Here we have instituted the principle of all human government. The sword of magisterial authority is, for the first time, committed into the hands of man. Before the flood, there does not seem to have been any recognized form of human government designed for the suppression of crime and the punishment of evil doers. Cain murdered his brother, but his own life was spared. Lamech also slew a man, but there is no hint that he had to defend himself before any tribunal that had been ordained by God. But now, after the flood, capital punishment as the penalty of murder *is* ordained, ordained by God Himself, ordained centuries before the giving of the Mosaic law, and therefore, universally binding until the end of time. It is important to observe that the *reason* for this law is not here based upon the well-being of man, but is grounded upon the basic fact that man is made "in the image of God." This expression has at least a twofold significance—a natural and a moral. The moral image of God in man was lost at the Fall, but the natural has been preserved as is clear from 1 Corinthians 11:7, and James 3:9. It is primarily because man is made in the image of God that it is sinful to slay him. "To deface the King's image is a sort of treason among men, implying a hatred against him, and that if he himself were within reach, he would be served in the same manner. How much more treasonable, then, must it be to destroy, curse, oppress, or in any way abuse the image of the King of kings!" (Andrew Fuller's Exposition of Genesis). As we have said above, God's words to Noah give us the institution of human government in the earth. The sword of magisterial authority has been given into the hands of man by God Himself, hence it is we read, "Let every soul be subject unto the higher powers. For there is no power but of God: the powers that be are ordained of God. Whosoever therefore resisteth the power, resisteth the ordinance of God" (Rom. 13:1, 2).

We turn now to the third of God's requirements—"And you, be ye fruitful, and multiply; bring forth abundantly in the earth, and multiply therein" (9:7). This was the renewal of God's word to Adam (1:28). The human family was starting out afresh. There was a new beginning. Noah stood, like Adam stood, as the head of the human race. The need for this word was obvious. The earth had been depopulated. The human family had been reduced to eight souls* (1 Pet. 3:20). If then the purpose of man's creation was to be realized, if the earth was to be replenished and subdued, then must man be "fruitful and multiply." "And the fear of you and the dread of you shall be upon every beast of the earth and upon every fowl of the air, upon all that moveth upon the earth, and upon all the fishes of the sea; *into your hand are they delivered"* (9:2) is further proof that Noah stood as the new head of the race, the lower orders of creation being delivered into his hands as they had been into the hands of Adam.

7. "And God said, This is *the token* of the covenant which I make between Me and you, and every living creature that is with you, for perpetual generations: I do set My bow in the cloud, and it shall be for a token of a covenant between Me and the earth. And it shall come to pass, when I bring a cloud over the earth, that the bow shall be seen in the cloud;....and *I will look upon it,* that I may remember the everlasting covenant between God and every living creature of all flesh that is upon the earth" (9:12-16). These verses bring before us the *token* of the covenant. In the giving of the rainbow God ratified the promise which He had made. The bow in the cloud was not only to assure man that no more would the earth be destroyed by a flood, but it was also the memorial of the new relationship which God had entered into with His creatures. "*His* eye," and not man's only, is upon the bow, and thus He gives them fellowship with Himself in that which speaks of peace in the midst of trouble, of light in the place of darkness; and what this bow speaks of it is ours to realize, who have the reality of which all figures speak.

"'God is light,' and that which doth make manifest is light." Science has told us that the colors which everywhere clothe the face of nature are but the manifold beauty of the light itself. The pure ray which to us is colorless is but the harmonious blending of all possible colors. The primary one—a trinity in unity—from which all others are

*It is something more than a coincidence that the word "covenant" is found in this connection just *eight* times, see Genesis 6:18; 9:9, 11, 12, 13, 15, 16, 17—eight being the numeral that signifies *a new beginning,* as the eighth day is the first of a new week.

produced, are blue, red, and yellow; and the actual color of any object is the result of its capacity to absorb the rest. If it absorb the red and yellow rays, the thing is blue; if the blue and yellow, it is red; if the red only, it is green; and so on. Thus the light paints all nature; and its beauty (which in the individual ray, we have not eyes for) comes out in partial displays wherein it is broken up for us and made perceptible.

"'God is light'; He is Father of lights." The glory, which in its unbroken unity is beyond what we have sight for, He reveals to us as distinct attributes in partial displays which we are more able to take in, and with these He clothes in some way all the works of His hands. The jewels on the High Priest's breastplate—the many-colored gems whereon the names of His people were engraved were thus the "Urim and Thummim"—the "Lights and Perfections," typically, of God Himself; for His people are identified with the display of those perfections, those "lights," in Him more unchangeable than the typical gems.

"In the rainbow the whole array of these lights manifests itself, the solar rays reflecting themselves in the storm; the interpretation of which is simple. "When I bring a cloud over the earth," says the Lord, "the bow shall be seen in the cloud; and I (not merely you) will look upon it." How blessed to know that the cloud that comes over our sky is of *His* bringing! and if so, how sure that some way He will reveal His glory in it! But that is not all, nor the half; for surely but once has been the full display of the whole prism of glory, and that in the blackest storm of judgment that ever was; and it is this in the cross of His Son that God above all looks upon and that He remembers" (F. W. Grant).

In the rainbow we have more than a hint of *grace*. As some one has said, "The bow is directed towards heaven, and arrow to it there is none, as if it had already been discharged." There are many parallels between the rainbow and God's grace. As the rainbow is the joint product of storm and sunshine, so grace is the unmerited favor of God appearing on the dark background of the creature's sin. As the rainbow is the effect of the sun shining on the drops of rain in a raincloud, so Divine grace is manifested by God's love shining through the blood shed by our blessed Redeemer. As the rainbow is the telling out of the varied hues of the white light, so the "*manifold* grace of God" 1 Pet. 4:10) is the ultimate expression of God's heart. As Nature knows nothing more exquisitely beautiful than the rainbow, so heaven itself knows nothing that equals in loveliness the wonderful grace of our God. As the rainbow is the union of heaven and earth—spanning the sky and reaching down to the ground—so grace in the one Mediator has brought together God and men. As the rainbow is a public sign of God hung out in the heavens that all may see it, so "the grace of God that bringeth salvation *hath appeared to all men*" (Titus 2:11). Finally, as the rainbow has been displayed throughout all the past forty centuries, so *in the ages to come* God will shew forth "the exceeding riches of His grace, in His kindness toward us, through Christ Jesus" (Eph. 2:7).

15. NOAH'S FALL AND NOAH'S PROPHECY

Genesis 9

In our last article we inquired into God's Covenant with Noah—its basis, its contents, its requirements, etc. We saw, in the emerging out of the ark that from Noah and his sons the human family started out afresh. The new beginning promised well. God entered into a covenant with Noah, declaring that the earth should not again be destroyed by a flood—thus did the Lord set the heart of His creatures at rest. Then, we learned that "God *blessed* Noah and his sons"; that He caused the fear and dread of man to fall upon every beast of the field, and "delivered" all the lower orders of creation into his hands. Further, we discovered that man was now vested with the sword of magisterial authority, the principle of human government being ordained and instituted by God Himself.

After such a merciful deliverance from the deluge, after witnessing such a solemn demonstration of God's holy wrath against sin, and after being started out with full provision and Divine assurance, one would have supposed that the human race, ever after, would adhere to the path of righteousness—but, alas! The very next thing we read is that "Noah began to be a husbandman, and he planted a vineyard: and he drank of the wine *and was drunken, and he was uncovered within his tent*" (Gen. 9:20, 21). Scholars tell us that the Hebrew word here for "uncovered" clearly indicates a deliberate act and not a mere unconscious effect of drunkenness. The sins of intemperance and impurity are twin sisters! No wonder the Psalmist was constrained to cry, "What is man that thou art mindful of him?" What a contrast there is between this section of Genesis and the last that we considered! Who would have imagined such a tragic sequel? How evident it is that truth is stranger than fiction.

Genesis 9 brings before us the inauguration of *a new beginning* and as we study and ponder what is recorded herein our minds revert to the first "beginning" of the human race, and careful comparison of the two reveals the fact that there is a most extraordinary resemblance in the history of Noah with that of Adam. We would here call attention to a tenfold correspondence or likeness. Adam was placed upon an earth which came up out of the "deep and which had previously been dealt with by God in judgment" (Gen. 1:12); so, also, Noah came forth onto an earth which had just emerged from the waters of the great Deluge sent as a Divine judgment upon sin. Adam was made lord of creation (Gen. 1:28) and into the hands of Noah God also delivered all things (Gen. 9:2). Adam was "blessed" by God and told to "be fruitful and multiply and replenish the earth" (Gen. 1:28), and, in like manner, Noah was "blessed" and told to "be fruitful and multiply and replenish the earth" (Gen. 9:1). Adam was placed by God in a garden to "dress and to keep it" (Gen. 2:15), and Noah "began to be a husbandman, and he planted a vineyard" (Gen. 9:20). In this garden Adam transgressed and fell, and the product of the vineyard was the occasion of Noah's sin and fall. The sin of Adam resulted in the exposure of his nakedness (Gen. 3:7), and so, too, we read "And he (Noah) was uncovered within his tent" (Gen. 9:21). Adam's nakedness was covered by another (Gen. 3:21); thus also was it with Noah (Gen. 9:23). Adam's sin brought a terrible curse upon his posterity (Rom. 5:12), and so did Noah's too (Gen. 24:24, 25). Adam had three sons—Cain, Abel and Seth, the last of which was the one through whom the promised Seed came; and here again the analogy holds good, for Noah also had three sons—Japheth, Ham and Shem, the last mentioned being the one from whom descended the Messiah and Saviour. Almost immediately after Adam's fall a wonderful prophecy was given containing in outline the history of redemption (Gen. 3:15); and almost immediately after Noah's fall, a remarkable prophecy was uttered containing in outline the history of the great races of the earth. Thus does history repeat itself.

Noah "planted a vineyard: and he drank of the wine and was drunken, and he was uncovered within his tent" (Gen. 9:21). As we read these words we are reminded of the Holy Spirit's comment upon the Old Testament Scriptures—"For whatsoever things were written aforetime were written for our learning" (Rom. 15:4). What then are we to "learn" from this narration of Noah's sad fall?

First, we discover a striking proof of the Divine inspiration of the scriptures. In the Bible human nature is painted in its true colors: the characters of its *heroes* are *faithfully* depicted, the *sins* of its most prominent personages are frankly recorded. It is human to err, but it is also human to conceal the blemishes of those we admire. Had the Bible been a human production, had it been written by uninspired historians, the defects of its leading characters would have been ignored, or if recorded at all, an attempt at extenuation would have been made. Had some human admirer chronicled the history of Noah, his awful fall would have been omitted. The fact that it *is* recorded and that no effort is made to *excuse* his sin, is evidence that the characters of the Bible are painted in the colors of truth and nature, that such characters were not sketched by human pens, that Moses and the other historians must have written by Divine inspiration.

Second, we learn from Noah's fall that man at his best estate is altogether vanity, in other words, we see the utter and total depravity of human nature. Genesis 9 deals with the beginning of a new dispensation, and like those which preceded it and those which followed it, this also *opened with failure.* Whatever the test may be, man is unable to stand. Placed in an environment which the besom of destruction had swept clean; a solemn warning of the judgment of heaven upon evil-doers only recently spread before him; the blessing of God pronounced upon him, the sword of magisterial authority placed in his hand, Noah, nevertheless, *fails to govern himself* and falls into open wickedness. Learn then that man is essentially "evil" (Matt. 7:11) and that naught avails but "a new creation" (Gal. 6:15).

Third, we learn from Noah's fall the danger of using *wine* and the awful evils that attend intemperance. It is surely significant and designed as a solemn warning that the *first* time wine is referred to in the Scriptures it is found associated with drunkenness, shame and a curse. Solemn are the denunciations of the Word upon drunkenness, a sin which, despite all the efforts of temperance reformers, is, taking the world as a whole, still on the increase. Drunkenness is a sin against *God,* for it is the *abusing* of His mercies; it is a sin against our *neighbors,* for it deprives those who are in want of their necessary supplies and sets before them an evil example; it is a sin against *ourself,* for it robs of usefulness, self-government and common decency. Moreover, drunkenness commonly leads to other evils. It did in Noah's case; Noah's sin gave occasion for his son to sin.

Fourth, in Noah's sin we learn *our* need of watchfulness and prayer. A believer is never immune from falling. The evil nature is still within us and nothing but constant dependency upon God can enable us to withstand the solicitations of the world, the flesh, and the devil. "Let him that thinketh he standeth take heed lest he fall" is a word that every saint needs daily to take to heart. Neither age nor character is any security in the hour of testing. Here was a man who had withstood the temptations of an evil world for six hundred years, yet nevertheless, he now succumbs to the lusts of the flesh. And this is one of the things which is written for *"our admonition"* (1 Cor. 10:11). Then let us not sit in judgment upon Noah with pharisaical complacency, rather let us "consider ourselves, lest we also be tempted" (Gal. 6:1). No experience of God's mercies in the past can deliver us from exposure to new temptations in the future.

Finally, Noah's fall utters a solemn warning to every *servant* of God. It is deeply significant that following this prophecy, recorded in the closing verses of Genesis 9, *nothing whatever* save his death is recorded about Noah after his terrible fall. The last three hundred years of his life are a blank! "But I keep under my body, and bring it into subjection; lest that by any means, when I have preached to others, I myself should be a castaway" (1 Cor. 9:27).

Having dwelt at some length upon Noah's fall and the lessons it is designed to teach us, we turn now to examine the prophecy which he uttered immediately after. Three things will engage our attention: the occasion of this prophecy, the meaning of this prophecy, and the fulfilment of it.

1. The *occasion* of Noah's prophecy. The setting of it is a remarkable one. The terrible fall of the illustrious patriarch and the wonderful prediction he uttered concerning the future history of the three great divisions of the human family are placed in juxtaposition. The fact that the Holy Spirit has thus joined these two together is a

striking illustration of the truth that God's ways are different from ours. The devout student of the Word has learnt that not only are the very words of Scripture inspired of God, but that their *arrangement* and *order* also evidence a wisdom that transcends the human. What then are we to learn from this linking together of Noah's fall and Noah's prophecy?

In seeking an answer to our last question we need to observe the *scope* of the prophecy itself. Noah's prediction contains an outline sketch of the history of the nations of the world. The great races of the earth are here seen in their embryonic condition: they are traced to their common source, through Shem, Ham and Japheth, back to Noah. The nature of the stream is determined by the character of the fountain—a bitter fountain cannot send forth sweet waters. The type of fruit is governed by the order of the tree—a corrupt tree cannot produce wholesome fruit. Noah is the fountain, and what sort of a stream *could* flow from *such* a fountain! Read again the sad recital of Noah's fall and of Ham's wickedness and then ask, what *must* be the fruit which springs from such a tree, what must be the harvest that is reaped from such a sowing? What will be the history of the races that spring from Noah's three sons? What can it be? A history that *began* by Noah abusing God's mercies; a history that *commenced* with the head of the new race failing, completely, to govern himself; a history that *started* with Ham's shameful impropriety can have only one course and end. It began with human failure, it has continued thus, and it will end thus. Here then is the answer to our question: Why is Noah's prophecy, which sketches the history of the three great races of mankind, linked to Noah's fall? The two are joined together as cause and effect, as premise and conclusion, as sowing and harvest!

It was written of old that "the wisdom of this world is foolishness with God." A striking illustration of this is discovered today in the wicked writings of the self-termed "Higher Critics." These blind leaders of the blind aim to degrade God's Word to the level of human productions and in this remarkable prophecy of Noah regarding his sons they see nothing more than a hasty ejaculation caused by the knowledge of his humiliation and expressed in this curse and blessing. That these words of Noah were not uttered to gratify any feeling of resentment, but were spoken under a Divine impulse is proven by the fulfilment of the prophecy itself. A very superficial acquaintance with the facts of ancient history will evidence the fact that there is far more in Noah's words than a local expression of indignation and gratitude. A careful comparison of other scriptures shows that this utterance of Noah was a *prophecy* and its remarkable fulfilment demonstrates that it was a Divine revelation.

"And he said, Cursed be Canaan; a servant of servants shall he be unto his brethren.

"And he said, Blessed be the Lord God of Shem; and Canaan shall be his servant.

"God shall enlarge Japheth, and he shall dwell in the tents of Shem; and Caanan shall be his servant" (Gen. 9:25-27).

2. Let us consider now the *meaning* of Noah's prophecy. This utterance consists of two parts: a malediction and a benediction. Noah's prediction concerning his sons corresponds with their conduct on the occasion of their father's drunkenness. Fearful had been the fall of Noah, but it was a still greater sin for Ham, on discovering the sad condition of his parent, to go out and report with malignant pleasure to his brethren. It is "fools" who "make a mock of sin" (Prov. 14:9). For a child to expose and sneer at his parent's fall was wickedness of the worst kind, and evidenced a heart thoroughly depraved.

In the curse passed upon Canaan we find an exceedingly solemn instance of the sins of the fathers being visited upon the children. In this day of human pride and scepticism, when everything is questioned and challenged, men have dared to criticise the ethics of this hereditary law. It has been termed unmerciful and unjust. The humble believer does not attempt to pry into things which are too deep for him, it is enough for him that the thrice holy God *has* instituted this law and therefore he *knows* it is a righteous one whether he can see the justice of it or no.

Ham's sin consisted of an utter failure to *honor his father*. He was lacking, altogether, in filial love. Had he really cared for his father at all he would have acted as his brothers did; but instead, he manifested a total disrespect for and subjection unto his parent. And mark the fearful consequence: he reaped exactly as he had sown—

Ham sinned as a *son* and was punished *in his son!* The punishment meted out to Ham was that his son *shall be* brought into subjection to others, his descendants shall be *compelled* to honor, yea, "serve" others—"servant of servants" (verse 25) implies the lowest drudgery, slavery.

It is to be noted that the "curse" uttered by Noah did not fall directly on Ham but upon one of his sons, the fourth—"Canaan" (Gen. 10:6). As we shall seek to show, this curse was not confined to Canaan but embraced *all* the descendants of Ham. It is highly probable that "Canaan" was specifically singled out from the rest of his brethren as a special *encouragement* to the Israelites who, centuries later, were to go up and occupy the Promised land. Moses would thus be taught by the Holy Spirit that a special curse rested upon the then occupants of the land, *i. e.,* the *Canaanites.* Yet, as we have said, *all* of Ham's children appear to have been included within the scope of this malediction as is evident from the fact that *no* blessing at all was pronounced upon Ham as was the case with each of his brothers.

"Blessed be the Lord God of Shem; and Canaan shall be his servant" (verse 26). The reward of Shem was in the sphere of *religious privileges.* The Divine title employed here supplies the key. In the following verse we read, "*God* shall enlarge Japheth," but here "Blessed be the *Lord God* of Shem," this being the title expressive of covenant relationship. God was to enter into covenant relationship with the children of Shem. The realization that *Jehovah* was to be the God of Shem caused Noah to break forth into thanksgiving—"*Blessed be* the Lord God of Shem."

"God shall enlarge Japheth" (verse 27). The word Japheth means "enlargement" so that here there was a play upon words. "And he shall dwell in the tents of Shem." This expression is somewhat ambiguous, the obscurity being occasioned by the difficulty to ascertain the antecedent. Scholars and students have differed as to whether the "he" refers to God or to Japheth dwelling in the tents of Shem. Personally, we incline toward the latter alternative, though we believe that each of them has been verified in subsequent history. May it not be that the Holy Spirit has designedly left it uncertain, to show that *both* interpretations are true? Sure it is that *God* did dwell in the tents of Shem, and equally sure is it that the descendants of Japheth are now doing so.

3. The *fulfillment* of Noah's prophecy. The wonderful prediction uttered by the builder of the Ark gives in a few brief sentences the history of the new world, and shows the positions that were delegated by God to the three great divisions of the human family. In the closing verses of Genesis 9 we have a remarkable unfolding of the future destinies of the new humanity. The various parts which are to be played in human history by its leading characters are now made known. The subjection of one, the religious preëminence of the second, and the enlarging of the third head of the postdiluvian race, is here revealed.

"Cursed be Canaan; a servant of servants shall he be unto his brethren" (verse 25). Above, we intimated that as no blessing at all was pronounced upon Ham as was the case with each of his brothers, it would seem that the curse was *not* intended to be *limited* to Canaan (there being a particular reason *why* Canaan should be thus singled out, namely, as an *encouragement* to the Israelites,) but included all of his children. By tracing the history of Ham's other sons it becomes evident that the scope of Noah's prophecy reached beyond Canaan. Nimrod sprang from Ham through Cush (Gen. 10: 6-8), and he founded the city and empire Babylon. Mizraim was another of Ham's children and he was the father of the Egyptians (Gen. 10: 6 and Ps. 78: 51). For a time Babylon and Egypt waxed great, but subsequently both of them were reduced to subjection, first by the Persians who descended from Shem, and later by the Greeks and Romans who were the children of Japheth. And from these early subjugations they have never recovered themselves. The whole of Africa was peopled by the descendants of Ham, and for many centuries the greater part of that continent lay under the dominion of the Romans, Saracens, and Turks. And, as is well known, the negroes who were for so long the slaves of Europeans and Americans, also claim Ham as their progenitor.

"Blessed be the Lord God of Shem; and Canaan shall be his servant" (verse 26). Two things are promised here: Jehovah was to be the God of Shem and Canaan was to be his servant. Shem was "the father of all the children of Eber," that is, the Hebrews (Gen. 10: 21). Thus, in the Hebrews, the knowledge and worship of God was preserved in the family of Shem. The fulfillment of this part of the prophecy is well known to our readers. God was in a peculiar sense the God of the Hebrews—"And I will dwell among the children of Israel, and will be *their God*" (Ex. 29:45). And again, "You only have I known of all the families of the earth" (Amos 3:2).

"And Canaan shall be his (Shem's) servant." This received its first fulfillment in the days of Joshua—"And Joshua made them (the Gibeonites) *hewers of wood and drawers of water* for the congregation" (Josh. 9:27). The following scriptures set forth its further accomplishment: "And it came to pass, when Israel was strong, that they *put the Canaanites to tribute*" (Judges 1:28). "And all the people that were left of the Amorites, Hittites, Perizzites, Hivites, and Jebusites, which were not of the children of Israel, their children that were left after them in the land, whom the children of Israel also were not able utterly to destroy, upon those did Solomon *levy a tribute of bond service* unto this day" (1 Kings 9:20, 21).

"God shall enlarge Japheth, and he shall dwell in the tents of Shem" (verse 27). Two things were also predicted of Japheth: first, he should be enlarged; second, he should dwell in the tents of Shem or, in other words, should receive blessing from Shem. The accomplishment of this prediction is witnessed to by history both sacred and secular. Those nations which have been most enlarged by God have descended from Japheth. The Greeks and the Romans who in their time dominated practically all of the then known world; and more recently the European Powers who have entered into the rich possessions of Asia (inhabited by the children of Shem); and, to-day, the Anglo-Saxon race, which occupies more territory than any other people, are all the descendants of Noah's firstborn! In Genesis 10, where a list of Japheth's sons is found, we read, "By these *were the isles of the Gentiles* divided in their lands."

"And he shall dwell in the tents of Shem" intimates that Japheth was to be Shem's guest, that he should share the rest and shelter of Shem's tabernacles. How remarkably has this prophecy been fulfilled spiritually! "The revelation which we prize is that of the God of *Israel;* the Saviour in whom we trust is the seed of *Abraham;* the Old Testament was written principally for Israel; and the New Testament though written in a Japhetic tongue, and, therefore for us, was penned by *Jewish fingers*" (Urquhart). To this may be added the words of our Lord, "Salvation is of the Jews" (John 4: 22); and that remarkable statement of the Apostle Paul's in Romans 11 where, writing of the Gentiles, he says, "And thou, being a wild olive tree, wert grafted in *among them* (Israel), and with them partakest of the root and fatness of the olive tree" (verse 17). Thus do we see Japheth "dwelling in the tents of Shem."

Who but He who knows the end from the beginning could have outlined the whole course of the three great divisions of the postdiluvian race so tersely and so accurately!

16. NIMROD AND THE TOWER OF BABEL

GENESIS 10, 11

In Genesis 10 and 11 we have the historical links which connect for us the time of Noah with the days of Abraham. Uninteresting as they may appear to the casual reader they furnish most valuable information to the prayerful student. Without these two chapters and the genealogies which they contain, we should be quite unable to trace the fulfillment of Noah's wonderful prophecy; we should be without any satisfactory solution to the ethnological problem presented by the variety and number of the different nations and tongues; and, we should be left in ignorance concerning the *cause* (from the human side) which led up to God abandoning His dealings with the nations and singling out Abram to be the father of His chosen people Israel.

Genesis 10 and 11 give us the history of the postdiluvian world; they show us the ways of men in this new world—in revolt against God and seeking to glorify and deify themselves; and they set before us the principles and judgments upon which this world is founded. For the understanding of the chapters it is necessary to pay careful attention to their *structure and chronology.* Chapter eleven *historically* antedates much of Genesis 10, furnishing us with a commentary upon it. Verses eight to twelve of chapter ten and verses one to nine of chapter eleven should be read as two *parentheses.* Reading them thus, we find, that outside of these parentheses, these chapters furnish us with the genealogical descent of Abram from Noah. Upon these genealogies and origins of the various nations we shall not now comment, preferring to dwell at some length on the parenthetical portions.

Like everything else in Genesis, the historical events recorded in these brief parentheses are remarkable in their typical significance and reach. In the clearer and fuller light of the New Testament we cannot fail to see that Nimrod foreshadowed the last great World-Ruler before our Lord descends to earth and ushers in His millennial reign It is deeply significant that the person and history of Nimrod are here introduced at the point immediately preceding

God calling Abram from among the Gentiles and bringing him into the Promised Land. So will it be again in the near future. Just before God gathers Abraham's descendants from out of the lands of the Gentiles (many, perhaps the majority of whom will be found dwelling at that very time in Assyria,—see Isaiah 11:11), there will arise one who will fill out the picture here typically outlined by Nimrod. We refer of course to *the Antichrist*. As the Antichrist is a subject of such interest and importance—his manifestation being now so near at hand—we digress for a moment to say one or two things about him.

To begin at the beginning. We need not remind our readers that Satan is the avowed and age-long enemy of God and that all through the course of human history he has been opposing his Maker and seeking to secure the scepter of earth's sovereignty. Further, we need not dwell upon the fact, so plainly revealed in Scripture, that Satan is an *imitator*, parodying and counterfeiting the ways and things of the Lord. But the climax of all Satan's schemes has not yet become history, though the inspired Word shows us clearly what form this climax will assume. God's purposes for this earth are to be realized and consummated in *a man*, "the man Christ Jesus" who will yet reign over it as King of kings and Lord of lords. Satan's designs will also head up in a man, "the man of Sin" who will for a short season reign over the earth as its acknowledged King. This man will be, preëminently, energized by Satan himself (2 Thess. 2:9). He will assume the right to enforce his autocratic dictates on all alike—"And he causeth all, both small and great, rich and poor, free and bond, to receive a mark in their right hand, or in their foreheads; and that no man might buy or sell, save he that had the mark, or the name of the beast, or the number of his name" (Rev. 13:16, 17). He it was who was before the Psalmist when he said, "He (Christ) shall wound *the head over many countries*" (Psa. 110:6). He was the one pictured by the prophet when he wrote—"Yea also, because he transgresseth by wine, he is *a proud man*, neither keepeth at home, who enlargeth his desire as hell, and is as death, and cannot be satisfied, but *gathereth unto him all nations, and heapeth unto him all people,*" etc., see Habakkuk 2:1-8. This Man of Sin (2 Thess. 2:3) will be the *super-man* of whom the world is even now talking about, and for whom it is so rapidly being prepared. He will be the "Lord of Light"—the great Mahatma—for whom Theosophists and Bahaists are looking.

The Antichrist is not only the subject of Old Testament prophecy, but he is also the subject of Old Testament *typology*. Most of the characters brought before us in Old Testament history are types of one of two men—the Christ or the Antichrist. Much attention has been paid to the study of and much has been written about those personages which foreshadowed our blessed Lord, but much less thought has been devoted to the consideration of those who prefigured the Man of Sin. A wide field here lies open for investigation, and we doubt not that as his appearing draws nigh the Holy Spirit will furnish additional light on this little studied subject.

One of those who foreshadowed the Antichrist was *Nimrod*. In at least seven particulars can the analogy be clearly traced. First: his very name describes that which will be the most prominent characteristic of all in the one whom he typifies. "Nimrod" means *"the Rebel,"* reminding us of one of the titles of the Antichrist, found in 2 Thessalonians 2:8—"The Lawless One"—R. V. Second: the *form* which Nimrod's rebellion assumed was to head a great confederacy in open revolt against God. This confederacy is described in Genesis eleven and that it was an organized revolt against Jehovah is clear from the language of Genesis 10:9—"Nimrod, the mighty hunter *before the Lord,"* which (as we shall see) means that he pushed his own designs in brazen defiance of his Maker. Thus it will be with the Antichrist; of him it is written, "And the King shall do according to his will, and he shall exalt himself and *magnify himself above every god* (ruler), and shall speak marvellous things against the God of Gods, and shall prosper till the indignation be accomplished; for that that is determined shall be done. Neither shall he regard the God of his fathers, nor the desire of women, nor regard any god, for he shall magnify himself above all" (Dan. 11:36, 37). Third: four times over the word "mighty" is used to describe Nimrod. Here again we are reminded of the Lawless One of whom it is said, "Even him whose coming is after the working of Satan *with all power* and signs and lying wonders" (2 Thess. 2:9). Fourth: Nimrod was a "hunter" (Gen. 10:9), probably a *hunter of men.* This is precisely what the Lawless One will be. In Psalm 5:6 he is denominated "the *bloody* and deceitful man." Fifth: Nimrod was a "king"—the beginning of his *kingdom* was Babel (Gen. 10:10), and, as we have seen in Daniel 11:36 the Antichrist is also termed "king." Sixth: Nimrod's headquarters were in *Babylon,* see Genesis 10:10 and 11:1-9; so also, we find the Man of Sin is called "the king of Babylon" (Is. 14:4), and in the Apocalypse he is connected with "mystery Babylon" (Rev. 17:3-5). Seventh: Nimrod's supreme ambition and desire was to make to himself a *name.* He had an inordinate desire for fame. Here, too the antitype agrees with the type. "Pride" is spoken of as the condemnation of the Devil: it was an impious ambition which brought about his downfall. The Man of Sin will be fully possessed by Satan, hence, an insatiable pride will possess him. It is this Satanic egotism which will cause him to oppose and "exalt himself above all that is called God, or that is worshipped; so that he as God sitteth in the temple of God, showing himself that he is God" (2 Thess. 2:4).

We have now prepared the way for a more detailed, yet brief, exposition of the two parenthetical portions of Genesis 10 and 11.

"And Cush begat Nimrod; he began to be a mighty one in the earth" (Gen. 10:8). The first thing we note here is that Nimrod was a descendant of *Ham,* through Cush; in other words, he sprang from that branch of Noah's family on which rested the "curse." Next, we observe that it is said, "he *began* to be mighty," which seems to suggest the idea that he *struggled for the preëminence,* and by mere force of will obtained it. Finally, we observe that he "began to be mighty in the earth." The intimation appears to be that of conquest or subjugation, as though he became a leader and ruler over men, as indeed he did.

"He was a mighty hunter before the Lord; wherefore it is said, Even as Nimrod the mighty hunter before the Lord" (Gen. 10:9). In so brief a description the *repetition* of these words, "mighty hunter before the Lord" are significant. Three times in Genesis 10 and again in 1 Chronicles 1:10 the word "mighty" is applied to Nimrod. The Hebrew word is "gibbor," and is translated in the Old Testament "chief" and "chieftain." The verse in Chronicles is in perfect agreement with these in Genesis

—"And Cush begat Nimrod; he began to be mighty upon the earth." The Chaldee paraphrase of this verse says, "Cush begat Nimrod who began to prevail in wickedness, for he slew innocent blood and rebelled against Jehovah." Observe, "a mighty hunter *before the Lord.*" If we compare this expression with a similar one in Genesis 6:11—"The earth also (in the days of Noah) was corrupt *before God,*" the impression conveyed is that this "Rebel" pursued his own impious and ambitious designs in brazen and open defiance of the Almighty. As we shall see, the contents of Genesis eleven confirm this interpretation.

"And the beginning of his kingdom was *Babel*" (Genesis 10:10). Here is the key to the first nine verses of the eleventh chapter. Here we have the first mention of Babel, and like the first mention of anything in Scripture this one demands careful consideration. In the language of that time Babel meant "the gate *of God*" but afterwards, because of the judgments which God inflicted there, it came to mean "Confusion," and from here onwards this is its force or meaning. By coupling together the various hints which the Holy Spirit has here given us we learn that Nimrod organized not only an imperial government over which he presided as king, but that he instituted a new and idolatrous worship. If the type is perfect, and we believe it is, then like the Lawless One will yet do, Nimrod demanded and received *Divine honors;* in all probability it is just here that we have *the introduction of idolatry.* Here, again, we learn how wonderfully the first mention of anything in Scripture defines its future scope; from this point Babylon in Scripture stands for that which is in opposition to God and His people—it was a *Babylonish* garment (Josh. 7:21) which led to the first sin in the promised land, while from Revelation 17 we learn that Romanism, which will gather into itself the whole of apostate Christendom, is termed "Mystery Babylon."

Out of that land he went forth into Assyria (marginal rendering) and builded Nineveh, and the city Rehoboth, and Calah, and Resen, between Nineveh and Calah; the same is a great city" (Gen. 10:11, 12). From these statements we gather the impression that Nimrod's ambition was to establish *a world-empire.* But we must turn now to the next chapter, asking our readers to study carefully the first nine verses in the light of what we have said above.

"And the whole earth was of one language, and of one speech. And it came to pass, as they journeyed *from the east,* that they found a plain in the land of Shinar; and they dwelt there" (11:1, 2). These geographical and topographical references have a *moral force,* just as we read of "going *down to Egypt,*" but "*up to* Jerusalem." Here we are told that men journeyed "from the east," *i. e.,* turned their backs upon the sunrise. Note further, "a *plain* (not a "mountain") in the land of Shinar."

Nimrod is not mentioned at all in Genesis 11, but from the statements made in the previous chapter we learn that *he* was the "chief" and "king" which organized and headed the movement and rebellion here described.

"And they said, Go to, let us build us a city, and a tower, whose top may reach unto heaven; and let us make us a name, *lest we be scattered abroad* upon the face of the whole earth" (11:4). Here we discover a most blatant defiance of God, a deliberate refusal to obey His command given through Noah. He had said, "Be fruitful, and multiply, and *replenish the earth*" (Gen. 9:1); but they said, "Let us make us a name lest we be scattered abroad upon the face of the whole earth."

As we have seen, Nimrod's ambition was to establish a *world-empire.* To accomplish this two things were necessary. First, a center of unity, a city headquarters; and second, a *motive* for the encouragement and inspiration of his followers. This latter was supplied in the "let us make us a name." It was an inordinate desire for fame. Nimrod's aim was to keep mankind all together under his own leadership "lest we be scattered." The idea of the "tower" (considered in the light of its setting) seems to be that of *strength*—a stronghold—rather than eminence.

"And the Lord said, Behold, the people is one, and they have all one language; and this they begin to do; and now nothing will be restrained from them, which they have imagined to do. Go to, let us go down, and there confound their language, that they may not understand one another's speech. So the Lord scattered them abroad from thence upon the face of all the earth; and they left off to build the city. Therefore is the name of it called Babel (Confusion); because the Lord did there confound the language of all the earth, and from thence did the Lord scatter them abroad upon the face of all the earth" (11:6-9). Another crisis had arrived in the history of the world.

Once again the human race was guilty of the sin of apostasy. Therefore did God intervene, brought Nimrod's schemes to naught by confounding the speech of his subjects and scattered them throughout the earth. Here was one of the mightiest and most far-reaching miracles of history. It finds no parallel until the outpouring of the Holy Spirit on the Day of Pentecost when another miracle of "tongues" was performed. The effect of God's intervention was the origination of the different nations and after the destruction of the Tower of Babel we get the formation of the "world" as we now have it. At this point the nations were abandoned to their own devices—"God gave them up" (Rom. 1)—but not until the race had twice enjoyed a revelation of God's mercy (first to Adam and then to Noah) and had twice forsaken Him before and now, after the Deluge.

To sum up. In Nimrod and his schemes we see Satan's initial attempt to raise up a universal ruler of men. In his inordinate desire for fame, in the mighty power which he wielded, in his ruthless and brutal methods—suggested by the word "hunter"; in his blatant defiance of the Creator, (seen in his utter disregard for His command to replenish the earth,) by determining to prevent his subjects from being scattered abroad; in his founding of the kingdom of Babylon—the Gate of God—thus arrogating to himself Divine honors; inasmuch as the Holy Spirit has placed the record of these things immediately before the inspired account of God's bringing Abram into Canaan—pointing forward to the re-gathering of Israel in Palestine immediately after the overthrow of the Lawless One; and finally, in the fact that the destruction of his kingdom is described in the words, "Let us *go down* and there confound their language" (11:7—foreshadowing so marvellously the *descent of Christ* from Heaven to vanquish His impious Rival, we cannot fail to see that there is here, beneath the historical narrative, something deeper than that which appears on the surface; yea, that there is here *a complete typical picture* of the person, work and destruction of the Anti-christ.

Much more might have been written upon this interesting and suggestive incident, but we trust sufficient has been said to indicate the broad outlines of its *typical* teaching and to stimulate others to further study for the filling in of the details.

17. THE CALL OF ABRAHAM

Genesis 12

We have now reached a section of this book which is of surpassing interest and one that is full of important lessons for those who are members of the household of faith. The passage for our present consideration introduces us to the third great section of Genesis. As its name intimates, Genesis is the book of Beginnings. Its literary structure is true to its title for the whole of its contents center around three beginnings. First there is the beginning of the human race in Adam; second, there is the new beginning on the post-diluvian earth in Noah and his sons; third, there is the beginning of the Chosen Nation in Abram. Thus in Genesis we have three great "beginnings," and therefore as three is the number of *the Godhead,* we see how in this first book of the Divine Library, the very autograph of Deity is stamped on the opening pages of Holy Writ as though anticipating and rebuking the modern assaults on this book by the Evolutionists and Higher Critics.

The relative importance (we do not say "value") of the three main divisions of Genesis is indicated by their respective dimensions. The first two divisions cover a period of not less than two thousand years, yet, but eleven chapters are devoted to this section of human history; whereas the third division, covering scarcely four hundred years, contains no less than thirty-nine chapters. More than three-fourths of the book is occupied with narrating the lives of Abram and the first three generations of his descendants.

While it is true that the first two *divisions* of the book are embraced by the first eleven chapters in Genesis, yet, from a literary viewpoint, it would really be more correct to regard these chapters as a *preface,* not only to the remaining twenty-nine chapters of Genesis, but also to the entire Old Testament, and, we may add, of the Bible as a whole. This Divine "preface" is given *to explain* that which is made known in all that follows. The first eleven chapters of Genesis are really *the foundation* on which rests the remainder of the Old Testament. They trace in rapid review the line of descent from Adam to Abram. It has been well said concerning the book of Genesis that "as the root to the stem so are chapters 1-11 to 12-50, and as the stem to the tree so is Genesis to the rest of the Bible." One of the main purposes of Genesis is to reveal to us the origin and beginnings of the Nation of Israel, and in the first eleven chapters we are shown the different steps by which Israel became a separate and Divinely chosen nation. In Genesis 10 and 11 the entire human race is before us, but from Genesis 12 onwards attention is directed to one man and his descendants.

Genesis 12 brings before us Abram—"the father of all them that believe." Abram whose name was subsequently changed to Abraham the most illustrious personage in ancient history. Abraham! venerated by Jews, Christians and Mohammedans. Abraham! the progenitor of the nation of Israel. Abraham! termed "the friend of God." Abraham! from whom, according to the flesh, our Lord came. Surely we shall be richly repaid if we devote our most diligent attention to the prayerful study of the life of such a man. The present article will serve to introduce a short series of papers which will be given to the consideration of the history of one who, in several respects, was the most eminent of all the patriarchs.

"Now the Lord *had said* unto Abram, Get thee out of thy country and from thy kindred, and from thy father's house, unto a land that I will show thee" (Gen. 12:1). The tense of the verb here looks back to an incident which was referred to by Stephen and which is recorded in Acts 7:2, 3—"The God of glory appeared unto our father Abraham, when he was in Mesopotamia before he dwelt in Charran, and said unto him, Get thee out of thy country, and from thy kindred and come into the land which I shall show thee." Three things here call for a brief comment; first, the Divine title used in this connection; second, the fact of the Lord's "appearing," and third, His communication to Abram.

The Divine title which is used here is found in only one other scripture, namely, Psalm 29, which is one of the Millennial Psalms—"The voice of the Lord is upon the waters, *the God of Glory* thundereth" (v. 3). That this is a *Millennial* Psalm is clear from verse 10—"The Lord sitteth upon the flood yea, the Lord sitteth *King* for ever." Closely connected with the above Divine title is the one by which the Lord Jesus is designated in Psalm 24 (another Millennial Psalm)—"Lift up your heads, O ye gates; and be ye lifted up, ye everlasting doors; and *the King of Glory* shall come in" (verse 7). Thus we see that this title is peculiarly a *Kingdom* title, and therefore, when Jehovah appeared to the father of *the Kingdom people,* it was as "The God of Glory." The *appropriateness* of this title is further evident from the religious state of Abram and his fathers at the time that God appeared to him, namely, a state of Idolatry. The "God of Glory" was in vivid contrast from the "other gods" mentioned in Joshua 24:2.

"The God of Glory *appeared* unto our father Abraham, when he was in Mesopotamia." This is the first recorded "appearing" of God after the banishment of our parents from Eden. It was probably the earliest of all the theophanic manifestations that we read of in the Old Testament and which anticipated the Incarnation as well as marked the successive revelations of God to men. We do not hear of God *appearing* to Abel or Noah. Great then was the privilege thus conferred upon the one who afterwards was termed the "friend of God." We turn now to consider the terms of the Divine communication received by Abram.

And God said unto him "Get thee out of thy country, and from thy kindred, and come into the land which I shall show thee." This command from God came to Abram in Mesopotamia, in the city of Ur of the Chaldees, which was situated near to the Persian Gulf. The *time* of Abram's call is significant. It occurred shortly after the destruction of Babel and dispersion of the nations. As we endeavoured to show in our last paper, even in that early day, men had added to their other offences against God, the sin of *idolatry.* A scripture which throws considerable light upon the religious conditions that prevailed throughout the earth in the days immediately preceding the Call of Abram is to be found in Roman 1—"When they knew God, they glorified Him not as God, neither were thankful; but became vain in their imaginations, and their foolish heart was darkened. Professing themselves to be wise, they became fools, and changed the glory of the incorruptible God into an image made like to corruptible man, and to birds, and four-footed beasts, and creeping things. Wherefore God also gave them up to uncleanness through the lusts of their own hearts to dishonor their own bodies between themselves: who changed the truth of God into a lie, and worshipped and served the creature more than the Creator, who is blessed for ever" (vs. 21-25, and read to end of v. 28). Three times over in this solemn passage we read "God gave them up," that is, He turned away from those who had first turned from Him. We believe the *historical* reference here is to Genesis 11. It was at that time God abandoned the nations, suffering them all to "walk in *their own* ways" (Acts 14:16, and compare Amos 3:3). The family from which Abram sprang was no exception to the general rule, his progenitors were idolaters too as we learn from Joshua 24:2—"Thus saith the Lord God of Israel, your fathers dwelt on the other side of the flood in old time even Terah, the father of Abraham and the father of Nachor and *they served other gods.*"

Here then is the setting of the incident now before us. Having *abandoned* (temporarily) the nations, God now singles out a man from whom the Chosen Nation was to spring. Having dealt in *judgment* (at Babel) God now deals in *grace.* This has been, and will ever be, true of all God's dealings. According to His infinite wisdom, judgment (which is His "strange" work) only serves to prepare the way for greater manifestations of His redeeming love. God's judgment upon Israel resulted in the enriching of the Gentiles. The outpouring of Divine wrath in the Tribulation period will be but the precursor of Millennial blessedness. And, we may add, the judgment of the great white throne will be followed by the new heaven and new earth wherein righteousness shall "dwell" and upon which the tabernacle of God shall be with men. Thus it was of old. The overthrow of Babel and the scattering of the nations was followed by the call of Abraham to be the father of a divinely governed nation which was to be a witness for God, the depository of His revelation, and ultimately, the channel through which His blessing should flow to all the families of the earth.

The lesson to be learned here is a deeply important one. The connection between Genesis eleven and twelve is highly significant. The Lord God determined to have a people of His own by the calling of grace, but it was not until all the claims of the natural man had been repudiated by his own wickedness that Divine clemency was free to flow forth. In other words, it was not until the utter depravity of man had been fully demonstrated by the antediluvians, and again at Babel, that God dealt with Abram in sovereign grace. That it was grace and grace alone, sovereign grace, which called Abram is seen in his natural state when God first appeared to him. There was nothing whatever in the object of His choice which commended him to God. There was nothing whatever in Abram which merited God's esteem. The *cause* of election must always be traced to God's will. Election itself is *"of grace"* (Rom. 11:5), therefore it depends in no wise upon any worthiness in the object—either actual or foreseen. If it did, it would *not be* "of grace." That it was not a question of worthiness in Abram is clear from the language of Isaiah 51:1, 2—"Hearken to me, ye that follow after righteousness, ye that seek the Lord: look unto the rock whence ye are hewn and to *the hole of the pit whence ye are digged. LOOK UNTO ABRAHAM your father,* and unto Sarah that bare you." While God's dealings are never arbitrary, yet their *raison d'etre* must ever be found in His own sovereign pleasure.

"Now the Lord had said unto Abram, Get thee out of thy country, and from thy kindred, and from thy father's house unto a land that I will show thee" (Gen. 12:1). As we have seen from Acts 7:3 this call from God came to Abram at his home in Mesopotamia. It was a call which demanded absolute confidence in and obedience to the word of Jehovah. It was a call of separation from the ties of the natural man. This is a marked advance upon that which we studied in connection with our previous patriarch. The connection between the histories and experiences of Noah and Abraham is most instructive. Noah passing through the judgment of the old world and coming forth upon a new earth, represents the acceptance of the believer in Christ, with a new standing ground before God. Abram called upon to separate himself from his home and kindred and bidden to go out into a place which afterwards God would give him for an inheritance, typifies the one whose citizenship is in heaven but who is still in the world, and in consequence, called upon to walk by faith and live as a stranger and pilgrim on the earth. In a word, Abram illustrates *the heavenly calling* of those who are members of the body of Christ.

In Abram we have exhibited the life of faith which is just what we shall expect, seeing that he is termed "the father of all them that believe." The *call* of Abram shows us the *starting-point* of the life of faith. The first requirement is *separation* from the world and from our place in it by nature. Abram was called upon to leave his "kindred" as well as his "country." Terah was an idolater, whereas Abram had become a believer in the living God, therefore it was expedient that Terah should be left behind for "how can two walk together except they be agreed" Even the closest ties of human affection cannot unite souls which are sundered by opposite motives, the one possessing treasure in heaven and the other having nought save that which moth and rust doth corrupt and which thieves may steal.

In order to learn what *response* Abram made to God's call it is necessary to revert again to the previous chapter —"And Terah took Abram his son, and Lot the son of Haran his son's son and Sarai his daughter-in-law, his son Abram's wife, and they went forth with them from Ur of the Chaldees, to go into the land of Canaan and they came unto Haran and dwelt there" (Gen. 11:31). From these words we discover a two-fold *failure* on Abram's part. Three things were commanded him by God; he was to leave his own country, he was to separate himself from his kindred, and he was to go forth *unto* a land which Jehovah had promised to show him. In respect to the first requirement Abram obeyed, but with reference to the last two he failed. He left Chaldea, but instead of separating himself from his kindred, Terah his father and Lot his nephew accompanied him. Terah means *"delay,"* and thus it proved. Terah's accompanying Abram resulted in a delay of at least five years in Haran, which word means "parched"!* Abram's response to God's call then, was partial and slow, for observe that in Isaiah 51:2 we are expressly told that God called Abram "alone," yet in the end he "obeyed." How beautiful it is to note that when we come to the New Testament Abram's *failure* is not mentioned—"By faith Abram, when he was called to go out into a place which he should after receive for an inheritance, *obeyed,* and he went out, not knowing whither he went" (Heb. 11:8), his obedience in leaving Ur is thus singled out, but no notice is here taken by the Holy Spirit of his *disobedience* in taking his "kindred" with him—that sin, with all of his others, had been "blotted out"!

*Haran was the point at which caravans for Canaan left the Euphrates to strike across the desert.

"Get thee out" was Jehovah's command, and His commands are not grievous. The Lord's commands are rarely accompanied with *reasons* but they are always accompanied with *promises,* either exprest or understood. So it was in Abram's case. Said the Lord: "And I will make of thee a great nation, and I will bless thee, and make thy name great; and thou shalt be a blessing" (Gen. 12:2). In the first place it is to be observed, however, that this promise was couched in very *general* terms and in a manner calculated to test Abram's faith. "Get thee out.....unto *a land,"* not unto a land flowing with milk and honey." And again, "unto a land that I will *show* thee" as yet there was no assurance that God was going to *give* it to him and his seed. In the second place it is to be noted that the *promise* corresponds closely with the *command.* The command included a threefold requirement and the promise embraced a threefold blessing." *"And I will make of thee a great nation,"* this was compensation for the loss of country. The nation from which he sprang had fallen into gross idolatry and ultimately perished beneath God's judgments; but from Abram God would make a great nation." *"And I will bless thee,"* the blessing of Jehovah would more than make up for any loss of carnal joys he would lose by leaving his "kindred." *"And make thy name great."* He was to leave his father's house, but God would make of him the head of a new house, even the house of Israel, on account of which he would be known and venerated the world over. In the third place, it should be pointed out that this promise included within its scope the call and blessing of the Gentiles. Abram's response to God's demand was to be the first link in a series of Divine interpositions by which God's mercy might be extended to the whole earth. *"And thou shalt be a blessing."* Abraham was not merely the subject of Divine blessing, but a medium of blessing to others. *"And I will bless them that bless thee, and curse him that* curseth thee." Here we see Jehovah identifying the cause of Abram with His own. *"And in thee shall all families of the earth be blessed."* This part of the promise received a partial fulfillment in the birth of Him who was according to the flesh, "the son of Abraham" (Matt. 1:1), but its complete and ultimate fulfilment looks forward to the Millennium, for then it will be that all families of the earth shall receive blessing through Abram and his seed.

"So Abram departed, as the Lord had spoken unto him; and Lot went with him; and Abram was seventy and five years old when he departed out of Haran" (Gen. 12:4). As we have seen, instead of journeying unto Canaan, Abram tarried at Haran. It was not until after Terah's death that Abram left Haran and came into Canaan. It was *death* which broke the link which bound Abram to Haran—"Then came he out of the land of the Chaldeans, and dwelt in Charran (Greek for "Haran") and from thence, *when his father was dead* he removed him into this land, wherein ye now dwell" (Acts 7:4). So it is with all his spiritual children. It is death which separates the believer from that which by nature unites him with the old creation—"But God forbid that I should glory, save in the cross of our Lord Jesus Christ, by whom *the world is crucified unto me and I unto the world*" (Gal. 6:14).

"And they went forth to go into the land of Canaan, and into the land of Canaan they came. And Abram passed through the land unto the place of Sichem, and unto the place (oak) of Moreh" (Gen. 12:5, 6). Abram did not enter into occupation of Canaan, he merely "passed through the land." As we read in Acts 7:5—"He (God) gave him none inheritance in it, *not so much as to set his foot on:* Yet He promised that He would give it to him for a possession and to his seed after him, when as yet he had no child." Abram first halted at Sichem (Shecham) which signifies "shoulder"—the place of strength, unto the oak of Moreh which means "instruction." How significant! What a lesson for us! It is only as we separate ourselves from the world and walk in the path marked out for us by God that we reach the place where strength is to be found, and, it is only thus that we can enter into fellowship with and learn from Him in whom are hid all the treasures of wisdom and knowledge. "And the Canaanite was then in the land" (v. 6)—to challenge and contest the occupation of it, just as the hosts of wickedness are in present occupancy of the heavenlies to wrestle with those who are partakers of the heavenly calling.

"And the Lord appeared unto Abram, and said, Unto thy seed will I give this land, and there builded he an altar unto the Lord, who appeared unto him" (Gen. 12:7). There is no record of Abram receiving any further revelation from God until His call had been fully obeyed, but now that he had left Ur and Haran behind him and had actually arrived in the land, Jehovah appeared once more unto him. At the first appearing God called him to go unto a land that He would *show* him, and now He rewards Abram's faith and obedience by promising to *give* this land unto his seed. Thus does the Lord lead His children step by step. At the first appearing the God of Glory called upon Abram to separate himself from his place by nature; but at this second appearing He reveals Himself to Abram for communion, and the result is that Abram erects an *altar.* There was no "altar" for Abram in Ur or Haran. It is not until there is real separation from the world that fellowship with God is possible. First the obedience of faith and then communion and worship.

"And he removed from thence unto a mountain on the east of Bethel, and pitched his tent, having Bethel on the west, and Hai on the east: and there he builded an altar unto the Lord, and called upon the name of the Lord" (Gen. 12:8). How significant! Bethel means "the house of God" while Hai signifies "a heap of ruin," and it was *between* them that Abram pitched his tent—typical of the sphere of the believer's present path, with the old creation (a ruin) on the one side and the house of God (on high) on the other. Observe the two objects here: "tent" and the "altar"—symbols of that which characterizes a walk in separation with God, the one speaking of the *pilgrim* life and the other of dependency upon and worship of God. Note, too, the order of mention: we must first be strangers and pilgrims on the earth before acceptable worship is possible.

And now we come to the second failure of Abram, namely, his leaving Canaan and going down into Egypt. Concerning this incident we can here say only a few words. First it is to be noted that, "Abram journeyed, going on still *toward the south*" (v. 9). This geographical reference is deeply significant: southward was Egyptward! When the "famine" overtook Abram his face was already *toward* Egypt.

"And there was a famine in the land: and Abram *went down* into Egypt to sojourn there; for the famine was grievous in the land" (v. 10). This is the first mention in Scripture of Egypt, and like all its subsequent references, so here, it stands for that which is a constant *menace* to the people of God symbolizing, as it does, alliance with the world and reliance upon the arm of flesh—"*Woe to them that go down to Egypt for help* and stay on horses, and trust in chariots, because they are many; and in horsemen, because they are very strong; but *they look not unto the Holy One of Israel,* neither seek the Lord!" (Isa. 31:1).

The famine was sent as a trial of Abram's faith. A famine in the Land of Promise. What a test of faith! "God would see whether he had such confidence in His goodness that even famine could not shake it. Alas, Abram did as we are all prone to do, he sought relief from all his difficulties, rather than profit by the trial" (Ridout). Observe that when this famine came there was no seeking counsel from the Lord. Abram was prompted by the wisdom of the flesh which ever suggests relief in means and human help, in fact, anything rather than in the living God. O, the inconsistencies of God's children! Faith in God with regard to our eternal interest, but afraid to confide in Him for the supply of our temporal needs. Here was a man who had journeyed all the way from Chaldea to Canaan on the bare word of Jehovah and yet was now afraid to trust Him in the time of famine. Sad that it should be so, but how like us today!

One sin leads to another. Failure in our love to God always results in failure in our love to our neighbor. Down in Egypt Abram practices deception and denies that Sarai is his wife, thus endangering the honor of the one who was nearest and should have been dearest to him. Alas! What is man? But Jehovah would not allow His purposes to be frustrated—"If we believe not, yet He abideth faithful: *He cannot deny Himself*" (2 Tim. 2:13). So it was here. The Lord interposed—"And the Lord *plagued* Pharaoh and his house with great plagues *because of Sarai,* Abram's wife" (v. 17). The sequel is found in the next chapter—"And Abram went up out of Egypt, he and his wife, and all that he had.....and he went on his journeys from the south even to Bethel, unto the place where his tent had been *at the beginning,* between Bethel and Hai; unto the place of the altar, which he had made there *at the first,* and there Abram called on the name of the Lord" (Gen. 13:1, 3, 4). He returned to the very place he had left. He repented and "did the first works." Abram's sojourn in Egypt was so much *lost time.*

We cannot close this paper without first seeking to gather up in a few words the practical and deeply important lessons here recorded for our learning. 1. The call which came to Abram comes to each one of his believing children —the call for absolute confidence in God; the call to take Him at His word and step out in simple and unquestioning faith; the call to separate ourselves from the world to a life of pilgrimage in dependency upon Jehovah. 2. The trial of Abram's faith is also the lot of all his children. Profession must be tested and at times the meal in the barrel will run very low. The failure of Abram is a solemn warning against being occupied with circumstances instead of with God. Look not at the famine but unto God's faithfulness. 3. Beware of going down to Egypt. The friendship of the world is enmity with God. Time spent in Egypt is wasted. Days lived out of communion with God produce nought but "wood, hay and stubble." 4. As you see in the failures of Abram the sad record of your own history, marvel anew at the long sufferance of God which deals in such infinite patience and grace with His erring and ungrateful children.

18. ABRAHAM AND LOT

Genesis 13

In our last article we followed Abraham from Ur of Chaldea to Haran, and from Haran to Canaan. We saw that after he had arrived in the land to which God called him, a famine arose, and his faith failing him in the hour of crisis, Abraham, accompanied by Lot, sought refuge in Egypt. Our present study reveals some of the *results* of the patriarch's backsliding. While God, in faithfulness and grace, restored His wandering child, yet the *effects* of his departure from the path of faith were manifested soon afterwards and continued to harass him the remainder of his days. The principle of sowing and reaping is of universal application and is true of believers equally as much as unbelievers. Two things Abraham obtained from his sojourn in Egypt, each of which proved a hindrance and curse, though in the end both were overruled by God for His own glory. We refer to them here in the inverse order of their mention in Genesis.

"And Sara, Abram's wife, took Hagar her maid, *the Egyptian,* after Abram had dwelt ten years in the land of Canaan, and gave her to her husband, Abram, to be his wife" (Gen. 16:3). During their stay in Egypt, Sarah took unto her the maid, Hagar. The strife, the jealousy, the trouble which Hagar introduced into the patriarch's household is well known, the climax of it all being seen in Ishmael (Hagar's son) "mocking Isaac" (Gen. 21:9) and his subsequent expulsion from Abram's tent.

The second thing which Abraham seems to have obtained in Egypt was great earthly possessions—"And Abram went up out of Egypt, he, and his wife and all that he had, and Lot with him, into the south. And Abram was very rich in cattle, in silver, and in gold" (Gen. 13:1, 2). This is the first time we read of Abram's "cattle," and it is deeply significant that shortly afterwards these very flocks and herds became the occasion of *strife* between him and his nephew. It also deserves to be noticed that this is the first mention of "riches" in Scripture, and, as now, so then, they pierced their possessor through with "many sorrows" (1 Tim. 6:10).

"And Lot also, which went with Abram, had flocks, and herds, and tents" (Gen. 13:5). Till now we hear nothing of Lot since he left Haran, but he appears to have been one of Abram's family and to have gone with him wherever he went. The characters and careers of Abram and Lot present a series of sharp antitheses. Throughout the biographical portions of Scripture we find the Holy Spirit frequently brings together two men of widely different character and placing them in juxtaposition so that we might the better learn the salutary lessons He would teach us. Abel and Cain, Moses and Aaron, Samuel and Saul, David and Solomon, are well known examples of this principle. In almost every respect Lot compares unfavorably with Abram. Abram walked by faith, Lot by sight. Abram was generous and magnanimous; Lot greedy and worldly. Abram looked for a city whose builder and maker was God; Lot made his home in a city that was built by man and destroyed by God. Abram was the father of all who believe; Lot was father of those whose name is a perpetual infamy. Abram was made "heir of the world" (Rom. 4:3), while the curtain falls upon Lot with all his possessions destroyed in Sodom, and himself dwelling in a "cave" (Gen. 19:30).

The history of Lot is a peculiarly tragic one and for that reason full of "admonition" for us upon whom the ends of the ages have come. We attempt nothing more than a rapid sketch of it, considering:

1. *Lot's Departure from Abram.*

This is described in Genesis 13: "And the land was not able to bear them, that they might dwell together, for their substance was great, so that they could not dwell together. And there was a strife between the herdmen of Abram's cattle and the herdmen of Lot's cattle" (vs. 6 and 7). How often "strife" between kinsmen has been brought about by earthly possessions and wealth! The record is very terse, but there can be little doubt as to *who* was to blame. The subsequent conduct of Lot and the Lord's rewarding of Abram indicate plainly that it was Lot who was in the wrong. Nor is the cause far to seek. Lot had brought with him out of Egypt something else besides "herds and flocks" —he had contracted its spirit and acquired a taste for its "fleshpots."

"And Abram said unto Lot, Let there be no strife, I pray thee, between me and thee, and between my herdmen and thy herdmen; for we are brethren. Is not the whole land before thee? Separate thyself, I pray thee, from me. If thou wilt take the left hand, then I will go to the right; or, if thou depart to the right hand, then I will go to the left" (vs. 8, 9). Abram foresaw there was danger of a falling out between himself and his nephew, that what had begun with the servants would probably end with the masters. Deprecating the thought of friction between brethren, he proposed that they should separate. The wisdom which is from above is first pure and then peaceable. In spirit, Abram carried out the letter of the Divine admonition: "As much as lieth in you, live peaceably with all men."

The proposal made by Abram to his nephew was exceedingly generous, and in his greed, Lot took full advantage of it. Instead of leaving the choice to Abram, we read: "And Lot lifted up his eyes, and beheld all the plain of Jordan, that it was well watered everywhere, before the Lord destroyed Sodom and Gomorrah, even as the garden of the Lord, like the land of Egypt, as thou comest unto Zoar. Then *Lot chose him* all the plain of Jordan; and Lot journeyed east, and they separated themselves the one from the other" (vs. 10, 11). Observe, that Lot *"Lifted up his eyes and beheld."* In other words, he preferred to walk by sight, rather than by faith. How impossible then for Lot to remain with Abram! How can two walk together except they be agreed? Abram "endured as seeing him who is invisible," while Lot's heart was set upon the things of time and sense. Hence, we are told, "they could not dwell together" (v. 6)—it was a *moral* impossibility.

Lot "lifted up his eyes." This was the commencement, outwardly, at least, of a decline which ended in the utmost shame. Eye-gate is one of the avenues through which temptations assail the soul: "For all that is in the world, the lust of the flesh, *and the lust of the eyes,* and the pride of life, is not of the Father, but is of the world" (1 John 2:16). Walking by sight is the cause of most of our failures and sorrows. So it was at the beginning: "And when the woman *saw* that the tree was good for food, and that it was *pleasant to the eyes,* and a tree to be desired to make one wise, *she took* of the fruit thereof" (Gen. 3:6). Mark, too, the confession of Achan: "When *I saw* among the spoils a goodly Babylonish garment and two hundred shekels of silver, and a wedge of gold of fifty shekels weight, then I coveted them and took them" (Joshua 7:21). How significant the order here—I saw, I coveted, I took! So it was with Lot: first he lifted up his eyes and beheld, and then he "chose him." How significant are the closing words of Genesis 13:10: "And Lot lifted up his eyes, and beheld all the plain of Jordan, that it was well watered everywhere....Even as the garden of the Lord, *like the land of Egypt,"* which shows us that Lot was still attached to "Egypt" in *heart.* But how true it is that "the Lord seeth not as man seeth" (1 Sam. 16:7)! To the worldly eye of Lot all the plain appeared "well watered and as the garden of the Lord," but to the holy eye of Jehovah the cities of the plain were peopled by those who were "wicked and sinners before the Lord exceedingly" (v. 13); "before the Lord," shows us *what* it was that His eyes dwelt upon. We consider next,

2. *Lot's Sojourn in Sodom*

"Then Lot chose him all the plain of Jordan; and Lot journeyed eastward: and they separated themselves the one from the other. Abram dwelt in the land of Canaan, and Lot dwelt in the cities of the plain, and pitched his tent toward Sodom" (vs. 11, 12). The various steps in the downward course of Lot are plainly marked out. First, he "lifted up his eyes and beheld." Second, he "chose him all the plain of Jordan." Third, he "separated" himself from Abram. Fourth, he "dwelt in the cities of the plain." Fifth, he "pitched his tent *toward* Sodom." Sixth, he "dwelt in Sodom" (14:12). Finally, we see him an alderman of Sodom, seated in its "gate" (19:1) and his daughters wedded to men of Sodom. Behold how great a fire a little matter kindleth. From a lifting up of the eyes to behold the land and seek pasturage for his flocks, to becoming an official in the city of wickedness! Like leprosy, sin has often a seemingly small beginning, but how rapid its spread, how loathsome its issue, how dreadful its end! Similar was the course of the Apostle Peter: the denial of his Lord was no sudden, isolated act, but the sequel and climax of an antecedent chain. There was first the boasting self-confidence, "Though all shall be offended, yet will not I" (Mark 14:29). Then there was the "sleeping" in the garden when he should have been watching and praying (Mark 14:37). Then there was the following Christ "afar off" (Matt. 26:58). Then there was the seating of himself at the fire in the presence of his Lord's enemies (Matt. 26:69). And then, amid these evil associates, came the awful denial and cursing.

And what did Lot gain by his separation from Abram and sojourn in Sodom? Nothing at all. Instead of gaining, he was the loser. The men of Sodom were "wicked and sinners before the Lord exceedingly" and Lot was "vexed with the filthy conversation of the wicked. For that righteous man dwelling among them, in seeing and hearing, vexed his righteous soul from day to day with their unlawful deeds" (2 Pet. 2:7, 8). Consider now,

3. *Lot's Deliverance from Sodom*

In the first place notice how, in His faithfulness and grace, God had given Lot a very definite *warning.* From Genesis 14 we learn that in the battle between the four kings with the five, "they took all the goods of Sodom and Gomorrah, and all their victuals, and went their way. And they took Lot, Abram's brother's son, who dwelt in Sodom, and his goods, and departed" (vs. 11, 12). Yet though Lot lost all his goods and seems to have been in imminent danger of losing his life but for the timely intervention of Abram with his armed servants, nevertheless, this experience failed to teach Lot the evil of being associated with the world, but he recovered his freedom and his property only to *return* unto Sodom. Alas! what is man? Even God's providential dealings are insufficient to move his heart.

The contents of Genesis 18 and 19 are so familiar to our readers that no lengthy exposition is needed. The Lord Himself makes known to His "friend" what He is about to do; but no such revelation was vouchsafed Lot who was altogether out of communion with Jehovah. The "secret of the Lord" is only with them that "fear Him." The two angels who accompanied the Lord to Abram's tent, go forward to Sodom, the Lord Himself remaining behind, and with Him Abram intercedes on behalf of the righteous who may be in the doomed city.

The two angels found Lot sitting in the gate of Sodom and in response to his request that they partake of his hospitality, said, "Nay, but we will abide in the street all night." Their reluctance to enter Lot's dwelling—in marked contrast with their fellowship with Abram—intimates the condition of Lot's soul. Observe, too, that it was "in the heat of the day" (Gen. 18:1) that they visited

Abram; whereas, it was "even" (19:1) when they appeared to his nephew. *The utter meanness and selfishness of Lot's character* was quickly exhibited in the contemptible proposal to sacrifice his daughters to the men of Sodom in order to secure his own preservation and peace (19:8). The *powerlessness of his testimony* appeared in the response made by his "sons-in-law" when he warned them that the Lord was about to destroy the city—"he seemed as one that mocked" (19:14); his *words* had now no weight because of his previous *ways.* The words "*while he lingered,* the men (the angels) laid hold upon his hand" (19:16) show plainly where his *heart* was. The summary judgment which overtook his wife and the fearful crime of his daughters was a terrible harvest from his sowing to the flesh.

The deliverance of Lot was a remarkable instance of God's care for His own. Lot was living far below his privileges, and manifestly was out of communion with the Lord, yet he was a "righteous man" (2 Pet. 2:7, 8) and therefore was he snatched as a brand from the burning. Blessed be His name, "He abideth faithful; He cannot deny Himself" (2 Tim. 2:13). Just as a shelter was provided for Noah, just as Israel was protected from the avenging angel, so with Lot. Said the angel to him, "I cannot do anything till *thou* be come thither" (Gen. 19:22).

We cannot leave this section without noticing the obvious connection between Lot's deliverance from Sodom and Abram's intercession for him. The particular word employed by Abram in his supplications was deeply significant. Said he, "Wilt Thou also destroy *the righteous* with the wicked?" (Gen. 18:23, and compare vs. 24, 25, 26, 28), which is the very word which the Holy Spirit employs in 2 Peter 2:8! May we not also see in Abram here a type of our blessed Lord? Lot was delivered from the kings by Abram's *sword* and from God's judgment upon Sodom by Abram's *supplications.* And are not these the instruments (if we may so speak) employed by our Saviour! He delivers His own from the (defilements of) the world by the Word—the sword—see John 13, and when they sin He acts as their Advocate with the Father (1 John 2:1).

It only remains for us now to point out a few of the leading lessons brought out in Genesis 13 and 19. Let us notice:

1. *The Certain Accomplishment of God's Purpose.*

Mysterious are the ways of Him with whom we have to do. The "strife" which God permitted to arise between the herdmen of Abram and Lot was designed for the carrying out of *His own* counsel. The declared purpose of God was to separate Abram from the land of his birth and from his own kinsmen, in order to educate him and his in the knowledge and obedience of Jehovah. God called Abram "alone" (Isa. 51:2), yet at least two of his relatives accompanied him when he left Ur of the Chaldees. But, in the end, God's purpose *was* realized. Terah, Abram's father, died at Haran. Lot accompanied him into the land of Canaan, but it is obvious that a worldly spirit like his, together with his own separate and large encampment imbued, no doubt, with the spirit of its chief and over which it would be difficult if not impossible for Abram to exercise authority, could not help forward the Divine purpose. In the separation of Lot from Abram, then, we see the departure of the last of his kinsfolk, and now Abram is left "alone" with God! Verily, "There are many devices in a man's heart; *nevertheless the counsel of the Lord that shall stand*" (Prov. 19:21). Let us consider,

2. *The Magnanimity of Abram.*

The proposal which Abram made to his nephew was exceedingly gracious and beautiful. Abram was the senior, and the one to whom God had promised to give the land (Gen. 12:7), yet, he generously waived his rights, and "with all lowliness and meekness, with long-suffering," he forebore with Lot in love. Note carefully his words, "Is not *the whole land* before *thee*" (13:9). Gladly did Abram surrender every claim and forego every right to put a stop to this strife between "brethren."

In the *waiving of his rights* Abram foreshadowed that One who was made, according to the flesh, "the son of Abraham" (Matt. 1:1). He who was in the form of God and thought it not robbery to be equal with God voluntarily waived His rights and took upon Him the form of a servant. All power in heaven and earth was His, yet He suffered Himself to be *led* as a lamb to the slaughter, and though He had the right to summon twelve legions of angels to come and do His bidding, He waived it and refused to give the command. Though He did no sin, had no sin, was without sin, and as such death had *no claim* upon Him, yet was He "made sin for us" and became obedient unto death, even the death of the cross. Yes, He "waived His rights" and He has left us an example that we should follow His steps.

3. *The Warnings Pointed by Lot's Failures.*

We mention three without dwelling upon them at any length:

First, *his choice of residence.* Surely this needed lesson is writ large across the story of Lot's life. He preferred the "well-watered" plains above Abram's "altar." He regarded temporal advantages only, and had no regard for his spiritual welfare. Alas! how many believers are there now who, when seeking a location for themselves and family follow his evil example. Seek ye *first* the kingdom of God and His righteousness ought to regulate our every decision.

Second, *his yielding to the spirit of worldliness.* Lot seems to be a type of that class of Christians who aim to make the best of both worlds, who are really occupied more with the things of earth than the things of heaven. Lot was a man who sowed to the flesh, and of the flesh he reaped corruption. Temporal prosperity was what he sought, but in the end he lost even his worldly possessions. His life on earth was a wretched failure, made up entirely of "wood, hay, stubble." There was no witnessing for God and no blessing of God upon his family. Lot is a concrete warning, a danger signal, for all Christians who feel a tendency to be carried away by the things of the world.

Third, *his miserable end.* Wretched, indeed, must have been the closing days of Lot—cowering in a cave, stript of all his earthly possessions, his sons-in-law destroyed in Sodom, his wife turned to a pillar of salt, and he left face to face with the fruit of his own awful sin.

19. ABRAHAM AND MELCHIZEDEK

Genesis 14

Our last chapter was concerned with Abraham and Lot. We touched upon the first part of Genesis 13, which records the strife that came between their herdmen, the prompt measures taken by the patriarch to put an end to the friction, the generous offer which he made his nephew, and Lot's leaving Abram and journeying to Sodom. In this present paper we continue our study of the career of the father of all that believe, resuming at the point where we left him in our last.

"And the Lord said unto Abram, after that Lot was separated from him, Lift up now thine eyes, and look from the place where thou art northward, and southward, and eastward, and westward: For all the land which thou seest, to thee will I give it, and to thy seed for ever. And I will make thy seed as the dust of the earth: so that if a man can number the dust of the earth, then shall thy seed also be numbered. Arise, walk through the land in the length of it and in the breadth of it; for I will give it unto thee" (Gen. 13:14-17). Abraham was now alone, and yet not alone, for the Lord was with him and gracious was the revelation that He made of Himself. It was with a true concern for God's glory that Abram had suggested Lot's separating from him. "There was a strife between the herdmen of Abram's cattle and the herdmen of Lot's cattle: *and the Canaanite and the Perizzite dwelt then in the land*" (v. 7). Abram could not endure the thought of "strife" between *brethren* in the presence of the Lord's enemies—would that God's children today were equally reluctant to bring reproach upon the holy name they bear.

God did not allow His child to lose by his magnanimous offer to Lot, made, as we have said, out of consideration for God's glory. To Lot Abram had said, "Is not the whole land before thee? Separate thyself, I pray thee, from me: if thou wilt take the left hand, then I will go to the right hand; or if thou depart to the right hand, then I will go to the left. And Lot lifted up his eyes, and beheld all the plain of Jordan," etc. (vs. 9, 10); and now Jehovah appears to Abram and says, "*Lift up now thine eyes* and look" (v. 14). O, what a contrast! Lot "lifted up his eyes" at the dictate of worldly interests; Abram lifted up his to behold the gift of God. Thus does our ever faithful God delight to honor those who honor Him. The student will note there are three passages in Genesis where it is said that Abram "lifted up his eyes." First, here in 13:14, when he beheld "the *land*"; second, in 18:2, when he beheld "three men," one of whom was *the Lord* Himself; third, in 22:13, when he beheld the *substitute*—"a ram caught in a thicket."

Above we have said that Abram was *now alone*. At last the purpose of God is realized. God "called him alone" (Isa. 51:2). He had said "Get thee out of thy country, and from thy kindred, and come into the land which I shall shew thee" (Acts 7:3), but to this command Abram had rendered but a tardy and partial obedience. Both his father and nephew accompanied him as he left Chaldea, and instead of journeying straight to Canaan, he stopped short at Haran where he "dwelt" until the death of Terah (11:31, 32). Yet even now the Divine command was not fully obeyed—into the land of God's call Abram came, *Lot still with him*. But now, at the point we have reached, Lot has taken his departure and Abram (with Sarai) is left alone with God. And is it not deeply significant that *not until now* did the Lord say, "For all the land which thou seest, *to thee will I give it*, and to thy seed for ever" (v. 15); Observe carefully the ascending scale in God's promises to Abram. In Chaldea God promised to "shew" Abram the land (Gen. 12:1). Then, when Abram had actually entered it and arrived at Sichem the Lord promised to "give" the land *unto his seed*—"And the Lord appeared unto Abram, and said, Unto thy seed will I give this land (12:7). But now—now that he is at last *separated from the last of his "kindred"*—God promises to give "all the land" unto Abram himself. Furthermore, it is to be noted that not until now does God say to Abram, "Arise, *walk through the land* in the length of it, and in the breadth of it" (v. 17), which intimated that God would have Abram appropriate His gift. Abram was to "feel at home" in the land as though the title deeds of it were already in his hands. Do we not discover in all this a striking illustration of an all important principle in God's dealings with His own people. How often our unbelief limits the outflow of Divine grace! An imperfect and circumscribed obedience prevents our enjoying much that God has for us. As a further illustration compare and contrast Caleb and the inheritance which he obtained for "following the Lord *fully*" (Num. 14:24).

In the words "Arise, walk through the land in the length of it and in the breadth of it" (v. 17) another important truth is suggested—*appropriation.* It was as though God had said to Abram, I have called you into this land, I have given it to you and your seed, *now enjoy it.* He was to travel through it, to look upon it as already his—his by faith, for he had God's word for it. As another has said, "He was to act towards it as if he were already in absolute possession." And is not this what God invites His people to do today? We, too, have received a call to separate ourselves from the world. We, too, have been begotten unto an inheritance, an inheritance which is "incorruptible, and undefiled, and that fadeth not away, reserved in heaven." And now we, too, are bidden tc "walk through the land in the length of it and in the breadth of it." In other words, we are called to *the exercise of faith;* to look not at the things that are seen, but at the things which are unseen; to set our affection upon things above, and not upon things below. In brief, we are to make our own, to appropriate and enjoy the things which God has *promised* us. It is unbelief which hinders us from enjoying to the full what is already ours in the purpose of God. Mark that word through the prophet Obadiah, "But upon Mount Zion shall be deliverance, and there shall be holiness; and the house of Jacob shall *possess their possessions*" (v. 17). In the Millennium Israel will fully "possess their possessions." We say "fully possess" for they have never done so in the past. And why? Because of unbelief. Then let us fear, lest there be in us also an evil heart of unbelief.

"Then Abram removed his tent, and came and dwelt in the plain of Mamre, which is in Hebron, and built there an altar unto the Lord" (13:18). The connection between this statement and the immediate context is also full of instruction. "Mamre" signifies *fatness* and "Hebron" means *fellowship.* Notice the opening word *"then":* it was not until Lot had left him and Abram was fully in the will of the Lord that Hebron—fellowship—is now mentioned for the first time! It is disobedience that hinders full fellowship with Jehovah. And, note, too, that Abram "built *there* an *altar* unto the Lord." Fellowship resulted in worship! This is ever the order: obedience, fatness of soul, fellowship, worship. Confirmatory of these remarks, is it not significant that this very "Hebron" became the inheritance and portion of Caleb who "followed the Lord *fully!*—"Hebron *therefore* became the inheritance of Caleb the son of Jephunneh the Kenezite unto this day; *because* that he wholly followed the Lord God of Israel" (Josh. 14:14).

Genesis 14 opens with a brief account of the first war mentioned in Scripture. It would be beside our purpose to pause and examine in detail what is here recorded of the four and five kings,* our present purpose is to note Abram's connection and dealings with them. The outcome of the conflict was the capture of Lot and his possessions (v. 12). As another has said, "He had laid up treasures for himself on earth, and the thieves had broken through." One who had escaped brought intelligence to Abram that his nephew had been captured.

It is beautiful to observe the effect of this intelligence upon our patriarch. Abram was not indifferent to his nephew's well-being. There was no root of bitterness in him. There was no callous, "Well, this is none of my doing: he must reap what he has sown." Promptly he goes to the aid of the one in distress. But note it was not in the energy of the flesh that he acted. It was no mere tie of nature that prompted Abram here—"When Abram heard that his brother (not his 'nephew') was taken captive." A *brother*—a spiritual brother—was in need, and so he "armed his trained servants, born in his own house, three hundred and eighteen, and pursued them unto Dan" (14:14). And has this no voice for us today? Surely the spiritual application is obvious. How often is a "brother" taken captive by the enemy, and the word comes, "Ye, which are spiritual *restore such an one* in the spirit of meekness, considering thyself, lest thou also be tempted (Gal. 6:1). But only too often the call falls upon ears that are dull of hearing. Only too often, our prided sep-

*A careful study of the order of mention and the meaning of the various proper names mentioned in Genesis 14:1-10 will well repay the devout student.

aration from evil leads to independence and indifference. Alas! that it should be so. How different from our blessed Lord, who leaves the ninety and nine and goes after the sheep that has strayed, and rests not until it is found and restored!

"The righteous are bold as a lion" (Prov. 28:1). When the news came that Lot was a prisoner in the hands of a mighty warrior, Abram showed no hesitation but immediately set out in pursuit of the victorious army, and taking the initiative was quickly successful in rescuing his nephew. "And he divided himself against them, he and his servants, by night, and smote them, and pursued them unto Hobah, which is on the left hand of Damascus. And he brought back all the goods, and also brought again his brother Lot, and his goods, and the women also, and the people. And the king of Sodom went out to meet him, after his return from the slaughter of Chedorlaomer and of the kings that were with him, at the valley of Shaveh, which is the kings' dale" (14:15-17).

It is just at this point that a very remarkable personage is brought before us, namely, Melchizedek. Much has been said and written about him. Some have thought he was Shem who was a contemporary of Abram's for a hundred years; but this cannot be, for we are distinctly informed concerning Melchizedek that he was "without father, without mother" (Heb. 7:3), which, as we shall see, means that Scripture is absolutely silent concerning his genealogy. This then disposes of the Shem theory, for we *do* know who *his* father was. Others have concluded that he was Christ Himself, but this supposition is equally unscriptural for we are told that Melchizedek is "made like unto the Son of God" and that Christ's priesthood is "after the similitude of Melchizedek" (Heb. 7:3, 15), which could not be said if Melchizedek were Christ Himself. Still others have supposed that he was some mysterious *celestial* being, but that is emphatically negatived by Hebrews 7:4, where Melchizedek is expressly called a "man."

In the words "made like unto the Son of God" (Heb. 7:3) we have the key to the mystery which centers around Melchizedek. Melchizedek was a *type of Christ,* and particularly a type of our Lord's priesthood. There are other points of resemblance which we shall consider below, but the first point of analogy between Melchizedek and the

Son of God singled out by the Holy Spirit in Hebrews 7 is that he is "without father, without mother, without descendant, having neither beginning of days nor end of life." This does not mean that Melchizedek was a supernatural, a divine being, but that *he is presented to us in the Old Testament as* without father or mother, etc. In other words, the *silence* of the Old Testament Scriptures concerning his parentage has a designed significance. The entire *omission* of any reference to Melchizedek's ancestry, birth or death, was ordered by the Holy Spirit (who "moved" Moses both in what he inserted and what he left out of the Genesis narrative) in order to present a perfect *type* of the Lord Jesus. No information concerning the genealogy of Melchizedek is recorded in Genesis, which is a book that abounds in genealogies. This is an instance where speech is silvern and silence golden. The silence was in order that there might be a nearer approximation between the type and the glorious antitype.

Not only was Melchizedek a type of our Lord in the fact that he is presented to us in Genesis as being "without father, without mother," but also in a number of other important particulars. Melchizedek was a *priest*—"the priest of the Most High God" (Gen. 14:18). But not only so, he was a *king*—"King of Salem"—and therefore a *royal priest*. In the person of Melchizedek the offices of priest and king were combined, and thus was he a notable type of our great High Priest who according to the flesh was not of the tribe of Levi, but of the tribe of Judah, the *royal* tribe (see Heb. 7:14). Not only was Melchizedek a type of the royal priesthood of Christ by virtue of his office as King of Salem (which means "peace") but his *name* also had a typical significance. "Melchizedek" means "king of righteousness." Here again there is a wonderful and blessed bringing together of things which out of Christ are divorced. Not only did Melchizedek combine in his *person* the offices of king and priest, but in his *titles* he united righteousness and peace. Melchizedek was both king of righteousness and king of peace and thus did he foreshadow the blessed result of the cross work of our adorable Lord, for it was at the Cross that "mercy and truth met together, and *righteousness and peace kissed each other*" (Ps. 85:10).

Observe the order of mention in Hebrews 7:2, "to whom also Abraham gave a tenth part of all; *first being* by interpretation King of Righteousness, and after that also King of Salem, which is, King of Peace." This is ever God's order. God cannot be at peace with guilty rebels until the claims of His throne have been met. Only upon a righteous basis can peace be established. "And the work of righteousness shall be peace; and the effect of righteousness, quietness and assurance forever" (Isa. 32:17). This is unfolded at length in the Epistle to the Romans, and particularly in 3:21-26, God's righteousness was "declared" at the Cross where the Lord Jesus made propitiation and fully satisfied every demand of the thrice holy God. There it is that the great "work of righteousness" was accomplished, the effect of which is peace. As it is written, "*Having made peace through the blood of His Cross*" (Col. 1:20). The benefits of this accrue to the believer through the channel of faith, for "being justified (pronounced righteous) by faith we have peace with God through our Lord Jesus Christ" (Rom. 5:1). The same order is found again in Romans 14:17—"For the Kingdom of God is not meat and drink; but righteousness, and peace, and joy, in the Holy Spirit."

In Hebrews 7:4 attention is called to the *greatness* of this man Melchizedek, his "greatness" being recognized and acknowledged by Abraham who "gave him tithes." In this also he is a type of the Lord Jesus Christ, our "*great* High Priest"—the only Priest so denominated in the Scriptures. The greatness of our Lord's priesthood inheres in His intrinsic glory which is in contrast with the feebleness of the perishable priests of the Levitical order who could not save. Two things prominently characterized the Levitical priests: first, they were personally unclean, and therefore needed to "offer for their *own* sins" (Heb. 7:27); and second, they were mortal, and therefore death put an end to their ministrations. Now in contradistinction, not only is our great High Priest sinless, but He is made "after the power of an endless life" (Heb. 7:16), and hence it is written concerning Christ, "Thou art a priest *for ever* after the order of Melchizedek" (Heb. 7:21). It is important to remark here that it is as risen and ascended that the Lord Jesus has received the eternal excellency of the Melchizedek title. His never-ending ministry of *blessing* dates its effectual beginning from the finished work of the Cross. Here again we note the accuracy of our type, for not only is the Genesis narrative silent concerning the origin of Melchizedek, but it *makes no mention of his death.*

Finally, it is to be noted that Melchizedek is termed "priest of *the Most High God*" (Gen. 14:18), a title which looks beyond all national relationships. Here is the final contrast between the two orders of priesthood—the Melchizedekian and the Aaronic. Aaron's priestly ministry never transcended the limits of Israel, and he was ever the priest of Jehovah as the God of *Israel.* But Melchizedek was priest of Jehovah under His more comprehensive title of the *Most High God, "Possessor of heaven and earth"* (Gen. 14:19), and therefore Melchizedek foreshadowed the *millennial glory* of Christ when "He shall be *a priest upon His throne*" (Zech. 6:13) and reign in righteousness and peace. As it is written, "Behold, the days come, saith the Lord, that I will raise unto David a righteous Branch, and a King shall reign and prosper, and shall execute judgment and justice in the earth. In His days Judah shall be saved, and Israel shall dwell safely: and this is His name whereby He shall be called THE LORD OUR RIGHTEOUSNESS" (Jer. 23:5, 6). Then shall the Divine Melchizedek rule as King of Righteousness and King of Peace. As it is written again, "His name shall be called Wonderful, Counsellor, The Mighty God, The Everlasting Father, The *Prince of Peace.* Of the increase of His government and peace there shall be no end, upon the throne of David, and upon His Kingdom, to order it, and to establish it with judgment and with justice (*righteousness*) from henceforth even for ever" (Isa. 9:6, 7).

That Melchizedek foreshadowed the *millennial glory* of Christ is further to be seen from *the occasion* when he appeared before Abram. The typical picture is wonderfully complete. Melchizedek met Abram as he was returning from the slaughter of the kings, having rescued from them his nephew Lot who foreshadows the Jewish remnant in the tribulation period.* Then it was that Melchizedek met Abram and *blessed* him (14:19). Thus it will be when our

*In the *federation* of the kings under Chedorlaomer we have foreshadowed the ten kingdomed Empire over which the Beast will rule, and surely it is more than a coincidence that here we find mentioned nine kings —"four kings with five" (v. 9)—which with Abram and his armed servants make in all *ten* contesting forces!

Lord returns to usher in the Millennium. He will overthrow the Beast and his forces in this same "King's dale," deliver Israel out of their hands and bless the descendants of Abraham, and just as Abram acknowledged the superiority of Melchizedek by paying him tithes, so will Israel acknowledge their Divine Melchizedek and own Him as their Priest and King.

It now only remains for us to consider here the immediate effects upon Abram of the appearing of Melchizedek before him and the blessing he had received from him. "And the King of Sodom said unto Abram, give me the persons, and take the goods to thyself" (Gen. 14:21). In the King of Sodom's offer we may discover one of the "wiles" of the devil for we are not ignorant of his "devices." The world is only too ready to offer God's children its subsidies so as to bring them under obligation to itself. But Abram was preëminently a man of faith and faith is "the victory that overcometh the world" (1 John 5:4).

"And Abram said to the King of Sodom, I have lifted up mine hand unto the Lord, the Most High God, the Possessor of heaven and earth.† That I will not take from a thread even to a shoelatchet, and that I will not take anything that is thine, *lest thou shouldest say I have made Abram rich.* Save only that which the young men have eaten, and the portion of the men which went with me, Aner, Eshcol, and Mamre; let them take their portion" (14:22-24). What noble words were these! With quiet dignity our patriarch refuses to be dependent in anywise upon the King of Sodom—what a contrast was Balaam and the offer made him by Balak! Abram knew that in heaven he had a "better and an enduring substance" (Heb. 10:34). The words, "I have lifted up mine hand unto the Lord" (compare Deut. 32:40) signify a vow or solemn oath, and seem to show that when he started out in pursuit of Lot's captors he promised the Lord that if He would give him success he would not enrich himself by his campaign; but it is beautiful to note that he did not forget or overlook the claims of those who had accompanied him and shared his perils. In the giving of tithes to Melchizedek, priest of the Most High God, Abram acknowledged God's grace in giving him the victory.

†The use of this Divine title here gives the lie to the wicked teaching of the higher critics who erroneously declare that the god of the patriarch and of Israel was a tribal or tutelary god. The God of Abram was no mere local deity but "The Possessor of heaven and earth."

20. ABRAHAM'S VISION

GENESIS 15

The connecting link between our present portion of Scripture and the one which we took for the basis of meditation in our last chapter is found in the opening words of Genesis 15—"*After these things* the Word of the Lord came unto Abram in a vision." Chedorlaomer, the King of Elam, had united his forces to those of three other kings in a league of conquest. Their military prowess seemed irresistible. The Rephaim, the Zuzim, the Emim, the Horites, the Amalekites and the Amorites were each defeated in turn (Gen. 14: 5-7). Five kings with their forces now combined and went forth to engage the armies of Chedorlaomer, but they also were overthrown, and in consequence the cities of Sodom and Gomorrah were sacked and Lot was taken prisoner. Then it was that Abram went forth at the head of his three hundred and eighteen armed servants and by a surprise night attack gained a signal victory. Chedorlaomer was slain, Lot was delivered, and the booty taken from Sodom and Gomorrah was recovered.

And now came the reaction, mental and physical. Abram had good reason to conclude that the remaining followers of the powerful King of Elam would not abandon the enterprise which had only been frustrated by a surprise attack at night—made by an insignificant force—but instead, would return and avenge their reverse. In defeating Chedorlaomer and his allies, Abram had made some bitter and influential foes. It was not likely that they would rest content until the memory of their reverse had been wiped out with blood. They who had been strong enough to capture the cities of Sodom and Gomorrah were too powerful to be set at defiance by Abram and his little colony. Thus alarmed and apprehensive Abram now receives a special word of reassurance: "After these things the Word of the Lord came unto Abram in a vision, saying, *Fear not, Abram, I am thy shield.*" Thus in tender grace did Jehovah quiet the troubled heart of the one whom He was pleased to call His "friend."

But further. In the remaining part of this opening verse—"I am....thy exceeding great *Reward*"—we have another word which looks back to the previous chapter; and a precious word it is. After Abram had defeated Chedorlaomer, and after he had been blessed and refreshed by Melchizedek, the King of Sodom offered to reward Abram by suggesting he take the recovered "goods" unto himself (14:21). But he who "looked for a city which hath foundations whose builder and maker is God" declined to accept anything from this worldling, saying, "I have lifted up mine hand unto the Lord, the Most High God, the possessor of heaven and earth, that I will not take from a thread even to a shoelatchet, and that I will not take anything that is thine, lest thou shouldest say, *I have made Abram rich*" (14:22, 23). Noble reply! And now we behold the *sequel.* God never permits His own to lose for honoring *Him* and seeking *His* glory. Abram had refused the spoil of Sodom, but God more than makes it up to him. Just as when our patriarch had shown his magnanimity to Lot by saying: "Is not the *whole* land before *thee*....if thou wilt take the left hand, then I will go to the right; or if thou depart to the right hand then I will go to the left," and the Lord appeared unto Abram and said, "Lift up now *thine eyes,* and look from the place where thou art northward, and southward, and eastward, and westward. For *all* the land which thou seest, to thee will I give it, and to thy seed forever" (13:9, 14, 15); so it was here. The refusal to be enriched by the king of Sodom is now compensated, more than compensated by a revelation from God which would greatly increase the joy of His servant. How important is the principle which here receives such lovely exemplification! How much are the Lord's people losing today because of *their acceptance* of the world's favors! Unto how few can the Lord now reveal Himself as He did here to Abram!

"I am thy shield and thy exceeding great Reward." We would fain tarry and extract some of the sweetness of these words. This is a special promise applicable to those who are "strangers and pilgrims on the earth." It is God's word to those who "choose rather to suffer affliction with the people of God, than to enjoy *the pleasures of sin* for a season, esteeming the reproach of Christ greater riches than the treasures in Egypt" for they have "respect unto the recompense of the *reward*" (Heb. 11:25, 26). Unto such, God promises to be their Shield, their Defense, the One behind whom faith shelters and trusts; as well as their Reward, their exceeding great Reward. So it was with our blessed Lord Himself. Refusing to accept from Satan the kingdoms of the world and their glory, He could say, "*The Lord* is the portion *of Mine inheritance,* and of My cup" (Ps. 16:5).

"And Abram said, Lord God, what wilt Thou give me, seeing I go childless, and the steward of my house is this Eliezer of Damascus? And Abram said, Behold, to me Thou hast given no seed; and, lo, one born in my house is mine heir" (vs. 2, 3). In hearing the words, "I am thy Shield and thy exceeding great *Reward,*" Abram's mind seems to have turned toward his *inheritance* and the fact that he had no seed of his own to enter into the promises of God. What Abram longed for was a *son,* for he rightly judged that to go childless was to lose the inheritance. In other words, the patriarch here recognizes that *heirship is based upon sonship,* and thus we have foreshadowed a truth of vital importance, a truth which is fully revealed in the Scriptures of the New Testament. There we read, "The Spirit Himself beareth witness with our spirit, that we are the children of God; and if children, *then heirs;* heirs of God, and joint heirs with Christ" (Rom. 8:16, 17). And again: "Having predestinated us unto the adoption of children by Jesus Christ to Himself....in whom also we have obtained an *inheritance*" (Eph. 1:5, 11).

We do not consider that in asking "What wilt thou give me," etc., that Abram was giving expression to unbelief. On the contrary we regard his words as the language of faith. Observe there was no rebuke given him by the Lord; instead, we are told, "And, behold, the Word of the Lord came unto him saying, This shall not be thine heir; but he that shall come forth out of thine own bowels shall be thine heir. And He brought him forth abroad, and said, Look now toward heaven, and tell the stars, if thou be able to number them; and he said unto him, So shall thy seed be" (vs. 4, 5). It is to be noted that in Genesis 13:15 God compared Abram's seed to the dust of the earth, but here, where *Christ* is contemplated (as well as a numerous offspring), the word is, "*Look now toward heaven,*" and his seed is likened to the "stars."

And now we come to those words which have been so precious unto multitudes: "And he believed in the Lord;

and He counted it to him for righteousness" (v. 6). A full exposition of this verse would lead us far beyond the limits of our present space, so we content ourselves with a few brief comments, referring the reader to Romans 4 for God's own exposition.

Literally rendered our verse reads, "And he *stayed himself upon* the Lord; and He counted it to him for righteousness." At the time God promised Abram that his heir should be one who came forth from his own bowels Abram's body was "as good as dead" (Heb. 11:12), nevertheless, he staggered not at the promise of God through unbelief; but was strong in faith, giving glory to God; and being fully persuaded that what He had promised, He was able also to perform" (Rom. 4:20, 21). Abram reasoned not about the *natural* impossibility that lay in the way of the realization of the promise, but believed that God would act just as He had said. God had spoken and that was enough. His own body might be dead and Sarah long past the age of child-bearing, nevertheless he was fully assured that God had power even to quicken the dead. And this faith was reckoned or counted unto him for righteousness; not that faith is accepted by God in lieu of righteousness as an equivalent for righteousness, else would faith be a meritorious thing, but that faith is the *recipient* of that righteousness by which we are justified. The force of the preposition is "unto" rather than "instead of"—it was "counted to him *unto* righteousness." Abram's case was a representative one. Today justification (to be declared righteous) is by faith, but with this important difference that whereas Abram believed God *would* give him a son through the quickening of his body, we believe that God *has* given us His Son, and through His death and quickening from the dead a Saviour is ours through faith.

Just here we would pause to consider what seems to have proven a real difficulty to expositors and commentators. Was not Abram a "believer" years before the point of time contemplated in Genesis 15:6? Not a few have suggested that prior to this incident Abram was in a condition similar to that of Cornelius before Peter preached to him. But are we not expressly told that it was "*By faith*" (Heb. 11:8) he had left Ur of the Chaldees and went out "not knowing whither he went"! Yet, why are we *here* told that "he believed in the Lord; and He counted it to him for righteousness"? Surely the answer is not far to seek. It is true that in the New Testament the Holy Spirit informs us that Abram was a believer when he left Chaldea, but his faith is *not there* (*i. e.,* Heb. 11:8) mentioned *in connection with his justification.* Instead, in the Epistles to the Romans and Galatians the incident which the Holy Spirit singles out as the occasion when Abram's faith was counted for righteousness is the one in Genesis 15 now before us. And why? Because in Genesis 15 Abram's faith is directly connected with God's promise respecting his "seed," which "seed" was *Christ* (see Gal. 3:16)! The faith which was *"counted for righteousness"* was the faith which believed what God had said concerning the promised Seed. It was *this* instance of Abram's faith which the Holy Spirit was pleased to select as the *model* for believing unto justification. There is no justification apart from Christ—*"Through this Man* is preached unto you the forgiveness of sins. And by *Him* all that *believe* are *justified* from all things" (Acts 13:38, 39). Therefore we say it was not that Abram here "believed God" for the first time, but that here God was pleased to *openly attest his righteousness* for the first time, and that for the reason stated above. Though Christians may believe God with respect to the common concerns of this life, such faith, while it evidences they have been justified is not the faith by which they were justified—the faith which justifies has to do directly with the person and work of our Lord Jesus Christ. This was the character of Abram's faith in Genesis 15; he believed the promise of God *which pointed to Christ.* Hence it is in Genesis 15 and not in Genesis 12 we read, "And He counted it to him for righteousness." How perfect are the ways of God!

"And He said unto him, I am the Lord that brought thee out of Ur of the Chaldees, to give thee this land to *inherit* it" (v. 7). Abram now ventures to ask for a sign by which he may know that by his posterity, he *shall* inherit the land. "And he said, Lord God, *whereby* shall I *know* that I shall inherit it?" (v. 8). We do not regard this question from Abram as arising from unbelief, but that having just been granted (v. 5) a sign or view of a numerous offspring he now desires a further sign or pledge by way of explanation. And now the Lord answers by putting *Christ,* in type, before him.

"And He said unto him, Take Me a heifer of three years old, and a she goat of three years old, and a ram of three years old, and a turtle dove, and a young pigeon. And he took unto him all these, and divided them in the midst, and laid each piece one against another, but the birds divided he not. And when the fowls came down upon the carcasses, Abram drove them away" (vs. 9-11). The typical picture is wonderfully complete. "Take Me," observe, for the sacrifice belongs to, is for *God.* It has been pointed out by another that each of the three animals named here were tame ones, not wild and needing to be captured by Abram; instead, they were the willing servants of man's need. Each one foreshadowed a distinctive aspect of Christ's perfections and work. The heifer of three years seems to have pointed to the freshness of His vigor; the goat, gave the sin-offering aspect; the ram is the animal that in the Levitical offerings was connected specially with consecration. The birds told of One from *Heaven.* The "three years," thrice repeated, suggested perhaps the *time* of our Lord's sacrifice, offered after "three years" of service! Note that death passed upon them all, for without shedding of blood is no remission and where no remission is there can be no inheritance. The "dividing" of the animals indicated that this sacrifice was to form the basis for a *covenant* (cf. Jer. 34:18, 19). The "driving away" of the fowls seems to have shown forth the energy of faith.

"And when the sun was going down, a deep sleep fell upon Abram; and, lo, a horror of great darkness fell upon him. And He said unto Abram, Know of a surety that thy seed shall be a stranger in a land that is not theirs, and shall serve them, and they shall afflict them four hundred years" (vs. 12, 13). A profound truth is here taught us in type. Abram now learns that the *inheritance* can be reached only through *suffering!* His heirs would have to pass through the furnace before they entered into that which God had prepared for them. In the "deep sleep" and the "horror of great darkness" Abram, as it were, entered in spirit into death, as that through which all his seed would have to pass ere they experienced God's deliverance after the death of the Paschal Lamb. First the suffering, the four hundred years' "affliction," and then the inheritance. How this reminds us again of Romans 8:17! "And if children, then heirs; heirs of God, and joint heirs with Christ; if so be that we *suffer* with Him, that we may be also glorified together." And again: "We must through much tribulation enter into the Kingdom of God" (Acts 14:22). Thus it was with our blessed Lord—first the "sufferings" and then "the glory." We call attention to the wonderful and perfect *order* of the typical teaching here: first the sacrifice (v. 9); second, "thy seed"—sons (v. 13); third, suffering—"affliction" (v. 13); fourth, entering into the inheritance—"come hither again" (v. 16). How *complete* the typical picture!

"And when the sun was going down, a deep sleep fell upon Abram; and, lo, a horror of great darkness fell upon him" (v. 12). By this *deep* sleep we learn how God was showing the patriarch, symbolically, that not during his *natural* life would he inherit the land; instead, he must go down into the grave and inherit it *together with* the Promised Seed. In his awaking from this "deep sleep" Abram received a veiled promise of *resurrection* from the dead and the horror of great darkness as of the grave (cf. Heb. 2:15) from which he was recalled again to the light of day. In a word, the way to blessing, to the inheritance, was through death and resurrection.

"And He said unto Abram, know of a surety that thy seed shall be a stranger in a land that is not theirs, and shall serve them; and they shall afflict them four hundred years. And also that nation, whom they shall serve, will I judge; and afterward shall they come out with great substance. And thou shalt go to thy fathers in peace; thou shalt be buried in a good old age. But in the fourth generation they shall come hither again; for the iniquity of the Amorites is not yet full" (vs. 13-16). These verses contain *a sevenfold prophecy* which received a literal and complete fulfillment. It had reference to the sojourn of Abram's descendants in the land of Egypt, their bondage there, and their deliverance and return to Canaan. We can do little more now than outline the divisions of this compound prophecy. First, Abram's descendants were to be strangers in a land not theirs (v. 13). Second, in that strange land they were to "serve" (v. 13). Third, they were to be "afflicted" four hundred years (v. 13)—note that Exodus 12:40 views the *entire* "sojourning" of the children of Israel in Egypt. They "dwelt" in Egypt four hundred and thirty years, but were "afflicted" for only four hundred years of that time. Fourth, the nation whom Abram's descendants "served" God would "judge" (v. 14). Fifth, Abram's offspring were to come out of Egypt with "great substance" (v. 14), cf. Ps. 105:37. Sixth, Abram himself was to be spared these afflictions—he should die in peace and be buried in a good old age (v. 15). Seventh, in the "fourth generation" Abram's descendants would return again to Canaan (v. 16). We take it that our readers are sufficiently well acquainted with the book of Exodus to know how wonderfully this prophecy was fulfilled, but we would point out here how accurately the *seventh* item was realized. By comparing Exodus 6:16-26 we find that it *was* exactly in the "*fourth* generation" that the children of Israel left Egypt and returned to Canaan. In this particular example the first generation was Levi, the son of Jacob, who entered Egypt at the time his father and brethren did (Ex. 6:16). The second generation was Kohath (Ex. 6:16), who was a son of Levi. The third generation was Amran, son of Kohath (Ex. 6:18). And the *fourth* generation brings us to Moses and Aaron, who were the sons of Amram (Ex. 6:20), and these were the ones who led Israel out of Egypt!

"And it came to pass, that, when the sun went down, and it was dark, behold a smoking furnace and a burning lamp that passed between those pieces" (v. 17). Much is suggested here which we have to pass by. The "smoking furnace" and the "burning lamp" symbolized the two leading features of the *history* of Abram's descendants. For the "furnace" see Jeremiah 11:3, 4, etc.; for the "burning lamp" see 2 Samuel 22:29; Psalm 119:105; Isaiah 62:1, etc. Note a "smoking furnace *and* a burning lamp." Did not this teach Abram that in Israel's sufferings God would be *with them;* and that in all their afflictions, He would be afflicted, too?

"In the same day the Lord made a covenant with Abram, saying, Unto thy seed have I given this land, from the river of Egypt, unto the great river, the river Euphrates" (v. 18). The covenant which God here made with Abram was based upon death, typically, the death of Christ. This covenant, based on sacrifice, was made by the Lord Himself; it concerned the land; and was absolutely unconditional. It has never yet been completely fulfilled. Note carefully its wording—"Unto thy seed *have I given* this land." Contrast these words with Genesis 13:15—"For all the land which thou seest to thee *will I give it.*" But now a sacrifice had been offered, blood had been shed, the purchase price had been paid, and hence the change from "I will" to "I have."

In these articles we are not attempting complete expositions. They are little more than "Notes"—"Gleanings"—and our prime endeavor is to indicate some of the broad outlines of truth in the hope that our readers will be led to fill in the details by their own personal studies. In concluding this paper it deserves to be noted that Genesis 15 is a chapter in which quite a number of important terms and expressions occur for the first time. The following is not a complete list, but includes some of the more important examples. Here for the first time we find that notable expression, "The word of the Lord came unto" (v. 1). Here is the first reference to a "vision" (v. 1). Here for the first time we read the words "Fear not" (v. 1), which, with their equivalent, "Be not afraid," occur in Scriptures almost one hundred and eighty times. Here is the first mention of God as a "Shield" (v. 1). Here is the first occurrence of the Divine title "Adonai Jehovah"—Lord God (v. 2). Here for the first time we find the words "Believed," "counted" or reckoned, and "righteousness." May writer and reader search the Scriptures daily and diligently so that each shall say, "I rejoice at Thy Word, as one that findeth great spoil" (Ps. 119:162).

21. ABRAHAM AND HAGAR

Genesis 16

It is difficult to imagine a greater contrast than what is presented in our present chapter from the one reviewed in our last article. In Genesis 15 Abram is seen as the man of faith, in chapter 16 as the man of unbelief. In Genesis 15 he "believed in the Lord," in Genesis 16 he "hearkened to the voice of Sarai." There he walks after the Spirit, here he acts in the energy of the flesh. Sad inconsistency! But One could say, "I do *always* these things that please Him" (John 8:29).

"Now Sarai, Abram's wife, bare him no children; and she had a handmaid, an Egyptian, whose name was Hagar. And Sarai said unto Abram, Behold now, the Lord hath restrained me from bearing. I pray thee, go in unto my maid, it may be that I may obtain children by her" (Gen. 16:1, 2). In this suggestion of Sarai's we witness a fresh *testing* of Abram. Again and again our patriarch was tried —tried, may we not say, at every point. First, his faith had to overcome the *ties of nature:* God's call was for him to leave his country and his kindred. Then, shortly after he had actually arrived in Canaan, his faith was tried by *stress of circumstances*—there was a famine in the land. Next, he had to meet a trial respecting *a brother:* Abram feared that the friction between his herdsmen and the herdsmen of his nephew might lead to "strife" between brethren, and how he met this by his magnanimous offer to Lot we have already seen in an earlier chapter. Later, there was a testing of Abram's *courage,* as well as his *love* for his nephew. Lot had been captured by a powerful warrior, but Abram hastens to his rescue and delivers him. Subsequently, there was a testing of his *cupidity.* The King of Sodom offered to "reward" him for overcoming Chedorlaomer. And now he is tested by a suggestion from his wife. Would he take matters out of the hand of God and act in the energy of the flesh with reference to the obtaining of a son and heir. Thus, at six different points (to this stage in his history) was the character of Abram tested. We might summarize them thus: There was the trying of the *fervor* of his faith—did he love God more than home and kindred. There was the trying of the *sufficiency* of his faith—was he looking to the living God to supply all his need, or was he depending on propitious circumstances? There was the trying of the *humility* of his faith—would he assert his "rights," or yield to Lot? There was the trying of the *boldness* of his faith—would he dare attempt the rescue of his nephew from the hands of a powerful warrior? There was the trying of the *dignity* of his faith—would he bemean himself by accepting honors from the King of Sodom? There was the trying of the *patience* of his faith—would he wait for God to fulfil His word in His own good time and way, or would he take matters into his own hand?

It is most instructive to note the *setting* of these various trials and temptations. Arrived in the land Abram was faced with a famine, and *Egypt* was at hand to lure the patriarch with its promise of relief from his anxiety. After his departure from Egypt and return to the path of God's will, the very next thing we read of is the *strife* between the herdsmen. Again: no sooner had Abram rescued Lot from his captors and been blessed by Melchizedek than he was tempted to dishonor God and bemean himself by a reward from the *King of Sodom.* And, immediately after Abram had received the wonderful revelation and promise of God recorded in Genesis 15, we read of this subtle temptation emanating from *his wife.*

It seems to be a general principle in the ways of God with His own to first bless and enrich and then to *test* the recipient. Elisha ardently desired to receive Elijah's mantle. His wish was granted; and the next thing we read of him is the facing of Jordan—the mantle had to be used at once! Solomon prayed for wisdom, and his prayer was heard, and at once his gift was called into exercise by the case of the two mothers each claiming the living child as hers. Thus it was, too, with our blessed Lord; no sooner had the Holy Spirit descended upon Him in the form of a dove than we read, "And *immediately* the Spirit driveth Him into the wilderness" (Mark 1:12), where He was tempted of the devil. It is highly necessary for *us* to take the lesson to heart—it is when we have received some special mark of the Lord's favor, or immediately after we have enjoyed some unusual season of communion with him, that we need most to be on our guard!

The evil suggestion that Sari made to Abram was a testing of the *patience* of his faith. God had said to Abram, "I will make of thee a great nation, and I will bless thee and make thy name great" (Gen. 12:2). He had said, further, "Look now toward heaven, and tell the stars, if thou be able to number them; and He said unto him, *So shall thy seed be*" (15:5), yet ten years had passed since the first of these promises and still Abram was *childless.* When the Lord repeated His promise "Abram believed in the Lord" (15:6), and now he was left to *wait* for the fulfillment of it. But waiting is just what the natural heart finds it so hard to endure. Rather than *wait* man prefers to take the management of his affairs into his own hands and use human expediencies to give effect to the Divine promise. It was thus with Jacob; the portion of the firstborn had been given to him and not to Esau, but instead of waiting for God to secure the inheritance for him, he sought to obtain it himself by his own dishonorable scheming. It was the same with Moses; God had declared that the descendants of Abram should be afflicted for 400 years in a strange country, and but 360 years had passed when Moses saw an Egyptian smiting a Hebrew, and taking matters into his own hands he smote and slew the Egyptian. It is one thing to "commit" our way unto the Lord, but it is quite another to *trust also* in Him," and *wait* till He brings it to pass.

"And Abram hearkened to the voice of Sarai" (v. 2). The father of mankind sinned by hearkening to his wife, and here the father of the faithful follows his example. These things are recorded for our learning. How often it is that a man's foes are those of his own household! How often those who are nearest to us by nature are snares and hindrances in the spiritual life! Hence, how deeply important to heed the Divine admonition and "Be not unequally yoked together."

"And Sarai, Abram's wife, took Hagar her maid, the Egyptian, after Abram had dwelt ten years in the land of Canaan, and gave her to her husband Abram to be his wife" (v. 3). Galatians 4:22-26 is the inspired commentary upon the doctrinal principles involved in this act and in Abram's response to it. The dispensational *significance* of Abram's fall has often been expounded by others so that it is unnecessary for us to dwell upon it here at any length. In refusing to wait upon the Lord, and in summoning to his aid this Egyptian maid for the fulfilling of the Divine promise, Abram took a step which only "gendered to bondage," just as now the believer does, if having begun in the Spirit he seeks to be made perfect by the flesh.

The *outcome* of Abram's yielding to the specious temptation from his wife was quickly evidenced. "And he went in unto Hagar, and she conceived; and when she saw that she had conceived, *her mistress was despised in her eyes*" (v. 4). The consequence was just what might have been expected. The Egyptian maid was elated at the honor (?) conferred upon her, and Sarai falls in her estimation. And now, when it is too late, Sarai repents and complains to her husband—"And Sarai said unto Abram, My wrong *be upon thee.* I have given my maid into thy bosom; and when she saw that she had conceived, I was despised in her eyes; *the Lord judge between me and thee*" (v. 5). How true to human nature (fallen human nature)—to throw the blame of wrong-doing upon another! Man ever seeks to shelve his responsibility and charge either God or Satan with what he terms his "misfortunes."

"But Abram said unto Sarai, Behold, thy maid is in *thy* hand; do to her as it pleaseth thee" (v. 6). Abram refuses to accept the responsibility of Sarai's "wrong" and leaves her to deal with the evil which was the fruitage of her own sowing. But observe how one evil leads to another; in wronging his wife, Abram now surrenders to her his position as *head* of the household.

"And when Sarai dealt hardly with her, she fled from her face" (v. 6). Was it to this Solomon had reference when he said, "It is better to dwell *in the wilderness,* than with a contentious and an angry woman" (Prov. 21:19)? Hagar, too, had to learn that the way of the transgressor is hard. "And the angel of the Lord found her by a fountain of water in the wilderness, by the fountain in the way to Shur" (v. 7). What *grace* was this, *Divine* grace, for we need not stop to prove that the "Angel of the Lord" (mentioned here for the first time) was God Himself in theophanic manifestation. The *place where He* found this poor Egyptian maid attracts our attention. It was "by a fountain of water in the wilderness," termed in verse 14 "the well." This is the first time we read of the "well" in Scripture. We pause to look at several other passages in the Old Testament where the "well" is mentioned, for the purpose of noting how beautifully they pointed to the One Who giveth the living water, that water of which those who drink shall never thirst" and which is in them a well of water springing up into "everlasting life" (John 4).

Ere turning to a few of those Scriptures, where the "well" is mentioned we pause to note first what is said of it here in Genesis 16. Three things are to be observed concerning *this* "well." First, it was located in the "wilderness." Second, the well itself was "by the fountain"—mark the repetition of these words in verse 7. And third, it was at this well that God revealed Himself to Hagar. Surely the symbols are easily interpreted. It is not amid the gaieties or the luxuries of the world that Christ is to be found. It is not while the soul is enjoying "the pleasures of sin for a season" that the Saviour is met with. It is in the *wilderness,* that is, it is as we withdraw from the attractions of earth and are in that state of soul which answers to the "wilderness" that the Lord meets with the sinner, and *where* is it that the needy one finds the Saviour? Where, but "by the fountain of water"—type of the written Word! Should these lines catch the eye of some sin-sick and troubled heart that is earnestly seeking the Lord Jesus, turn, we beseech thee, away from man, and "search the Scriptures," for they are they which testify of Him. Finally, note that it was here at the "well" that God was *revealed*—"and she called the name of the Lord that spake unto her, Thou God seest me; for she said, Have I also here looked after Him that seeth me? Wherefore the well was called Beer-lahai-roi—the well of Him that liveth and seeth me" (vs. 13, 14). So Christ—of whom the "well" speaks —"He that hath seen Me hath seen the Father." It is in Him that God is fully revealed.

The next Scripture in which the "well" is found is Genesis 21:19, again in connection with Hagar: "And God opened her eyes, and she saw a well of water." How plain is the type! "No man can come to Me, except the Father which hath sent Me draw him" (John 6:44). And not only so, but none can *see* Christ with the eyes of the heart until they are opened by God. "And Jesus answered and said unto him, Blessed art thou, Simon Bar-jona; for flesh and blood hath not *revealed it unto thee* (*i. e.,* that Jesus was the Christ, the Son of the living God), but My Father which is in heaven" (Matt. 16:17). As it was here with Hagar—"God *opened her eyes, and she saw* a well"—so also was it with Lydia, "*whose heart the Lord opened,* that she attended unto the things which were spoken of Paul" (Acts 16:14), and as it was with Lydia so is it with all who believe.

"Then Jacob went on his journey, and came into the land of the people of the East. And he looked, and behold a well in the field, and, lo, there were three flocks of sheep lying by it; *for out of that well they watered the flocks*" (Gen. 29:1, 2). Comment here is needless. The "well" is the place where the *sheep* were watered and refreshed. So, again, with the antitype. Not only does our Lord give life—His own life—but He *refreshes* our parched souls day by day.

"And from thence they went to Beer: that is the well whereof the Lord spake unto Moses, Gather the people together, and I will give them water. Then Israel sang this song, *Spring up, O well: sing ye unto it*" (Num. 21:16, 17). What a word is this! It reminds us of Genesis 22:8 compared with Isaiah 53:7. In the former passage the promise is that "God will provide Himself a lamb," and in the latter, the Lamb is definitely identified—"*He* was led as a lamb to the slaughter." And so here. The "well" is *personified*—"Sing ye unto it"! Note, too, that the well was here made the *gathering center* of Israel. O, may *we,* as we gather around our blessed Lord, "sing" unto Him that loved us, and washed us from our sins in His own blood.

"Now Jonathan and Ahimaaz stayed by En-rogel, for they might not be seen to come into the city; and a wench went and told them; and they went and told King David. Nevertheless, a lad saw them, and told Absalom; but they went both of them away quickly, and came to a man's house in Bahurim, which had a well in his court; whither they went down. And the woman took and spread a covering over the well's mouth, and spread ground corn thereon; and the thing was not known" (2 Sam. 17:17-19). Thus the "well" was a place of *protection* for Jonathan and his servant. They were *securely hidden* in the well. How this reminds us of that word, "Your life is *hid with Christ* in God" (Col. 3:3).

Summarizing the typical teaching of the Scriptures we have little more than glanced at, we learn: First, that the "well" is to be found "by the fountain of water," which, to interpret, signifies, that Christ is to be found in the written Word. Second, that it is at the well God revealed Himself, just as in Christ God is now fully told out. Third, it was not until God opened the eyes of Hagar, that she "saw" the well. So it is not until the eyes of our heart are opened by God the Spirit that we are enabled to see Christ as the One we need and as the Fairest among ten thousand. Fourth, that it is at the well the "sheep" are "watered." So it is in communion with Christ our souls are refreshed. Fifth, that the well was the place where Israel were gathered together by the Word of Jehovah through Moses. So Christ is now the appointed Gathering-Center when we come together for worship. Sixth, unto the well Israel were bidden to "sing." So throughout time and eternity our adorable Lord will be the Object and Subject of our praises. Seventh, the well was the place where Jonathan and his servant found protection from their enemies. So in Christ we find shelter from every foe and refuge from every storm.

"And the angel of the Lord found her by a fountain of water in the wilderness, by the fountain in the way to Shur. And he said, Hagar, Sarai's maid, whence camest thou? and whither wilt thou go? And she said, I flee from the face of my mistress Sarai. And the angel of the Lord said unto her, *Return* to thy mistress, and *submit* thyself under her hands" (vs. 7-9). "Grace reigns through righteousness." It was grace that *sought* her, it was righteousness that thus *counselled* her. Grace is never exercised at the expense of righteousness. Grace upholds rather than ignores our responsibilities toward God and toward our neighbor. The grace of God that bringeth salvation, *teaches* us to deny ungodliness and worldly lusts, and to live soberly, righteously, and godly, in this present world (Titus 2:12). Note two things here in connection with Hagar. First, the angel of the Lord addresses her as "Sarai's maid," thus disallowing her marriage (?) with Abram; and second, she is bidden to "return" to her mistress. The day would come when God Himself would open the door, and send Hagar out of Abram's house (21:12-14), but till then she must "submit" herself to the authority of Sarai. For another thirteen years she must patiently endure her lot and perform her duty. In the meantime, the Lord cheers Hagar's heart with a promise (see v. 10). Is there a word here for any of our readers? Is there one who has fled from the post of duty? Then to such the Lord's word is, "Return ....submit." If we have done wrong, no matter what the temptation or provocation may have been, the only way to Divine blessing, to peace and happiness, is to retrace our footsteps (as far as this is possible), in repentance and submission.

"And the angel of the Lord said unto her, Behold, thou art with child, and shalt bear a son, and shalt call his name Ishmael; because the Lord hath heard thy affliction. And he will be a *wild* man; his hand will be against every man, and every man's hand against him" (vs. 11, 12). This prophecy seems to have had reference more to his posterity than to Ishmael himself. It is well known how accurately its terms have been fulfilled in the Arabs who, in all ages, have been a wild and warlike people, and who, though surrounded by nations that have each been conquered in turn, yet have themselves been unsubdued by the great Powers unto this day.

"And she called the name of the Lord that spake unto her, Thou God seest me; for she said, Have I also here looked after Him that seeth me. Wherefore, the well was called, The well of Him that liveth and seeth me" (vs. 13, 14). May the Lord Himself find *us* at the "well" as He did Hagar of old, and may it be ours as it was hers to hear and see *Him.*

22. ABRAHAM AT NINETY AND NINE

Genesis 17

We have reached another of the important crises in the history of our patriarch and are to behold again the matchless grace of Jehovah in His dealings with the father of all them that believe. Thirteen years had elapsed (see 17:25) since Abram, in his impatient unbelief had "hearkened to the voice of Sarah." Significant number this! In Scripture thirteen is invariably found in an evil connection signifying, as it does in the language of numerics, unbelief, rebellion, apostasy. The first time this numeral is met with in the Word is Genesis 14:4, where we read, "Twelve years they served Chedorlaomer, and in the thirteenth year they *rebelled.*" How closely Abram's own experience resembled this! Abram was seventy-five years of age when God's call had come to leave home and kindred and to tread the highway of faith, and for practically twelve years he had endured as seeing Him who is invisible. But at the age of eighty-six (Gen. 17:1, ninety-nine, less the thirteen years for the age of Ishmael, 17:25) Abram turned aside from the path of faith and resorted to the devices of the flesh, hearkening to the suggestion of Sarah to obtain a son by Hagar her Egyptian maid. And now *another thirteen years* pass, during which time there is no mention of any appearing of the Lord unto him. This interval is passed over in silence; it is a blank, a period of spiritual barrenness; apparently a season which brought forth nothing but wood, hay and stubble. Thus we find that the first two mentionings of this numeral thirteen are associated, respectively, with rebellion and impatient unbelief in resorting to carnal efforts instead of waiting upon God. And it will be found that thirteen is an *evil number* right through the Scriptures (see 1 Kings 7:1 and contrast 6:38; Esther 3:12, 13, etc.). The same is true of instances where the numeral is not specifically mentioned as, for example, the marching of Israel thirteen times around the defiant Jericho; also the thirteen "judges" enumerated in Judges, which is the book of apostasy (see 21:25); so, too, of Mark 7:21-23, where the Lord specifies just thirteen of the evil characteristics and products of the depraved heart of man; other examples might be added such as the fact that the term "Dragon" is found exactly thirteen times in the apocalypse. Again, the same uniform evil significance of this numeral is discovered in cases where *multiples* of thirteen occur in Scripture: thus Jacob says to Pharaoh, "The days of the years of my pilgrimage are a hundred and thirty years (13 x 10): few and *evil* have the days of the years of my life been" (Gen. 47:9). In Numbers 16, which records the *rebellion* of Korah, Dathan and Abiram and the visitation of God's *wrath* upon them and their followers, we find there perished 250 (Num. 16:35) plus 14,700 (Num. 16:49) or 14,950 in all, which is 13 x 1,150. In Deuteronomy 14 there is a list of the *unclean* animals and birds which the Israelites were forbidden to eat, and a careful count shows there were just 26 or 13 x 2, which were prohibited (see vs. 7-19). At the hands of his *unbelieving* countrymen the Apostle Paul received "forty stripes save one" (2 Cor. 11:24), or 39, that is 13 x 3. The Epistle of Jude which treats of the *apostasy of Christendom* is the twenty-sixth book of the New Testament. And so on. In the light of these examples it is surely not without deep meaning that we learn there was an interval of just thirteen years between the incident mentioned in Genesis 16 and that recorded in Genesis 17, between Abram hearkening to the voice of Sarah and the Lord's appearing to him anew, and that this interval is one of spiritual barrenness and is passed over in silence. Ere we turn and consider the gracious revelation which the Lord made to Abram at the close of this interval let us first ask and ponder an important question:

Why had Abram to wait all this while before the Lord appeared to him again? Why must so many years drag their weary course before Jehovah reveals Himself once more and makes promise of giving him Isaac? Is not the answer to be found in Romans 4:19? "And being not weak in faith; he considered not his own body *now dead,* when he was about an hundred years old, neither yet the *deadness* of Sarah's womb." God was about to act in grace, but ere grace can be displayed the creature has first to come to the end of himself: ere divine power is put forth man must learn his own impotency. Not till Israel were driven to desperation and despair at the Red Sea did the word come, "Stand still and see the salvation of the Lord." So here. Not till Abram's body was "dead" would God fulfil His word and give him a son. God's opportunity does not come until man's extremity is reached. This is a lesson we sorely need to take to heart, for it is of great practical importance. It might be tersely expressed thus: the Lord has a reason for all His *delays.* God not only does that which is right and best but He always acts at the right and best time. Mark, it was not until "the *fulness* of time had come, God sent forth His Son, made of a woman" (Gal. 4:4). Is not this the explanation of what is a sore problem to many hearts? We mean, God's delay in sending back His Son the *second* time. Like one of old, we are often tempted to ask, "Why is His chariot so long in coming? Why tarry the wheels of His chariots?" (Judges 5:28). Ah! here is the answer—the "*fulness* of time" has not yet arrived. God has a wise and good reason for the delay. What that is we learn from 2 Peter 3:9: "The Lord is not slack concerning His promise (to send back His Son—see v. 4), as some men count slackness; but is long-suffering to usward, not willing that any should perish, but that all should come to repentance." God's delay in sending back His Son is due to His *long-sufferance,* not willing that any should perish.

Let us repeat what we have said above and apply it to another perplexing problem. God has a reason for His delays. Not until man comes to the end of himself will God put forth His power. Not until man's extremity is reached does God's opportunity arrive. Not until our own powers are "*dead*" will God act in grace. What is the great lesson of Psalm 107 but this? "They wandered in the wilderness in a solitary way; they found no city to dwell in. Hungry and thirsty, their soul *fainted* in them. *Then* they cried unto the Lord in their trouble, and He delivered them out of their distresses....Therefore He brought down their heart with labor; they fell down, *and there was none to help. Then* they cried unto the Lord in their trouble, and He saved them out of their distresses....They that go down to the sea in ships, that do business in great waters; These see the works of the Lord, and His wonders in the deep. For He commandeth, and raiseth the stormy wind, which lifteth up the waves thereof. They mount up to the heaven, they go down again to the depths: their soul is melted because of trouble. They reel to and fro and stagger like a drunken man, and are *at their wit's end. Then* they cry unto the Lord in their trouble, and He bringeth them out of their distresses" (Ps. 107:4-6, 12, 13, 23-28). Ah! it is when we are at our "wit's end," when all our own devices have failed and all our own efforts come to nought, that we "cry unto the Lord in our trouble," and "then" He bringeth us out of our distresses.

Beloved reader, apply now this principle *to your own individual life.* Are you anxiously exercised over God's *delay?* He has some wise purpose for it. He had with Abram, and He has with you. From seventy-five—his age when he left Haran—to one hundred—when Isaac was born—was a long time to wait, but the sequel evidenced the Lord's wisdom. God has more than one reason for His delays. Often it is to test the faith of His children, to develop their patience, to bring them to the end of themselves. His delays are in order that when He does act His delivering power may be more plainly evident, that what He does may be more deeply appreciated, and that in consequence He may be more illustriously glorified.

"And when Abram was ninety years old and nine, the Lord appeared to Abram, and said unto him, I am the Almighty God; walk before Me, and be thou perfect" (Gen. 17:1). These words are to be regarded first as a *reproof.* It was as though the Lord had said, "Have recourse no more to unbelieving expedients; keep now to the path of uprightness, and leave Me to fulfil My promise in My own good time and way." This opening verse of Genesis 17 needs to be read in the light of God's original promise to Abram to give him a "seed" (Gen. 13:15, 16) and the attempt made by our patriarch to obtain fulfilment by his own efforts. What Abram needed to be reminded of was God's *Almightiness.* It was for want of considering this that he had had recourse to crooked devices. Another lesson this which *we* do well to mark—never to employ unlawful means in seeking to promote the cause of God. How much the Lord's *servants* need to heed this truth! Like Abram, they are longing for seed, spiritual seed, but it comes not; and only too often they resort to unworthy methods to produce seed of themselves, arguing that the end justifies the means. Here is the effectual cure for all impatient anxiety—to reckon on One who is all-gracious, all-powerful, all-sufficient.

"And when Abram was ninety years old and nine, the Lord appeared to Abram, and said unto him, I am the Almighty God; walk before Me, and be thou perfect" (Gen. 17:1). But again. These words must be regarded as a blessed exhibition of *Divine Love.* It is written that "Love suffereth long, and is kind." How this was exemplified in God's dealings with the patriarchs of old! How they tried that love! How often they grieved it! How often they acted unworthily of it! Yet, notwithstanding, as it was with the apostles so it was with the patriarchs—"Having loved His own which were in the world, He loved them to the end" (John 13:1). How patiently God bore with Abram! It was *love* that "suffered long" with Abram's failings! It was *love* that persisted with him in spite of every check and drawback. It was *love* that now met him and promised to grant the desire of his heart, and in old age give him a son. And, Christian readers, is it not Divine Love that still "suffers long" with each of us! Would we not have perished long ago were it not that nothing is able to separate us from the love of God in Christ Jesus? Ah, note the last three words. It is the love of God *in Christ Jesus.* That love is a *righteous* love and not a sickly sentimentality at the expense of holiness. In the epistle which tells us that God is Love, we *first* read that "God is *Light*" (see 1 John 1:5; 4:8). But to return to Genesis 17:1.

"And when Abram was ninety years old and nine, the Lord appeared to Abram and said unto him, I am *the Almighty God.*" The revelation which God here made of Himself was well suited to the occasion. This was the first time that He revealed Himself as "the Almighty." None but *One* who possessed all power could meet Abram's need at this time. Ninety and nine years of age, his body dead; Sarah barren and long past the age of child-bearing—how could they hope to have a son? But with God all things are possible. And why? Because He is El Shaddai, the All-Sufficient One. The "Almighty" is a title which strikes terror into the hearts of the wicked, but to the righteous it is a haven of rest. "The name of the Lord is a strong tower: the righteous runneth into it, and is safe" (Prov. 18:10).

The second time that the Lord revealed Himself as El Shaddai was under circumstances very similar to those found in Genesis 17:1 and context. "And God appeared unto Jacob again, when he came out of Padam-aram, and blessed him. And God said unto him, Thy name is Jacob: thy name shall not be called any more Jacob, but Israel shall be thy name; and He called his name Israel. And God said unto him, I am God Almighty: be fruitful and multiply; a nation and a company of nations shall be of thee, and kings shall come out of thy loins" (Gen. 35:9-11). It will be noted that when God revealed Himself as *the Almighty* to Abram, He changed his name from Abram to Abraham; so here, He changes the name of his grandson from Jacob to Israel. To Abram God said, "And I will make My covenant between Me and thee, and *will multiply thee exceedingly*....and thou shalt be a father of many nations" (17:2, 4); to Jacob He said, "Be fruitful and multiply; a nation and a *company of nations* shall be of thee" (35:11). Again, we are told that God "appeared" to Abram (17:1), literally "was seen to Abram," and here in 35:9 the same word is used—this is the more striking for, excepting 12:7, these are the only occasions in Genesis where we read of God "appearing" to the patriarchs, as though to emphasize the importance of this Divine title. Finally, in noting the parallelisms between Genesis 17 and 35, we may observe that at the close of this Divine interview we read "And He left off talking with him, and God *went up* from Abraham" (Gen. 17:22) and in 35:13 we are told, "And God *went up* from him in the place where He talked with him."

It is blessed to remember that this same divine title is found in the Church epistles: "Wherefore come out from among them (as Abram did from Chaldea), and be ye separate saith the Lord, and touch not the unclean thing (as Abram did with Hagar); and I will receive you, And will be a Father unto you, and ye shall be My sons and daughters, saith *the Lord Almighty*" (2 Cor. 6:17, 18). It is because *our* God and Father is the "Almighty" that *"He is able* also to save them to the uttermost that come unto God by Him"—Christ (Heb. 7:25). It is because our God and Father is the "Almighty" that *"He is able* to succor them that are tempted" (Heb. 2:18). It is because our God and Father is the "Almighty" that nothing "shall *be able* to separate us from the love of God which is in Christ Jesus our Lord" (Rom. 8:39). It is because our Saviour is "Almighty" that He shall "change our vile body, that it may be fashioned like unto His glorious body, according to the working whereby *He is able* even to subdue all things unto Himself" (Phil. 3:21). It is because our God is the "Almighty" that He "*is able* to do exceeding abundantly above all that we ask or think, according to the power that worketh in us" (Eph. 3:20). It is because our Lord is "Almighty" that He "*is able* to keep us from falling, and to present us faultless before the presence of His glory with exceeding joy (Jude 24).

"And when Abram was ninety years old and nine, the Lord appeared to Abram, and said unto him, I am the Almighty God; *walk before Me,* and be thou perfect" (Gen. 17:1). We would call attention to four passages which refer to the walk of the Lord's people in which a different preposition is used. Here in Genesis 17:1 Abram is bidden to "walk *before*" Almighty God. The children of Israel were exhorted to "walk *after*" the Lord: "Ye shall walk after the Lord your God, and fear Him, and keep His commandments" (Deut. 13:4). Of Enoch and Noah it is witnessed that they "walked *with* God" (Gen. 5:24; 6:9). But of those who are members of the Body of Christ the word is, "As ye have therefore received Christ Jesus the Lord, so walk ye *in* Him" (Col. 2:6). To walk *before* is suggestive of a child running ahead and playing in the presence of his father, conscious of his perfect *security* because he is just behind. To walk *after* becomes a servant following his master. To walk *with* indicates fellowship and friendship. To walk *in* denotes union. As to *how* we are to walk in Christ, the Holy Spirit tells us in the words which immediately follow the exhortation: "Rooted and built up in Him" (Col. 2:7). We might summarize these varied aspects of the believer's walk as intimated by the four different prepositions thus: we walk "before" God as *children;* we walk "after" Him as *servants;* we walk "with" Him as His *friends;* we walk "in" Him as *members of His body.*

"Be thou perfect." The careful reader will notice that the words "upright" and "sincere" are supplied in the margin as alternatives for "perfect," but it seems to us there is no need for this, that the word in the text is a legit-

imate rendering of the Hebrew "tamin." The same word occurs in Psalm 19:7: "The Law (Word) of the Lord is *perfect,* converting the soul." It is the same word which is translated forty-four times "without blemish." Then, did God really say to Abram, "Be thou *perfect?*" He certainly did. And how could He say anything less? What lower standard than that of perfection can the Perfect One set before His creatures? Only too often men whittle down the Word to make it square with their own conceptions. All through the Scriptures, the standard of *perfection* is set before us. The law required that Israel should love the Lord their God with *all* their hearts. The Lord Jesus bade His disciples, "Be ye therefore perfect as your Father which is in heaven is perfect" (Matt. 5:48). And the teaching of the Epistles is all summed up in that Word, "Christ also suffered for us, leaving us an example, that ye should follow His steps" (1 Pet. 2:21). Is not that the standard of perfection? Brethren, such *is* the standard set before us. This is that which we are constantly to strive after. With nothing short may we be satisfied. It is because *such* is the standard that none in the flesh have ever realized it, that each and all must say with the apostle, "Not as though I had already attained, either were already perfect; but I follow after, if that I may apprehend that for which also I am aprehended of Christ Jesus. Brethren, I count not myself to have apprehended: but this one thing I do, forgetting those things which are behind, and reaching forth unto those things which are before, I press toward the mark for the prize of the high calling of God in Christ Jesus" (Phil. 3:12-14). Yet, nevertheless, the Word to us today is the same as that to Abram of old: "Be thou perfect." Does some one murmur, "An impossible standard!" Then remember that it was El Shaddai who gave it. Who dares to talk of "impossibilities" when the Almighty is our God? Has He not said "My grace is sufficient for thee"? Then, do not charge Him with setting before us an unattainable standard: rather let us charge ourselves with failure to rest upon His Almighty arm, and confess with shame that the blame is ours through not appropriating His all-sufficient grace.

"And Abram *fell on his face:* and God talked with him" (Gen. 17:3). It seems to us that this act of Abram in prostrating himself before the Lord must be looked at in the light of his ways as recorded in the previous chapter—his taking of matters into his own hands instead of leaving them with God; his resorting to fleshly expediences instead of patiently waiting for Him to act. And now that Jehovah condescends to reveal Himself again to Abram, he is overwhelmed at such grace. Thus we regard Abram's falling on his face not so much due to confusion as to wonderment at the divine favor shown him notwithstanding his unbelief.

We cannot now comment upon the remaining verses of the chapter, but in closing would call attention to one other feature. It is to be noted that in connection with the revelation of Himself as the "Almighty" the Lord God made Abram a composite promise in which *seven times* He said "I will"—"And *I will* make thee exceeding fruitful, and *I will* make nations of thee, and kings shall come out of thee. And *I will* establish My covenant between Me and thee and thy seed after thee in their generations, for an everlasting covenant to be a God unto thee and to thy seed after thee. And *I will* give unto thee, and to thy seed after thee the land wherein thou art a stranger, all the land of Canaan, for an everlasting possession; and *I will* be their God....And God said, Sarah thy wife shall bear thee a son indeed: and thou shalt call his name Isaac: and *I will* establish my covenant with him for an everlasting covenant, and with his seed after him....But My covenant *will I* establish with Isaac" (vs. 6, 7, 8, 19, 21). The relationship between this compound promise and the title of Deity used on the occasion of its utterance is the pledge of its fulfilment. It is because all power is at His disposal, it is because He is sufficient in Himself, that the performing of all He has said is sure. What God says He will do. So sure is the fulfilment that in verse 5 the Lord says, "for a father of many nations *have I* made thee" (not "will I make thee"), just as in Romans 8:30 it is "whom He justified them He also glorified," and yet in experience the glorification is yet future.

With the above seven "I wills" of God should be compared the seven "I wills" of Exodus 6:6-8, "Wherefore say unto the children of Israel, I am the Lord, and *I will* bring you out from under the burdens of the Egyptians, and *I will* rid you of their bondage, and *I will* redeem you with a stretched out arm, and with great judgments: and *I will* take you to be a people, and *I will* be to you a God:

and ye shall know that I am the Lord your God, which bringeth you out from under the burdens of the Egyptians. And *I will* bring you in unto the land, concerning the which I did sware to give it to Abraham, to Isaac and to Jacob; and *I will* give it you for a heritage : I am the Lord." Our purpose in calling attention to this latter passage is that in Genesis 16 the Lord revealed Himself to Abram as the Almighty and followed the revelation with a sevenfold promise, and here in Exodus 6 He reveals Himself as Jehovah (v. 3) and follows this revelation with another sevenfold promise. Perfect are the ways and perfect is the Word of Him with whom we have to do.

23. ABRAHAM AT GERAR

Genesis 20

In our last chapter we considered at some length the revelation which God made of Himself to Abraham as the Almighty, together with the sevenfold promise which accompanied this revelation, including, as it did, that Abraham and Sarah should be given Isaac in their old age. In Genesis 18 we behold the Lord in full fellowship with the one He thrice terms His "friend," eating at his table, and making known his purpose concerning Sodom; while at the close of the chapter Abraham is seen as an intercessor before God. And now, in Genesis 20, we are to witness a sad and dramatic change. There is a return to the miserable policy which he followed down in Egypt. Afraid that his life may be taken from him on account of his wife, he causes her to pose as his sister, and only through a direct interposition by God is she delivered from the effects of his sin.

"And Abraham journeyed from thence toward the south country and dwelt between Kadesh and Shur, and sojourned in Gerar. And Abraham said of Sarah his wife, She is my sister: and Abimelech, King of Gerar, sent and took Sarah" (Gen. 20:1, 2). The contents of Genesis 20 furnish a striking proof of the Divine inspiration of the Scriptures. No fictitious historian would have recorded this dark blot on the life of such an illustrious personage as Abraham. The tendency of the human heart is ever toward hero worship, and the common custom of biographers is to conceal the defects and blemishes in the careers of the characters which they delineate, and this, had it been followed, would naturally forbid the mention of such a sad fall in the life of one of the most venerated names on the scroll of history. Ah! but herein the Bible differs from all other books. The Holy Spirit has painted the portraits of Scripture characters in the colors of nature and truth. He has given a faithful picture of the human heart such as is common to all mankind.

At first sight it seems incredible that Abraham should have acted as recorded here in Genesis 20, but further reflection will convince any honest Christian that the picture here drawn is only too true to life: "As in water face answereth to face, so the heart of man to man" (Prov. 27:19). The remaining of the old nature in the believer, the occasional manifestations of it in God-dishonoring activities, the awful backslidings which God's children have been subject to in all ages, and the reviewing of our own sad departures from the path of faith and righteousness, are quite enough to *explain* the deplorable and seemingly unaccountable conduct of the father of all who believe. And if the reader knows nothing of such departures and backslidings let him not boast of *his* faithfulness and superior piety, rather let him ascribe all glory to the matchless grace of Him that is *able* to keep us from falling.

Sad indeed, inexpressibly sad, was Abraham's conduct. It was not the fall of a young and inexperienced disciple, but the lapse of one who had long walked the path of faith that here shows himself ready to sacrifice the honor of his wife, and what is worse, give up the one who was the depositary of all the promises. "What then is man, and what hope for him except in God None, surely. And it is to ground us well in this that we are given to see the sad and terrible failures of these honored servants of God. Not to discourage but to lead us to the Source of all comfort and strength. Only in realized weakness do we find this. Only when unable to do without God for a moment do we find what He is for us moment by moment" (F. W. Grant).

What made the matter so much worse in Abraham's case was that it was not a question of being surprised into a sudden fault. It was the recurrence of an old sin. Long ago he had followed the same wicked course in Egypt, where his duplicity had been discovered and from whence he was banished in disgrace. But the experience profited him not. Some twenty or twenty-five years had passed since then, and in the interval he had built an altar unto the Lord, had vanquished Chedorlaomer, had been blessed by Melchizedek the priest of the Most High God, had repulsed the offer of the King of Sodom to be enriched at his hands, and had received wondrous revelations and promises from God; yet now we see him leaving God out of his reckoning, and ensnared by the fear of man, resorting to the most shameful deception. How then shall we account for this? The explanation is obvious: until the time referred to in Genesis 20 Abraham had not been in circumstances to call into exercise the evil that was in his heart.

"The evil was not *fully brought out*—not confessed, not got rid of—and the proof of this is, that the moment he again finds himself in circumstances which could act upon *his weak point,* it is at once made manifest that the weak point is there. The temptation through which he passed in the matter of the King of Sodom was not by any means calculated to touch this peculiar point; nor was anything that occurred to him from the time that he came up out of Egypt until he went down to Gerar calculated to touch it, for had it been touched it would no doubt have exhibited itself.

"We can never know what is in our hearts until circumstances arise to draw it out. Peter did not imagine he could deny his Lord, but when he got into circumstances which were calculated to act upon his peculiar weakness, he showed that his weakness was there.

"It required the protracted period of forty years in the wilderness to teach the children of Israel 'what was in their hearts' (Deut. 8:2); and it is one of the grand results of the course of discipline through which each child of God passes, to lead him into a more profound knowledge of his own weakness and nothingness. 'We had the *sentence of death in ourselves,* that we should not trust in ourselves but in God which raiseth the dead' (2 Cor. 1:9). The more we are growing in the sense of our infirmities, the more shall we see our need of clinging more closely to Christ—drawing more largely upon His grace, and entering more fully into the cleansing virtue and value of His atoning blood. The Christian, at the opening of his course never knows his own heart; indeed, he could not bear the full knowledge of it; he would be overwhelmed thereby. 'The Lord leads us not by the way of the Philistines lest we should see war,' and so be plunged into despair. But He graciously leads us by a circuitous route, in order that our apprehension of His grace may keep pace with our growing self-knowledge" (C. H. M.).

As we have seen, it was *stress of circumstances* which revealed the state of Abraham's heart, as it is of ours. Though the wording of it might be improved, we thoroughly agree with the sentiment of a preacher who long ago said, "We possess no more religion than what we have in the time of trouble." It is comparatively easy to trust God while everything goes along pleasantly, but the time of disappointment, of loss, of persecution, of bereavement, is the time of testing; and then how often we fail! Here is where the Lord Jesus is in such striking *contrast* from all others. Stress of circumstances only served to display the *perfections* of His heart. When He was a hungered, and tempted by Satan to make bread to supply His own need, He lived by every word of God. When He sat by the well, worn with His journey, He was not too weary to speak words of grace and life to the poor Samaritan woman. When the cities in which His mightiest works had been done rejected His message, He meekly submitted, saying "Even so, Father: for so it seemed good in Thy sight" (Matt. 11:23-26). When He was reviled, He reviled not again. And in the supreme crisis, on the cross, His perfections were fully displayed—praying for the forgiveness of His enemies, speaking the word of acceptance to the repentant thief, making provision for His widowed mother, yielding up His spirit into the hands of the Father. Ah! *our* garments (symbols of conduct, habits, ways) are at best, so much patchwork, but *His* were "*without seam,* woven *from the top* throughout" (John 19:23). Yes, in *all things* He has the preëminence.

Light is thrown upon Abraham's fall by the thirteenth verse of our chapter—"And it came to pass, when God caused me to wander from my father's house, that I said unto her, This is thy kindness which thou shalt shew unto me; at every place whither we shall come, say of me, He is my brother." It is to be noted that this arrangement entered into by Abraham with his wife, was made *before* they left Chaldea. It was therefore something which they brought with them from the place of their birth! In other words, it was that which was attached to the *old* man and, as we have seen, something which had never been *judged.* Let us learn then from this, the vileness of the flesh, the utter corruption of the old nature, the hideousness of the old man. Truly there is need for us to "mortify" our members which are on the earth.

Plainly, the evil compact which Abraham made with Sarah was due to the feebleness of his faith in God's power to take care of them. And once more, let not writer or reader sit in pharisaic judgment upon Abraham, but see a picture of himself. Abraham did but illustrate what is all too sadly common among the Lord's people—that which might be termed the *inconsistency* of faith. How often those who are not afraid to trust God with their souls, *are* afraid to trust Him with regard to their bodies! How often those who have the full assurance of faith in regard to eternal things, are full of unbelief and fear when it comes to temporal things! We have believed in the Lord and it has been counted unto us for righteousness; yet, how often, like Abraham, in the matter of the practical concerns of our daily life, we too, have more confidence in our own wisdom and scheming than we have in the sufficiency of God.

And how did God act? Did He lose patience with Abraham, and cast off one so fickle and inconsistent? Manifestly Abraham had dishonored the Lord in acting as he did, in setting such an evil example before these heathen (Philistines). Yet, behold the *grace* of Him with whom we have to do. Instead of casting him off, God interposed and delivered Abraham and his wife from the peril which menaced them. Not only did God not forsake Abraham, but He would not abandon him to his foes. Ah! the gifts and calling of God are "without repentance." And why? Because they are bestowed altogether without respect to any worthiness in the recipient, and hence, because God's gifts are free and we do nothing to merit them, we can do nothing to demerit them.

"The soul that on Jesus hath leaned for repose,
I will not, I will not desert to his foes;
That soul, though all Hell should endeavor to shake,
I'll never, no never, no never forsake."

"But God came to Abimelech in a dream by night, and said to him, Behold, thou art but a dead man, for the woman which thou hast taken; for she is a man's wife" (Gen. 20:3). This statement may appear very commonplace to the casual reader—the mere narration of a detail lacking in importance. But the meditative mind discovers here an exemplification of a truth of profound importance and high value, though one that is now generally lost sight of. We refer to the *universality* of God's rule; the *absolute* control which he has over His creatures; the *ease* with which He can move men to accomplish His will. God has access to *all* minds and can impress them by a dream, an affliction, or in any way He thinks proper. In the above case God used a dream to instruct Abimelech, to show him the wrong he had unconsciously done, and to point out to him his immediate duty. Abimelech was a Philistine, and, so far as we know to the contrary, a heathen. He knew nothing of the fact that Sarah was the one chosen to be the mother of the Jewish race, and the one from whom, according to the flesh, the Messiah was to come. Appearances seemed to show that Jehovah's purpose was in immediate danger of being foiled. But how simply God dealt with the situation! By means of a *dream,* nothing more, Sarah is delivered, the seeming hindrances to God's purpose is removed, the situation is saved! What we here desire to emphasize is the perfect ease with which God can move men *when He pleases.* All this modern talk about man's "freedom" and man's going his own way in defiance of God's secret counsels leaves God out entirely. To say that God wants to influence men but that men will not let Him is to reduce the Almighty to a helpless spectator, full of gracious intentions but lacking in power to make them good. But what saith the Scriptures? Hear them: "The king's heart is in the hand of the Lord, as the rivers of water: He turneth it whithersoever He will" (Prov. 21:1). Yes, and so easily can He turn the king's heart, that when He pleases He needs employ nothing more than a "dream"!

"And God said unto him in a dream, Yea, I know that thou didst this in the integrity of thy heart; for I also withheld thee from sinning against Me: therefore suffered I thee not to touch her" (Gen. 20:6). In these words we have (as so often in Scripture) an apparently incidental statement which throws great light upon a difficult problem and which positively refutes the proud reasoning of the philosophic theologians. How often it has been said that in endowing Adam with the power of choice God was *unable* to prevent his fall. But how untenable are such theorizings in the face of the above passage! If God could "withhold" Abimelech from sinning against Him, then had He pleased He could have done the same with our first parents. Should it be asked *why* He did not "withhold" Adam from sinning, the answer must be that He permitted sin to enter that opportunity might be given to display His *grace.*

"Therefore Abimelech rose early in the morning, and called all his servants, and told all these things in their ears and the men were sore afraid. Then Abimelech called Abraham, and said unto him, What hast thou done unto us? and what have I offended thee, that thou hast brought on me and on my kingdom a great sin? thou hast done deeds unto me that ought not to be done'' (Gen. 20:8, 9). It is important to note that Abimelech recognized fornication as a ''great sin.'' Unquestionably the heathen are aware of the criminality of many of the sinful acts which they commit—''their conscience also bearing witness, and their thoughts the meanwhile *accusing* or else excusing one another'' (Rom. 2:15).

A brief consideration of one other thought and our space is exhausted. Notice how differently God looked at and spoke of Abraham from Abimelech's words concerning him —''Now therefore restore the man his wife; for he is a *prophet,* and he shall *pray for thee* and thou shalt live.'' All that Abimelech saw in our patriarch was a man guilty of barefaced deception. But God looked at Abraham in Christ, and therefore speaks of him as a ''prophet'' (one who has His mind), and makes Abimelech debtor to his prayers! This is how God ever vindicates His own before the unbelieving. It was a similar case to what He said through Balaam concerning Israel at a later date—''He hath not beheld iniquity in Jacob, neither hath He seen perverseness in Israel'' (Num. 23:21). In some such way as this is now being answered on high the charges of the enemy who accuses the brethren before God day and night. Oh! blessed fact, ''There is therefore now *no condemnation* to them which are in Christ Jesus.'' Will this encourage careless living? God forbid, ''For sin shall not have dominion over you: for ye are not under the law, but under grace.''

24. ABRAHAM "THE FATHER OF US ALL"

It is to be feared that many who read the Old Testament, particularly its earlier books, look upon these Scriptures as little more than historical narratives, as simply containing a description of certain events that happened in the far distant past, and that when they come to the record of the lives of the patriarchs they discover nothing beyond a piece of ancient biography. But surely this is very dishonoring to God. Is it not obvious that when we relegate to a remote date in the past what we are told about Abraham, Isaac, Joseph, etc., and see in the inspired record little or nothing applicable to ourselves today, that we virtually and practically reduce Genesis to a *dead book?* Suppose we express this in another way: If Genesis is a part of "The Word *of Life*" (Phil. 2:16), then it is a living book, charged with vitality; a book which must have about it a *freshness* which no other book, outside of the Sacred Canon, possesses; a book which speaks to *our* day, which is pertinent and applicable to *our own* times.

Let us now follow out another line of thought which will lead us to the same point at which we arrived at the close of the preceding paragraph. One truth which Scripture reveals about God is, that He changes not, for He is "the same yesterday, and today, and forever." Therefore, it follows that, fundamentally, His *ways* are ever the same; that is to say, He deals through all time with men, especially His own people, upon the same principles. It is this which explains the well-known fact that so often history *repeats* itself. Having stated the broad principle, let us now apply it. If what we have just said is correct, should we not expect to find that God's dealings with Abraham forecast and foreshadow His dealings *with us?* That, stripped of their incidental details, the experiences of Abraham illustrate *our* experiences? Grant this, and we reach a similar conclusion (as we anticipated) to the one expressed at the close of the preceding paragraph. Let us now *combine* the two conceptions.

Because the Bible is a living book no portion of it is *obsolete,* and though much that is recorded in it is ancient, yet none of it is *antiquated*. Because the Bible is a living book, every portion of it has some message which is applicable and appropriate to our own times. Because God changes not, His ways of old are, fundamentally, His ways today. Hence, God's dealings with Abraham, in the general, foreshadow His dealings with us. Therefore, to read most profitably the record of Abraham's life, we must see in it a portrayal of our own spiritual history. Before we attempt to particularize, let us take one other starting point and lead up to the place where we here leave off.

"Therefore it is of faith, that it might be by grace; to the end the promise might be sure to all the seed; not to that only which is of the law, but to that also which is of the faith of Abraham; who is the father of us all" (Rom. 4:16). *How* is Abraham the "father" of *us* all? *In what sense* is he such? Not, of course, literally, by procreation, but figuratively, by typification. Just as naturally the son inherits certain traits from his father, just as there is a *resemblance* between them, just as Adam "begat a son in his own likeness, after his image" (Gen. 5:3), so there is a resemblance and likeness between Abraham and those who are "Abraham's seed and heirs according to the promise" (Gal. 3:29). In a word, Abraham is to be regarded as a *sample believer*. Thus there will be a close correspondence, in the broad outline, between Abraham's history and ours. And here, once more, we reach the same point as at the close of each of the above paragraphs. We are now prepared to test the accuracy of these conclusions and follow them out in some detail.

I read, then, the life of Abraham as recorded in Genesis, not *merely* as a piece of inspired *history* (though truly it is such), not as an obsolete narrative of something which happened in the far distant past, but also, and specially, as a portrayal of the experiences of Abraham's children in all ages, and as a description of God's dealings with His own in all time. To particularize: What was Abraham at the beginning? A lost sinner; one who knew not God; an idolator. So were we: "Wherefore remember, that ye being in time past Gentiles....that at that time ye were without Christ, being aliens from the commonwealth of Israel, and strangers from the covenants of promise, having no hope, and without God in the world" (Eph. 2:11, 12). What happened? The God of glory appeared unto him (Acts 7:2). So it was with us. He revealed Himself to us. What was the next thing? God's call to Abraham to separate himself from everything which pertained to his old life. Such is God's call to us—to separate ourselves from the world and everything of it. Did Abraham obey? At first only imperfectly. Instead of leaving his kindred as commanded, Terah his father and Lot his nephew accompanied him as he left Chaldea. Has this no voice for us? Does it not solemnly condemn Abraham's "children"? Has not *our* response to God's call of separation been tardy and partial? To proceed: Soon after Abraham arrived in Canaan painful circumstances try his faith—a "famine" arose. How did this affect him? Did he make known his need to God and look to Him to meet it? Ah, can we not supply the answer from *our own* sad experience? Have we not turned to the world for help and deliverance in the hour of emergency, as Abraham turned to Egypt? See Abraham again in Genesis 16. He is childless. God has promised that his seed should inherit the land. But years have passed and Sarah is still barren. What does Abraham do? Does he patiently wait upon God and go on waiting? Suppose the Bible had not told us, could not our own experience supply the answer once more? Abraham has recourse to *fleshly* means, and drags in Hagar to *assist* God (?) in the furtherance of His purpose. And what was the outcome? Did *God* lose patience? Well He might. But *did* He cast off His erring child? Has He dealt thus with us? No, indeed, "If we believe not, yet He *abideth* faithful" (2 Tim. 2:13). We need not review Abraham's life any further. Do you not see now, dear reader, *why* Abraham is termed the "*father* of us all"? Is not the saying of the world—"Like father, like son"—true here? But let us look at one other line in the picture ere we leave it. Look at Abraham in Genesis 22, offering up Isaac. Does this apply to us? Is there anything in the experiences of Christians today which corresponds with the scene enacted on Mount Moriah? Surely, but note *when* this occurred—not at the beginning, but near the *close* of Abraham's pilgrimage. Ah! life's discipline had not been in vain: the fire had done its work, the gold had been refined. At the last Abraham had reached the place where he is not only willing to give up Terah and Lot at the call of God, but where he is ready to lay his *Isaac* upon the altar! In other words, he resigns *all* to God, and places at *His* feet the dearest idol of his heart. Grace had triumphed, for grace alone can bring the human heart into entire submission to the Divine will. So will grace triumph with us in the end. See, then, in Abraham's up and down experiences, his trials, his failures, a representation of *yours.* See in God's patient dealings with Abraham a portrayal of His dealings with *you.* See in the final triumph of grace in Abraham the promise of its ultimate triumph in *you,* and thus will Genesis be a *living* book by translating it into the *present.*

Deeply important are the lessons to be learned from the life of Abraham, and many are the precious truths which are seen illustrated in his character and career. Having looked at him as a simple believer, let us next consider him as a *Man of Faith.* In Hebrews 11, the great faith chapter, Abraham is given striking prominence. Only once do we read "By faith Isaac," and only once do we read "By faith Jacob"; but *three times* the faith of Abraham is mentioned (see vs. 8, 9, 17). Probably it is no exaggeration to say that Abraham's faith was tried more severely, more repeatedly, and more varisomely than that of any other human being. First, he was called upon to leave the land of his birth, to separate himself from home and kindred, and to set out on a long journey unto a land which God promised to "show" him, and, we are told, "he went out not knowing whither he went." After his arrival in the new land he did not enter into occupation of it, but instead, sojourned there as a stranger and pilgrim. All that he ever *owned* in it was a burying-place. Dwelling in tents with Isaac and Jacob, he remained there well-nigh a century. Again, his faith was tested in connection with God's promise to give him a son by Sarah. His own body "dead," and his wife long past the age of child-bearing, nevertheless "he staggered not at the promise of God through unbelief; but was strong in faith, giving glory to God; and being fully persuaded that, what He had promised, He was able also to perform" (Rom. 4:20, 21). Finally, the supreme test came when he was bidden to offer up his son Isaac, but, "By faith Abraham, when he was tried, offered up Isaac: and he that had received the promises offered up his only begotten son.... accounting that God was able to raise him up, even from the dead" (Heb. 11:17, 19).

But did Abraham's faith never waiver? Alas, it did. He was a man of like passions to ourselves, and in him, too, there was an evil heart of *unbelief*. The Spirit of God has faithfully portrayed the dark as well as the fair side, and were it not that we are painfully conscious of the tragic history of our own spiritual lives, we might well marvel at the strange mingling of faith and unbelief, obedience and disobedience. By faith Abraham *obeyed* when God called him to leave Chaldea; yes, but by unbelief he *disobeyed* in that his father and nephew accompanied him in direct contravention of Jehovah's express command. By faith he left Chaldea, but by unbelief he stopped short at Haran (Gen. 11:31). By faith he *entered* the land of promise, but as soon as a famine arose he *forsook* it and went down to Egypt (Gen. 12:10). By faith he returned and sojourned in the land of promise, but by unbelief he took to himself the maid Hagar rather than wait for God to put forth His power and give him a son by Sarah. By faith he went forth against Chedorlaomer and his armies to rescue Lot, but later, by unbelief he lied to Abimelech about his wife (Gen. 20:21). What a sad exemplification is all this of the *two* natures in the believer!

How terribly *inconsistent* are the lives of God's saints! By faith Israel crossed the Red Sea, but a little later, in unbelief, they feared they had been brought into the wilderness to perish from hunger. With heart stayed upon the Lord, David feared not to engage the mighty Goliath, yet the time came when he fled from Saul. Filled with confidence in Jehovah, Elijah, single-handed, faced the four hundred prophets of Baal, but within a few hours he ran in terror from an angry woman. Peter was not afraid to step out on to the sea, nor was he intimated in the presence of the Roman soldiers, but drew his sword and smote off the ear of the high priest's servant; yet, the same night, he trembled before a maid and dared not to confess his Lord. Oh! the God dishonoring ways of unbelief! Unbelief! Surely this is the sin which doth *so easily* beset us.

Do not the above histories *and their sequels bring* out the marvelous and gracious *long-suffering* of Him with whom we have to do? How patiently God deals with His people! Israel *did not* perish with hunger in the wilderness, even though they murmured against God; instead, they were fed with "angel's food" (Ps. 78:25)! David *was not* slain by

Saul, even though he did flee from him; instead, he was afterwards exalted to the throne of Israel! Elijah *did not* fall a victim to the wrath of Jezebel, though his faith did fail him; instead, he was afterwards taken to heaven without seeing death at all! Peter *was not* disowned because he denied his Lord, nay, after his restoration, he had the signal honor of opening the door of the kingdom both to the Jews and to the Gentiles! So it was with Abraham. God did not abandon him when his faith faltered, but dealt gently and patiently with him, leading him on step by step, disciplining him in the school of experience, until by wondrous grace He enabled him to do by faith on Mount Moriah that which was a type of Calvary itself!

The divine dealings with Abraham wonderfully demonstrated *God's Sovereignty.* A unique honor was conferred upon our patriarch, for he was chosen by God to be the father of the chosen nation, that nation from which, according to the flesh, Christ was to come. And mark how God's Sovereignty was displayed in the *character* of the one selected by Him. There was nothing in Abraham by nature to commend him to Jehovah. By descent he belonged to a family of idolaters. Ere he left Chaldea, in response to God's call, he entered into an evil compact with his wife (Gen. 12:7). As though to give special emphasis to their *unworthiness,* God said to Israel, "Look unto Abraham, your father, and unto Sarah that bore you: for I called him alone—look unto the rock whence ye are hewn, and to *the hole of the pit* whence ye are digged" (Isa. 51:2, 1). And Abraham, the father of us all, was a pattern or sample case. God's choice before the foundation of the world was not determined by any good or merit foreseen in ourselves. Election itself is of "*grace*" (Rom. 11:5). It is all of grace from beginning to end, sovereign grace, gratuitous grace, matchless grace.

Consider next Abraham as an object of God's *Love.* The history of our patriarch was one of strange vicissitudes. On no flowery beds of ease was he permitted to luxuriate. Painful were the trials he was called upon to endure. Again and again he passed through the waters and the fire, but there was ever One by him that forsook him not. As the father of them that believe, Abraham was, as we have seen, a representative believer. In kind though not in character the experiences of Abraham are the same we meet with.

Faith has to be tried that it may work patience: the gold has to be put in the crucible that it may be refined. God had one Son without sin, but none without suffering and sorrow. Whom the Lord *loveth* He chasteneth, and scourgeth *every* son whom He receiveth. First, Abraham had to endure the severance of nature's ties; at the call of God he had to leave home and kindred. And the word comes to us, too, "He that loveth father or mother more than Me, is not worthy of Me" (Matt. 10:37). Called to leave the land of his birth, to be a stranger and pilgrim in a foreign land, he was taught, as we are, that "Our citizenship is in heaven" (Phil. 3:20). The "strife" which arose between the herdmen of Abraham and Lot, necessitating the separation between our patriarch and his nephew, illustrates the fact that the path of faith is ofttimes a *lonesome* one, and that frequently we are obliged to walk apart from those loved by the flesh. The years of waiting that Abraham experienced ere the longing of his heart was gratified and a son was given him, exemplified that lesson, so hard to learn, that we must wait *only* upon Him with our expectation from Him. Finally, as Abraham was called upon to relinquish his Isaac and offer to God his only son, so we are required to place our all at His disposal, and in doing this we shall not be the losers any more than Abraham was. See, then, the love of God exercised toward the father of all who believe; love displayed in faithful chastening, and issuing in the peaceable fruit of righteousness.

There are many facets to this precious jewel. We have noted how God's long-sufferance, His sovereignty, His love were manifested toward Abraham; now observe His *matchless grace.* Is not this the only appropriate word to use here? Was it not *grace* that made Abraham the "*friend* of God"? Oh, wondrous condescension that should stoop so low as to lay hold of a worm of the earth! Oh, matchless benignity that should bring one of His own creatures into such intimate relationship with Himself! Oh, undeserved and unmerited favor that made him "the friend of God"! And mark *how* this friendship was exhibited. See how the Lord makes known to His "friend" what shall happen to his descendants for a long time (Gen. 15:13-16). Mark, again, how He takes him into His confidence and counsels respecting what He was about to do with Sodom (Gen. 18:17). Observe the Lord in intimate fellowship with Abraham, eating and drinking at his board (Gen. 18:8). Finally, consider how marvelously God took him into the *fellowship of His heart* (Gen. 22). Probably no other human being ever entered so deeply into the meaning and movements of the Father's heart at Calvary as did Abraham on Mount Moriah.

In the last place, let us look upon Abraham as a *typical character.* We do not know of any Old Testament personage who was such a *multifarious* type as was Abraham. First, he was a type of *the Father.* This is seen in his desire for children (compare Eph. 1:5); in his making a "feast" at the weaning of Isaac (compare Matt. 22:2-4); in the offering up of his only son Isaac (compare John 3:16); in his sending for a bride for his son (compare Rev. 21:9); in appointing his son heir of all things (25:5). Second, Abraham was a type of *Christ.* This is seen in him leaving his father's house at the call of God; in that he is the one in whom all the families of the earth are to be blessed; in that he is the kinsman—redeemer of Israel; in that he is the holder of headship of the nations. Third, he is a type of *the Church.* This is seen, particularly, in that he was a *stranger and pilgrim* in the earth. Observe that though he left his home in Chaldea he did not find another in Canaan; instead, he was the man of the tent. Note how this comes out toward the end of his life. When he needed a burying-place he purchased it of the children of Heth (Gen. 23:3, 4). He preferred to *buy* it rather than receive it as a gift from these worldlings. He would not be enriched by them any more than he would be a debtor to and accept favors from the king of Sodom. The *strangership* of Abraham was also displayed in the seeking of a wife for Isaac. He was a stranger in Canaan, so he sent to Haran! Thus, though he tabernacled in Canaan, he was sharply distinguished from the people of the land—he was *among* them but not *of* them. Fourth, Abraham was a type of *Israel.* This is seen in that he was the one to whom God gave Palestine; the one with whom God entered into a covenant; the one who was divinely preserved while dwelling in a strange country (Gen. 20); the one who, after a checkered career, was supernaturally quickened in old age, and the one who was ultimately joined to the Gentiles (Gen. 23).

May divine grace enable writer and reader to walk by faith and not by sight, to live in complete separation from the world as strangers and pilgrims, to render unto God a more prompt and unreserved obedience, to submit to His will and hold all at His disposal, and then shall we find with Abraham that the path of the just shineth more and more unto the perfect day.

25. THE BIRTH OF ISAAC

GENESIS 21

The birth of Isaac marked a pivotal point in the outworking of God's eternal purpose. The coming of this son to Abraham and Sarah was the second great step toward the fulfillment of Jehovah's plan. This purpose and plan was to have a people of His own, separate from the surrounding nations; a people to whom should be entrusted the Holy Oracles, a people of whom as concerning the flesh the Saviour was to be born; a people who should ultimately become the medium of blessing to all the earth. In the realization of this plan and purpose the first great step was the *selection* of Abram to be the father of the chosen nation, the *call* which separated him from the idolatrous people among whom he lived, and the *migration* unto the land which Jehovah promised to give him.

Some twenty-five years had now passed since Abram had left Ur of the Chaldees, and during these years he had received promise from the Lord that He would make of him a great nation (Gen. 12:2) and that He would make his seed as the dust of the earth (Gen. 13:16). But years went by and Abram remained childless: the promised seed had not been given and Abram was exercised and perplexed. "And Abram said, Lord God, what wilt Thou give me, seeing I go childless, and the steward of my house is this Eliezar of Damascus? And Abram said, Behold, to me Thou hast given no seed: and, lo, one born in my house is mine heir" (Gen. 15:2, 3). To these questions the Lord returned answer, "This shall not be thine heir; but he that shall come forth out of thine own bowels shall be thine heir" (Gen. 15:4). Another interval passed and yet no child appeared, and "Sarai said unto Abram, Behold, now, the Lord hath restrained me from bearing: I pray thee, go in unto my maid; it may be that I may obtain children by her. And Abram hearkened to the voice of Sarai, and he went in unto Hagar, and she conceived" (Gen. 16:2, 4). A further thirteen years dragged their weary course and

"God said unto Abraham, as for Sarai thy wife, thou shalt not call her name Sarai, but Sarah shall her name be. And I will bless her, and give thee a son also of her: yea, I will bless her, and she shall be a mother of nations: Kings of people shall be of her. Then Abraham fell upon his face, and laughed, and said in his heart, Shall a child be born unto him that is a hundred years old? And shall Sarah, that is ninety years old, bear? And Abraham said unto God, O that Ishmael might live before Thee! And God said, Sarah thy wife shall bear thee a son indeed; and thou shalt call his name Isaac" (Gen. 17:15-19). Shortly after this the Lord, accompanied by two angels, appeared unto His servant in the plains of Mamre and, "they said unto him, Where is Sarah thy wife? And he said, Behold, in the tent. And He said, I will certainly return unto thee according to the time of life; and, lo, Sarah thy wife shall have a son. And Sarah heard it in the tent door, which was behind him. Now Abraham and Sarah were old and well stricken in age; and it ceased to be with Sarah after the manner of women. Therefore Sarah laughed within herself, saying, After I am waxed old shall I have pleasure, my lord being old also? And the Lord said unto Abraham, Wherefore did Sarah laugh, saying, Shall I of a surety bear a child, which am old? Is any thing too hard for the Lord? At the time appointed I will return unto thee, according to the time of life, and Sarah shall have a son" (Gen. 18: 9-14).

And now the appointed hour for the fulfillment of God's promises to Abraham and Sarah had struck, and we read, "And the Lord visited Sarah as He had said, and the Lord did unto Sarah as He had spoken. For Sarah conceived, and bare Abraham a son in his old age, at the set time of which God had spoken to him" (Gen. 21:12). Thus we reach, as we have said, the second stage in the accomplishment of Jehovah's purpose. The birth of Isaac marked an important crisis in connection with the history of the chosen line, for not in Ishmael but in Isaac was Abraham's seed to be called (Gen. 21:12).

Many are the important truths illustrated in the above Scriptures, and many are the profitable lessons to be learned therefrom. We name a few of them without attempting to enlarge. We see from the above that *God is in no hurry* in the working out of His plans. Man may fret and fume, hurry and bustle, but Jehovah has all eternity at His disposal and works leisurely and with deliberation. Well for us to mark this attentively—"he that believeth shall not make haste" (Is. 28:16). Again, we note here ***God's Almightiness.*** Nothing can hinder or thwart the out-working of His purpose. Abraham may be old, Sarah may be barren, but such trifles present no difficulty to Him who is infinite in power. Abraham may seek to obtain an heir through Hagar, but Jehovah's plan cannot be foiled: Sarah's son *shall be* his heir, not Ishmael. Behold, too, the *faithfulness* of God. The Lord had *said* Sarah *shall have* a son, and what He promised He performed. His promise may seem unreasonable and impossible to the carnal mind, but His word is *sure.* Learn, also, how *faith is tried and tested.* This is in order to display its *genuineness.* A faith that is incapable of enduring trial is no faith at all. A hard thing was promised to Abraham but, "he considered not his own body now dead, when he was about an hundred years old, neither yet the deadness of Sarah's womb: he staggered not at the promise of God through unbelief, but was strong in faith, giving glory to God" (Rom. 4:19, 20). Finally, note that *God has a set time* for the accomplishing of His will and the fulfilling of His word. Nothing is left to chance. Nothing is *contingent* on the creature. Everything is definitely fixed beforehand by God. "For Sarah conceived, and bare Abraham a son in his old age, *at the set time* of which God had spoken to him" (Gen. 21:2). Mark how this is emphasized by repetition—"But my covenant will I establish with Isaac, which Sarah shall bear unto thee *at this set time* in the next year" (Gen. 17:21); *"At the time appointed* I will return unto thee, according to the time of life, and Sarah shall have a son" (Gen. 18:14). So also we read in another connection, "For the vision is yet for *an appointed time,* but at the end it shall speak" (Hab. 2:3). Compare Gal. 4:4.

Isaac was the child of *promise.* The Lord took great interest in the birth of this boy. More was said about him *before* his birth than about any other, excepting only Abraham's greater Son. God first made promise to Abraham; "As for Sarai thy wife, thou shalt not call her name Sarai, but Sarah shall her name be. And I will bless her, and give thee a son also of her" (Gen. 17:15, 16). The response of the aged patriarch is recorded in the next verse

—"Then Abraham *fell upon his face,* and laughed." Later, the promise was renewed in the hearing of Sarah, "And He said I will certainly return unto thee according to the time of life; and, lo, Sarah thy wife shall have a son" (Gen. 18:10). Then we are told, "Therefore Sarah laughed within herself, saying, Shall I of a surety bear a child, which am old?" How *reason* ever opposes the promises of God. The "laughter" of Abraham was the laughter of worshipful joy, that of Sarah was credulous unbelief. There *is* a laughter which *the Lord* fills the mouth with, when, at some crisis, He comes to our relief. "When the Lord turned again the captivity of Zion, we were like them that dream. Then was our mouth filled with *laughter,* and our tongue with singing: then said they among the heathen, *the Lord* hath done great things for them" (Ps. 126:112). But there is also the laughter of cynicism and unbelief. The former we are not afraid to avow; the latter makes us, like Sarah, cowards and liars. But are we not told "Through *faith* also Sarah herself received strength to conceive seed, and was delivered of a child when she was past age, because *she judged him faithful* who had promised" (Heb. 11:11). How shall we harmonize this with her laugh of unbelief? To the infidel this would appear a contradiction, but the believer has no difficulty in reconciling these two, for he knows from experience there is a continual struggle going on in his heart between faith and unbelief, sometimes the one and sometimes the other being uppermost. But is it not beautiful and blessed to note that in the New Testament Sarah's unbelief is *passed over,* just as nothing is said there of Rahab's deception (Heb. 11:31), or of Job's impatience (Jas. 5:11).

Isaac was the child of *miracle.* Sarah's womb was *"dead"* (Rom. 4:19) and ere she could conceive a supernatural "strength" must be given her (Heb. 11:11). In this, of course, we discover a foreshadowment of the miraculous birth of the Lord Jesus—now, alas, so generally denied. We are tempted to digress here but must refrain. Certain it is that the vital importance of the virgin birth of our Saviour cannot be overestimated. Well did Sir Robert Anderson say, "The whole Christian system depends upon the truth of the last verse of Matthew one" ("The Coming Prince"). Returning to the miraculous birth of Isaac, do we not see in it, as also in the somewhat similar cases of

Rachel, the mother of Samson, Hannah, and Elisabeth, not only a foreshadowing of the supernatural birth of Christ, but also the gracious way of God in *preparing* Israel to believe in it, facilitating faith in the Divine incarnation. If God quickened a dead womb and caused it to bear, why should it be thought a thing incredible if He made the *virgin* give birth to the Child!

The birth of Christ was markedly foreshadowed by that of Isaac and this in *seven* ways at least. First, Isaac was the *promised* seed and son (Gen. 17:16); so also was Christ (Gen. 3:15; Is. 7:14). Second, *a lengthy interval* occurred between God's first promise to Abraham and its realization. When we are told, "And the Lord visited Sarah *as he had said*" (Gen. 21:1), the immediate reference is to 17:16 and 18:14, but the remote reference was to the original promise of 12:7. So also was there a lengthy interval between God's promise to send Christ and the actual fulfillment of it. Third, when Isaac's birth was announced, his mother asked, "Shall I of a surety bear a child, which am old?" (Gen. 18:13), to which the answer was returned, "Is anything too hard for the Lord?" and the striking analogy is seen in the fact that when the angel of the Lord made known unto Mary that she was to be the mother of the Saviour, she asked, "How shall this be, seeing I know not a man?" (Luke 1:34), to which query the answer was returned, "With God nothing shall be impossible" (Luke 1:37): so that *in each case* God's *omnipotency* was affirmed following the annunciation of the birth of the child. Fourth, Isaac's *name* was specified *before* he was born—"And thou shalt call his name Isaac" (Gen. 17:19); compare with this the words of the angel to Joseph before Christ was born—"And thou shalt call his name Jesus" (Matt. 1:21)! Fifth, Isaac's birth occurred at God's *appointed* time (Gen. 21:2) "at the set time"; so also in connection with the Lord Jesus we read "But when *the fullness of time* was come, God sent forth His Son, born of a woman" (Gal. 4:4). Sixth, as we have seen above, Isaac's birth required a *miracle* to bring it about; so also was it with the incarnation of Immanuel. Seventh, the name Isaac (given unto him by Abraham and not Sarah, Gen. 21:3), which means laughter, declared him to be *his father's delight;* so also was the one born at Bethlehem—"this is My beloved Son in whom I am well pleased." Need we remark how strikingly this sevenfold type evidences the Divine inspiration of Scripture, and demonstrates that the book of Genesis—so much attacked by the critics—was written by one "moved by the Holy Spirit."

It has been noticed by others that in Abraham we have a striking illustration of *election,* while in Isaac we get, typically, the precious truth of *sonship.* Abraham was the one chosen and called by God; Isaac was the one promised and born of God's power. The *historical* order of Genesis is thus the *doctrinal* order of the New Testament. Thus we read in Eph. 1:4, 5, "According as He hath *chosen us* in Him before the foundation of the world, that we should be holy and without blame before Him: in love having predestinated us *unto the adoption of children* by Jesus Christ to Himself, according to the good pleasure of His will." Isaac brings before us in type *regeneration,* and it is this which will now engage our attention.

The first point we would here dwell upon is that before Isaac was born *the power and activities of nature were made an end of.* Abraham and Sarah had come to the end of themselves. Abraham's body was "dead," and so too was Sarah's womb (Rom. 4:19). And in order for Isaac to be born that which was *dead* must be *quickened,* quickened by God. This is a very humbling truth; one which is thoroughly distasteful to man; one which nothing but the grace of God will enable us to receive. The state of the natural man is far worse than *he* imagines. It is not only that man is a sinner, a sinner both by nature and by practice, but that he is "*alienated* from the *life* of God" (Eph. 4:18). In a word the sinner is *dead*—dead in trespasses and sins. As the father said of the prodigal, "This my son was *dead,* and is alive again; he was lost, and is found" (Luke 15:24).

That the natural man is dead in trespasses and sins is no mere figure of speech; it is a solemn *reality,* an awful *fact.* It is ignorance and the denial of this fact which lies at the root of so much of the false teaching of our day. What the natural man needs first and foremost is not education or reformation, but *life.* It is because the sinner is dead that he needs to be born again. But how little this is pressed today! The unspeakably dreadful state of the natural man is glossed over where it is not directly repudiated. For the most part our preachers seem *afraid* to insist upon the utter ruin and total depravity of human nature. This is a *fatal* defect in any preaching: sinners will never be brought to see their need of a Saviour until they realize their *lost* condition, and they will never discover their lost condition until they learn that they are *dead* in sin.

But what does Scripture mean when it says the sinner is "dead"? This is something which seems *absurd* to the natural man. And to him *it is* absurd. "The natural man receiveth not the things of the Spirit of God: for they are *foolishness unto him*: neither can he know them, because they are spiritually discerned" (1 Cor. 2:14). To the natural man it *seems* that he is very much *alive.* Yes, and Scripture itself speaks of one that lives in pleasure as being "*dead while she liveth*" (1 Tim. 5:6). Herein lies the key to the meaning of that expression employed by our Lord in His teaching upon the Good Samaritan. Describing the condition of the natural man under the figure of one who had fallen among thieves, who had stripped him of his raiment and left him wounded by the wayside, the Saviour termed him "*half dead*" (Luke 10:30). Mark then the absolute *accuracy* of Christ's words. The sinner *is* "half *dead*": he is alive manward, worldward, sinward, but he is *dead Godward!* The sinner is alive naturally—physically, mentally, morally—but he is *dead spiritually.* That is why the new birth is termed a "passing from death unto life" (John 5:24). And just as the deadness of Abraham and Sarah—in their case *natural* deadness, for they but *foreshadowed* spiritual truths—had to be quickened by God before Isaac could be born, so has the sinner to be quickened by God into newness of life before he can become a son of God. And this leads us to say.

Second, before Isaac could be born God had to perform a *miracle.* As we have said, Abraham's body was "dead" and Sarah was long past the age of child-bearing. How then could *they* have a son? Sarah *laughed* at the mention of such a thing. But what was beyond the reach of nature's capacity was fully within the scope of Divine power. "Is there anything too hard for the Lord?" (Gen. 18:14). No, indeed. "Ah, Lord God, behold! Thou hast made the heaven and the earth by Thy great power and stretched out arm, and there is nothing too hard for Thee" (Jer. 32:17).

As it was with Isaac so it is with every Christian. Before any of us could be born again God had to work a miracle.

Make no mistake on this point; regeneration is the direct result of the *supernatural* operation of God. This needs to be stressed today, for regeneration has been so misrepresented by modern evangelists that to the popular mind the "new birth" signifies nothing more than a process of reformation. But the new birth is no mere turning over of a new leaf and the endeavor to live a better life. The new birth is very much more than going forward in a religious meeting and taking the preacher's hand; very much more than signing a card and "joining the church." The new birth is an act of God's creative power, the impartation of spiritual life, the communication to us of the Divine nature itself.

Abraham and his wife—each of them nearly a hundred years old—desiring a son—what could *they* do? Nothing! absolutely nothing. God had to come in and work a miracle. And thus nature had *nothing* to glory in. So it is with us. The natural man is not only a sinner, a lost sinner, but he is a *helpless* sinner—impotent, unable to do anything of himself. If help comes it *must* come from *outside* of himself. He is, like Abraham and Sarah, *shut up to God.*

Third, the coming of Isaac into Abraham's household *aroused opposition and produced a conflict.* "And Sarah saw the son of Hagar the Egyptian, which she had borne unto Abraham, *mocking*" (Gen. 21:9). In the epistle to the Galatians we are shown the *dispensational* meaning and application of this, and there we read, "But as then he that was born after the flesh (Ishmael) *persecuted* him that was born after the Spirit, *even so it is now*" (Gal. 4:29); but it is with the *individual* application of this type that we are now concerned. Ishmael exemplifies the one born after the flesh: Isaac the one born after the Spirit. When Isaac was born *the true character* of Ishmael was manifested; and so when we are born again and receive the new nature, the old nature, the flesh, then comes out in its true colors.

Just as there were *two* sons in Abraham's household, the one the product of nature, the other the gift of God and the outworking of Divine power, each standing for a totally different principle, so in the believer there are two natures which are distinct and diverse. And just as there was a *conflict* between Ishmael and Isaac, so the flesh in us lusteth against the spirit and the spirit against the flesh (Gal. 5:17).

It is of first importance that the Christian, especially the young Christian, should be clear upon the two natures in the believer. The new birth is not the *improving* of the old nature, but the receiving of a new; and the receiving of the new nature does not in any wise improve the old. Not only so, the old and the new natures within the believer are in open antagonism the one to the other. We quote now from the works of one deeply respected and to which we are much indebted: "Some there are who think that regeneration is a certain change which the old nature undergoes; and, moreover, that this change is gradual in its operation until, at length, the whole man becomes transformed. That this idea is unsound, can be proved by various quotations from the New Testament. For example: The carnal mind is enmity against God. How can that which is thus spoken of ever undergo any improvement? The apostle goes on to say, "It is not subject to the law of God, *neither indeed can be*." If it *cannot be* subject to the law of God, how can it be improved? How can it undergo any change? Do what you will with flesh, and it is flesh all the while. As Solomon says, "Though thou shouldst bray a fool in a mortar among wheat with a pestle, yet will not his foolishness depart from him" (Pro. 27:22). "There is no use seeking to make foolishness wise. You must introduce heavenly wisdom into the heart that has been hitherto only governed by folly" (C. H. M.).

Fourth, it is to be noted that it was the birth of Isaac which *revealed* the true character of Ishmael. We know practically nothing of Ishmael's life *before* the birth of Isaac, but as soon as this child of promise made his appearance the real nature of Hagar's son was made manifest. He may have been very quiet and orderly before, but as soon as the child of God's quickening-power came on the scene, Ishmael showed what he was by persecuting and mocking him. Here again the type holds good. It is not until the believer receives the *new* nature that he discovers the *real* character of the old. It is not until we are born again we learn what a horrible and vile thing the flesh is. And the discovery is a painful one: to many it is quite unsettling. To those who have supposed that regeneration is an *improving* of the old nature, the recognition of the awful depravity of the flesh comes as a shock and often destroys all peace of soul, for the young convert quickly concludes that, after all, *he* has *not* been born again. The truth is that the recognition of the true character of the flesh and a corresponding *abhorrence* of it, is one of the plainest evidences of our regeneration, for the unregenerate man is *blind* to the vileness of the flesh. The fact that I have within me a *conflict* between the natural and the spiritual is the proof there are two natures present, and that I find the Ishmael-nature "persecuting" the Isaac-nature is only to be expected. That the Ishmael-nature appears to me to be growing *worse* only goes to prove that I now have capacity to *see* its real character, just as the *real* character of Ishmael was not revealed until Isaac was born.

Fifth, we read, "And Abraham *circumcised* his son Isaac being *eight* days old, as God had commanded him" (Gen. 21:4). Our space is exhausted and we must be very brief on these last points. The circumcising of Isaac, and later of the Israelites, was a foreshadowing of our *spiritual* circumcision: "And ye are complete in Him, which is the Head of all principality and power: in whom also ye are *circumcised* with the circumcision *made without hands,* in putting off the body of the sins of the flesh *by the circumcision of Christ*" (Col. 2:10, 11). *Judicially we have been* circumcised and God no longer looks at us in the flesh but in Christ, for circumcision—typically and spiritually—is separation from the flesh, and the *eighth* day brings us on to resurrection ground—in Christ. Compare Col. 3:9, etc.

Sixth, "And the child *grew,* and was *weaned*: and Abraham made a great feast the same day that Isaac was weaned" (Gen. 21:8). Here again the type holds good. Isaac "grew" by feeding on his mother's milk. Thus, too, is it with the believer. By the new birth we are but spiritual *babes,* and our growth is brought about by feeding on the milk of the Word. "As new-born babes, desires the sincere milk of the Word, that ye may *grow thereby*" (1 Pet. 2:2). We cannot now touch upon the significance of the "great feast" above.

Seventh, "And Sarah saw the son of Hagar the Egyptian, which she had borne unto Abraham mocking. Wherefore she said unto Abraham, Cast out this bondwoman and her son: for the son of this bondwoman shall not be heir with my son, even with Isaac. And the thing was very grievous in Abraham's sight because of his son. And God said unto Abraham, let it not be grievous in thy sight because of the lad, and because of thy bondwoman; in all that Sarah hath said unto thee, hearken unto her voice; for in Isaac shall thy seed be called. And also of the son of the bondwoman will I make a nation, because he is thy seed. And Abraham rose up early in the morning, and took bread, and a bottle of water, and gave it unto Hagar, putting it on her shoulder, and the child, and sent her away" (Gen. 21: 9-14). At last the conflict is over. He who "persecuted" Isaac is now *"cast out"* (Gal. 4: 29). So it will yet be with us. Judicially the life of the flesh is *already ended* for us, but practically it is still here with us and in us. But blessed be God what is true now judicially shall soon be true experimentally also. When Christ returns for us, the flesh shall be put off for ever, just as Elijah left behind him *his* earthly mantle. But mark how *accurate* our type is: not till Isaac "grew" and was "weaned" was the persecuting Ishmael cast out! Let this be our closing thought. Soon *our* Ishmael shall be cast out. Soon shall this vile body of ours be made like unto the body of Christ's glory (Phil. 3: 21). Soon shall the Saviour return and we shall be *"like Him,"* for we shall see Him as He is (John 3: 2). Blessed promise! Glorious prospect! Does not the presence of the vile flesh within us now only serve to intensify the longing for our blessed Lord's return? Then let us continue to cry daily, "Come quickly. Even so, come Lord Jesus."

26. THE OFFERING UP OF ISAAC

Genesis 22

"And it came to pass *after these things,* that God did tempt (try) Abraham" (Gen. 20:1). These words refer us back to the context, a context that is rich in typical significance. The immediate context is the twenty-first chapter, where we have recorded the Birth of Isaac—a remarkable type which, with what follows it, needs to be viewed from two standpoints: its *individual* application, and its *dispensational* application. In our last paper we considered the former, here we shall deal briefly with the latter.

The birth of Isaac awakened the enmity of Ishmael, and in consequence Sarah came to Abraham saying, "Cast out this bondwoman and her son; for the son of this bondwoman shall not be heir with my son, even with Isaac" (21:10). From the Epistle to the Galatians (4:22-31) we learn there was a profound meaning to the act here requested by Sarah, that it possessed a dispensational significance. It is to be noted first that Sarah refers to the "inheritance"—the son of Hagar should not be "*heir* with Isaac." Now Isaac, as we have shown in our last, not only foreshadowed the Lord Jesus in His miraculous birth, but also pointed forward to those who now become the children of God through faith in Christ Jesus. In a word, Isaac stands for Divine *sonship.* Only the *spiritual* family of promise answers to Isaac, and takes the title of "*heirs* of God and joint heirs with Christ." Israel, *nationally,* does not inherit with the church. Hence, as Isaac in Genesis 21 foreshadowed those who are members of the Body of Christ, *Ishmael* stands for *the Nation of Israel* which is now "*cast out*" during the time that God is visiting the Gentiles and taking from among *them* a people for His name (Acts 15:14). With this key in hand let us turn to the second part of Genesis 21 and note how the course of Israel as a nation is pursued in the type.

1. "And Abraham rose up early in the morning and took bread and a bottle of water, and gave unto Hagar, putting it on her shoulder, and the child, *and sent her away,* and she departed and wandered in the wilderness of Beer-Sheba" (21:14). First we note (and we shall be as brief as possible) that Hagar and her son *became wanderers in the*

wilderness. How true the picture. Such has been Israel's portion ever since she rejected Abraham's greater Son, the Lord of Glory. Throughout all these centuries, during which God has been building the Church, the Jews have dwelt in the wilderness, and "wanderers" well describes "the nation of the weary foot!"

2. "And the water was spent in the bottle, and she cast the child under one of the shrubs" (21:15). In type, *the Holy Spirit is here taken from Israel*—the *water* was *spent.* This it is which explains the tragic "veil" which is over the heart of the Jews as they read the Scriptures (2 Cor. 3:15), for without the Spirit none can understand or draw refreshment from the Word of God.

3. "And she went and sat her down over against him a good way off, as it were a bowshot: for she said, Let me not see the death of the child. And she sat over against him and lifted up her voice *and wept*" (21:16). We see here a foreshadowment of *Jerusalem bemoaning her desolations,* and at this point the lamentations of Jeremiah are most appropriate to her condition. O, how the above type anticipated the poor Jews "wailing" before the gates of Jerusalem!

4. "And God *heard the voice of the lad;* and the angel of God called to Hagar out of heaven and said unto her, What aileth thee, Hagar? Fear not; for God hath heard the voice of the lad where he is" (21:17). And here is where *hope* begins. It is not until the Jew *bewails his sins* (see Hosea 5:15, etc.), confesses his dreadful crime of crucifying the Son of God, not until after much bitter humiliation they shall cry, "Blessed is He that cometh in the name of the Lord" (Matt. 23:39), that Jehovah will take up again His covenant people.

5. "And God opened her eyes, and she saw a well of water; and she went and filled the bottle with water and gave the lad drink" (21:19). In type *the Spirit is given once more to Israel.* Just as God here "opened the eyes of Hagar," so in a near-coming day will He open the eyes of the Jews, and even during the days of the now rapidly approaching tribulation, a pious remnant shall keep the testimony of God and wash their garments in the blood of the Lamb (Rev. 14:3, 4; 20:4).

6. "And God was with the lad; and he grew, and dwelt in the wilderness, and became an archer" (21:20). Couple

with this the promise of verse 18, "For I will make him *a great nation.*" How accurate the type! Thus it will be with Israel in the Millennium after God has taken into favor again the chosen race.

7. "And he dwelt in the wilderness of Paran" (21:21). Paran means "Beauty or Glory," speaking in type of Palestine, the dwelling place of Israel in the Millennium, when the wilderness shall be made to blossom as the rose, for the curse now resting on the material creation shall then be removed; and then the Shekinah Glory shall once more be in their midst.

8. "And his mother took him a wife out of the land of Egypt" (21:21). In type this allies Israel with Egypt, and thus will it be during the Millennium—"In that day shall Israel be the third *with Egypt* and with Assyria, even a blessing in the midst of the land; whom the Lord of hosts shall bless, saying, Blessed be *Egypt my people,* and Assyria the work of My hands, and Israel Mine inheritance" (Is. 19:24, 25).

9. "And it came to pass *at that time,* that Abimelech and Phichol the chief captain of his host spoke unto Abraham saying, *God is with thee* in all that thou doest" (21:22). How this reminds us that in the Millennium the Gentile will seek out the Jew, because conscious that Jehovah is once more in their midst! As it is written, "Thus saith the Lord of hosts, In those days it shall come to pass that ten men shall take hold out of all languages of the nations, even shall take hold of the skirt of him that is a Jew, saying, "We will go with you, for we have heard that *God is with you*" (Zech. 8:23).

10. Note the close of this chapter: "And Abraham *planted a grove in Beer-Sheba*" (21:33). This action of the patriarch was deeply significant when viewed typically. It marked the change from strangership to possession. Abraham, who stands figuratively as the federal head of the nation plants a "grove" in *Beer-Sheba,* which means, "Well of the oath," for all is founded upon *the Covenant,* and thus *takes possession of the land,* for the planting of a tree emblemizes settled and long continuance—"They shall not build, and another inhabit; they shall not plant, and another eat: for *as the days of a tree* are the days of My people, and Mine elect *shall long enjoy* the work of their hands' (Is. 64:22).

11. "And Abraham planted a grove in Beer-Sheba, and called there on the name of the Lord, *the Everlasting God*" (21: 33). Here Abraham calls not on Jehovah, nor on the Almighty, but on the Lord, "the Everlasting God." So will it be when the Kingdom comes in power and glory. Instead of ceaseless change and decay in all around we see, as now, there shall be fixity, permanence, peace and blessing. Then shall Israel say, "Thou art the same, and Thy years shall have no end. The children of Thy servants shall continue, and their seed shall be established before Thee" (Is. 102: 27, 28).

12. One more notice is given to this type and it *completes* the picture—"These are the sons of *Ishmael*, and these are their names, by their towns and by their castles; *twelve princes* according to their nations" (25: 16). In the Millennium the whole of the *twelve tribes of Israel* will be restored and raised to *princely* dignity among the nations.

And now what follows this marvellous sketch of Israel's course?—for marvellous it surely is to the anointed eye. What follows? why, that unparalleled foreshadowing of the Saviour's Death and Resurrection. And why this linking of the two together? To show us, and later the Jews, that Israel owes her Millennial blessedness, as we do our present and eternal blessings, to the precious Sacrifice of the Lamb of God. But we must leave the dispensational application of the type, and turn and consider once more its *individual* application.

In our last article we pointed out how that in seven particulars the birth of Isaac was a type of the Birth of the Lord Jesus. Now, we are to see how the offering up of Isaac upon the altar pointed forward to the Cross of Calvary.

This twenty-second chapter of Genesis has ever been a favorite one with the saints of God, and our difficulty now is to single out for mention that in it which will be most precious to our hearts and most profitable for our walk. Ere examining it in detail it should be said that this is, we believe, the only type in the Old Testament which distinctly intimated that God required a *human sacrifice*. Here it was that God first revealed the necessity for a human victim to expiate sin, for as it was man that had sinned, it must be by man, and not by sacrifice of beasts, that Divine justice would be satisfied.

1. "And He said, "Take now thy son, thine only son Isaac, whom thou lovest, and get thee into the land of Moriah, and offer him there for a burnt offering upon one* of the mountains which I will tell thee of" (Gen. 22:2). This is one of the very few Old Testament types that brings before us not only God the Son but also *God the Father.* Here, as nowhere else, are we shown the *Father's heart.* Here it is that we get such a wonderful foreshadowment of the *Divine* side of Calvary. Oh! how the Spirit of God lingers on the offering and the offerer, as if there must be a thorough similitude in the type of the antitype—*"thy son—thine only son—whom thou lovest"!* Here it is we learn, in type how that God "spared not His own Son" (Rom. 8:32). Really, this is *central* in Genesis 22. In this chapter Abraham figures much more prominently than Isaac—Isaac is shown simply (and yet how sweetly!) obeying his father's will. It is the affections of the father's heart which are here displayed most conspicuously.

2. "And Abraham rose up early in the morning, and saddled his ass, and took two of his young men with him, and Isaac his son, and clave the wood for the burnt offering, and rose up, and went unto the place of which God had told him" (22:3). Here we see in type *the Father setting apart the Son for sacrifice.* Just as we find the passover-lamb was separated from the flock four days before it was to be killed (Ex. 12:3), so here Isaac is taken by Abraham three days before he is to be offered upon the altar. This brings before us an aspect of truth exceedingly precious, albeit deeply solemn. The seizure and crucifixion of the Lord Jesus was something more than the frenzied act of those who hated Him without a cause. The cross of Christ was according to "the determinate counsel and foreknowledge of God" (Acts 2:23). Herod, Pontius Pilate, the Gentiles and Jews only did "whatsoever" God's hand and counsel "determined before to be done" (Acts 4:28). Christ was the Lamb "without blemish and without spot, who verily was foreordained before the foundation of the world" (1

*The writer has little doubt that the particular "mountain" upon which Isaac was bound to the altar was Calvary itself. Here, the mountain is not denominated, it was "one of the mountains" in the "land of Moriah" (it is significant that "Moriah" means "the Lord will provide"), and Calvary *was* one of the mountains in the land of Moriah. What seems to identify Isaac's mountain with Calvary is not only that the marvelous fullness and accuracy of *this* type would seem to *require* it, but the fact that in Gen. 22:14 *this* mount on which Isaac was offered is distinctly termed "the mount *of the Lord.*" Surely this establishes it, for what other save Calvary could be thus named!

Pet. 1:20). Yes, the Lord Jesus was marked out for sacrifice from all eternity. He was, in the purpose of God, "the Lamb slain from the foundation of the world" (Rev. 13:8). And note how this is suggested by our type, "And Abraham rose up *early* in the morning" (22:3).

3. "And Abraham said unto his young men, Abide ye here with the ass, and I and the lad will go yonder and worship, and come again to you" (22:5). Here we see in type that what took place on that mount of sacrifice *was a transaction between the Father and the Son* ONLY. How jealously God guarded these types! Nothing whatever is said of Sarah in this chapter though she figures prominently in the one before and is mentioned in the one succeeding. Abraham and Isaac must be alone. Up to the time the appointed place enters their range of vision "*two* young men" (22:3) accompany Isaac; but as they near the scene of sacrifice they are left behind (22:5). Is it without a reason we are told of these *two* men journeying with Abraham and Isaac just so far? We think not. Two is the number of witness, but there is more in it than this. These two men witnessed Isaac carrying the wood on his shoulder up the mountain, but what took place between him and his father at the altar they were not permitted to see. No; no human eye was to behold *that*. Look now at the *Antitype*. Do you not also see *there* "two men," the two thieves who followed Abraham's greater son so far but who, like all the spectators of that scene, were *not permitted* to behold what transpired between the Father and the Son on the altar itself—the three hours of darkness concealing from every human eye the Divine Transaction.

4. "And Abraham took the wood of the burnt offering, and laid it upon Isaac his son" (22:6). This was no half grown boy (as pictures so often represent Isaac), but a full-grown man who is here brought before us, one who could, had he so wished, have easily resisted the aged patriarch. But instead of resisting, Isaac quietly follows his father. There is no voice of protest raised to mar the scene, but he acquiesces fully by carrying the wood on his *own* shoulder. How this brings before us the Peerless One, gladly performing the Father's pleasure. There was no alienated will in Him that needed to be brought into subjection: "Lo, *I come to do* Thy will, O God," was His gladsome cry. "I *delight* to do Thy will" revealed the per-

fections of His heart. Christ and the Father were of one accord. Note how beautifully this is brought out in the type—"And they went both of them *together*:" twice repeated. We need hardly say that Isaac carrying "the *wood*" foreshadowed Christ bearing His cross.

5. "And he took the fire in his hand and a knife; and they went both of them together" (22:6). And he (Abraham) took *the fire* in *his* hand. Here, as everywhere in Scripture, "fire" emblemizes *Divine judgment*. It expresses the energy of Divine Holiness which ever burns against sin. It is the perfection of the Divine nature which cannot tolerate that which is evil. This was first manifested by the *flaming* sword which turned every way, to keep the way of the tree of life (Gen. 3:24). And it will be finally and eternally exhibited in *the Lake which burneth* with fire and brimstone. But here in our type it pointed forward to that awful storm of Divine judgment which burst upon the head of the Sin-Bearer as He hung upon the Cross, for there it was that sin, *our* sin, Christian reader, was being dealt with. Just as Isaac's father took in his hand the fire and the knife, so the beloved Son was "smitten *of God*, and afflicted" (Is. 53:4).

6. And Isaac spake unto Abraham his father and said, My father: and he said, Here am I, my son. And he said, Behold the fire and the wood: but where is the lamb for a burnt offering? And Abraham said, My son, God will provide Himself a lamb for a burnt offering: So they went both of them together" (22:7, 8). These words of Abraham have a *double* meaning. They tell us that God was the One who should *"provide"* the "lamb," and they also make known the fact that the lamb was *for Himself*. God alone could supply that which would satisfy Himself. Nothing of man could meet the Divine requirements. If sacrifice for sin was ever to be found God Himself must supply it. And mark, the "lamb" was not only provided *by* God but it was also *for* God. Before blessing could flow forth to men the claims of Divine holiness and justice must be met. It is true, blessedly true, that Christ died for sinners, but He first died (and this is what we are in danger of forgetting) *for God*, i. e., as the Holy Spirit expresses it through the apostle. "to declare *His* righteousness . . . that He might be just, *and* the justifier of him which believeth in Jesus" (Rom. 3:26). Note how this comes out in our passage: it is

not "God Himself will provide a lamb," but "God will *provide Himself* a lamb"—put this way, abstractly, so as to take in *both* of these truths.

7. "And they came to the place which God had told him of; and Abraham built an altar there, and laid the wood in order, and bound Isaac his son, and laid him on the altar upon the wood. And Abraham stretched forth his hand, and took the knife to slay his son. And the Angel of the Lord called unto him out of heaven, and said, Abraham, Abraham, and he said, Here am I. And he said, Lay not Thine hand upon the lad, neither do thou anything unto him: for now I know that thou fearest God, seeing thou hast not withheld thy son, thine only son, from me. And Abraham lifted up his eyes, and looked, and beheld behind him a ram caught in a thicket by his horns: and Abraham went and took the ram, and offered him up for a burnt offering in the stead of his son. And Abraham called the name of that place Jehovah-Jireh: as it is said to this day. In the mount of the Lord it shall be seen" (22:9-14). Here the type passes from Isaac to the ram offered up—"*offered up in his stead*"—a beautiful foreshadowment of Christ dying in the stead of sinners who are, as Isaac was, *already in the place of Death,* "bound," unable to help themselves, with the knife of Divine justice suspended over them. Here it was that the *Gospel* was "preached unto Abraham" (Gal. 3:8). Similarly in other scriptures we find this *double* type (both Isaac and the ram) as in the sweet savor and the sin offerings, the two goats on the Day of Atonement, the two birds at the cleansing of the leper.

8. "By faith Abraham, when he was tried, offered up Isaac: and he that had received the promises offered up his only begotten son, of whom it was said, In Isaac shall thy seed be called, accounting that God was able to raise him up, even from the dead, *from whence also he received him in a figure*" (Heb. 11:17-19). From this scripture we learn that Gen. 22 presents to us in type not only Christ offered upon the altar, but Christ raised again from the dead, *and that on the third day, too,* for it was on "the third day" Abraham received Isaac back again, for during the three days that elapsed from the time Abraham received command from God to offer him up as a burnt offering, his son was as good as dead to him. And now to complete this won-

derful picture, observe how Gen. 22 anticipated, in type, *the Ascension of Christ!* It is very striking to note that after we read of Isaac being laid upon the altar (from which Abraham received him back) *nothing further is said of him in Gen. 22.* Mark carefully the wording of verse 19 —"So Abraham returned unto his young men, and they rose up and went together to Beer-Sheba." Our type leaves Isaac *up in the mount!*

This article would not be complete did we say nothing about the remarkable trial of Abraham's faith and of the Divine grace which sustained him, yet, a very brief word is all we now have space for.

The spiritual history of Abraham was marked by four great crises, each of which involved the surrender of something which was *naturally* dear to him. First, he was called on to separate himself from his native land and kindred (Gen. 12:1); Second, he was called on to give up Lot (Gen. 13:1-18); Third, he had to abandon his cherished plan about Ishmael (Gen. 17:17, 18); Fourth, God bade him offer up Isaac as a burnt offering. The life of the believer is a series of tests, for only by discipline can Christian character be developed. Frequently there is one supreme test, in view of which all others are preparatory. So it was with Abraham. He had been tested again and again, but never as here. God's demand is, "Son, give Me thine heart (Pro. 23:26). It is not our intellect, our talents, our money, but our *heart,* God asks for first. When we have responded to God's requirement, He lays His hand on something especially near and dear to us, to prove the *genuineness* of our response, for God requireth truth in the inward parts and not merely on the lips. Thus He dealt with Abraham. Let us consider now, *The Time of Abraham's Trial.*

It was "after these things" that God did try Abraham; that is, it was after the twenty-five years of waiting, after the promise of a seed had been frequently repeated, after hope had been raised to the highest point, yea, after it had been turned to enjoyment and Isaac had reached man's estate. Probably Abraham thought that when Isaac was born his trials were at an end; if so, he was greatly mistaken. Let us look now at, *The Nature of Abraham's Trial.*

Abraham was bidden to take his *son*—and what? Deliver him to some other hand to sacrifice? No: be thou thyself the priest; go, offer him up for a burnt offering.

This was a staggering request! When Ishmael was thirteen years old, Abraham could have been well contented to have gone without another son, but when Isaac was born and had entwined himself around the father's heart, to part with him thus must have been a fearful wrench. Add to this, the three days' journey, Isaac having to carry the wood and Abraham the knife and fire up the mountainside, and above all, the cutting question of the son asked in the simplicity of his heart, without knowing he himself was to be the victim—"Behold the fire and the wood: *but where* is the lamb for a burnt offering?" (22:8)—this would seem to be more than the human heart could bear. Yet, this shock to Abraham's natural affection was not the severest part of the trial. What must it have been to his *faith.* It was not only that Isaac was his son, but *the promised seed,* the one in whom all the great things spoken of the seed were to be fulfilled. When he was called to give up his other son God condescended to give him a reason for it, but here no reason was given. In the former case, though Ishmael must go, it was because he was not the child of promise ("in Isaac shall thy seed be called"), but if Isaac goes who shall substitute for him? To offer up Isaac was to sacrifice the very object of faith! Turn now and consider, *Abraham's Response.*

Mark his *promptitude.* There was no doubt or delay, and no reluctance or hesitation; instead, he "rose up *early* in the morning." There was no opposition either from natural affection or unbelief, rather did he bow in absolute submission to the will of God. Faith triumphed over natural affection, over reason, and over self-will. Here was a most striking demonstration of the efficacy of Divine grace which can subdue every passion of the human heart and every imagination of the carnal mind, bringing all into unrepining acquiescence to God. And what was the effect of this trial upon Abraham? He was amply rewarded, for he discovered something in God he never knew before, or at most knew imperfectly, namely, that God was Jehovah-Jireh—*the Lord who would provide.* It is only by passing through trials that we learn what God is—His grace, His faithfulness, His sufficiency. May the Lord grant both writer and reader more of that power of faith which, with open hand, takes every blessing which God gives us, and with open hand gives back to Him, in the spirit of worship.

27. THE MAN ISAAC

Genesis 26

In our last two articles we have been occupied more particularly with the *person* of Isaac, now we are to review his *history*. It is noticeable that though Isaac lived the longest of the four great patriarchs yet less is recorded of him than of the others: some twelve chapters are devoted to the biography of Abraham, and a similar number each to Jacob and Joseph, but excepting for one or two brief mentionings, before and after, the *history* of Isaac is condensed into a single chapter. Contrasting his character with those of his father and son, we may remark that of Isaac there is noted less of Abraham's triumphs of faith and less of Jacob's failures.

As we have seen in our previous studies Isaac, typically, represents *sonship*. In perfect consonance with this we may note how he was appointed *heir* of all things. Said Eliazer to Bethuel, "And Sarah my master's wife bare a son to my master when she was old: *and unto him hath he given all that he hath*" (24:36). Observe how this is repeated for sake of emphasis in 25:5—"And Abraham gave all that he had unto Isaac." In the type this pointed first to Abraham's greater Son, "Whom He (God) hath appointed Heir of all things" (Heb. 1:2). But it is equally true of all those who are through faith the children of Abraham and the children of God—"And if children, *then heirs:* heirs of God, and joint-heirs with Christ" (Rom. 8:17). As with Isaac, so with us: all the wealth of the Father's house is ours! But Isaac not only represented the believer's sonship and heirship, but he also foreshadowed *our heavenly calling.* As is well known to most of our readers, the land of Canaan typified the Heavenlies where is our citizenship (Phil. 3:20) and our spiritual warfare (Eph. 6:12). Hence it was that Isaac alone of the patriarchs *is never seen outside the Land.* This is the more noticeable and striking when we remember how that Abraham, Jacob and Joseph each did leave the Land, for a time at least.

Having looked at Isaac *mystically* we shall now consider him *morally.* The first thing we read about him after the remarkable scene pictured in Gen. 22 is that "Isaac came from the way of the well Lahai-roi; for he dwelt in the south country. And Isaac went out to meditate (or pray) in the field at the eventide" (24: 62, 63). This gives us a good insight into Isaac's character. He was of the quiet and retiring order. He had not the positive, active, aggressive disposition of his eminent father, but was gentle and retiring and unresisting. In One only do we find *all* the Divine graces and perfections.

Isaac was essentially the man of the well. Abraham was markedly the man of the altar, Jacob specially the man of the tent but that which was most prominent in connection with Isaac was the "well." The first thing said of Isaac after he was bound to the altar (Gen. 22) is, "Isaac came from the way of the well Lahai-roi" (24: 62). This is very striking coming as *the next* mention of Isaac after we have seen Christ typically slain, resurrected and ascended (compare our last article on Gen. 22). Hence that which follows here in the type is the figure of *the Holy Spirit's operations*—as succeeding Christ's Ascension! But returning to Isaac and the well. The next time he is referred to we are told, "And it came to pass after the death of Abraham, that God blessed his son Isaac; and Isaac dwelt by the *well* Lahai-roi" (25: 11). And again we read, "And Isaac departed thence, and pitched his tent in the valley of Gerar, and dwelt there. And Isaac digged again *the wells* of water which they had digged in the days of Abraham his father; for the Philistines had stopped them" (26: 18, 19). For further references see Gen. 26: 20, 21, 22, 25. It is very striking and significant that the name of Isaac is associated with "wells" just *seven* times, not less, not more. Undoubtedly there is some important lesson to be gathered from this.

A well differs from a cistern, in that it is the place of *running* water. What a marvelous hint of the *typical* meaning of Isaac's well is that found in 26: 19!—"And Isaac's servants digged in the valley, and found there a well of *springing* water," the margin gives, "of *living* water"! Water is imperative for the maintenance of the natural life; so, too, is it with the spiritual. The first need of the believer is the "living water," that is, the Spirit acting through the Word. "The way that water ministers to life and growth is indeed a beautiful type of the Spirit's action. Without water a plant will die in the midst of abundance of food in actual contact with its roots. Its office is to make food to be assimilated by the organism, and to give power to the system itself to take it up" (F. W. G.).

The *first* well by which Isaac is seen is that of Lahai-roi (24:62; 25:11), the meaning of which is, "Him that liveth and seeth me" (See 16:14). It told of the unfailing care of the ever-living and ever-present God. And where is such a "well" to be found to-day? Where is it we are brought to *realize* the presence of this One? Where but in the Holy Scriptures! The Word of God ministered to us by the power and blessing of the Spirit is that which reveals to *us* the presence of God. The "well," then, typifies the place to which the son is brought—into the presence of God. His *remaining* there, practically, depends upon his use of and obedience to the Word.

We have just looked at Isaac by the Well of Lahai-roi; did he *remain* there? What do you suppose is the answer, reader? Could you not supply it from your own experience! "And there was a famine in the land, besides the first famine that was in the days of Abraham. And Isaac *went unto Abimelech,* king of the Philistines unto Gerar" (26:1). Isaac's departure from the well Lahai-roi to Gerar typifies the *failure* of the son (the believer) to maintain his standing in the presence of God and his enjoyment of Divine fellowship. But is it not blessed to read next, "And the Lord appeared unto him, and said, Go not down into Egypt; dwell in the land which I shall tell thee of. Sojourn in this land, and I will be with thee, and will *bless* thee, for unto thee, and unto thy seed, I will give all these countries, and I will perform the oath which I sware unto Abraham thy father" (26:2, 3). Apparently, Isaac was on his way to *Egypt,* like his father before him in time of famine, and would have gone there had not the Lord appeared to him and arrested his steps. In passing, we would remark that here we have a striking illustration of the *sovereign ways* of God. To Isaac the Lord appeared and stayed him from going down to Egypt, yet under precisely similar circumstances He appeared not unto Abraham!

"And Isaac dwelt in Gerar" (26:6). Gerar was the *borderland* midway between Canaan and Egypt. Note that God had said to Isaac, "*Sojourn* in this land" (v. 3), but

Isaac *"dwelt"* there (v. 6), and that "a *long* time" (v. 8). Mark now the *consequence* of Isaac settling down in Gerar —type of the believer *out of* communion. He *sinned* there! "And the men of the place asked him of his wife; and he said, She is my sister: for he feared to say, She is my wife; lest, said he, the men of the place should kill me for Rebekah; because she was fair to look upon" (26:7). Isaac thus repeated the sin of Abraham (Gen. 20:1, 2). What are we to learn from Isaac thus following the evil example of his father? From others we select two thoughts. First, the readiness with which Isaac followed in the way of Abraham suggests that it is much easier for children to imitate the vices and weaknesses of their parents than it is to emulate their virtues, and that the sins of the parents are frequently perpetuated in their children. Solemn thought this! But, second, Abraham and Isaac were men of vastly different temperament, yet each succumbed to the same temptation. When famine arose each *fled to man* for help. When in the land of Abimelech each was afraid to own his wife as such. Are we not to gather from this that no matter what our natural temperament may be, unless the grace of God supports and sustains us we shall inevitably fall! What a warning!

"Then Isaac sowed in that land, and received in the same year a hundred-fold: and the Lord blessed him. And the man waxed great, and went forward, and grew until he became very great" (26:12, 13). Most of the commentators have had difficulty with these verses and have resorted to various ingenuities to explain this prosperity of Isaac while he was out of communion with God. But the difficulty vanishes if we look at the above statement in the light of v. 3, where the Lord had said, "I will bless thee"—a promise given *before* Isaac had practised this deception upon Abimelech. That this is the true interpretation appears from the word "bless." God had said, "I will bless thee" (v. 3), and v. 12 records the fulfillment of God's promise, for here we read, "And the Lord *blessed* him." The failure of Isaac between the time when God made promise and its fulfillment only affords us a striking illustration of that blessed word, "He is *faithful* that promised" (Heb. 10:23)! Yes, blessed be His name, even "if we believe not, yet He abideth faithful: He cannot deny Himself" (2 Tim. 2:13).

Next we are told, "And Abimelech said unto Isaac, *Go from us;* for thou art much mightier than we" (26:16). Was not this *God* speaking to Isaac, speaking *at a distance* (through Abimelech) and not yet directly!

"And Isaac departed thence, and pitched his tent in the valley of Gerar, and dwelt there. And Isaac digged again the wells of water, which they had digged in the days of Abraham his father; for the Philistines had stopped them after the death of Abraham; and he called their names after the names by which his father had called them" (26: 17, 18). In digging again these wells of Abraham which had been stopped up by the Philistines, Isaac appears to typify Christ who, at the beginning of the New Testament, dispensation re-opened the Well of Living Water which had, virtually, been blocked up by the traditions and ceremonialism of the Pharisees.

"And Isaac's servants digged in the valley, and found there a well of springing water. And the herdsmen of Gerar did *strive* with Isaac's herdmen, saying, The water is ours....And they digged another well and strove for that also.....And he *removed* from thence and digged another well" (26:19-22). Again we would ask, Was not this "strife" God's way of leading his child back to Himself again! But note also the lovely moral trait seen here in Isaac, namely, his nonresistance of evil. Instead of standing up for his "rights," instead of contending for the wells which he had dug, he quietly "removed" to another place. In this he beautifully points out the path which the Christian should follow: "For this is thankworthy, if a man for conscience toward God endure grief, suffering wrongfully. For what glory is it, if, when ye be buffeted for your faults, ye shall take it patiently? but if, when ye do well, ye suffer for it, ye take it patiently, this is acceptable with God" (1 Pet. 2:19, 20). We need hardly remind the reader that the attitude displayed by Isaac, as above, was that of the Saviour who "when He was reviled, reviled not again."

"And he went *up* from thence *to Beersheba*" (26:23). Mark here the topographical reference which symbolized Isaac's moral ascent and return to the place of communion, for "Beersheba" means the Well of the Oath. In full accord with this behold the blessed sequel—"And the Lord appeared unto him *the same night* and said, I am the God of Abraham thy father; fear not, for I am with thee, and will bless thee, and multiply thy seed for My servant Abraham's sake'' (26:24). On the very night of Isaac's return to Beersheba the Lord ''appeared unto'' him!

''And he builded an altar there, and called upon the name of the Lord, and pitched his tent there: and there Isaac digged a well'' (26:25). Mark how the ''altar'' is mentioned before the ''tent''—there was no mention of any altar in Gerar! How striking, too, that next we read, ''Then Abimelech went to him from Gerar, and Ahurzzath one of his friends, and Phichol the chief captain of his army'' (26:26). Personal blessings from the Lord was not the only result of his return to Beersheba. Abimelech seeks him out, not now to distress him (we no longer read of any ''striving'' for *this* last well), but to ask a favor. And they said, ''We certainly saw that the Lord was with thee: and we said, Let there be now an oath betwixt us, even betwixt us and thee, and let us make a covenant with thee'' (26:28). Now that our patriarch has entered again the path of God's will, those who formerly were his enemies seek him and bear witness to the presence of God with him. An illustration is this that ''when a man's ways please the Lord, He maketh even his enemies to be at peace with him'' (Pro. 16:7).

''And he (Isaac) made them a *feast,* and they did eat and drink. And they rose up betimes in the morning, and sware one to another: and Isaac sent them away, and they departed from him in peace'' (26:30, 31). Above we called attention to how meekly Isaac suffered wrong when the Philistines strove for his wells, but here we may mark his failure to manifest another grace which ought always to accompany meekness. There is a meekness which is according to nature, but usually this degenerates into weakness. The meekness which is of the Spirit will not set aside the requirements of righteousness, but will maintain the claims of God. And here Isaac failed. To forgive is Christian, but with that there must be faithfulness in its season. ''If thy brother trespass against thee, *rebuke* him; and if he repent, forgive him'' (Luke 17:3). Abimelech had clearly wronged him, but instead of dealing with Abimelech's conscience, Isaac made him a ''feast.'' This was amiable, no doubt, but it was not upholding the claims of righteousness. Contrast the conduct of Abraham under similar circumstances—"And Abraham *reproved* Abimelech because of a well of water, which Abimelech's servants had violently taken away" (Gen. 21:25)!

"And Esau was forty years old when he took to wife Judith, the daughter of Beeri *the Hittite,* and Bashemath, the daughter of Elon the Hittite: which were *a grief* of mind unto Isaac and to Rebekah" (26:34 and 35). This is sad, and points a solemn warning to us. Marriage is a momentous undertaking, and for one of the Lord's people to unite with a worlding is to court disaster as well as to dishonor Christ. Jehovah's instructions to Israel were very pointed: under no circumstances must they marry a Canaanite (Deut. 7:3). In the times covered by the book of Genesis, though apparently no divine law had been given respecting it, yet the mind of God was clearly understood. This is evident from the care which Abraham took to secure Isaac a wife from among his own people (Gen. 24), thus did he prevent Isaac from marrying a daughter of Canaan. But Isaac was careless about this matter. He failed to watch over his children so as to anticipate mischief. Esau married a daughter of the Hittites. God could not say of Isaac as he had of his father, "For I know him, that he will command his children and his household after him, and they shall keep the way of the Lord" (Gen. 18:19). However, that Isaac had within him a righteous soul to be "vexed" is clear from the words, "which were *a grief of mind* unto Isaac and to Rebekah" (26:35).

We reserve for our next article a detailed examination of Genesis 27. Suffice it now to refer barely to the incident which is well known to our readers. Isaac was one hundred and forty years old and was fearful that death might soon overtake him. He therefore prepares to perform the last religious act of a patriarchal priest and bestow blessing upon his sons. But mark how that instead of seeking guidance from God in prayer his mind is occupied with a feast of venison. Not only so, but he seeks to reverse the expressed will of God and bestow upon Esau what the Lord had reserved for Jacob. But whatsoever a man soweth *that* shall he also reap. Isaac acts in the energy of the flesh, and Rebekah and Jacob deal with him on the same low level. And here the history of Isaac terminates! After charging Jacob not to take a wife from the daughters of Canaan (28:1) he disappears from the scene and nothing further is recorded of him save his death and burial (35:27-29). As another has said, "instead of wearing out, Isaac rusted out," rusted out as a vessel no longer fit for the master's use.

"Was Isaac, I ask, a vessel marred on the wheel? Was he a vessel laid aside as not fit for the Master's use? or at least not fit for it any longer? His history seems to tell us this. Abraham had not been such an one. All the distinguishing features of 'the stranger here,' all the proper fruits of that energy that quickened him at the outset, were borne in him and by him to the very end. We have looked at this already in the walk of Abraham. Abraham's leaf did not wither. He brought forth fruit in old age. So was it with Moses, with David, and with Paul. They die with their harness on, at the plough or in the battle. Mistakes and more than mistakes they made by the way, or in their cause, or at their work; but they are never laid aside. Moses is counselling the camp near the banks of the Jordan; David is ordering the conditions of the Kingdom, and putting it (in its beauty and strength) into the hand of Solomon; Paul has his armour on, his loins girded. When, as I may say, the time of their departure was at hand, the Master, as we may read in Luke 12, found them 'so doing,' as servants should be found. But thus was it not with Isaac. Isaac is laid aside. For forty long years we know nothing of him; he had been, as it were, decaying away and wasting. The vessel was rusting till it rusted out.

"There is surely meaning in all this, meaning for our admonition. And yet—such is the fruitfulness and instruction of the testimonies of God—there are others in Scripture, of other generations, who have still more solemn lessons and warnings for us. It is humbling to be *laid aside* as no longer fit for use; but it is sad to be left merely to *recover ourselves,* and it is terrible to remain to *defile ourselves.* And illustrations of all this moral variety we get in the testimonies of God. *Jacob,* in his closing days in Egypt, is not as a vessel laid aside, but he is there recovering himself. I know there are some truly precious things connected with him during those seventeen years that he spent in that land, and we could not spare the lesson which the Spirit reads to us out of the life of Jacob in Egypt. But still, the moral of it is this—a saint, who had been under holy discipline, recovering himself, and yielding fruit, meet for recovery. And when we think of it a little, that is but a poor thing. But *Solomon* is a still worse case. He lives to defile himself; sad and terrible to tell it. This was neither Isaac nor Jacob—it was not a saint simply laid aside, nor a saint left to recover himself. Isaac was, in the great moral sense, blameless to the end, and Jacob's last days were his best days; but of Solomon we read, 'It came to pass, *when Solomon was old,* that his wives turned away his heart after other gods,' and this has made the writing over his name, the tablet to his memory, equivocal, and hard to be deciphered to this day.

"Such lessons do Isaac and Jacob and Solomon, in these ways, read for us, beloved—such are the minute and variour instructions left for our souls in the fruitful and living pages of the oracles of God. They give us to see, in the house of God, vessels fit for use and kept in use even to the end—vessels laid aside, to rust out rather than to wear out —vessels whose best service is to get themselves clean again —and vessels whose dishonor it is, at the end of their service, to contract some fresh defilement." (J. G. Bellett, "The Patriarchs.")

28. ISAAC BLESSING HIS SONS

Genesis 27

Let us look at the two sons who were to receive the blessing. They are first brought before us in Gen. 25:20-26—"And Isaac was forty years old when he took Rebekah to wife, the daughter of Bethuel the Syrian of Padan-Aran, the sister to Laban the Syrian. And Isaac entreated the Lord for his wife, because she was barren and the Lord was entreated of him, and Rebekah his wife conceived. And the children struggled together within her; and she said, If it be so, why am I thus? And she went to enquire of the Lord. And the Lord said unto her, Two nations are in thy womb, and two manner of people shall be separated from thy bowels; and the one people shall be stronger than the other people; and the elder shall serve the younger. And when her days to be delivered were fulfilled, behold, there were twins in her womb. And the first came out red, all over like a hairy garment; and they called his name Esau. And after that came his brother out, and his hand took hold on Esau's heel; and his name was called Jacob: and Isaac was three-score years old when she bare them." We reserve our comments on this passage until our next article on Jacob, and pass on now to the well-known incident of Esau selling his birthright.

"And the boys grew: and Esau was a cunning hunter, a man of the field; and Jacob was a plain man, dwelling in tents. And Isaac loved Esau, because he did eat of his venison: but Rebekah loved Jacob. And Jacob sod pottage: and Esau came from the field, and he was faint: And Esau said to Jacob, Feed me, I pray thee, with that same red pottage; for I am faint: therefore was his name called Edom. And Jacob said, Sell me this day thy birthright. And Esau said, Behold, I am at the point to die: and what profit shall this birthright do to me? And Jacob said, Swear to me this day; and he sware unto him: and he sold his birthright unto Jacob. Then Jacob gave Esau bread and pottage of lentiles; and he did eat and drink, and rose up, and went his way. Thus Esau despised his birthright." (Gen. 25:27-34.) There is far more beneath the surface here (as in all Scripture) than meets the eye at first glance. Esau and Jacob are to be considered *as representative characters.* Esau typifies the unbeliever, Jacob the man of faith. Every line in the brief sketch that is here given of their characters is profoundly significant.

Esau was "a cunning hunter" (v. 27). The "*hunter*" tells of the roving, daring, restless nature that is a stranger to peace. A glance at the concordance will show that the word "hunter" is invariably found in an *evil* connection (cf. 1 Sam. 24:11; Job 10:16; Psa. 140:11; Prov. 6:26; Micah 7:2; Ezek. 13:18). "*Search*" is the antithesis, the *good* word, the term used when God is *seeking* His own. Only two men in Scripture are specifically termed "hunters," namely, Nimrod and Esau, and they have much in common. The fact that Esau is thus linked together with Nimrod, the rebel, reveals his true character.

Next we are told that Esau was "a man of the field" (v. 27). In the light of Matt. 13:38—"The field is the world"—it is not difficult to discern the spiritual truth illustrated in the person of Esau. He was, typically, a man of the world. In sharp contrast from what we are told of Esau two things are said of Jacob:—he was "a plain man; dwelling in tents" (v. 27). The Hebrew for "plain" is "tam," which is translated in other passages "perfect," "upright," "undefiled." The reference is to his character. The "dwelling in tents" denotes that he was a stranger and pilgrim in this scene; having here no abiding city, but seeking one to come.

"And Jacob sod pottage: and Esau came from the field and he was faint." Here again the contrast between the two sons of Isaac is sharp and instructive. Jacob was occupied with the affairs of the *house,* cooking a meal, and enjoying his portion,* whereas Esau was again connected with the "field" and is "faint." Remembering what we have seen above, namely, that Esau is to be viewed as *a representative character,* a man of the world, this next line in the picture is highly suggestive. Esau returns from the field without his venison, hungry and faint. Such is ever the case with the worldling. There is nothing to be found in the "field" which can satisfy, or, to drop the figure, the world affords nothing that is able to meet man's spiritual needs, for be it noted, that man in contrast from the beasts, is essentially a spiritual being. No; over all the systems of this poor world it is written "Whosoever drinketh of this

*Note in 2 Kings 4:: 38-40 "pottage" was the food of God's *prophets.*

water shall thirst again." It cannot be otherwise. How can a world into which *sin* has entered, which is *away from God,* and which *"lieth in the Wicked One"* furnish anything which can truly meet the need of the heart that, consciously or unconsciously, ever panteth after God! Esau's experience was but that of Solomon at a later date, and of many another since—vanity and vexation of spirit is the only portion for those who seek contentment "*under* the sun." So it is now. Only the Jacobs—the objects of God's grace—possess that which appeases the hunger of the inner man.

"And Esau said to Jacob, Feed me, I pray thee, with that same red pottage for I am faint." It is a pity that the translators of our noble King James Version should have obscured the meaning here by inserting in italics the word "pottage." As it so frequently the case the words in italics, put in to convey a better sense, only *hide* the real sense. So it is here. In v. 29 the word "pottage" *is* employed by the Holy Spirit to denote the portion which Jacob enjoyed. But here in v. 30 what Esau really says is "Feed me, I pray thee, with that same red," and this was all he said. He was *ignorant* of even the name of that which was Jacob's. No doubt he was thoroughly versed in the terms of the chase, but of the things of the house, of the portion of God's chosen, he *knew not*—"Therefore the world knoweth us not, because it knew Him not" (1 John 3:1).

"And Jacob said, Sell me this day thy birthright," etc. (v. 31). Here Jacob offers to *buy from* Esau what was his by the free bounty of God. A word now concerning this "birthright." The birthright was a most cherished possession in those days. It consisted of the excellency of dignity and power, usually a double portion (see Gen. 49:3 and Deut. 21:17). In connection with the family of Abraham there was a peculiar blessing attached to the birthright: it was spiritual as well as temporal in its nature. "The birthright was a spiritual heritage. It gave the right of being the priest of the family or clan. It carried with it the privilege of being the depository and communicator of the Divine secrets. It constituted a link in the line of descent by which the Messiah was to be born into the world." (F. B. M.)

Esau reveals his true character by saying "Behold, I am going to die: and what profit shall this birthright do to me?" These words show what a low estimate he placed upon "the blessing of Abraham." *This* birthright he contemptuously termed it. We think, too, that in the light of the surrounding circumstances Esau's utterance here explains the word of the Holy Spirit in Heb. 12:16—"Lest there be any fornicator, or *profane* person, as Esau, who for one morsel of meat sold his birthright." Surely Esau did not mean he would die of hunger unless he ate immediately of the pottage, for that is scarcely conceivable when he had access to all the provisions in Isaac's house. Rather does it seem to us that what he intended was, that in a little time at most, he would be dead, and then of what account would the promises of God to Abraham and his seed be to him—I cannot live on promises, give me something to eat and drink, for to-morrow I die, seems to be the force of his words.

The next time Esau is mentioned is at the close of Gen. 26: there we read "And Esau was forty years old when he took to wife Judith the daughter of Beeri the Hittite, and Bashemath the daughter of Elon the Hittite: which were a grief of mind unto Isaac and to Rebekah." We cannot do better than quote from Mr. Grant:—"This is the natural sequel of a profanity which could esteem the birthright at the value of a mess of pottage. These forty years are a significant hint to us of a completed probation. In his two wives, married at once, he refuses at once the example and counsel of his father, and by his union with Canaanitish women disregarded the Divine sentence, and shows unmistakably the innermost recesses of the heart."

We are now ready to look at the sad scene which Gen. 27 presents to us. "And it came to pass, that when Isaac was old, and his eyes were dim, so that he could not see, he called Esau his eldest son, and said unto him, My son: and he said unto him, Behold, here am I. And he said, Behold now, I am old, I know not the day of my death: Now therefore take, I pray thee, thy weapons, thy quiver and thy bow, and go out to the field, and take me some venison; And make me savory meat, such as I love, and bring it to me, that I may eat; that my soul may bless thee before I die" (Gen. 27:1-4). Why was it that Isaac desired to partake of venison from Esau *before* blessing him? Does not Gen. 25:28 answer the question—"And Isaac loved Esau *because* he did eat of his venison." In view of this statement it would seem, then, that Isaac desired to enkindle or intensify his affections for Esau, so that he might bless him with all his heart. But surely Isaac's eyes were "dim" spiritually as well as physically. Let us not forget that what we read here at the beginning of Gen. 27 follows immediately after the record of Esau marrying the two heathen wives. Thus it will be seen that Isaac's wrong in being partial to Esau was greatly aggravated by treating so lightly his son's affront to the glory of Jehovah—and all for a meal of venison! Alas, what a terrible thing is the flesh with its "affections and lusts" *even in a believer,* yea, more terrible than in an unbeliever. But worst of all, Isaac's partiality toward Esau was a plain disregard of God's word to Rebekah that Esau should "serve" Jacob (Gen. 25:23). By comparing Heb. 11:20 with Rom. 10:7 it is certain that Isaac had himself "heard" this.

"And Rebekah heard when Isaac spake to Esau his son .....and Rebekah spake unto Jacob her son.....Now therefore, my son, obey my voice according to that which I command thee. Go now to the flock, and fetch me from thence two good kids of the goats; and I will make them savory meat for thy father, such as he loveth: And thou shalt bring it to thy father, that he may eat, and that he may bless thee before his death" (vs. 6-10). How like Sarah before her, who, in a similar "evil hour" imagined that she could give effect to the Divine promise by fleshly expediences (Gen. 16:2). As another has suggested "they both acted on that God dishonoring proverb that 'The Lord helps those who help themselves,'" whereas the truth is, the Lord helps those who have come to the *end* of themselves. If Rebekah really had confidence in the Divine promise she might well have followed tranquilly the path of duty, assured that in due time God would Himself bring His word to pass.

"And Jacob said to Rebekah his mother, Behold, Esau my brother is a hairy man, and I am a smooth man: My father peradventure will feel me, and I shall seem to him as a deceiver; and I shall bring a curse upon me, and not a blessing" (vs. 11, 12). How the character of Jacob comes out here! He reveals his native shrewdness and foresight, but instead of shrinking back in horror from the sin, he appears to have been occupied only with what might prove its unpleasant consequences.

"And his mother said unto him, Upon me be thy curse, my son: only obey my voice, and go fetch me them. And he went and fetched, and brought them to his mother: and his mother made savory meat, such as his father loved. And Rebekah took goodly raiment of her eldest son, Esau, which were with her in the house, and put them upon Jacob her younger son: And she put the skins of the kids of the goats upon his hands, and upon the smooth of his neck: And she gave the savory meat and the bread, which she had prepared, into the hand of her son Jacob" (vs. 13-17). It is difficult to say who was most to blame, Jacob or his mother. Rebekah was the one to whom God had directly made known His purpose respecting her two sons, and, be it noted, the wife of Isaac was no heathen but, instead, one who knew the Lord—cf. "She went to enquire of the Lord" (25:22). Her course was plain: she should have trusted the Lord to bring to nought the carnal design of Isaac, but she took the way of the flesh, plotted against her husband, and taught her son to deceive his father. Yet in condemning Rebekah we are reminded of Rom. 2:1, "Therefore thou are inexcusable O man, whosoever thou art that judgest: for wherein thou judgest another, thou condemnest thyself; for thou that judgest doest the same things."

We refrain from quoting at length the verses that follow. Jacob complies with his mother's suggestion, and adds sin to sin. First he impersonates his brother, tells lies to his father, and ends by going the awful length of bringing in the name of the Lord God (v. 20). To what fearful lengths will sin quickly lead us once we take the first wrong step! A similar progression in evil is seen (by way of implication) in Psa. 1:1: the one who "walks" in the counsel of the ungodly will soon be found "standing" in the way of sinners, and then it will not be long ere he is discovered "sitting" in the seat of the scornful.

At first suspicious, Isaac's fears were allayed by his son's duplicity, and the blessing was given, "and he came near and kissed him: and he smelled the smell of his raiment, and blessed him, and said, See, the smell of my son is as the smell of a field which the Lord hath blessed: Therefore God give thee of the dew of heaven, and the fatness of the earth, and plenty of corn and wine: Let people serve thee, and nations bow down to thee: be lord over thy brethren, and let thy mother's sons bow down to thee: cursed be every one that curseth thee, and blessed be he that blesseth thee" (vs. 27-29). It is to be noted that the "blessing" which Jacob here receives from the lips of his father was far below the blessed string of promises which he received directly from God when wholly cast upon His grace (see 28:13-15).

We need not tarry long on the pathetic sequel. No sooner had Jacob left his father's presence than Esau comes in with his venison and says, "let my father arise and eat of his son's venison, that thy soul may bless me." Then it is that Isaac discovers the deception that has been practiced upon him, and he "trembled very exceedingly." Esau learns of his brother's duplicity, and with a great and exceeding bitter cry says, "Bless me, even me also, O my father," only to hear Isaac say, "Thy brother came with subtlety, and hath taken away thy blessing....behold I have made him thy lord." Esau renews his request saying, "Hast thou but one blessing, my father? Bless me, even me, also." Then it was that Isaac uttered that prophecy that received such a striking fulfillment in the centuries that followed—"Behold, thy dwelling shall be the fatness of the earth, and of the dew of heaven from above; And by thy sword shalt thou live, and shalt serve thy brother: and it shall come to pass when thou shalt have the dominion, that thou shalt break his yoke from off thy neck" (vs. 39, 40). For Esau "serving his brother" *see* 2 Sam. 8:14 (David was a descendant of Jacob); and for "thou shalt break his yoke from off thy neck" *see* 2 Chron. 21:8.

Above we have noticed that when Isaac discovered that he had blessed Jacob instead of Esau he "trembled very exceedingly." This was the turning point in the incident, the point where, for the first time, light breaks in on this dark scene. It was horror which was awakened in his soul as he now fully realized that he had been pitting himself against the expressed mind of Jehovah. It is beautiful to notice that instead of "cursing" Jacob (as his son had feared, see v. 12) now that Isaac discovers how God had graciously overruled his wrong doing, he bowed in self-judgment, and "trembled with a great trembling greatly" (margin). Then it was that faith found expression in the words "And he *shall* be blest" (v. 33). He knew now that God had been securing what He had declared before the sons were born. It is this which the Spirit seizes on in Heb. 11:20, "*By faith* Isaac blest Jacob and Esau concerning things to come."

Many are the lessons illustrated and exemplified in the above incident. We can do little more than name a few of the most important. 1. How many to-day are, like Esau, bartering Divine privileges for carnal gratification. 2. Beware of doing evil that good may come. What shame and sorrow they do make for themselves who in their zeal for good do not scruple to use wrong means. Thus it was with Rebekah and Jacob. 3. Let us seek grace to prevent natural affections overriding love for God and His revealed will. 4. Remember the unchanging law of Sowing and Reaping. How striking to observe that it was Rebekah, not Isaac, who sent her beloved child away! She it was who led him into grievous sin, and she it was whom God caused to be the instrument of his exile. She, poor thing, suggested that he find refuge in the home of Laban her brother for "some days." Little did she imagine that her favorite child would have to remain there for twenty years, and that never again should she behold him in the flesh. Ah! the mills of God grind slowly, but they grind exceeding small, and we might add "surely." And during those long years Jacob was to be *cheated* by Laban as he had cheated Isaac. 5. Learn the utter futility of seeking to foil God: "So then it is not of him that willeth, nor of him that runneth, but of God that showeth mercy" (Rom. 9:16); neither Isaac's "willing" nor Esau's "running" could defeat the purpose of Jehovah. "There are many devices in a man's heart; nevertheless the counsel of the Lord that shall stand" (Prov. 19:21). Man proposes but God disposes.

Finally, have we not here, deeply hidden, a beautiful picture of the Gospel. Jacob found acceptance with his father and received his blessing because he sheltered behind the name of the father's firstborn, beloved son, and was clothed with his garments which diffused to Isaac an excellent odor. In like manner, we as sinners, find acceptance before God and receive His blessing as we shelter behind the name of *His* beloved Firstborn, and as we are clothed with the robe of righteousness which we receive from Him thus coming before the Father in the merits of His Son who "hath given Himself for us an offering and a sacrifice to God for *a sweet smelling savor*" (Eph. 5:2).

29. THE MAN JACOB

Genesis 28

Jacob and his experiences may be viewed from two chief viewpoints: as a picture of the believer, and as a type of the Jewish nation. We shall take up the latter first. As to Jacob foreshadowing the history of the Jews we may note, among others, the following analogies:

1. Jacob was markedly the object of God's election: Rom. 9:10. So, too, was the Jewish nation. See Deut. 6: 7; 10:15; Amos 3:2.

2. Jacob was loved before he was born, Rom. 9:11-13. Of the Jewish nation it is written, "Thus saith the Lord, the people which were left of the sword found grace in the wilderness; even Israel, when I went to cause him to rest, the Lord hath appeared of old unto me, saying, Yea, I have loved thee with an everlasting love" (Jer. 31:2, 3).

3. Jacob was altogether lacking in natural attractiveness. This is singularly true of the Jewish people.

4. Jacob was the one from whom the Twelve Tribes directly sprang.

5. Jacob is the one after whom the Jewish race is most frequently called. See Isaiah 2:5, etc.

6. Jacob was the one whom God declared should be "served," Gen. 25:23; 27:29. Of the Jews the prophetic scriptures affirm, "Thus saith the Lord God, Behold, I will lift up Mine hand to the Gentiles, and set up My standard to the people, and they shall bring thy sons in their arms, and thy daughters shall be carried upon their shoulders. And kings shall be thy nursing fathers, and their queens thy nursing mothers; they shall *bow down to thee* with their face to the earth, and lick up the dust of thy feet" (Is. 49:22, 23). And again it is written of Israel, "And they shall *bring* all your brethren for an offering unto the Lord out of all nations upon horses, and in chariots, and in litters, and upon mules" (Is. 66:20).

7. Jacob was the one to whom God gave the earthly inheritance, Gen. 27:28; 28:13. So, too, the Jews.

8. Jacob suffered a determined effort to be *robbed* of his inheritance, Gen. 27: Isaac and Esau. So have the Jews.

9. Jacob valued the blessing of God, but sought it in carnal ways, totally opposed to faith, Gen. 26:27. So it is

written of the Jews, "For I bear them record that they have a zeal of God, *but not according to knowledge.* For they being ignorant of God's righteousness, and going about to establish their own righteousness, have not submitted themselves unto the righteousness of God" (Rom. 10:2, 3).

10. Jacob was exiled from the land as the result of his *sin,* Gen. 28:5. So have the Jews been.

11. Jacob spent much of his life as a wandering exile from the land; such has been the history of his descendants

12. Jacob was distinctly the *wanderer* among the patriarchs, and as such a type of the wandering Jew!

13. Jacob experienced, as such, the sore chastenings of a righteous God. So, too, the Jews.

14. Jacob had no "altar" in the land of his exile: thus also is it written of the Jews, "For the children of Israel shall abide many days without a King, and without a prince, *and without a sacrifice*" (Hosea 3:4).

15. Jacob set his heart upon the land while exiled from it. His yearning for home is strikingly expressed in his words to Laban: "Send me away, that I may go unto mine own place, and to my country," (30:25). How we behold the same yearning among the Zionists today, as they appeal to American and British statesmen to make it possible for them to return in safety to Palestine!

16. Jacob was unjustly dealt with in the land of exile, Gen. 29:23; 31:41, 42.

17. Jacob developed into a crafty schemer and used subtle devices to secure earthly riches, Gen. 30:37, 43.

18. Jacob while in exile receives promise from God that he shall return unto the promised land, Gen. 28:15.

19. Jacob received no further revelation from God during all the years of his exile, until at length bidden by Him to return, Gen. 31:3.

20. Jacob was graciously preserved by God in the land of his exile and was the object of His ceaseless providential care.

21. Jacob became wealthy while in the land of exile, Gen. 30:43.

22. Jacob, because of this, had stirred up against him the enmity of those among whom he sojourned, Gen. 31:1.

23. Jacob ultimately returned to the land bearing with him the riches of the Gentiles, 31:18.

24. Jacob is seen at the end *blessing* the Gentiles (Gen. 47:7), and acting as God's prophet, Gen. 49. In all these respects Jacob was a striking type of the Jew.

We shall next look at Jacob as a picture of the believer. It is intensely interesting to mark how each of the patriarchs foreshadowed some distinct truth in the believer. In Abraham we see the truth of Divine sovereignty, and the life of faith; in Isaac Divine sonship, and the life of submission; in Jacob Divine grace, and the life of conflict. In Abraham, election; in Isaac, the new birth; in Jacob, the manifestation of the two natures. Thus we find the *order* of these Old Testament biographies foreshadowed accurately what is now fully revealed in the New Testament. Again, we may remark further that, typically, Jacob is the *servant*. This is ever the Divine order. Abraham, the chosen object of God's sovereign purpose, necessarily comes first, then Isaac, the *son* born supernaturally, the heir of the father's house, followed by Jacob, the *servant*. It is needful to call special attention to this order to-day, though we cannot here enlarge upon it. Man would place sonship at the *end* of a long life of service, but God places it at the *beginning*. Man says, Serve God in order to become His son; but God says, You must first be My son in order to serve Me acceptably. The apostle Paul expressed this order when he said: "Whose I am, *and* whom I serve" (Acts 27:23). How carefully this order is guarded in our type appears further in the fact that *before* Jacob commenced his service at Padan-aram he first tarried at Bethel, which means "the House of God"—we must first enter God's household before we can serve Him! That Jacob *does*, typically, represent *service* is clear from, Hosea 12:12, where we are told, "And Jacob fled into the country of Syria, and Israel *served* for a wife, and for a wife he kept sheep." The *history* of this we get in Genesis 29 and 30. As a servant with Laban, Jacob was singularly *faithful*. Here is his own challenge, "These twenty years have I been with thee; thy ewes and thy she goats have not cast their young, and the rams of thy flock have I not eaten. That which was torn of beasts I brought not unto thee; I bare the loss of it; of my hand didst thou require it, whether stolen by day, or stolen by night. Thus I was, in the day the drought consumed me, and the frost by night."

There is still another way in which this *progressive order* in the typical foreshadowings of the three great patriarchs comes out. This has been forcefully set forth by Mr. F. W. Grant who, when commenting on the words of the Lord to Moses at the burning bush—"say unto the children of Israel, the God of Abraham, and the God of Isaac, and the God of Jacob sent me unto you"—says, "In Abraham we find manifested the type of the Father, and in Isaac admittedly that of the Son, in Jacob-Israel we find a type and pattern of the Spirit's work which is again and again dwelt on and expanded in the after-scriptures. Balaam's words as to the people, using this double—this natural and this scriptural—name, are surely as true of the nation's ancestors. 'It shall be said of Jacob, and of Israel, what hath God wrought?' What God hath *wrought* is surely what in the one now before us we are called in an especial way to acknowledge and glory in. For Jacob's God is He whom we still know as accomplishing in us by almighty power the purposes of sovereign grace."

While it is true that each of the three great patriarchs exemplified in his own person some fundamental truth of Divine revelation, yet it is to be particularly noted that each succeeding individual carried forward what had gone before, so that nothing was lost. In Abraham we behold the truth of election—God's singling of him out from all the people on the earth; yet in Isaac the *same* truth is manifested, as is evident from the passing by of Ishmael and God's declaration that "In Isaac shall thy seed be called." Isaac represents the truth of Divine sonship, born supernaturally by the intervention of God's power. Now in Jacob both of these truths, with important additions, are also to be observed. Even more notably than in the cases of Abraham and Isaac, Jacob is the object of God's sovereign choice: "Jacob gives occasion to the exercise of God's sovereignty as to the twin children of Isaac and Rebekah. 'For they being not yet born, nor having done any good or bad, that the purpose of God according to election might stand, not of works, but of Him that calls, it was said to their mother, the elder shall serve the younger.' It had been shown before in casting out the bond-woman and her son; but so it was now far more emphatically in Jacob chosen, not Esau. No flesh shall glory in His sight; in Jehovah certainly, as it ought to be. Is man *only to think and talk of his* rights? Sinful man! Has God alone no rights? Is He to be a mere registrar of man's wrongs? Oh! his wrongs, not rights: this is the truth, as no believer should forget from the dawn of a vital work in his soul!" ("Jacob," by W. Kelly).

As the above truth is now so much controverted we subjoin a further quotation from the pen of one who is regarded as one of the leading orthodox teachers of our day: "In all this we see the marvel and glory of the Divine sovereignty. Why the younger son should have been chosen instead of the elder we do not know. It is, however, very striking to find the same principle exercised on several other occasions. It is pretty certain that Abraham was not the eldest son of Terah. We know that Isaac was the younger son of Abraham, and that Joseph was not the eldest son of Jacob. All this goes to emphasize the simple fact that the order of nature is not necessarily the order of grace. All through, *God decided to display the sovereignty of His grace* as contrasted with that which was merely natural in human life. The great problem of Divine sovereignty is of course insoluable by the human intellect. It has to be accepted as a simple fact. It should, however, be observed that it is not merely a fact in regard to things spiritual; it is found also in nature in connection with human temperaments and races. All history is full of illustrations of the Divine choice, as we may see from such examples as Cyrus and Pharaoh. *Divine election is a fact, whether we can understand it or not* (italics ours). God's purposes are as certain as they are often inscrutable, and it is perfectly evident from the case of Esau and Jacob that the Divine choice of men is entirely independent of their merits or of any pre-vision of their merits or attainments (Rom. 9:11). It is in connection with this subject that we see the real force of St. Paul's striking words when he speaks of God as acting 'according to the *good pleasure* of His will' (Eph. 1:5), and although we are bound to confess the '*mystery* of His will' (Eph. 1:9), we are also certain that He works all things 'after the *counsel* of His will' (Eph. 1:11—italics not ours). There is nothing arbitrary about God and His ways and our truest wisdom when we cannot understand His reasons is to rest quietly and trustfully, saying, 'Even so, Father, for so it seemeth good in thy sight.' 'In His

Will is our peace' " (Dr. Griffith-Thomas, Commentary on Genesis).

Not only is the Divine sovereignty illustrated in Jacob, as in Abraham, but we also see typified in him the truth of regeneration (as in the case of Isaac) inasmuch as *nature* was set aside, and only in answer to prayer and by Divine intervention was Rebekah enabled to bear Jacob: see Gen. 25:21.

That which is most prominent in the Divine dealings with Jacob was the matchless *grace* of God, shown to one so unworthy, the marvellous *patience* exercised toward one so slow of heart to believe, the changeless *love* which unweariedly followed him through all his varied course, the *faithfulness* which no unfaithfulness on Jacob's part could change, and the *power* of God which effectively preserved and delivered him through numerous dangers and which, in the end, caused the spirit to triumph over the flesh, transforming the worm Jacob into Israel the prince of God. How these Divine perfections were displayed will be discovered as we turn our attention to the various scenes in which the Holy Spirit has portrayed our patriarch. We turn now to look briefly at Jacob in Genesis 28.

In our last article we dwelt upon Jacob deceiving his father, now we see how quickly he began to suffer for his wrongdoing! "And Isaac called Jacob, and blessed him, and said unto him, Thou shalt not take a wife of the daughters of Canaan. *Arise, go* to Padan-aram, to the house of Bethuel thy mother's father; and take thee a wife from thence of the daughters of Laban, thy mother's brother" (28:1, 2). Jacob is sent away from home, to which he returns not for many years. In our studies upon Isaac we have seen how he foreshadowed those who belong to the *heavenly* calling, whereas, as we have pointed out above, Jacob typified the people of the earthly calling. This comes out in many incidental details. Isaac was forbidden to leave Canaan (type of the Heavenlies)—24:5, 6—and his bride was brought to him, but Jacob *is sent forth out of Canaan* to the house of his mother's father in quest of a wife, and thus was signified the evident contrast between Isaac and Jacob, and Jacob's *earthly* place and relationship.

"And Jacob went out from Beersheba, and went toward Haran. And he lighted upon a certain place, and tarried there all night, because the sun was set; and he took of the stones of that place, and put them for his pillows, and lay down in that place to sleep. And he dreamed, and behold a ladder set up on the earth, and the top of it reached to heaven: and behold the angels of God ascending and descending on it. And, behold, the Lord stood above it, and said, I am the Lord God of Abraham thy father, and the God of Isaac; the land whereon thy liest to thee will I *give* it, and to thy seed; and thy seed shall be as the dust of the earth; and thou shalt spread abroad to the west, and to the east, and to the north, and to the south; and in thee and thy seed shall all the families of the earth be blessed. And, behold, I am with thee, and will keep thee in all places whither thou goest, and will bring thee again into this land; for I will not leave thee, until I have done that which I have spoken to thee of" (28:10-15). There is much here that might be dwelt upon with profit to our souls, but we can do little more than mention one or two things.

Here we behold the marvellous *grace* of God, which delights to single out as its objects the most unlikely and unworthy subjects. Here was Jacob a fugitive from his father's house, fleeing from his brother's wrath, with probably no thought of God in his mind. As we behold him there on the bare ground with nothing but the stones for his pillow, enshrouded by the darkness of night, asleep—symbol of death—we obtain a striking and true picture of *man in his natural state.* Man is never so *helpless* as when asleep, and it was while he was in *this* condition that God appeared unto him! What had Jacob done to *deserve* this high honor? What was there in him to *merit* this wondrous privilege? Nothing; absolutely nothing. It was God in *grace* which now met him for the first time and here *gave* to him and his seed the land whereon he lay. Such is ever His way. He pleases to choose the foolish and vile things of this world: He selects those who have nothing and gives them everything: He singles out those who deserve naught but judgment, and bestows on them nothing but blessing. But note—and mark it particularly—the recipient of the Divine favors must first take his place *in the dust,* as Jacob here did (on the naked earth) before God will bless him.

And under what similitude did the Lord now reveal Himself to the worm Jacob? Jacob beheld in his dream a *ladder* set up on the earth, whose top reached unto heaven, and from above it the voice of God addressed him. Fortunately we are not left to our own speculations to determine the signification of this: John 1:51 interprets it for us. We say fortunately, for if we could not point to John 1:51 in proof of what we advance, some of our readers might charge us with indulging in a wild flight of the imagination. The "ladder" pointed to *Christ Himself,* the One who spanned the infinite gulf which separated heaven from earth, and who has in His own person provided a Way whereby we may draw near to God. That the "ladder" reached from earth to heaven, told of the *complete* provision which Divine grace has made for sinners. Right down to where the fugitive lay, the ladder came, and right up to God Himself the "ladder" reached!

In His address to Jacob, the Lord now repeated the promises which He had made before to Abraham and Isaac, with the additional assurance that He would be with him, preserving him wherever he went, and ultimately bringing him back to the land. In perfect harmony with the fact that Jacob represented the earthly people we may observe here that God declares Jacob's seed shall be "as the dust of the earth," but *no reference* is made to "the stars of heaven!"

The sequel to this vision may be told in few words. Jacob awoke and was afraid, saying, "How dreadful is this place! This is none other but the house of God, and this is the gate of heaven" (v. 17). Next, he took the stone on which his head had rested and poured oil upon it. Then he changed the name of the place from Luz to Bethel. It is instructive to note this change of name, Luz—its original name, signifies "separation," while Bethel, its new name, means "the house of God." Is it not beautiful to mark the typical force of this? God calls us to *separate from the world,* but in leaving the world *we enter His house!* "Never do we part from ought at His call, but He far more than makes it up to us with His own smile" (W. Lincoln).

Finally, we are told, "And Jacob vowed a vow, saying, If God will be with me, and will keep me in this way that I go, and will give me bread to eat, and raiment to put on, so that I come again to my father's house in peace; then shall the Lord be my God. And this stone, which I have set for a pillar, shall be God's house, and of all that Thou shalt give me *I will surely give* the tenth unto Thee" (28: 20-22). How true to life this is! It was not only characteristic of Jacob personally, but typical of *us* representatively. *Jacob failed to rise to the level of God's grace* and was filled with fear instead of peace, and expressed human legality by speaking of what *he* will do. Oh, how often *we* follow in his steps! Instead of resting in the goodness of God and appropriating His free grace, like Jacob, we bargain and enter into conditions and stipulations. May the God of Grace enlarge our hearts to receive His grace, and may He empower us to magnify His grace by refusing to defile it with any of our own wretched additions.

30. JACOB AT PADAN-ARAM

Genesis 29

In our last article we followed Jacob as he left his father's house and commenced his long journey to Padan-aram where lived Laban, his mother's brother. On his first night out from Beersheba he lit upon a certain place and making a pillar of the stones lay down to sleep. Then it was that he dreamed, and in the dream the Lord appeared unto him, probably for the first time in his life, and after promising to give him the land whereon he lay and to make his seed as numerous as the dust of the earth and a blessing to all families, he received the comforting assurance that God would be with him, would keep him in all places whither he went, and ultimately bring him back again to the land given to him and his fathers. In the morning Jacob arose, poured oil on the stone pillar, and named the place Bethel, which means "The House of God."

The effect of this experience on Jacob is briefly but graphically signified in the opening words of Genesis 29, where we read, "*Then* Jacob *lifted up his feet,* and came into the land of the people of the East" (marginal rendering). The heaviness with which he must have left home had now gone. Assured of the abiding presence and protection of Jehovah, he went on his way light-heartedly. It deserves to be noted that the journey which Jacob had scarcely begun the previous day was an arduous and difficult one. From Beersheba, Isaac's dwelling-place, to Padan-Aram, his destination, was a distance of something like five hundred miles, and when we remember that he was on foot and alone we can the better appreciate the blessed grace of Jehovah which met the lonely fugitive the first night, and gave him the comforting promise that He was with him and would keep him in *all* places whither he went (28:15). Little wonder, then, that now Jacob goes forth so confidently and cheerfully. As a Jewish commentator remarks, "His heart lifted up his feet." And, reader, do not we need to be reminded that *our* Lord has promised, "Lo, I am with you always, even unto the end"? If our hearts drew from this cheering and inspiring promise the comfort and incentive it is designed to convey should not we "lift up" *our* feet as we journey through this world? Oh! it is unbelief, failure to rest upon the "exceeding great and precious promises" of our God, and forgetfulness that He is ever by our side, that makes our feet leaden and causes us to drag along so wearily.

The remainder of the long journey seems to have passed without further incident, for the next thing we read of is that Jacob had actually come into that land which he sought. And here we find a striking *proof* that the Lord *was* with him indeed, for he was guided to a well where he met none other than the daughter of the very man with whom he was going to make his home! It was not by chance that Jacob lit upon that well in the field, nor was it by accident that Rachel came to that well just when she did. There are no chance-happenings or accidents in a world that is governed by God. It was not by chance that the Ishmaelites passed by when the brethren of Joseph were plotting his death, nor was it an accident they were journeying down to Egypt. It was not by chance that Pharoh's daughter went down to the river to bathe, and that one of her attendants discovered there the infant Moses in the ark of bullrushes. It was not by chance that upon a certain night, critical in the history of Israel, that Ahasuerus was unable to sleep and that he should arise and read the state-records which contained an entry of how Mordecai had foiled an attempt on the King's life, which led, in turn, to the saving of Mordecai's life. So, we say, it was not by chance that Jacob now met Rachel. No; we repeat, there cannot be any chance-happenings in a world that is governed by God, still less can there be any accidents in the lives of those He is constantly "with." My reader, there are no chance-happenings, no chance-meetings, no chance delays, no chance losses, no chance anythings in *our* lives. *All* is of Divine appointment.

But while we have called attention to God's faithfulness in guiding Jacob to the well where he met Rachel, we must not ignore Jacob's personal failure, a noticeable failure of *omission.* As he had come so near to the end of his journey and had almost arrived at his destination we would have thought, as he reached this well, that now was the time for him to very definitely commit himself into the hands of God, especially in view of the fact that he was engaged in the important and momentous undertaking of seeking a wife. Years before, when the servant of Abraham was upon a similar mission, seeking a wife for Isaac, when *he* arrived at a well we are told that "he said, O Lord God of my master Abraham, I pray Thee, send me good speed this day" (24:12). But here in connection with Jacob we read of no prayer for Divine guidance and blessing, instead, we find him interrogating the Haran shepherds.

"And he looked, and behold a well in the field, and, lo, there were three flocks of sheep lying by it; for out of that well they watered the flocks: and a great stone was upon the well's mouth. And thither were all the flocks gathered: and they rolled the stone from the well's mouth, and watered the sheep, and put the stone again upon the well's mouth in his place. And Jacob said unto them, My brethren, whence be ye? And they said, Of Haran are we. And he said unto them, Know ye Laban the son of Nahor? And they said, We know him. And he said unto them, Is he well? And they said, He is well: and, behold, Rachel his daughter cometh with the sheep" (29:2-6). Without doubt there is a spiritual meaning to each detail here. It cannot be without some good reason that the Spirit of God has told us this was in a *field,* that there were *three* flocks of sheep lying by it, and that there was a *great stone* upon the well's mouth. But we confess we discern not their significance, and where spiritual vision be dim it is idle, or worse, to speculate.

"Behold, Rachel his daughter cometh with the sheep." At mention of Rachel, Jacob acted in a thoroughly characteristic manner: "And he said, Lo, it is yet high day, neither is it time that the cattle should be gathered together: water ye the sheep, *and go* and feed them" (29:7). Jacob's design is evident; he sought to send the shepherds away, so that he might be alone when he met Rachel. But his design was foiled, "and while he yet spake with them, Rachel came with her father's sheep: for she kept them." And then follows a touching description of the meeting between Jacob and this young woman who was to become his wife.

"And it came to pass, when Jacob saw Rachel the daughter of Laban his mother's brother, and the sheep of Laban his mother's brother, that Jacob went near, and rolled the stone from the well's mouth, and watered the flock of Laban his mother's brother. And Jacob kissed Rachel, and lifted up his voice, and wept. And Jacob told Rachel that he was her father's brother, and that he was Rebekah's son: and she ran and told her father" (29:10-12). These verses shed an interesting light on Jacob's natural character. Rachel's appearance awakened within him all the warmth of natural feeling. He courteously rolled away the stone, watered the sheep, kissed Rachel and burst into tears. The remembrance of home and the relationship of his *mother* to Rachel overpowered him—note the threefold reference to his mother in verse 10: "When Jacob saw Rachel the daughter of Laban *his mother's* brother, and the sheep of Laban *his mother's* brother, that Jacob went near, and rolled the stone from the well's mouth, and watered the flock of Laban *his mother's* brother." Jacob, then, was no cold, calculating stoic, but was of a warm disposition, and everything that revived the memory of his mother went to his heart. What a lovely human touch this gives to the picture! Nothing is trivial with God.

"And it came to pass, when Laban heard the tidings of Jacob his sister's son, that he ran to meet him, and embraced him, and kissed him, and brought him to his house. And he told Laban all these things. And Laban said to him, Surely thou art my bone and my flesh. And he abode with him the space of a month" (29:13, 14). The plan of Jacob's mother seemed to be working very well. Everything appeared to be running very smoothly. Esau had been left behind at a safe distance, the long journey from Beersheba to Padan-aram had been covered without harm, little or no difficulty had been experienced in locating his mother's brother. Rachel had shown no resentment at Jacob's affectionate greeting, and now Laban himself had accorded the fugitive a warm welcome, and for a whole month nothing seems to have broken their serenity. *And what of God?* What of His moral government? What of the law of retribution? Was Jacob to suffer nothing for his wrongdoing? Was the deception he had practiced upon Isaac to escape unnoticed? Would it, in his case, *fail* to appear that "the way of the transgressor is hard"? (Pro. 13:15). Ah! be not deceived; God is not mocked. Sometimes the actions of God's government may appear to move slowly, but sooner or later they are sure. Often-times this is overlooked. Men take too short a view: "Because sentence against an evil work is not executed *speedily,* therefore the heart of the sons of men is fully set in them to do evil" (Ecc. 8:11).

It is in the sequel that God is vindicated. History in fragments denies God, but history as a whole is seen to be His story. Look at the cruel Egyptian task-masters and at the helpless Hebrews. They cried to Heaven, and for years it seemed as though Heaven was deaf. But *the sequel* showed God *had* seen and heard, and *in* the sequel His righteous government was vindicated. We have had striking illustrations of this abiding principle in the history of our own times. A few years ago we were horrified by the Belgian atrocities on the Congo, and equally so by the cruel inhumanities practiced by the Russians upon the Jews. But behold *the sequel*—mark Belgium and Russia today! Yes, the way of the transgressor is hard, and so Jacob found it in the sequel.

"And Laban said unto Jacob, Because thou art my brother, shouldest thou therefore *serve* me for nought? Tell me, what shall thy *wages* be?" (29:15). Here was the first cloud on Jacob's horizon, and the first appearing of the Divine rod of chastisement. Here, too, was a most striking example of the law of righteous retribution. Jacob was about to begin reaping that which he had sown. Perhaps this is not apparent on the surface, so we tarry to explain. It will be remembered that the end before Jacob and his mother in their scheming and lying was that he should secure from Isaac the blessing which was the portion of the first born. What this blessing was we know from the words of the Lord to Rebekah before her sons were born, words which expressly declared that Jacob *should* receive the first-born's portion—"the elder *shall serve* the younger" (25:23). That, then, upon which Jacob had set his heart, and that which he had sought to obtain from Isaac by a wicked device, was the position of dignity and honor. Instead of serving he wanted to be served. How striking, then, to note that the very first word spoken by Laban after Jacob had enjoyed the hospitality of his house for a month, concerned that of *service!* How significant that Jacob should have fallen into the hands of a *crafty schemer!* Laban was glad to receive Jacob into his household, but even though his nephew he did not intend that he should remain on indefinitely as a guest. No, he meant to profit by Jacob's presence, and so seeks to strike a bargain, lets Jacob know that if he remained with him it must be in the capacity of a *servant,* and so raises the question of "wages." This must have been a bitter portion for Jacob and a painful blow to his pride. He was beginning to learn that the way of the transgressor is hard.

But what follows is even more remarkable: "And Laban had two daughters: the name of the elder was Leah, and the name of the younger was Rachel. Leah was tender-eyed; but Rachel was beautiful and well favored. And Jacob loved Rachel; and said, I will serve thee seven years for Rachel thy younger daughter. And Laban said, It is better that I give her to thee, than that I should give her to another man: abide with me. And Jacob served seven years for Rachel; and they seemed unto him but a few days, for the love he had to her. And Jacob said unto Laban, Give me my wife, for my days are fulfilled, that I may go in unto her. And Laban gathered together all the men of the place, and made a feast. And it came to pass in the evening, that he took Leah his daughter, and brought her to him; and he went in unto her. And Laban gave unto his daughter Leah Zilpah his maid for an handmaid. And it came to pass, that in the morning, behold it was Leah: and he said to Laban, What is this thou hast done unto me? did not I serve with thee for Rachel? wherefore then hast thou beguiled me? And Laban said, It must not be so done in our country, to give the younger before the first-born. Fulfil her week, and we will give thee this also for the service which thou shalt serve with me yet seven other years. And Jacob did so, and fulfilled her week: and he gave him Rachel his daughter to wife also" (29:16-28). The quotation is a lengthy one but it was necessary to give it in full so that the reader might be able to follow our remarks upon it. In the preceding paragraph we have seen how that the first lesson God was now teaching Jacob was that of humble *submission*—if he had refused to submit to God then he must submit to "serve" a human master. Here, in this quotation, we discover the second lesson that Jacob must learn was to *respect* the rights of the *first-born!* This was just what Jacob had disregarded in connection with Esau, so that which he had ignored concerning his brother he must bow to in connection with his wife. In the third place, mark how God was correcting the *impatience* of our patriarch. It was because he had refused to *wait God's time* for the fulfillment of His promise (as per 25:23) that he had involved himself in so much trouble, and had to leave home and flee from Esau; how fitting then he should now be obliged *to wait seven years* before he could obtain Rachel, and that he should be made to serve a further seven years for her after they were married!

In drawing this article to a close we would seek to expand briefly what seems to us to be the outstanding principle in the scripture we have just examined, namely, the principle of Divine retribution. "Even as I have seen, they that plough iniquity, and sow wickedness, *reap the same*" (Job 4:8). In Laban's treatment of Jacob we see the deceiver deceived! This principle that whatsoever a man soweth *that shall* he also reap is writ large across the pages of Holy Scripture and is strikingly, nay marvelously, illustrated again and again. Pharaoh, King of Egypt, gave orders that every son of the Hebrews should be *drowned* (Ex. 1:22), and so in the end *he* was drowned (Ex. 14:28). Korah caused a cleft in the Congregation of Israel (Num. 16:2, 3), and so God made a cleft in the earth to swallow him (Num. 16:30). Again, we read of one Adoni-bezek that he fled, "and they pursued after him, and caught him, and cut off his thumbs and his great toes. And Adoni-bezek said, Three score and ten kings, having their thumbs and their great toes cut off, gathered their meat under my table: *as I* have done, *so God* hath requited me!" (Judges 1:6, 7). Wicked Ahab caused Naboth to be slain and the dogs came and licked up his blood (1 Kings 21:19), accordingly we read that when Ahab died he was buried in Samaria, "And one washed the chariot (in which he had been slain) in the pool of Samaria; and the dogs licked up *his* blood" (1 Kings 22:38). King Asa caused the prophet to be placed in "the house of *the stocks*" (2 Chron. 16:10 R. V.), and accordingly we read later that God punished *him* by a disease in his *feet* (1 Kings 15:23). Haman prepared a gallows for Mordecai, but was hanged upon it himself (Esther 7:10). Saul of Tarsus stood by and consented to the *stoning* of Stephen, and later we read that at Lystra the Jews *stoned* Paul (Acts 14:19)—this is the more noticeable because Barnabas who was with him escaped!

But the most striking example of what men term "poetic justice" is the case of Jacob himself. First, he deceived his father and was, in turn, deceived by his father-in-law: Jacob came the younger for the elder to deceive Isaac, and has the elder daughter of Laban given instead of the younger for a wife. Second, we may mark the same principle at work in Jacob's wife. In deceiving Jacob in the matter of Leah, Laban tricked Rachel; later we find Rachel tricking Laban (31:35). Again, we note how a mercenary spirit actuated Jacob in buying the birthright from Esau for a mess of pottage; the sequel to this was the mercenary spirit in Laban which caused him to change Jacob's wages ten times (see 31:41). Finally we may remark, what is most striking of all, that Jacob deceived Isaac by allowing his mother to cover his hands and neck with "the skins of *the kids of the goats*" (27:16), and later Jacob's sons deceived him by dipping the coat of Joseph in the blood of "a *kid of the goats*" (37:31) and making him believe an evil beast had devoured him: note, too, that Jacob deceived Isaac in regard to his favorite son (Esau), and so was Jacob deceived in regard to *his* favorite son (Joseph).

While it is true that very often *the connection between* evil-doing and its evil consequences is not so apparent as in the above examples, nevertheless, God has given us, and still gives us, sufficient proof so as to provide us with solemn warnings of the fact that He is *not mocked,* that He *does* observe the ways of men, that He *hates* sin wherever it is found, and that His righteous government requires that "*every* transgression and disobedience" shall receive "a just recompense of reward" (Heb. 2:2). This "just recompense of reward" is visited upon His own children here in this world, not sent in anger but in love, not in judgment but directed to the conscience and heart so as to bring them to judge themselves for their evil doing. With the wicked it is often otherwise. Frequently they flourish here as a green bay tree, but at the Great White Throne the books shall be opened and every one of them shall be "judged *according to their works.*"

Should one who is out of Christ, a lost sinner, have read this article, let it be unto him as a voice crying "Flee from the wrath to come;" flee to the Lord Jesus, the Saviour, the only Refuge, who came into this world to save sinners. And, let the Christian reader learn anew the exceeding sinfulness of sin, and earnestly seek grace to enable him to crucify the flesh with its affections and lusts so that he may "sow to the Spirit," then shall he "of the Spirit reap life everlasting."

31. JACOB AT PADAN-ARAM, CONTINUED

GENESIS 29, 30

Jacob's stay at Padan-Aram was a lengthy one, much longer than he imagined when he first went there, so little do any of us know what the immediate future holds for us. We move to some place expecting to settle there, and lo, in a short time, God calls us to strike our tents and move to another region. Or, we go to a place thinking it is only for a transient visit, but remain there many years. So it was with Jacob. How blessed to remember, "My times are in *Thy* hand" (Ps. 31: 15).

A somewhat lengthy account is given describing Jacob's sojourn in Laban's home. It is not our aim to expound in detail this section of Genesis—abler pens have done that; rather shall we proffer a few general remarks upon some of the outstanding features which are of special interest and importance.

The thirtieth chapter of Genesis is not pleasant reading, yet is it, like every other in the Old Testament, recorded for our learning. No reflecting Christian mind can read through this chapter without being disgusted with the fruitage and consequences of *polygamy* as therein described. The domestic discords, the envies and jealousies between Jacob's several wives, forcibly illustrate and demonstrate the wisdom and goodness of God's law that each man should have his own wife, as well as each woman her own husband. Example is better than precept, and in Gen. 30 the Holy Spirit sets before us an example of what a plurality of wives must necessarily result in—discord, jealousy and hatred. Let us thank God, then, for giving to us His written precepts to regulate the marriage relationship, the observance of which is necessary not only for the protection of the purity of the home but for its peace and happiness as well.

Though the strifes and jealousies of Jacob's wives were indeed distressing and disgusting yet, we must not attribute their desire for children, or the devices they resorted to in order to obtain them, to mere carnal motives. Had there been nothing more than this the Holy Spirit would not have condescended to record them. There can be little doubt that the daughters of Laban were influenced by the promises of God to Abraham, on whose posterity were entailed the richest blessings, and from whom the Messiah Himself, in the fullness of time, was to descend. It was faith in these promises which made every pious woman of those times desirous of being a mother, and that explains why we read so often of Hebrew women praying so earnestly for this honor.

In the previous article we dwelt at some length on the law of retribution as it was exemplified in the history of Jacob. In an unmistakable and striking manner it is shown again and again in the inspired narrative how that he reaped just what he had sown. Yet it must be borne in mind that in dealing retributively with Jacob God was not acting in wrath but in love, holy love it is true, for Divine love is never exercised at the expense of holiness. Thus, in this evident retribution God was speaking to our Patriarch's conscience and heart. A further illustration of the righteousness of God's governmental dealings is here seen, in that, now Jacob had obtained Laban's first-born daughter his desire was thwarted—she was barren. As another has remarked, "God would have His servant Jacob learn more deeply in his own wounded affections the vileness of self-seeking deceit, and hence He permitted what He would use for chastening and good in the end." (W. K.)

That which occupies the most prominent place in the passage we are now considering is the account there given of the birth and naming of Jacob's twelve sons by his different wives. Here the record is quite full and explicit. Not only is the name of each child given, but in every instance we are told the meaning of the name and that *which occasioned* the selection of it. This would lead us to conclude there is some important lesson or lessons to be learned here. This chapter traces the stream back to its source and shows us the beginnings of the twelve Patriarchs from which the twelve-tribed Nation sprang. Then, would not this cause us to suspect that the *meaning* of the names of these twelve Patriarchs and that which *occasioned* the selection of each name, here so carefully preserved, must be closely connected with the early history of the Hebrew Nation? Our suspicion becomes a certainty when we note the *order* in which the twelve Patriarchs were born, for the circumstances which gave rise to their several names correspond exactly with *the order* of the history of the Children of Israel.

Others before us have written much upon the twelve Patriarchs, the typical significance of their names, and the order in which they are mentioned. It has been pointed out how that the Gospel and the history of a sinner saved by grace is here found in veiled form. For example: Reuben, Jacob's first-born, means, *See, a Son!* This is just what God says to us through the Gospel: to the Son of His love we are invited to look—"Behold the lamb of God." Then comes Simeon whose name signifies *Hearing* and this points to the reception of the Gospel by faith, for faith cometh by hearing, and the promise is, "Hear, and your soul shall live." Next in order is Levi, and his name means *Joined,* telling of the blessed *Union* by which the Holy Spirit makes us one with the Son through the hearing of the Word. In Judah, which means *Praise,* we have manifested the Divine life in the believer, expressed in joyous gratitude for the riches of grace which are now his in Christ. Dan means *Judgment,* and this tells of how the believer uncompromisingly passes sentence upon himself, not only for what he has done but because of what he is, and thus he reckons himself to have died unto sin. Naphtali means *Wrestling* and speaks of that earnestness in prayer which is the very breath of the new life. Next is Gad which means *a Troop or Company,* speaking, perhaps of the believer in fellowship with the Lord's people, and Jacob's eighth son announces the effect of Christian fellowship, for Asher means *Happy.* Issachar means *Hire,* and speaks of *service,* and Zebulon which signifies *Dwelling* reminds us that we are to "occupy" till Christ comes; while Joseph which means *Adding* tells of the *reward* which He will bestow on those who have served diligently and occupied faithfully. Benjamin, the last of Jacob's sons, means *Son of my right hand,* again speaking directly of Christ, and so the circle ends where it begins—with our blessed Lord, for He is "The First and the Last."

There is, then, a typical significance behind the meaning of the names of Jacob's twelve sons, and we believe there is also a prophetic significance behind the carefully preserved record of the words used by the mothers upon the naming of their sons, a significance which must be apparent to all, once it is pointed out. In view of the fact that the Hebrew nation became known as the children of Israel, it is to be expected that we should look closely at the children of Jacob, from whom the nation took its name. And further, in view of the fact that Gen. 29, 30 records the *early* history of Jacob's twelve sons, we should expect to find their history in some way corresponds with the *early* history of the Nation descended from them. Such is indeed the case, as we shall now endeavor to set before the reader.

What we have written above in connection with the typical significance of the names of Jacob's twelve sons is no doubt, with perhaps slight variations, well known to our readers. But it is to be noted that in addition to the naming of the twelve Patriarchs, Gen. 29 and 30 records the *circumstances* which gave rise to the selection of their respective names, for in each case a *reason* is given *why* they received the names they did, yet, so far as we are aware, little or no attention at all has been paid to this feature. We are fully satisfied, however, that the words uttered by the respective mothers of these twelve sons on the occasion of their births, is not without some special significance, and it behooves us to enquire prayerfully into the Spirit's purpose in so carefully preserving a record of them.

Jacob's first son was born to him by Leah, and was named Reuben, and upon giving her son this name she said, "Surely the Lord hath *looked* upon my *affliction*" (Gen. 29:32). The second son was also borne by Leah and was named Simeon, and her reason for thus naming him was as follows, "Because the Lord hath *heard* that I was hated" (Gen. 29:33). The striking resemblance between these two utterances and what is recorded in Exodus in connection with the sufferings of Israel in Egypt is at once apparent. First, we read that "God *looked* upon the Children of Israel" (Ex. 2:25). Then, unto Moses He said, "I have surely seen the *affliction* of My people which are in Egypt" (Ex. 3:7). Then, corresponding with the words of Leah when Simeon was born, He adds, "And have *heard* their cry" (Ex. 3:7). It is surely something more than a mere coincidence that at the birth of Israel's *first* two sons their mother should have spoken of "affliction," which she said the Lord hath "looked upon" and "heard," and that these identical words should be found in the passage which describes the *first* stage in the national history of the Children of Israel who were then "hated" and "afflicted" by the cruel Egyptians. When the Lord told Moses He had seen the "affliction" of His people Israel and had "heard" their cry, did He not have in mind the very words which Leah had uttered long years before!

Jacob's third son was named Levi, and at his birth his mother said, "This time will my *husband* be *joined* to me" (Gen. 29:34). Again these words of the mother point us forward to the beginning of Israel's national history. When was it that Jehovah was "joined" to Israel, and became her "husband"? It was on the eve of their leaving Egypt on the night of the Passover when the lamb was slain and its blood shed and sprinkled. Then it was Jehovah was "joined" to His people—just as now God is joined to us and becomes one with us only in Christ: it is in the Lamb slain, now glorified, that God and the believing sinner meet. And then it was that Jehovah entered into covenant relationship with the chosen Nation, and became their "Husband." Note how this very word is used in Jeremiah, and mark how this reference points back to the Passover night: "Behold, the days come, saith the Lord, that I will make a new covenant with the House of Israel, and with the House of Judah: Not according to the covenant I made with their fathers in the day that I took them by the hand to bring them out of the land of *Egypt;* which My covenant they brake, although I was an *Husband* unto them, saith the Lord" (Jer. 31:31, 32).

Jacob's fourth son was Judah, and upon his birth the mother said, "Now will I *praise* the Lord" (Gen. 29:35). As Leah's words at Levi's birth point us back to the Passover, so her words at Judah's birth carry us forward to the crossing of the Red Sea, where Israel celebrated Jehovah's victory over their foes in song and praised the Lord for their wondrous deliverance. Then it was that, for the first time, Israel sang: "Who is like unto Thee, O Lord, among the gods? Who is like Thee, glorious in holiness, fearful in *praises,* doing wonders?" (Ex. 15:11.) Mark, too, that the Psalmist when referring back to this momentous event said, "And the waters covered their enemies: there was not one of them left. Then believed they His words: they sang His *praise*" (Psa. 106:11, 12).

Next comes Dan, and upon his birth Rachel said, "God hath *judged* me" (Gen. 30:6). If the line of interpretation and application we are now working out be correct, then these words of Rachel, following those of Leah at the birth of Judah, which as we have seen carry us, prophetically, to the Red Sea, will bear upon the early experiences of Israel in their Wilderness wanderings. Such, indeed, we believe to be the case. Do not the above words of Rachel, "God hath *judged* me," point us to the displeasure and "wrath" of God against Israel when, in response to their "murmuring" He sent the "quails," and when again they provoked His wrath at the waters of Massah and Merribah?

At the birth of Jacob's sixth son Rachel exclaimed, "With great *wrestlings* have I wrestled with my sister, and I have *prevailed*" (Gen. 30:8). How strikingly this corresponds with Israel's history! The very next thing we read of after that God "judged" Israel for their sin at Merribah was their conflict or "wrestling" with Amalek, and again be it particularly noted that the self-same word used by Rachel at the birth of Napthali is used in describing the "wrestling" between Israel and Amalek, for in Ex. 17:11 we read, "And it came to pass, when *Moses* held up his hand, that Israel *prevailed*: and when he let down his hand, Amalek *prevailed*." Surely it is something more than mere coincidence that the very word used by the mother of Napthali should occur twice in the verse which records that in Israel's history which her words prophetically anticipated; the more so, that it agrees so accurately with *the order* of events in Israel's history.

The utterances of the mother of the seventh and eighth sons of Jacob may be coupled together, as may also those connected with the birth of his ninth and tenth sons. At the birth of Gad it was said, *"A troop cometh"* (Gen. 30:11), which perfectly agrees with the order of Israel's history, for after the Wilderness had been left behind and the Jordan crossed, a "troop" indeed "came" to meet Israel, the seven nations of the Canaanites seeking to oppose their occupation of the promised land. The words of the mother of Asher, the next son, *"Happy am I"* (Gen. 30:13), tell of Israel's joy following the overthrow of their foes. Then, the words of Leah at the birth of Jacob's ninth and tenth sons, namely "God, hath given me my hire" (Gen. 30:18), and "God hath endued me with a good dowry" (Gen. 30:20), tell of Israel's *occupation* of the goodly inheritance with which Jehovah had "endowed" them. Then, just as there was a break or interval before the last two sons were born, and just as these two *completed* Jacob's family, and *realized* his long cherished desire, inasmuch as *they* were born to him by his beloved Rachel, so her words, "The Lord shall add to me another son" (Gen. 30:24), and "The son of my sorrow" changed by the father to "Son of my right hand" (Gen. 35:18), would point to the *completion* of Israel's history as an *un*divided nation and the *realization* of their long cherished desire, in the giving to them a King, even David, to whom was "added" only one "other," namely, Solomon; and the *double* sentence uttered at Benjamin's birth was surely appropriate as a prophetic intimation of Solomon's course—so bright, yet so dark—for while in his reign the Kingdom attained its highest dignity and glory (the position signified by the "right hand"), yet, nevertheless, from the time of Solomon's coronation began Israel's *sorrowful* decline and apostasy.

Thus we have sought to show how the utterances of the mothers of Jacob's twelve sons were so many prophetic intimations of the course of the history of the Nation which descended from them, and that the *order* of the sayings of these mothers corresponds with the *order* of Israel's history, outlining that history from its beginning in Egypt until the end of the undivided Kingdom in the days of Solomon, for it was *then* the history of Israel as a nation terminated, the ten tribes going into captivity, from which they have never returned, almost immediately after.

To complete the study of this hidden but wonderful prophecy, particular attention should be paid to the way in which Jacob's sons were *grouped* under their different mothers, for this also corresponds exactly with *the grouping* of the outstanding events in Israel's history. The first four sons were *all borne* by Leah, and her utterances all pointed forward to *one group* of incidents, namely, Israel's deliverance from Egypt and the Egyptians. The fifth and sixth sons were borne by a different mother, namely, Bilhah, and her utterances pointed to a *distinct* series of events in Israel's history, namely, to their experiences in the Wilderness. The seventh and eighth sons were borne by Zilpah, and the ninth and tenth by Leah, and their utterances, closely connected yet distinct, pointed, prophetically, to Israel's occupation and enjoyment of Canaan. The eleventh and twelfth sons were *separated* from all the others, being borne by Rachael, and so also that to which her words at their births pointed forward to, was also clearly *separated* from the early events of Israel's history, carrying us on to the establishment of the Kingdom in the days of David and Solomon.

In drawing this article to a close, one or two reflections upon the ground we have covered will, perhaps, be in place:

First, What a striking proof of the Divine inspiration of Scripture is here furnished! Probably no uninspired writer would have taken the trouble to inform us of the words used by those mothers in the naming of their boys—where can be found in all the volumes of secular history one that records *the reason why* the parent gave a certain name to his or her child? But there *was* a good and sufficient reason why the words of Jacob's wives *should be* preserved—unknown to themselves their lips were guided by God, and the Holy Spirit has recorded their utterances because they carried with them a hidden, but real, prophetic significance; and in that recording of them, and their perfect agreement with the outstanding events in the history of Israel, in which, though centuries afterward, these prophetic utterances received such striking fulfillment, we have an unmistakable proof of the Divine inspiration of the Scriptures.

Second, What an object lesson is there here for us that nothing in Scripture is trivial or meaningless! It is to be feared that many of us dishonor God's Word by the unworthy thoughts which we entertain about it. We are free to acknowledge that much in the Bible is sublime and Divine, yet there is not a little in it in which we can see no beauty or value. But that is due to the dimness of our vision and not in anywise to any imperfection in the Word. "*All* Scripture" is given by inspiration of God, the proper nouns as much as the common nouns, the genealogical lists equally as much as the lovely lyrics of the Psalmist. Who would have thought that there was anything of significance in *the meaning* of the names of Jacob's sons? Who would have supposed that it was of first importance that we should note *the order* in which they were born? Who would have imagined there was a wondrous prophecy beneath the words used by the mothers on *the occasion* of them naming their sons? Who? Each and all of us *ought* to have done so. Once we settle it for good and all that there is nothing in the Bible which is trivial and meaningless, once we are assured that *everything* in Scripture, each word, has a significance and value, then we shall prayerfully ponder every section, and *expect* to find "hid treasures" (Prov. 2:4) in every list of names, and according unto our faith so it will be unto us.

Third, What a remarkable illustration and demonstration of the absolute Sovereignty of God is found here in Genesis 29 and 30! What a proof that God *does* rule and overuie! What a showing forth of the fact that even in our smallest actions we are controlled by the Most High! All unconsciously to themselves, these wives of Jacob in naming their babies and in stating the reasons for these names, were outlining the Gospel of God's Grace and were prophetically foreshadowing the early history of the Nation which descended from their sons. If then these women, in the naming of their sons and in the utterances which fell from their lips at that time were unknown to themselves, *guided by God,* then, verily, God is *Sovereign* indeed. And so affirms His Word, *for OF HIM,* and through Him, and to Him, *are all things."* (Rom. 11:36.)

32. JACOB'S DEPARTURE FROM HARAN

Genesis 31

Before Jacob had ever set foot in Padan-Aram Jehovah, the God of Abraham and the God of Isaac, had said to him, "Behold, I am with thee, and will keep thee in all places whither thou goest, and will bring thee again into this land; for I will not leave thee until I have done that which I have spoken to thee of." (Gen. 28:15.) And now the time had drawn near when our patriarch was to return to the promised land. He was not to spend the remainder of his days in his uncle's household; God had a different purpose than that for him, and all things were made to work together for the furtherance of that purpose. But not until God's hour was ripe must Jacob leave Padan-Aram. Some little while before *God's* time *had* come, Jacob assayed to leave: "And it came to pass, when Rachel had borne Joseph, that Jacob said unto Laban, *send me away,* that I may go unto mine own place, and to my country." (30:25.) Apparently Laban was reluctant to grant this request, and so offered to raise his wages as an inducement for Jacob to remain with him, "And Laban said unto him, I pray thee, if I have found favor in thine eyes, tarry: for I have learned by experience that the Lord hath blessed me for thy sake. And he said, Appoint me thy wages, and I will give it." (30:27, 28.) Ere proceeding with the narrative the above words of Laban deserve to be noticed. This was a remarkable confession of Jacob's uncle—"The Lord hath blessed me *for thy sake.*" Laban was not blessed for his own sake, nor on account of any good deeds *he* had done; but he was blessed "for the sake" of another. Was not God here setting forth under a figure the method or principle by which He was going to bless sinners, namely, for the sake of another who was dear to Him? Do not these words of Laban anticipate the Gospel? and point forward to the present time when we read "God *for Christ's sake* hath forgiven you" (Eph. 4:32), and again in 1 John 2:12 "your sins are forgiven you *for His name's sake.*" Yes, this is the blessed truth foreshadowed in Gen. 30:27: God blessed Laban for Jacob's sake. So again we read in Gen. 39:15 concerning Potiphar, "The Lord blessed the Egyptian's house *for Joseph's sake.*" And again we have another beautiful illustration of this same precious fact and truth in 2 Sam. 9:1: "And David said, Is there yet any that is left of the house of Saul, that I may show him kindness *for Jonathan's sake.*" Reader, have *you* apprehended this saving truth? *That for which we are accepted and saved by God* is, not any work of righteousness which we have done, nor even for our believing—necessary though that be—but simply and solely *for Christ's sake.*

The sequel would seem to show that Jacob accepted Laban's offer, and decided to prolong his stay. Instead, however, of leaving himself at the mercy of his grasping and deceitful uncle, who had already "changed his wages ten times" (see Gen. 31:7), Jacob determined to outwit the one whom he had now served for upwards of twenty years by suggesting a plan which left him master of the situation, and promised to greatly enrich him. (See Gen. 30:31-42.) Much has been written concerning this device of Jacob to get the better of Laban and at the same time secure for himself that which he had really earned, and varied have been the opinions expressed. One thing seems clear: unless *God* had prospered it Jacob's plan had failed, for something more than sticks from which a part of the bark had been removed was needed to make the cattle bear "ringstreaked, speckled, and spotted" young ones. (Gen. 30:39.)

The outcome of Jacob's device is stated in the last verse of Gen. 30: "And the man increased exceedingly, and had much cattle, and maidservants, and menservants, and camels, and asses." This intimates that some little time must have elapsed since our patriarch suggested (30: 25) leaving his uncle. Now that prosperity smiled upon him Jacob was, apparently, well satisfied to remain where he was, for though Laban was no longer as friendly as hitherto, and though Laban's sons were openly jealous of him (31: 1, 2) we hear no more about Jacob being anxious to depart. But, as we have said, God's time for him to leave had almost arrived; and so we read, "And the Lord said unto Jacob, *Return* unto the land of thy fathers, and to thy kindred; and I will be with thee." (31: 3.)

God timed this word to Jacob most graciously. The opening verses of Gen. 31 show there was not a little envy and evilmindedness at work in the family against him. Not only were Laban's sons murmuring at Jacob's prosperity, but their father was plainly of the same mind and bore an unkindly demeanor toward his nephew—"And Jacob beheld the countenance of Laban, and behold, it was not toward him as before." The Lord had promised to be with Jacob, and to keep him in all places whither he went, and he now makes good His word. Like a watchful friend at hand, He observes his treatment and bids him depart. As another has well said, "If Jacob had removed from mere personal resentment, or as stimulated only by a sense of injury, he might have sinned against God, though not against Laban. But when it was said to him 'Return unto the land of thy fathers and to thy kindred, and I will be with thee,' his way was plain before him. In all our removals, it becomes us to act as that we may hope for the Divine presence and blessing to attend us; else, though we may flee from one trouble, we shall fall into many, and be less able to endure them." (Andrew Fuller.)

"And the Lord said unto Jacob, Return unto the land of thy fathers, and to thy kindred; and I will be with thee." (31: 3.) What a showing forth of God's wondrous grace was this! In all that is told us about Jacob during the twenty years he spent at Padan-Aram there was not a word which intimates he had any dealings with God during that time. There is no mention of any "altar," no reference to prayer, nothing to distinguish him from a thorough worldling. It needs to be remembered that the "altar" speaks not only of sacrifice but of *communion* too. The altar pointed forward to Christ, and it is only in Him that God and the redeemed sinner meet and commune together. Jacob, then, had no altar in Padan-Aram because he was out of communion with Jehovah. "Although God in His faithfulness be with us, we are not always with Him." (J. N. D.) But if Jacob had forgotten the Lord, Jehovah had not forgotten him; and now that Jacob begins to be in real need the Lord spoke the suited word. Yet mark the other side.

Having been warned of God to depart, Jacob sends for his wives into the field, where he might converse with them freely on the subject, without danger of being overheard. (See 31: 4-13.) The reasons he names for leaving were partly the treatment of Laban, and partly the intimations of God—"I see your father's *countenance* that it is not toward me as before." Mr. Fuller's practical observations on these words are so good we cannot refrain from quoting them: "It is wisely ordered that the countenance should, in most cases, be an index to the heart; else there would be much more deception in the world than there is. We gather more of men's disposition toward us from their looks than their words; and domestic happiness is more influenced by the one than by the other. Sullen silence is often more intolerable than contention itself, because the latter, painful as it is, affords opportunity for mutual explanation. But while Jacob had to complain at Laban's cloudy countenance he could add, 'The God of my father hath been with me.' God's smiles are the best support under man's frowns; if we walk in the light of His countenance we need not fear what man can do unto us."

Having talked the matter over with his wives, and obtained their consent to accompany him, the next thing was to prepare for their departure. Had Laban known what was in his nephew's mind there is reason to fear he would have objected, perhaps have used force to detain him, or at least deprived him of the greater part of his possessions. Acting with his usual caution, Jacob waited until Laban was a three days' journey away from home, absent at a sheep-shearing. Taking advantage of this, Jacob, accompanied by his wives, his children, and his flocks, "stole away unawares to Laban." (31: 20.) How little there was of Divine guidance and of faith in Jehovah in this stealth! Not of him could it be said "For ye shall not go out with haste, nor by flight; for the Lord will go before you; and the God of Israel will be your rearward." (Isa. 52:12.) That the Holy Spirit was *not* here leading is made still more evident by what is told us in verse 19: "And Rachel had stolen the teraphim that were her father's." It may be of interest to some of our readers if we here digress again and contemplate these teraphim in the light of other scriptures.

Scholars tell us that the word "teraphim" may be traced to a Syrian root which means "to enquire."* This explains the reason *why* Rachel took with her these family "gods" when her husband stole away surreptitiously from her home —it was to *prevent* her father from "enquiring" of these idol "oracles" and thus discovering the direction in which they had gone. Mark that Laban calls these teraphim his

*Probably the name "teraphim" was originally a corruption of cherubim.

"gods." (31: 30.) The next reference to the "teraphim" in Scripture confirms the idea that they were used for oracular consultation. In Judges xvii: 5 we read: "And the man Micah had a house of gods, and made an ephod, and teraphim, and consecrated one of his sons who became his priest"; next we are told "In those days there was no king in Israel, but every man did that which was right in his own eyes" and "Micah consecrated the Levite; and the young man became his priest, and was in the house of Micah." (Verse 6, 12.) Then, in the chapter that follows, we read of the tribe of Dan seeking an inheritance to dwell in, and sending out spies to search out the land; and they came to "the house of Micah (who had the teraphim) and said to his priest, *Ask counsel,* we pray thee, of God, that we may know whether our way which we go shall be prosperous." (Judges 18: 6.) That it was of the "teraphim" they wished him to enquire, and not of the Lord, is clear from what follows, for when the spies returned to their tribe and made their report (which was adopted), the tribe on going forth to secure their inheritance carefully saw to it that Micah's "priest" with his "graven image, and the ephod, and the teraphim" accompanied them, so that we are told he became their "priest." (See 18: 8-20.) Next we read in 1 Sam. 19:13: "And Michal took a teraphim and laid it in the bed, and put a pillow of goat's hair for his bolster, and covered it with a cloth." This scripture not only reveals the sad fact that Saul's daughter was an idolator and practiced necromancy, but also intimates that by this time the "teraphim" were *fashioned after the human form*—hence Michal's selection of one of these to appear like the figure of her sleeping husband.* Ezek. 21: 21 also makes it clear that the "teraphim" were used for oracular consultation—"The king of Babylon . . . consulted with teraphim." Later scriptures indicate that after Israel had apostatized from Jehovah they turned to the "teraphim" more and more—"For the teraphim have spoken vanity, and the diviners have seen a lie, and have told false dreams; they comfort in vain." (Zech. 10: 2.) Hence it was in pronouncing sentence on recreant Israel, God said: "For the children of Israel shall abide many days without a king, and without a prince, and without a sacrifice, and *without a*

*This one must have been much largor than those which Rachael concealed under her saddle.

teraphim." What a terrible analogy to all this we behold in our own day! Just as in olden time Israel turned from Jehovah to the "teraphim" of the heathen, so today, now that Christendom has apostatized, men on all sides are turning away from the Holy Scriptures which are the Oracles of God, and are giving heed to seducing spirits and the deceptions of Satan.

That Laban harbored in his home these "teraphim" shows that the idolatry of Babylonia still clung to his family, notwithstanding he had some knowledge of the true God. (See 31: 53.) Laban appears to have been a man much after the order of those of whom it is written: "They sware by the Lord and by Malchom" (a heathen god). (Zeph. 1: 5.) This strange contradiction in Laban's religious life appears to throw light upon a passage and person that has long puzzled Bible students. We refer to Balaam. This mysterious prophet seems to have been a heathen soothsayer, and yet it is evident he also had some dealings with Jehovah. If Balaam was a descendant of Laban this would account for this religious anomoly. Now in Num. 23: 7 we learn that Balaam came from "Aram," which may possibly be identical with Padan-Aram where Laban dwelt. Balaam prophesied only some 280 years after Jacob's departure from Laban's home, and may then have been an old man, at any rate in those days 280 years covered only about two generations. The Targum of Jonathan on Num. 27:5, and the Targum on 1 Chron. 1:44 make Balaam to be Laban himself; and others say he was the son of Beor, the son of Laban. Bearing in mind that Laban employed the "teraphim" as his "gods," if Balaam were one of his descendants then it would explain why he did not utterly disown Jehovah while yet practicing the abominations of the heathen.

To return to the narrative. It was not long after Jacob's stealthy departure that Laban heard of what had taken place, and gathering together what was, no doubt, a considerable force, he immediately set out in pursuit. But on the night before he overtook Jacob's party, God appeared to him in a dream, and warned him against even speaking to Jacob "good or bad." Thus did Jehovah, once again, make good His original promise to our patriarch and manifest His preserving Presence with Jacob. The measure in which Laban respected the word of God is seen in the charges he brought against Jacob when they met the next day. We refrain from commenting on the lengthy colloquy between Jacob and his uncle. Though considerable feeling was evidenced by both parties, the interview terminated happily, and the final leave-taking was quite affecting. But it is remarkable that at the close of their interview each man revealed himself and his true condition of heart. It is by the seemingly little things that our characters are shown —"By thy *words* thou shalt be justified, and by thy words thou shalt be condemned." (Matt. 12: 37.) So it was here. When Jacob took a stone and "set it up for a pillar" to be a witness of the covenant made between them (31: 44-46) *Laban* called it "Jegar-sahadutha" which is *Chaldean* for "heap of witness," thus speaking in the language of *heathendom;* whereas, Jacob termed it "Galeed" which was *Hebrew* for "heap of witness." Only the true believer can speak the language of God's people; of the worldling, the godless idolator, it must be said of him as the maid said of Peter when he was *denying* his Lord, "Thy *speech* betrayeth thee." (Matt. 26: 73.)

The closing verses of our chapter present briefly another beautiful typical picture: "Then Jacob offered sacrifice upon the mount, and called his brethern to eat bread; and they did eat bread, and tarried all night in the mount. And early in the morning Laban rose up, and kissed his sons and his daughters, and blessed them; and Laban departed and returned unto his place." First a covenant of peace was proposed, then it was ratified by a sacrifice, and last it was commemorated by a feast. So it was in Egypt. God made promise to Moses, then the lamb was slain, and then the people feasted upon his roasted flesh. Thus it is with us. God entered into a covenant of peace before the foundation of the world, in the fullness of time the great Sacrifice was offered and accepted, and this is now commemorated at the "feast" of the Lord's Supper. (I Cor. v: 8.) Note, too, it was not Laban the elder, but Jacob his nephew who "offered sacrifice upon the mount."

One practical observation on the circumstance of Jacob leaving Padan-Aram and we conclude. It has been suggested by Dr. Griffith-Thomas that this incident supplies us with valuable principles for regulating the believer in his daily life when in doubt concerning the will of God. How often one is puzzled to know whether God would have us take a certain course or not. How may I be sure of God's will concerning some issue which confronts me? An important question; one that is frequently met with, and one which must find answer in the Word alone. Surely God has not left us without something definite for our guidance. Not that we must always look for a passage of Scripture whose terms are absolutely identical with our own situation, but rather must we search for some passage which sets forth some clearly defined *principles* which are suited to meet our case. Such indeed we find here in Gen. 31.

Jacob was in a strange land. He had been there for twenty years, yet he knew he was not to spend the remainder of his days there. God had assured him he should return to Canaan. How much longer then was he to tarry at Padan-Aram? When was he to start out for his old home? How could he be sure when *God's time* for him to move had arrived? Pressing questions these. Note how the answer to them is found here in three things: first, a definite *desire* sprang up in Jacob's heart to return home—this is evident from Gen. 30: 25. But this in itself was not sufficient to warrant a move, so Jacob must wait a while longer. Second, *circumstances* became such that a move seemed the wise thing; the jealousy of Laban and his sons made his continued stay there intolerable. (Gen. 31: 1, 2.) This was ordered of God who makes all things "work together" for the good of His own people. But still something more was needed ere Jacob was justified in leaving. So, in the third place there was a clear *word from God*—"The Lord said unto Jacob, Return unto the land of thy fathers." (Gen. 31: 3.)

It is not always that God gives us a manifestation of these three principles, but whenever they *do* combine and are evident we may be sure of His will in any given circumstance. First, a definite conviction in our hearts that God desires us to take a certain course or do a certain thing. Second, the path He would have us take being indicated by outward circumstances, which make it (humanly) possible or expedient we should do it. Then, third, after definitely waiting on God for it, some special word from the Scriptures which is suited to our case and which by the Spirit bringing it manifestly to our notice (while waiting for guidance) is plainly a message from God to our individual heart. Thus may we be assured of God's will *for us*. The most important thing is to *wait on God.* Tell Him your perplexity, ask Him to prevent you from making any mistake, cry earnestly to Him to make "plain His way before your face" (Psa. 5: 8), and then "wait patiently" till He does so. Remember that "whatsoever is not of faith is sin." (Rom. 4: 23.) If you are sincere and patient, and pray in faith, then, in His own good time and way, He will most certainly answer, either by removing the conviction or desire from your heart, and arranging your circumstances in such a manner that your way is blocked—and then you will know *His time* for you to move has not arrived—or, by deepening your conviction, so ordering your circumstances as that the way is opened up *without your doing anything yourself,* and by speaking definitely through His written Word. "Commit thy way unto the Lord, trust also in Him, and He shall bring it to pass. (Psa. 37: 5.) The *meek* will He guide in judgment; and the *meek* will He teach His way." (Psa. 25: 9.) "He that believeth shall not make haste." May writer and reader be permitted by Divine grace to enjoy that blessed peace that comes from knowing we are in the will—that "good and perfect and acceptable will"—of God.

33. JACOB AT MAHANAIM

GENESIS 32

In our last article we contemplated Jacob, in obedience to the word of the Lord who bade him "return unto the land of thy fathers, and to thy kindred, and I will be with thee" (Gen. 31: 3), as then leaving Padan-Aram and starting out for Canaan. We also paid some attention to Laban's pursuit of our patriarch, and of the affectionate leave-taking which eventually ensued. Here we are to consider another important incident which befell Jacob by the way.

"And Jacob went on his way, and the angels of God met him." (Gen. 32:1.) Jacob was now in the path of obedience and therefore God favored him with another revelation to strengthen his faith and inspire him with courage for what lay before him—the meeting with Esau and his four hundred men. While in the path of obedience we must expect to encounter that which will test our faith, and not the least of such trials will be that to all outward appearances God Himself is against us; yet as we *start out* along any path He has appointed, God in His grace, usually encourages us with a plain revelation from Himself, a token of His approval, a strengthener to faith; and at *the end* we find the path of the just is as the shining light that shineth more and more unto the perfect day. So it proved with Jacob.

"And Jacob went on his way, and the angels of God *met* him." The word "met" here suggests a beautiful thought. It is not that the angels "appeared" to him, but they "met" him. Jacob is returning from his long exile, returning to the land given to his fathers (and later to himself) by Jehovah. These angels then came forward to greet him, as it were. God sent these messengers of His in advance to *welcome* his servant home, and to express to him His good-will. On his journey out from Canaan to Padan-Aram the Lord Himself met Jacob and gave him a vision of the angels; and here, now that he is on his way back from Padan-Aram to Canaan, the angels met him, followed immediately afterwards by the Lord appearing to him.

"And Jacob went on his way, and the angels of God met him. And when Jacob saw them, he said, This is God's host; and he called the name of that place Mahanaim."

(Gen. 32:1, 2.) Once again we note how *timely* are God's interventions. Jacob had just escaped from one company of his enemies (Laban and his brethren—Gen. 31: 22, 23), and another was now advancing to meet him, namely, Esau with his four hundred men. But at this juncture God's host made its appearance, as though to show him to whom he owed his recent escape, and as if to further assure him that He who *had* delivered, *did* deliver, and he might safely trust *would* deliver him. It is to be remarked that the angels (32: 1) which appeared on this occasion were termed by Jacob "God's host" in the singular number, but from the name which Jacob gave to the place—Mahanaim—it is evident they were divided into two companies, for Mahanaim signifies *two hosts.* It would seem, then, there was one host of these "angels" of God, but divided into two companies, probably encompassing him both before and behind. Was not this God's provision for the two hosts of Jacob's adversaries, which at the same time, and no doubt with the same violent designs, were coming against him! The one had already been sent back without striking a blow (Laban and his company), and the other should yet also be. While this was not expressly revealed to Jacob, nevertheless, this host of angels before him, as well as the one behind, was most evidently a comforting assurance from God that He was with His child and would preserve him whithersoever he went. How it reminds us of the experience of the Children of Israel in the wilderness, centuries later, when the Pillar of Cloud went before them by day, and the Pillar of Fire protected their rear by night.

"And Jacob sent messengers before him to Esau, his brother, unto the land of Seir, the country of Edom. And he commanded them, saying, Thus shall ye speak unto my lord Esau; Thy servant Jacob saith thus, I have sojurned with Laban, and stayed there until now; and I have oxen, and asses, flocks, and men-servants, and women-servants; and I have sent to tell my lord, that I may find grace in thy sight." (Gen. 32: 3-5.) As yet Jacob had heard nothing of his brother Esau, save that he was now settled in the land of Seir; but recalling the past, remembering the angry threat of the man, he was plainly apprehensive of the consequences of meeting him again. He, therefore, decided to send messengers before him, much as an army which is marching through an enemy's country sends on spies in advance. These messengers were evidently instructed to sound Esau (for they returned to Jacob with their report), and if needs be to appease his anger. These messengers were carefully instructed what they should say to Esau, how they should conduct themselves in his presence, and the impression they must aim to make upon him—all designed to conciliate. While they were coached to say nothing but what was strictly true, nevertheless, the *craftiness* of Jacob comes out plainly in the words he puts into the mouths of his messengers:

"And he commanded them, saying, Thus shall ye speak unto my lord Esau; Thy servant Jacob saith thus, I have sojourned with Laban, and staved there until now; and I have oxen, and asses, flocks, and men servants, and women servants; and I have sent to tell my lord, that I may find grace in thy sight." (Gen. 32: 4, 5.) Jacob does not insist on the fulfillment of the blessing which he had obtained from his father. Isaac had said, "Be lord *over* thy brother, and let thy mother's sons bow down *to thee.*" But here Jacob refuses to press the claim of his precedency, and instead of requiring that Esau should "bow down" unto him, he refers to Esau as "*his* lord" and takes the place of a servant"! Note, too, nothing is said of the reason why he had fled to Padan-Aram—all reference to his outwitting of Esau is carefully passed over—instead, he naively says, "I have *sojourned* (not found refuge) with Laban, and stayed there until now." Once again be it remarked, Jacob would have Esau plainly to understand that he had not come to *claim the double portion,* nor even to seek a division of their father's inheritance—he had no need for this, for God had given him plenty of this world's goods. How plainly the native shrewdness of our patriarch comes out in all this needs not be argued.

"And the messengers returned to Jacob, saying, We came to thy brother Esau, and also he cometh to meet thee, and four hundred men with him." (Gen. 32: 6.) It would seem from the sequel that the messengers sent out by Jacob never delivered their message, but only went far enough to discover that Esau was advancing toward them accompanied by four hundred men—to them, no doubt, with hostile intentions. It must have come upon Jacob as a terrible shock to learn that his brother was already acquainted with his movements. It could only be about a fortnight at most since Jacob had left his uncle's farm, and as his journey had been conducted with all possible secrecy (in order to escape from Laban), how could Esau have learned of it at all? Was his thirst for revenge upon his brother so great that he had had him watched all these years? Was there some spy of his in the employ of Laban, who had now secretly communicated with Esau? Someone must have informed him, and the fact that Esau was now advancing upon him was disquieting news indeed. "*Then* Jacob was greatly afraid and distressed" (32: 7)—a guilty conscience needs no accusing.

"And he divided the people that was with him, and the flocks, and herds, and the camels, into two bands; and said, If Esau come to the one company, and smite it, then the other company which is left shall escape." (32: 7, 8.) There seemed no time to be lost, so Jacob acted promptly, and with accustomed shrewdness. First he divided his people and his flocks into two bands, so that if Esau came up with one and smote it, the other at least might escape. Second he betook himself to prayer. Ere condemning Jacob here, let us examine our own hearts and remember our own ways. How often we come to God only as a *last resort!* How often we scheme and plan, and not until *afterwards* do we cry unto God. Alas, how often we act on the principles of that God-dishonoring proverb that "God helps those who help themselves"—as though anybody was sufficient to "help himself" without God first helping him! The truth is rather, and how blessed, that God is ever ready to help those who have learned by sad experience that they are quite *unable* to "help themselves." His promise is "He giveth power to the faint; and to them that have no might He increaseth strength." (Isa. 40:29.)

There is not a little in the prayer of Jacob which is worthy of close attention, the more so as it was a prevailing prayer, and that it is the *first* recorded real prayer in the Bible. "And Jacob said, O God of my father Abraham, and God of my father Isaac, the Lord which saidst unto me, Return unto thy country, and to thy kindred, and I will deal well with thee; I am not worthy of the least of all the mercies, and of all the truth, which thou hast showed unto thy servant; for with my staff I passed over this Jordan; and now I am become two bands. Deliver me, I pray thee, from the hand of my brother, from the hand of Esau; for I fear him, lest he will come and smite me, and the mother with the children. And thou saidst, I will surely do thee good, and make thy seed as the sand of the sea, which cannot be numbered for multitude." (32: 9-12.) Notice first the God to whom he prayed. He approached God not merely as God the Creator, but as "the God of his father Abraham and the God of his father Isaac." It was God in *Covenant relationship.* This was laying hold of the Divine faithfulness; it was the prayer of faith. It means much to approach God thus; to appeal to Him on the ground of a sure and established relationship. *We* come before God not as the God of our forefathers, but as the God and Father of the Lord Jesus Christ, and therefore *our* "God and Father." It is as we plead *this* relationship He is pleased to bless us.

Second, Jacob *cast himself on the sure Word of Jehovah,* pleading before Him His promise. He humbly reminded the Lord how He had said, "Return unto thy country, and to thy kindred, and *I will* deal well with thee." Here again we do well to learn from Jacob. The Scriptures contain many promises given to believers in general, and it is our individual privilege to plead them before God in particular, the more so when, like our patriarch, we encounter difficulties and opposition in the way wherein He has directed us to walk. Jacob pleaded a definite promise; so must we. In 2 Cor. 12: 9 we read, "My grace is sufficient for thee." Come to the Throne of Grace at the beginning of each day, reverently and believingly remind the Lord of this declaration of His, and then say with one of old, "Do as Thou hast said." (2 Sam. 7: 25.) Again, we read in Phil. 4: 19, "My God shall supply all your need." Tell the Lord of this in the hour of emergency, and say, Lord "Do as Thou hast said."

Third, Jacob *fully acknowledged his own utter lack of desert.* He confessed that the Lord was in no wise *his* debtor. He took a lowly place before the Most High. He owned that *"he was not worthy of the least* of all God's mercies." Mark this well, dear reader, for very little teaching is heard in these days that leads to self-abasement. It has become a rarity to hear a saint of God confessing his *un*worthiness. There is so much said about living on a high plane of spirituality, so much Laodicean boasting, that many are afraid to acknowledge before other believers that *they* are "not worthy of the least of God's mercies." One sometimes wonders if this is the chief reason why so few of us have any real power in prayer today. Certain it is that we must get down into the dust before God if we would receive His blessing. We must come before Him as empty-handed supplicants, if He is to fill us. We must own our ill deserts, and be ready to receive from Him on the ground of grace *alone* if we are to have our prayers answered.

Finally, notice *the motive* which actuated Jacob in presenting the petition he did. That for which he made request was expressed as follows: "Deliver me, I pray thee, from the hand of my brother, from the hand of Esau; for I fear him, lest he will come and smite me, and the mother with the children." At first glance it would appear that our patriarch was moved by nothing higher than the natural affections of the human heart. It would seem that this was the petition of a kind husband and a tender father. But as we re-read this request of Jacob in the light of the closing words of his prayer, we shall discover he was prompted by a far worthier and higher motive. He at once added "And thou saidst, I will surely do thee good, and make *thy seed* as the sand of the sea, which cannot be numbered for multitude." In this conclusion to the prayer we may see not only a further pleading of God's promise, but an eye to *God's glory.* Jehovah had promised to make Jacob's seed as the sand of the sea, but if his wife and children were slain how then could God's promise be fulfilled! Now it is natural, and by no means wrong, for us to be deeply concerned over the salvation of our loved ones; but our chief concern must center itself not in the well-being of those who are united to us by the ties of blood or intimate friendship, but for *the glory of God.* "*Whatsoever* ye do (in prayer, as in everything else) do all to the glory of God"—to this everything else must be subordinated. Here, then, is a searching test: Why am I so anxious to see certain ones saved?—simply because they are near and dear to me? or that God may be glorified and Christ magnified in their salvation? May Divine grace purge us of selfishness and purify our *motives* in prayer. And may God use these few words and cause both writer and reader to cry, with ever increasing fervor, "Lord, teach us to pray."

34. JACOB AT PENIEL

Genesis 32

In our last article we contemplated Jacob as he continued on his way home from Padan-Aram where he had lived as an exile for so long. As Jacob went on his way "the angels of God met him," apparently in two distinct companies or "hosts," probably one of them to his rear and the other before him. It was suggested that there was a symbolic meaning to this ordering of the angels; that as God had just delivered our patriarch from Laban and his company, who were now left behind, so would he deliver him from Esau and his company which were ahead of him. After the angels had disappeared, Jacob sent out messengers to meet Esau, to pacify him with friendly overtures, and thus prepare for their meeting. Shortly afterwards these messengers returned to Jacob bringing with them the discomforting news that Esau was advancing, accompanied by no less than four hundred men. Jacob was "greatly afraid and distressed," and after dividing his party and possessions into two bands, he at once betook himself to earnest prayer. We considered this prayer at some length, and sought to point out some of its striking and suggestive features. It was a prayer of faith, and one which, in its general principles, we do well to copy.

What followed Jacob's prayer is now to engage our attention. A striking contrast is immediately presented to our notice, a contrast which seems unthinkable but for the sad fact that it is so often repeated in our own experiences. Jacob at once turns from the exercise of faith to the manifestation of unbelief, from prayer to scheming, from God to his own fleshly devises. "And he lodged there that same night; and took of that which came to his hand a present for Esau his brother." (32: 13.)

There was nothing inherently wrong in thus sending a present to his advancing brother; it was the *motive* which actuated him which is censurable, and which is "written *for our admonition.*" (1 Corinthians 10: 11.) In the verses which follow the Holy Spirit lays bare for us the heart of Jacob, that we may the better become acquainted with our own deceitful and wicked hearts. Had Jacob's motive been a righteous and praiseworthy one there was no need for him to have been at so much care and trouble in arranging his present for Esau. First he divided his extravagant present into three parts, or droves (for it consisted of cattle), putting a space between each and thus spreading them out to the best advantage, with the obvious intention of making as great an impression as possible upon his brother. Next, he commanded the servants who were entrusted with the care of his present, that when they should meet Esau and he enquired who these flocks and herds belonged to, they should say, "these be thy *servant's* Jacob's; it is a present sent unto my *lord* Esau." Clearly, the message which Jacob sent to Esau was utterly beneath the dignity of a child of God; such fawning phrases as "my lord Esau" and "thy servant Jacob" tell their own sad tale. This obsequious servility before a man of the world evidenced the state of his heart. Clearly, Jacob was *afraid* of Esau, and was no longer exercising confidence in God. Finally, Jacob's real design is made still more evident when we note his own soliloquizing—"For he said I will appease him with the present that goeth before me, and afterward I will see his face; preadventure he will accept of me." (32. 20.)

Instead of trusting in the Lord to work in him a spirit of conciliation, he undertook himself to propitiate Esau—"I" will appease him. But mark carefully, dear reader, that after all his scheming and devising he could say only "*peradventure* he will accept of me!" So it is still; after all our fleshly efforts have been put forth there is *no confidence* begotten thereby, nothing but an uncertain "peradventure" for our pains. How different from the way of faith, and the calm but certain assurance which is the blessed fruit of resting on the Divine promise and trusting God to undertake *for us?*

Ere proceeding further we would pause to consider a pertinent and pressing question which naturally arises out of what we have seen above: How was it possible for Jacob to turn to fleshly scheming and efforts of his own to appease Esau when just before he had prayer with such earnestness? to God, and had not failed to plead the Divine promises? Was Jacob after all an *un*-believer? Surely not—God's dealings with him previously dispel the idea. Had he then "fallen from grace" and *become* an unbeliever? And again we must reject any such suggestion, for the Scriptures are plain and explicit on the point that one who has been born again cannot be unborn—an unfaithful and unworthy child of God I may be, but I am still *His child,* nevertheless. The gifts and calling of God are "without repentance"—"without change of mind." (Romans 11: 29.) Once a sinner has been called out of darkness into God's marvelous light, and once God has given to him light and salvation, he never undoes that calling or withdraws His gift, for the sinner did nothing whatever of himself to *merit* God's gift, and he can do nothing to *demerit* it. The basis on which God bestows His gifts is not that of works and human desert, but that of sovereign grace alone. This does not argue that we shall therefore be careless and free to sin as much as we want, for that would only go to prove that *we* had never received God's "gift" of salvation; rather shall we become more careful and have a greater hatred of sin, not because we are afraid of the consequences of wrong doing, but because we are desirious of showing our deep gratitude to God, by a life which *is* pleasing to Him, in return for His abounding mercy and goodness to us.

But this still leaves unanswered our question concerning Jacob. Jacob *was* a believer in God—a careful study of his prayer as recorded in Genesis 32: 9-12 evidences that. But though Jacob was a believer there still remained the "flesh," the old evil nature in him. And to this he gave way. The flesh is ever unbelieving, and where it is not constantly judged breaks forth in God-dishonoring activities. The clearest exemplification and demonstration of the two natures in the believer is to be seen in the history of Jacob recorded faithfully by the Holy Spirit not for our emulation but for our "warning." The same two natures are in every child of God today, the spiritual and the carnal, the one which believes God and the other which disbelieves. It is because of this we need to cry daily, "Lord, I believe; *help Thou* mine unbelief." (Mark 9: 24.)

"So went the present over before him; and himself lodged that night in the company. And he rose up that night, and took his two wives, and his two women-servants, and his eleven sons, and passed over the ford Jabbok. And he took them, and sent them over the brook, and sent over that he had. And Jacob was left alone; and there wrestled a man with him until the breaking of the day." (32: 21-24.) This passage introduces us to a most important crisis in the life of Jacob. The book of Genesis presents our patriarch in two characters, as he is exhibited to us as Jacob and as Israel; the one looking at the natural man, and the other at the spiritual man, the one telling of how Divine grace found him and the other of what Divine grace made him—this will become clearer as we continue these studies, if the Lord will. We are now to consider the memorable occasion when Jacob formally received his new name of Israel, when he who was rightly termed "the supplanter" became known as "God commands."

The circumstances under which Jacob formally received his new name are worthy of the closest attention. He was, as we have seen, in great distress. News had come to hand that Esau, accompanied by four hundred men, was on the way to meet him. That for which he had labored so hard and so long to obtain in Padan-Aram seemed about to be wrested from his hands; his wives and his children appeared to be in imminent danger, and his own life in peril. As a precautionary measure he had sent his family over the brook Jabbok,* and now he was left alone—more desolate than when twenty years before he had left his father's house. Night had fallen, when suddenly a mysterious stranger appeared, and in the darkness grappled with him. All through the night this strange conflict continued.

"And Jacob was left alone." In this sentence we have the first key to the incident we are now considering. On these words it has been well said, "To be left alone with God is the only true way of arriving at a just knowledge of ourselves and our ways. We can never get a true estimate of nature and all its actings until we have weighed them in the balances of the sanctuary, and there we may ascertain their real worth. No matter what we may think about ourselves, nor yet what man may think about us, the great question is, What does God think about us? And the answer to this question can only be learned when we are 'left alone.' Away from the world, away from self, away from all the thoughts, reasonings, imaginings, and emotions of mere nature, and 'alone with God,'—thus, and thus alone, can we get a correct judgment about ourselves." (C. H. M.)

"And there wrestled a man with him." In Hosea 12: 4 this "man" is termed "the angel"; that is, we take it; "*the* Angel of the Covenant," or, in other words, the Lord Jesus

*Jabbok signifies "emptying"—appropriate name, for it emphasizes the fact that Jacob was "left alone."

Himself in theophanic manifestation. It was the same One who appeared unto Abraham just before the destruction of Sodom. In Genesis xviii: 2 we read of "three men," but later in the chapter one of them is spoken of as "the Lord." (5:13.) So here in Genesis 32, at the close of the conflict between this "Man" and our patriarch, Jacob called the name of the place Peniel, saying, "For I have *seen God* face to face." (32: 30.)

"And there wrestled a Man *with him.*" Note we are not told that Jacob wrestled with the mysterious Visitor, but "there wrestled a Man *with him,*" that is, with Jacob. This incident has often been referred to as an illustration and example of a saint's power in prayer, but such a thought is wide of the mark. Jacob was not wrestling with this Man to obtain a blessing, instead, the Man was wrestling with Jacob to gain some object from him. As to what this object is the best of the commentators are agreed—it was to reduce Jacob to a sense of his nothingness, to cause him to see what a poor, helpless and worthless creature he was; it was to teach us through him the all important lesson that in recognized weakness lies our strength.

"And there wrestled a Man with him *till the breaking of the day.*" From dark till dawn the mysterious conflict continued. There are those who have taken exception to the view set forth above, and who argue that if it was God who was wrestling with Jacob for the purpose of bringing him to a sense of his impotency He would have taken a shorter cut and arrived at the designed end much quicker. But such an objection loses sight of the wondrous patience which God ever exercises toward His own. He is "*long suffering* to usward." Long does He bear with our fleshly struggling, but in the end He accomplishes His purpose and grace triumphs. The delay only serves to provide opportunity for Him to display His infinite forbearance.

"And when He saw that He prevailed not against him, He touched the hollow of his thigh; and the hollow of Jacob's thigh was out of joint as He wrestled with him." This shows us how quickly and how easily God could, when it so pleased Him, bring to an end Jacob's resistance and reduce him to helplessness; all He had to do was but to "*touch* the hollow of his thigh," and in a moment Jacob's power to continue wrestling was gone! And here we get the second key to the incident. Jacob was now brought to the end of his own resources. One swift stroke from the Divine hand and he was rendered utterly powerless. And *this* is the purpose God has before Him in His dealings with us. One of the principal designs of our gracious heavenly Father in the ordering of our path, in the appointing of our testings and trials, in the discipline of His love, is to bring us to the end of ourselves, to show us our own powerlessness, to teach us to have no confidence in the flesh, that His strength may be perfected in our conscious and realized weakness.

"And He said, Let me go, for the day breaketh. And he said, I will not let thee go, except thou bless me." (32:26.) Here is the third key which unlocks to us the precious contents of our narrative. Here we see the object of the Heavenly Wrestler accomplished. No longer could Jacob wrestle; all he could do was *cling*. The mysterious Stranger brought Jacob to the point where he had to *lean his entire weight on Him!* Hitherto Jacob had sought to order his own life, planning, scheming and devising; but now he was "left alone" he is shown what a perfectly helpless creature he was in himself. "The seat of his strength being touched, he learnt to say, 'I will not let *Thee* go'—'other refuge have I none; clings my helpless soul to Thee.' This was a new era in the history of the supplanting, planning, Jacob. Up to this point he had held fast by his own ways and means, but now he is brought to say 'I will not let *thee* go.' " But mark carefully, it was not until "the hollow of his thigh was touched" that Jacob said this; and, it is not until we fully realize our own helplessness and nothingness that we are brought to cling to God and really *seek* His blessing, for note, not only did Jacob say "I will not let Thee go," but he added "except Thou *bless me.*"

"And He said unto him, What is thy name? And he said, Jacob. And He said, Thy name shall be called no more Jacob, but Israel; for as a prince *hast thou* power with God and with men, and *hast* prevailed." (32:27, 28.) We cannot but feel that these verses have been generally misunderstood by most of the commentators. Why should the Divine Wrestler ask our patriarch his name, if not to emphasize and press upon the conscience of Jacob the force of it, namely, supplanter or contender. And in the new name here given him, it seems to us Jacob received a *rebuke,* though its meaning also well sums up the central teaching of this incident which describes the occasion when he received it. But what is the significance of "Israel," his new name? The marginal reading of the R. V. gives "God striveth" which we believe conveys the real thought, though, "God *commandeth*" would probably be a happier alternative. One who was a profound Hebrew scholar tells us that "names compounded with 'El' have that of the nominative when the other part of the name is a verb as here. Out of some forty Hebrew names compounded with 'El' or 'Jah,' God is always the Doer of what the verb means. Thus, Hiel=God liveth; Daniel=God judgeth; Gabriel=God is my strength." Israel would, therefore, be "God commandeth." Does not this furnish a most appropriate significance to the name of the Nation which were and will be again the center of God's *governmental* dealings on earth—Israel, "God commandeth!"

"And He said, Thy name shall be called no more Jacob, but Israel; for as a prince hast thou power with God and with men, and hast prevailed." (32:28.) *"As a prince"* —as a deposer, orderer (see the various renderings of the Hebrew word: rendered "ruler" thirty-three times); used not to dignify but to reproach. *"Hast thou power"*—hast thou contended (the Hebrew cognate is translated "rebellion," "revolt," etc.); Jacob had contended with Esau in the womb and thus got his name "Jacob." And long had Jacob, "the orderer" of his life *contended* "with God and with men." *"And hast prevailed"* or succeeded. To quote from the Companion Bible: "He had contended for the birthright and had succeeded. (25:29-34.) He had contended for the blessing and succeeded. (27.) He had contended with Laban and succeeded. (31.) He had contended with 'men' and succeeded. Now he contended with God (the Wrestler), and fails. Hence his new name was changed to Isra-el, God *commands,* to teach him the greatly needed lesson of dependance upon God." Jacob had arranged everything for meeting and appeasing his brother Esau. Now, God is going to take him in hand and order all things for him. To learn this lesson, and take this low place before God, Jacob must be humbled. He must be lamed as to his own strength, and made to limp. Jacob's new name was to be henceforth the constant reminder to him that he had learned, and was never to forget this lesson; that it was not he who was to order and arrange his affairs, but God; and his *new name,* Israel, henceforth to be, him, that "God commandeth." As Jacob *he* had "prevailed," but now as Israel *God* would command and prevail.

In the above incident then—together with its setting and sequel—we have a most striking and typical picture of the "flesh" in a believer, its vitality and incurability, God's marvelous forbearance toward it and dealings with it and victory over it. First, in choosing and arranging the present for Esau we see the *character* and *activities* of the "flesh"—devising and scheming. Second, in Jacob's experience we are shown the *worthlessness* and *helplessness* of the "flesh." Third, we learn that *our nothingness* can be discovered only as we get "alone" with God. Fourth, in the Man coming to wrestle with Jacob we see *God subduing* the "flesh" in the believer, and in the prolongation of the wrestle all through the night we have more than a hint of the patience He exercises and the *slowness* of His process—for only *gradually* is the "flesh" subdued. Fifth, in the touching of the hollow of Jacob's thigh we are enabled to discern the *method* God pursues, namely, the bringing us to a vivid *realization* of our utter helplessness. Sixth, in the clinging of Jacob to the God-man we discover that it is not until He has written the sentence of death on our members that we shall *cast ourselves* unreservedly on the Lord. Seventh, in the fact that Jacob's name was now changed to Israel we learn that it is only after we have discovered our nothingness and helplessness that we are *willing and ready for* God to command and order our lives for us. Eighth, in the words, "and He blessed him *there,*" we learn that when God "commands" *blessing* follows. Ninth, behold the lovely sequel —"And as he passed over Penuel *the sun rose upon him.*" (32:31.) Does not this defiine or rather describe (symbolically) the spiritual nature of the "blessing!" Tenth, note how accurate is the picture—"The sun rose upon him, and he *halted* upon his thigh. Therefore the children of Israel eat not of the sinew which shrank, which is upon the hollow of the thigh, unto this day; because He touched the hollow of Jacob's thigh *in the sinew that shrank.*" (32:31, 32.) The sinew only "shrank," it was not *removed.* Nor is the "flesh" eradicated from the believer!

Many are the important lessons taught in the Scripture we have been examining, but for lack of space we can but barely name some of them: (1) It is *natural* to the "flesh" to plan and scheme and to desire the ordering of our lives.

(2) The mind of the flesh deems itself fully competent *to order* our life. (3) But God in His faithfulness and love determines to correct this habit in His child. (4) Long does He bear with our self-confidence and self-sufficiency, but He must and will bring us to the end of ourselves. (5) To accomplish this He lays *His hand on us,* and makes us conscious of our utter helplessness. (6) This He does by "withering" us in the seat of our creature strength, and by writing the sentence of death on our flesh. (7) As the result we learn to *cling* to Him in our weakness, and seek His "blessing." (8) What a lesson is this! The "flesh" cannot be subdued, but must be "withered" in the very sinew of its power—"because the carnal mind is enmity against God; for it is not subject to the law of God, *neither indeed can be.*" (9) That which hinders us in our growth in grace is not so much our spiritual weakness as it is confidence in our natural strength! (10) Not until these truths are apprehended shall we cease to be "contenders," and shall we gladly take our place as *clay* in the hands of the Potter, happy for Him to "command" and order our lives for us. (11) Then will it be with us, as with Jacob—"And He *blessed* him there." (12) And so will the sequel, too, prove true of us—"The sun rose upon him," for "the path of the just shineth more and more unto the perfect day."

35. JACOB MEETING ESAU

Genesis 33

"And Jacob lifted up his eyes, and looked, and, behold, Esau came, and with him four hundred men. And he divided the children unto Leah, and unto Rachel, and unto the two handmaids. And he put the handmaids and their children foremost, and Leah and her children after, and Rachel and Joseph hindermost. And he passed over before them, and bowed himself to the ground seven times, until he came near to his brother." (33:1-3.) Here again we meet with one of those strange and sudden transitions in this living narrative of our patriarch's history. Truth is stranger than fiction, it is said, and no doubt this is so, but certainly truth is more accurate than fiction. In the Epistle of James the one who is a hearer of the Word and not a doer is said to be "like unto a man beholding his natural face in a glass" (1:24.) There is no other book in the whole range and realm of literature which so marvelously uncovers the innermost recesses of the human heart, and so faithfully delineates its workings. In the biographical portions of Scripture the Holy Spirit, as everywhere, paints human nature in the colors of truth. An uninspired writer would have followed Jacob's wondrous experience at Peniel by a walk which was henceforth flawless. But not so the Holy Spirit. He has recorded just what did happen, and shows us Jacob distrusting God and yielding to the fear of man. Thus it is all through. Abraham in faith-obedience to the call of God went ont "not knowing whither he went," but after his arrival in Canaan, when a famine arose, he seeks refuge in Egypt. Elijah displays unexampled courage on Mt. Carmel, as alone he confronted the four hundred priests of Baal; but the next we hear of him he is fleeing from Jezebel! David dares to meet Goliath, but later, he runs away from Saul And thus we have recorded the sad inconsistencies of the noblest of God's saints. So it was again here with Jacob: what a change from clinging to the Divine Wrestler to prostrating himself before Esau!

There is a lesson and warning for each of us here which we do well to take to heart. It is one thing to be privileged with a special visitation from or manifestation of God to us, but it is quite another to live in the power of it. Jacob's experience at this point reminds us of the favored disciples who were with Christ in "the holy mount." They were deeply impressed with what they saw and heard, and Peter, acting as spokesman, said, "Lord, it is good for us to be here." But observe the sequel. Next day a father brought his lunatic son to the disciples, but "they could not cure him," (Luke) and when they asked the Lord the cause of their failure He said, "Because of your *unbelief.*" Is not the juxtaposition of these two scenes—the Transfiguration witnessed by the disciples, and their failure in the presence of need—intended to teach us the lesson that unless faith remains active we shall cease to live in the power of the Vision of Glory. Such is also the lesson we learn from Jacob's failure following immediately the visitation from God from Peniel. Ah, there was but One who could say "I do *always* those things that please Him." (John 8:29.)

Let us mark for our instruction just *wherein* Jacob failed. He failed to use in faith the blessedness of his new name. The lessons which the all-night wrestle ought to have taught him were the worthlessness and futility of all his own efforts; that instead of putting confidence in the flesh, he needed to cling to God; and in the new name he received—Israel, God commands—he should have learned that God is the Orderer of our lives and can well be trusted to undertake for us at every point. But O, how slow we are to appropriate and live in the blessedness of the meaning of the new names which God has given *us* "Saint!" "Son!" "Heir!" How little we live our daily lives under the comfort, the inspiration, the strength, the elevation, which such titles ought to bring to us and produce from us. Instead of trusting God to manage Esau for him Jacob at once resorts to his old devisings and subtleties.

Hardly had Jacob passed over the brook Jabbok and regained his family when, lifting up his eyes, he beheld his brother approaching accompanied by four hundred men. To flee was impossible; so at once he took whatever precautionary measures were possible under the circumstances. He had just sufficient time before Esau came up to arrange his family, placing his different children with their respective mothers, and putting those in the rear that he had the most love for. This shows that though outwardly he appeared to treat Esau with confidence, nevertheless, he was secretly afraid of him. He was obliged, however, to put the best face he could upon it, and goes out at the head of his company to meet his brother—"And he passed over before them, and bowed himself to the ground seven times, until he came near to his brother." This betokened the fact that Jacob was ready to take the place of *complete submission* to his elder brother. His action reveals plainly the real state of Jacob's heart, he was anxious to impress upon Esau that he intended to make no claim of preëminence but rather was willing to be subordinate to him. This will be even more apparent when we attend to the words he used on this occasion.

"And Esau ran to meet him, and embraced him, and fell on his neck, and kissed him" (33:4.) It seems to us that most of the commentators have missed the point of this. Instead of discovering here the power, goodness, and faithfulness of God, they see only the magnanimity of Esau. Personally we have no doubt that had Esau been left to himself his reception of his erring brother would have been very different from what it was. But he was *not* left to himself. Jacob had prayed earnestly to God and had pleaded His promise. And now, He in whose hands is the king's heart and who "turneth it whithersoever He will" (Proverbs 21:1), inclined the fierce and envious heart of Esau to deal kindly with Jacob. Mark it: and he "fell on his neck and kissed him!" Is not the hand of God further to be seen in the fact that Jacob's wives and children *all* uniformly "bowed" too, to Esau—"Then the handmaidens came near, they and their children, and they bowed themselves. And Leah also with her children came near, and bowed themselves; and after came Joseph near and Rachel, and they bowed themselves." (33:6-7.)

"And he said, What meanest thou by all this drove which I met? And he said, These are to find grace in the sight of my lord." (33:8.) Esau desired to know the meaning of those droves of cattle which had been sent on to him earlier as a present. Jacob's answer is quite frank, but it shows what it was in which he placed his confidence—he was depending on his present, rather than upon God, to conciliate his brother. Note, too, as in verse 5 he had spoken of himself to his brother as "thy *servant*," so here, he terms Esau "my *lord*." Such obsequious cringing ill-became a child of God in the presence of a man of the world. The excessive deference shown to the brother he had wronged evidenced a servile fear: the fawning obloquy was manifestly designed to imply that he was fully prepared to acknowledge Esau's seniority and superiority.

"And Esau said, I have enough, my brother; keep that thou hast unto thyself." (33:9.) Whether we are to admire these words of Esau or not is not easy to determine. They may have been the language of independency, or they may, which is more likely, have expressed the generosity of his heart. Esau was no pauper; in any case, no such present from Jacob was needed to heal the breach between them. Such was the plain implication of Esau's words, and in them we are shown the futility and needlessness of Jacob's scheming. Jacob had devoted much thought to the problem how *he* could best propitiate the brother whose anger he feared, and had gone to much expense and trouble to this end. But it accomplised nothing! It was all labor lost as the sequel shows. *God* had "appeased" Esau, just as before *He* had quietened Laban! How much better then had Jacob just been "still" and trusted in the Lord to act for him. Let us seek grace to learn this important lesson, that not only are all our fleshly plannings and efforts dishonoring to God, and that they are quite uncalled for and unnecessary, but also that in the end God sets them aside as they accomplish NOTHING.

Jacob was not satisfied with the generous words of his brother, and proceeded to press his present upon him, urging him to receive it as a token of good-will. "And Jacob said, Nay, I pray thee, if now I have found grace in thy sight, then receive my present at my hand; for therefore I have seen thy face, as though I had seen the face of God, and thou wast pleased with me." (v. 10.) The receiving of a present at the hands of another has always been regarded as a pledge of amity and good-will. None will receive a present from the hand of an enemy. The same principle underlies God's dealings with us. *He* will receive no offering from His sinful creatures until they are reconciled to Him by faith in the Atonement of His Son. Let the reader make no mistake upon this score. The Lord God will receive nothing from your hands until you have first received from His hands, received the Saviour which His love has provided for sinners. Many there are who suppose they must first bring something to God in order to win His favor. But no matter how beautiful their offering may be, no matter what self-sacrifice it has entailed, if Christ is still rejected God will not accept it. To offer God your own works while continuing to despise Christ is but to *insult* Him and to walk in the way of Cain. The teaching of Scripture on this point is most emphatic—"The sacrifice of the wicked is an abomination to the Lord." (Proverbs 15:8.)

Jacob continues to press his suit. To have his present accepted would be proof to him that his brother no longer bore him any ill-will. Hence, he continues to assure him how highly his favor was regarded, yea, to have seen his face, was, he says, "as though I had seen the face of God." Finally, he adds "take, I pray thee, my blessing that is brought to thee; because God hath dealt graciously with me, and because I have enough." (v. 11.) In the end, he prevailed upon Esau to accept his present—"And he urged him, and he took it."

"And he said, Let us take our journey, and let us go, and I will go before thee. And he said unto him, My lord knoweth that the children are tender, and the flocks and herds with young are with me; and if men should overdrive them one day, all the flock will die. Let my lord, I pray thee, pass over before his servant; and I will lead on softly, according as the cattle that goeth before me and the children be able to endure, until I come unto my lord unto Seir." (33:12-14.) If there can be any question raised as to Jacob's secret fears when he met his brother, what we read of in these verses surely settles the point. The old Jacob is here very evident. Now that his brother had accepted his present, he was only too anxious for them to separate again. Esau suggests they resume the journey in each other's company. But this was not what Jacob wanted. Old memories might revive in Esau's mind, and when that time came Jacob wished to be far away. However, he could not afford to offend his brother, so Jacob, at once, begins to frame excuses as to why they should journey separately. Then Esau suggested that some of his own company should stay behind with Jacob—"And Esau said, Let me now leave with thee some of the folk that are with me." This was probably to afford protection for Jacob and his herds while passing through a wild and dangerous country. But Jacob seems to have suspected some unfriendly design lay behind Esau's offer, and so he declined it—"What needeth it? Let me find grace in the sight of my lord."

The sequel is indeed a sad and humbling one. Not only was Jacob distrustful of his brother but he lied unto him. Jacob had said "let my lord, I pray thee, pass over before his servant . . . until I come unto my lord unto Seir." (v. 14.) But after Esau had taken his departure we read, "And Jacob journeyed to Succoth and built him a house, and made booths for his cattle." (v. 17.) Instead of making for Seir, the appointed meeting-place, he journeyed in another direction entirely. Even after the unexpected cordiality which Esau had displayed, Jacob would not believe that God had permanently subdued his brother's enmity; therefore did he mistrust Esau, refusing his offer of protection, and sought to avoid another meeting by a deliberate untruth. Alas, what is man! How true it is "that every man at his best state is altogether vanity." (Psalm 39:5.)

Jacob's unbelief explains why his journey back to the Land was delayed, for instead of pressing on home he settled down in Succoth. Not only so, but we are told that "Jacob came to Shalem, a city of Shechem, which is in the land of Canaan, when he came from Padan-Aram; and pitched his tent before the city. And he bought a parcel of a field, where he had spread his tent, at the hand of the children of Hamor, Shechem's father, for a hundred pieces of money." (33:18-19.) And this in the very face of God's word "return unto the land of thy fathers, *and to thy kindred,* and I will be with thee." (31:3.) But he had to pay a dear price for his unbelief and disobedience. Divine retribution did not sleep. We have only to read what happened to his family while Jacob abode at Shechem to discover how, once more, Jacob was called upon to reap that which he had sown—Jacob's sojourn in Succoth was followed by the ruining of his only daughter!

Little light seems to have been given as yet upon the closing verse of our chapter—"And he erected there an altar, and called it God the God of Israel." (33:20.) That this was an act of faith on the part of Jacob cannot be doubted, but as to how high his faith rose the best of the expositors are not agreed. When Jacob denominated this altar "God the God of Israel" was he losing sight of Jehovah's *convenant relationship* with Abraham and his seed, and thinking of God merely as *his* God? Or, was he appropriating to himself his new name of Israel? Whichever view be the true one it should be carefully noted that in the very next word our patriarch received from the Lord it concerned the "altar" and intimated that God was not pleased with the altar he had erected in Succoth—"and God said unto Jacob, arise, go up to Bethel, and dwell *there*, and make *there* an altar unto God." (35:1.) But this belongs to our next Genesis study. In the meantime may Divine grace open our eyes fully to see the wickedness, as well as the vanity of placing any confidence in our fleshly devisings and bring us to trust the Lord with all our heart.

36. JACOB AT BETHEL AGAIN

Genesis 35

In our last article we closed with Jacob parting from Esau and failing to keep his word and rejoin his brother at Seir. We pass over the sad record of the intervening chapter, asking our readers to turn to it for themselves. After passing through the grievous experiences narrated in Genesis 34, we might well have supposed that Jacob had been in a hurry to leave Shechem—yet, *whither* would he flee! Laban he had no desire to meet again. Esau he wished to avoid. And now from the Shechemites also he was anxious to get away. But whither should he go? Poor Jacob! He must have been in a grand quandary. Ah, but man's extremities are God's opportunities, and so it was shown to be here. Once more God appeared to him, and said, "Arise, *go up* to Bethel, and dwell there: and make there an altar unto God, that appeared unto thee when thou fledest from the face of Esau thy brother." (Genesis 35:1.)

In studying the above passage we have arrived at the conclusion that God's word to Jacob on this occasion was one of admonition. The reference to him "fleeing" from the face of Esau, takes us back, of course, to the time when Jacob first fled from home fearful of his brother's anger at the deception practiced on him in winning from their father the coveted blessing. On the first night out the Lord had appeared to our patriarch in a dream in which He promised to keep him in all places whither he went, and to bring him again into the land and unto his kindred. When Jacob awoke he said, "Surely the Lord is in this place" (28:16), and rising up early in the morning he took the stone on which his head had rested during the night and set it up for a pillar, pouring oil on the top of it, and calling the name of the place Bethel, which means "House of God." And there, we are told, "And Jacob vowed a vow, saying, If God will be with me, and will keep me in this way that I go, and will give me bread to eat, and raiment to put on, so that I come again to my father's house in peace; then shall the Lord be my God: And this stone, which I have set for a pillar, shall be God's house." (Genesis 28:20-22.)

Probably thirty years at least had passed since Jacob had had that vision of the "ladder," and now God *reminds* him of the pledge which our patriarch had failed to redeem. God here addressed Himself to Jacob's conscience, with respect to his neglect in performing his vow. God had performed *His* part, but Jacob had failed. God had preserved him whithersoever he had journeyed, and *had* brought him back safely to the land of Canaan; but now that Jacob had been in the land at least seven years (for in less time than this Simeon and Levi could not have reached man's estate—34:25), yet, he had *not* gone up to Bethel.

That God's word to Jacob recorded in Genesis 35:1, was a *reproof* is further evidenced by the immediate effect which it had upon him. Not only had Jacob failed to go to Bethel, but, what was worse, while Jehovah had been his personal God, his household was defiled by *idols*. Rebekah's stolen "teraphim" had proven a snare to the family. At the time Laban overtook them Jacob seems to have known nothing about these gods; later, however, he was evidently aware of their presence, but not until aroused by the Lord appearing to him did he exert his parental authority and have them *put away*. It is striking to note that though God Himself said nothing, directly, about the "teraphim" yet, the immediate effect of His words was to stir Jacob's conscience about them—"*Then* Jacob said unto his household and to all that were with him, Put away the strange gods that are among you, and be clean, and change your garments" (35:2.) These words show that Jacob *was* aware of the corrupt practices of his family, and had only too long connived at them.

There is good reason to believe that the troubles into which Jacob fell at Shechem were due immediately to his failure in this very particular, and had he gone directly to Bethel his household had been purged the more promptly of the "strange gods" that were in it, and his children had escaped the taint which these of necessity must impart. Furthermore, had he gone sooner to Bethel his children would have been kept out of the way of temptation (34:1), and then the impure and bloody conduct of which they were guilty had been prevented. Mark, too, how this second verse of Genesis 35 illustrates the awful spread of the leprosy of sin. At first the teraphim were hidden by Rachel. and none of the family except her seem to have known of them: but now Jacob had to command his "household" and "*all* that were with him" to "put away the strange gods" which were among them. The moral is evident: spiritual neglect and trifling with temptation can issue only in evil and disaster. Let us not neglect God's House, nor delay to keep His commandments.

"And let us arise, and go up to Bethel; and I will make there an altar unto God, who answered me in the day of my distress, and was with me in the way that I went" (35:3). Jacob not only commands his household to put away their idols, but seeks to impress them with his own sentiments, and urges them all to accompany him to Bethel. His reciting to them how that God had "answered him in the day of his distress" not only argued the propriety of the step he was urging upon them, but would excite a hope that God might disperse the cloud which *now* hung on them on account of the late lamentable transactions in Shechem.

"And they gave unto Jacob all the strange gods which were in their hand, and all their ear-rings which were in their ears; and Jacob hid them under the oak which was by Shechem" (35:4). It is pleasing to observe the readiness with which his family acceded to Jacob's command. They not only gave up their "gods" but their *"ear-rings"* also. These, too, were frequently converted to the use of idolatrous practices, as is evident not only from the example of Aaron who made the calf out of the "golden ear-rings" (Exodus 32:2), but from Hosea 2:13 as well—"And I will visit upon her the days of Baalim, wherein she burned incense to them, and she decked herself with her *ear-rings* and her jewels, and she went after her lovers, and forgat Me, saith the Lord." That Jacob *buried* the teraphim and ear-rings, instead of attempting to convert them to a more honorable use, teaches us that the things of Satan must not be employed in the service of God, and that we need to forsake even the appearance of evil. There can be no doubt that in the readiness with which the family acted in response to Jacob's command we are to see *the hand of the Lord.* In fact the power of God is evident at every point in this incident: the immediate effect of God's word to Jacob to go to Bethel (the effect on his conscience, evidenced by the prompt purging of his household); the unanimous response of his family; and further, what we read of in verse 5 all demonstrate this—"and they journeyed; and the terror of God was upon the cities that were round about them, and they did not pursue after the sons of Jacob."

In the scripture last quoted we find a striking illustration of the sovereign control which God exercises over and upon men, even upon those who are not His people. Evidently the Shechemites were so enraged against Jacob and his family that had not God put forth His power they had promptly avenged the wrong done them. But not a hand can be raised against any of the Lord's people without His direct permission, and even when our enemies are incensed against us, all God does is to put His "terror" upon them and they are impotent. How true it is that "the king's heart is in the hand of the Lord, as the rivers of water: He turneth it whithersoever He will" (Proverbs 21:1). *And God is still the same:* living, ruling, almighty. There is no doubt in the writer's mind that in the authenticated reports of "the Angels at Mons" we see in the terror which caused the German cavalry to turn about and flee from the outnumbered English a modern example of what we read of in Genesis 35:5—"And the terror of God was upon the cities that were round about them, *and they did not pursue* after the sons of Jacob."

"So Jacob came to Luz, which is in the land of Canaan, that is, Bethel, he and all the people that were with him. And he built there an altar, and called the place El-Bethel; because there God appeared unto him, when he fled from the face of his brother" (35:6, 7). It is significant that Bethel is here first called by its original name, "Luz" which means "departure." From God Jacob had departed for (as previously pointed out) Jacob built no "altar" during all the years he sojourned in Padan-Aram, and only now does he return to God, to the "house of God," to the altar of God, and in order to do this he must needs retrace his steps and return to the place from which he had "departed." So it was with Abraham before him, for after he left Egypt (whither he had gone in unbelief) we read, "And he went on his journeys from the south even to Bethel, unto the place where his tent had been *at the beginning,* between Bethel and Ai; unto the place of the altar, which he had made there *at the first*" (Genesis 13:3, 4). And so it has to be with us.

"But Deborah, Rebekah's nurse, died, and she was buried beneath Bethel under an oak, and the name of it was called Allon-Bachuth. And God appeared unto Jacob again, when he came out of Padan-Aram and blessed him" (35:8, 9). In principle these two verses are inseparably connected.

No mention is made of Deborah in the sacred narrative from the time Jacob left his father's house until the time when he had now returned to Bethel. The departure and the return of Jacob are thus linked together for us by the mention of Deborah "*Rebekah's* nurse." The same thing is seen again in the verse which follows. "And God appeared unto Jacob *again, when he came out of* Padan-Aram." God had appeared to him just before he entered Padan-Aram, and He now appeared "again" when he came out of Padan-Aram. All the years spent with Laban were lost, as were also those lived in Succoth and Shechem. The twenty years he served with his father-in-law were so much "wood, hay and stubble." We find another illustration of this same sad principle in Hebrew 11:29-30, where we read, first, "*by faith* Israel passed through the Red Sea," and the next thing we read is, "*by faith* the walls of Jericho fell down." The forty years wandering in the wilderness in unbelief is passed over! Nothing of "faith" was to be found in *that* period of Israel's history. The forty years was so much *lost time!* Ah, my reader, when our records are reviewed at the Judgment-seat of Christ methinks there will be similar tragic *blanks* in most, possibly all, of *our* lives.

The sequel of Jacob's return to Bethel is very beautiful, but we cannot here dwell much upon the details. God appeared unto Jacob again, reaffirmed that he should be called by his new name Israel, revealed Himself as the "Almighty" or "All-Sufficient One," bade him to be "fruitful and multiply," assuring him that "a nation and a company of nations should be of him, and kings should come out of his loins;" and, finally, ratifying the gift of the land unto his fathers, unto himself, and unto his sons (35:11, 12).

That Jacob was now fully restored to communion with God is seen from the fact that he now once more "set up a pillar" in the place where he had talked with God and poured oil theron (35:14, and cf. 28:18).

Next, we are told "And they journeyed from Bethel; and there was but a little way to come to Ephrath." How significant and how beautiful is the moral order here: Ephrath is Bethlehem (verse 19), and Bethlehem signifies "House of Bread." Note carefully the words, "There is *but a little way* (*i. e.* from Bethel) to come to Ephrath." Yes, it is but a short distance from the place where the soul is *restored* to communion with God to the place where nourishment and satisfaction of heart are to be found!

"And Rachael died, and was buried in the way to Ephrath, which is Bethlehem" (35:19). Thus the leading link of Jacob's life at Padan-Aram was now severed! The "teraphim" had been "hid under the oak" (verse 4), Deborah (the link with his old unregenerate life) had also been "buried under an oak" (verse 8), and now Rachael is "buried." Death is written large across this scene. And we too must have "the sentence of death" written on our members if we would walk in full communion with God and dwell in the house of bread. And is it not lovely to mark that from the dying Rachael there came forth *Benjamin*—"the Son of the right hand!"

Having considered some of the moral lessons which the 35th chapter of Genesis inculcates, we would in closing point out how that once again we have here another of those marvelous typical pictures in which this first book of Scripture abounds; this time a dispensational foreshadowment of the coming *restoration of Israel.*

1. Just as Jacob left the house of God (Bethel—Genesis 28) for the land of exile, so has the Nation which had descended from him. 2. Just as God said to Jacob "Arise, go up to Bethel," return to the place of Divine communion and privilege, so will He yet call to Israel. 3. Just as the immediate effect upon Jacob of God's "call" was to purge his house from idolatry and to issue in a change of his ways (emblemized by "changing of *garments*"—35:2), so the Nation will yet be purged from their final idolatry (in connection with Antichrist) and be changed in their ways and walk. 4. Just as Jacob acknowledged that God had "answered him in the day of his *distress*" (35:3), so will Israel when He responds to their cry in the great Tribulation. 5. Just as the "terror of God" fell upon the Shechemites (35:5), so will His terror fall once more upon the Gentiles when He resumes His dealings with His covenant people. 6. Just as when Jacob returned to Bethel he built another "altar," so will Israel once more worship God acceptably when they are restored to His favor. 7. Just as now the link with Jacob's past was severed (the death of Rebekah—35:8), so will Israel die to their past life. 8. Just as God now appeared unto Jacob "again," so will He, in the coming day, manifest Himself to Israel as of old. 9. Just as God then

said "Thy name shall not be called any more Jacob, but Israel shall be thy name" (35:10), so his descendants shall no more be called Jews, but as Israel shall they be known. 10. Just as God now for the first time discovered unto Jacob his name "Almighty," so on Israel's restoration will the Messiah be revealed as "the wonderful Counsellor, *the mighty God.*" 11. Just as national prosperity was here assured unto Jacob—"be fruitful and multiply, a nation and a company of nations shall be of thee" 35:11—so shall the prosperity and blessings promised through the prophets become theirs. 12. Just as God here said unto Jacob "the land which I gave Abraham and Isaac, to thee will I give it and to thy seed after thee" (35:12), so will He say to the restored nation. 13. Just as Jacob poured oil on the pillar he erected at Bethel, so will God pour the Holy Spirit upon Israel and upon all flesh. 14. Just as Jacob found Bethel to be but a little way from Bethlehem, so shall Israel at last find the Bread of Life once they have had their second Bethel. 15. Just as Benjamin *now* took his place in Jacob's household, so will the true Benjamin—"Son of his mother's sorrow, but also of his father's right hand"—take His rightful place among redeemed Israel. There are other points in this typical picture which we leave for the reader to search out for himself. Surely as the Christian ponders the wondrous and blessed future which yet awaits the Israel of God he cannot do less than heed that earnest word—"Ye that make mention of the Lord, keep not silence, and give Him no rest, till He establish, until He make Jerusalem a praise in the earth" (Isaiah 62:6, 7)!

37. THE SUNSET OF JACOB'S LIFE

Genesis 37-49

It is not easy to decide which of the two is the more wonderful and blessed—the grace of God which has given the believer a perfect standing in Christ, or the grace which ever bears with the believer who fails so miserably in making his state correspond with his standing. Which is the more remarkable—that, judicially, my sins are all put away forever, or, that in His governmental dealings God treats so leniently with my sins as a saint? Though it is true we reap as we sow, it also remains true concerning believers that God "hath not dealt with us after our sins, nor rewarded us according to our iniquities" (Ps. 103:10).

That is a marvelous word which is found in Numbers 23:21, a word that has been of untold comfort to many of the saints—"He hath not beheld iniquity in Jacob, neither hath He seen perverseness in Israel." These words were spoken by God through the mouth of Balaam, spoken of that very people who so frequently were wayward and filled with murmuring. Mark, the prophet does not say that iniquity and perverseness were not in Jacob. That would not give the believer confidence, which is the very thing God desires to give. It could never assure my poor heart to be told there was no sin in me for, alas I know too well there is. What I am to rest in is the wondrous fact that God sees no sin on me—that gives the conscience peace. God saw no perverseness and iniquity on Israel because He looked at them as under the Blood of the Lamb. And why is it that God sees no sin on believers? It is because "the Lord hath laid on Him (on Christ) the iniquities of us all" (Isa. 53:6).

In view of this, what a walk ought to be ours. Surely we can do nothing now which would displease the One who has dealt so wondrously toward us. Surely we ought now to render a ready and joyful obedience to Him who has done so much for us. Surely we ought to abstain even from every appearance of evil. And yet that word "ought" condemns us, for it implies our failure. I would not say to one who was fulfilling his duty, You ought to do so and so. Should I say to any one, You ought to do this, the plain inference is that he is not doing it. How wondrous then, how heart-affecting, is the patience of grace which bears with our failures, with our base ingratitude, with our Christ-dishonoring ways! And so we say again, it is difficult to determine which is the more amazing: whether the love which hath washed us from our sins, or the love which loves us "to the end" despite our unloveliness.

These are the reflections suggested by a review of Jacob's history. As we have followed the Holy Spirit's record of Jacob's life we have marvelled again and again at the matchless patience of God in His dealings with one so intractable and unworthy. Surely none but the "God of all grace" (1 Pet. 5:10) would have borne with such an one so long. Ah! such is equally true of the reader and of the writer. The only way in which it is possible to account for God's dealings with you and with me, these many years, is the fathomless and matchless grace of our God. Truly He is "long suffering to usward" (2 Pet. 3:9).

Not only is it affecting to trace the dealings of God through the changing scenes of Jacob's life, but it is also beautiful to mark the triumphs of Divine grace as these are exemplified in his closing days. The path of the just "shineth more and more unto the perfect day" (Prov. 4:18). And plainly is this manifested in the case of our patriarch. So feeble were the manifestations of the Divine life in Jacob in his early and middle life, so much did he walk in the energy of the flesh, that it is difficult to determine exactly when his spiritual life really began. But as he draws near the end of his earthly pilgrimage it becomes increasingly evident in him as in us that "though our outward man perish, yet the inward man is renewed day by day" (2 Cor. 4:16). The sunset of Jacob's life reveals the triumph of God's mighty grace and the marvelous transforming effects of His power which works upon material that seemed so unpromising. It is to some of the fruits of the Divine life in Jacob that we would now direct attention.

And what is it which produces these fruits? One answer to the question is found in Heb. 12—"My son, despise not thou the chastening of the Lord, nor faint when thou art rebuked of Him: For whom the Lord loveth He chasteneth, and scourgeth every son whom He receiveth . . . Now no chastening for the present seemeth to be joyous, but grievous: nevertheless, afterward it yieldeth the peacable fruit of righteousness unto them which are exercised thereby'' (Heb. 12:5, 6, 11). Do not these scriptures furnish a key to the closing scenes in the life of our patriarch! How plainly we may discern God's chastening hand upon him. First there is the death of the faithful nurse Deborah (35:8), and this is followed almost immediately by the decease of his beloved Rachel (35:19), next we read that his eldest son "went and lay with Bilhah his father's concubine" (35:22), and then Isaac dies (35:29). Poor Jacob! sorrows came upon him thick and fast, but the hand of Divine chastisement is soon to fall still heavier. Jacob is touched now in his tenderest spot—Joseph, his favorite son, is taken from him, and mourned for as dead. This was indeed a severe blow, for we read "And Jacob rent his clothes, and put sackcloth upon his loins, and mourned for his son many days. And all his sons and all his daughters rose up to comfort him; but he refused to be comforted; and he said, For I will go down into the grave unto my son mourning. Thus his father wept for him" (Gen. 37:34-35).

How are these afflictions to be viewed? As marks of the Divine anger? As judgment from God? Surely not. Not so does God act toward His own. Whom the Lord loveth He chasteneth. Even afflictions are among his love-gifts, sent in faithfulness, sent for our blessings, sent to exercise our hearts, sent to wean our affections from things of earth, sent to cast us more upon God that we may learn, experimentally, His sufficiency. The losses which Jacob suffered and the trials he was called upon to meet were among the "all things" which worked together for his good.

But not immediately did God's disciplinary dealings with our patriarch yield the peaceable fruit of righteousness—that comes "afterward" (Heb. 12:11). At first, we see only the resistance of the flesh. When Jacob's sons returned from Egypt Simeon was not with them, and what was worse, they informed their father that the lord of Egypt's granaries required them to bring Benjamin with them when they came back again. Listen to the petulent outburst from Jacob's lips when he hears these tidings, "And Jacob their father said unto them, Me have ye bereaved: Joseph is not, and Simeon is not, and ye will take Benjamin away: all these things are against me" (42:36). Poor Jacob! He is looking at the things that are seen, rather than at the things unseen. He is walking by sight rather than by faith. It does not seem to have occurred to him that God might have a wise purpose in all these events. He judged by 'feeble sense.' But ere undertaking to pass sentence upon Jacob let us remember that word in Rom. 2:1, "Therefore thou art inexcusable, O man, whosoever thou art that judgeth: for wherein thou judgeth another, thou condemneth thyself; for thou that judgeth doest the same things."

Not long, however, does Jacob continue in such a state of mind. The next thing recorded of him reveals a better spirit: "And the famine was sore in the land. And it came to pass, when they had eaten up the corn which they had brought out of Egypt, their father said unto them, Go again, buy us a little food" (43:1-2). The relief which had been obtained by the first journey to Egypt of Jacob's sons and the corn they had brought back was soon exhausted. The famine was yet "sore in the land." Jacob bids his sons "Go again, buy us a little food." Does not this word "little "evidence the beneficent effects of God's disciplinary dealings with him? Unbelief and avarice would have wished for much food so as to hoard against a prolongation of the famine. But Jacob is contented with "little." No longer do we see him, as aforetime, selfish and greedy; instead, he is desirous that others, whose stores were running low, should have a part as well as himself; and, so far as the unknown future was concerned, he would trust God.

But now a difficulty presented itself. Jacob's sons could not go down to Egypt unless Benjamin accompanied them, and this was the last thing his father desired. A struggle ensued in the breast of our patriarch; the affections of the father are pitted against the calls of hunger. To allay Jacob's fears, Judah offers to stand as surety for his younger brother. And Jacob yielded, though not without a measure of reluctance. Yet, it is sweet to notice the manner in which the aged patriarch acquiesced. It was not the sullen consent of one that yielded to an inexorable fate when, in heart, he rebelled against it. No, he yielded in a manner worthy of a man of God. After arranging that every possible means should be employed to conciliate the lord of Egypt, he committed the whole issue to God.

"Take also your brother, and arise, go again unto the man: And God Almighty give you mercy before the man, that He may send away your other brother, and Benjamin: If I be bereaved of my children, I am bereaved" (43: 13, 14.) Note how Jacob speaks of God—"God Almighty," or

"God, the Sufficient One." This was the name under which Abraham was blessed (17: 1). This was the name used by Isaac in blessing Jacob, "God Almighty bless thee," etc., (28: 3). In using this name here, then, Jacob rests on the covenant promise and blessing, and thus we see that his prayer was a prayer of faith. Note further, his confidence in God's sovereign power, seen in his request that God would so move upon the man at the head of Egypt that he would be made willing to send Jacob's sons away. Finally, mark here his spirit of resignation—"If I be bereaved, I am bereaved."

Is it not lovely to mark the sequel. Jacob committed Benjamin into the hands of God, and he was returned safely to his father. When God deals with His saints He usually touches them in their tenderest parts. If there be one object around which the heart has entwined itself more than any other and which is likely to be God's rival, this it is of which we must be deprived. But if, when it is taken from us, we humbly resign it into God's hands, it is not unusual for Him to return it. Thus Abraham on giving up Isaac, received him again; so David, on giving himself up to God to do as seemed Him best, was preserved in the midst of peril; and so, in the present case of Benjamin, who later was returned to Jacob.

When Jacob's sons returned home they brought with them a strange tale—Joseph was yet alive, in fact governor over all the land of Egypt. Little wonder that at first Jacob refused to believe his sons, for the news seemed too good to be true. But we read "And they told him all the words of Joseph, which he had said unto them: and when he saw the wagons which Joseph had sent to carry him, the spirit of Jacob their father revived. And Israel said, It is enough; Joseph my son is yet alive; I will go and see him before I die" (45: 27, 28). It is beautiful to note the change here from Jacob to Israel, especially as this is carried on into the next verse, "And Israel took his journey with all that he had, and came to Beersheba, and offered sacrifices unto the God of his father Isaac" (46: 1). Thus, the first thing recorded of Jacob after his long journey to Egypt had begun, was the offering of sacrifices to God. Long years of discipline in the school of experience had, at last, taught him to put God first; ere he goes forward to see Joseph he tarries to worship the God of his father Isaac!

Beautiful, too, is it to note that here God met him for the seventh and last recorded time (see 28:13; 31:3; 32:1; 32:24; 35:1; 35:9), and said, "Jacob, Jacob. And he said, Here am I. And He said, I am God, the God of thy father; fear not to go down into Egypt; for I will there make of thee a great nation. I will go down with thee into Egypt; and I will also surely bring thee up again; and Joseph shall put his hand upon thine eyes" (46: 2-4).

Arrived in Egypt, restored to Joseph the aged patriarch is brought before Pharaoh: "And Joseph brought in Jacob his father, and set him before Pharaoh; and Jacob blessed Pharaoh" (47: 7). The aged and feeble patriarch stands before the monarch of the mightiest empire of the world. And what dignity now marks Jacob! What a contrast from the day when he bowed himself seven times before Esau! There is no cringing and fawning here. Jacob carries himself as a child of God. He was a son of the King of kings, and ambassador of the Most High. Brief is the record, yet how much the words suggest when we remember that "the less is blessed of the better" (Heb. 7: 7). Note, further, "And Jacob said unto Pharaoh, the days of the years of my pilgrimage are a hundred and thirty years" (49:7). At last Jacob has learned that his home is not here, that he is but a stranger and sojourner on earth. He sees now that life is but a journey, with a starting point and a goal—the starting point, regeneration; the goal, heavenly glory.

In Heb. 11: 21 we read, "By faith Jacob, when he was a dying, blessed both the sons of Joseph; and worshipped, leaning upon the top of his staff." It is striking to observe that here the Holy Spirit passes by the feebler struggles of Jacob's faith and goes on to mention the brightness of its setting glory, as it beautified the closing scenes of this vessel of God's choice. Two distinct acts of Jacob are here singled out: the former is recorded in Gen. 48, the latter in Gen. 47: 31. Into the probable reasons for this reversal of the historical order we cannot now enter, but a brief word concerning these two manifestations of faith will be in place.

"And the time drew nigh that Israel must die: and he called his son Joseph, and said unto him, If now I have found grace in thy sight, put, I pray thee, thy hand upon my thigh and deal kindly and truly with me: bury me not, I pray thee, in Egypt: But I will lie with my fathers, and thou shalt carry me out of Egypt, and bury me in their burying place. And he said, I will do as thou hast said. And he said, Swear unto me. And he sware unto him. And Israel bowed himself on the top of his staff." It is exceedingly beautiful to notice this act of worship and what occasioned it. There is more here than meets the eye at first glance. This was no mere sentimental whim of the aged patriarch. God had promised, many years before, to give to Jacob and to his seed the land of Canaan, and now His promise is "embraced," Jacob had never possessed the land, and now he is about to die in a strange country. But he knows God's word cannot fail, and his faith looks forward to resurrection. At last the easily besetting sin (unbelief) is laid aside, and faith triumphs. Having secured from Joseph the assurance that he should not be buried in Egypt, but that his remains should be carried up out of Egypt and placed in the sepulchre of his fathers, Jacob "worshipped (bowing himself) on the top of his staff." It was a blessed exhibition of faith, and of his confidence in God, that He would do all that He had said and perform all that He had promised.

The second act of Jacob to which the Holy Spirit calls attention in Heb. 11 is rceorded in Gen. 48. All through this chapter we may see how God was now in all Jacob's thoughts, and how His promises were the stay of his heart. He recounts to Joseph how God had appeared to him at Luz (v 3) and how He had promised to give the land of Canaan to him and his seed for an everlasting possession. He spoke of God as the One who "fed me all my life long unto this day" (v 15), and as the One "which redeemed me from all evil," which was only another way of acknowledging that "goodness and mercy" had "followed" him "all the days of his life."

Jacob was now about to die, and he wishes to bless the two sons of Joseph. Joseph had his own desires and wishes on this subject, and his desire was that Manasseh, the firstborn, should receive the blessing. Accordingly, he placed Manasseh at Jacob's left hand and Ephraim at his right, so that Jacob's right hand might rest on the head of Manasseh and his left on Ephraim. But though Jacob's natural eyesight was dim, his spiritual discernment was not. Deliberately, Jacob crossed his hands "guiding his hands wittingly" (48: 14), or, as the Hebrew reads, literally, "he made his hands to understand." Note it is expressly said that "Israel" did this: it was the new man that was acting, not the old man, "Jacob." And "by faith" he blessed both the sons of Joseph. Truly, it was not by sight or reason. What was more unlikely than that these two young Egyptian princes, for this is virtually what they were, should ever forsake Egypt, the land of their birth, and migrate to Canaan! How unlikely, too, that each should become a separate tribe. And how improbable that the younger should be exalted above the elder, both in importance and number, and should become "a multitude of peoples" (48:19). How impossible for him to foresee (by any human deduction) that long centuries afterwards Ephraim should become representative of the kingdom of "Israel," as distinct from "Judah." But he had heard God, rested on His word, and believed in the sure fulfilment of His promise. What a grand display of faith! Nature's eyes might be dim, but faith's vision was sharp: in his bodily weakness the strength of faith was perfected.

After blessing Joseph's sons, Jacob turns to their father and says, "Behold, I die: but God shall be with you, and bring you again unto the land of your fathers" (48:21). How utterly unlikely this appeared! Joseph was now thoroughly established and settled in Egypt. But no longer is Jacob walking by sight. Firm indeed was his confidence, and with an unshaken faith he grasps firmly the promises of God (that his seed should enter Canaan), and speaks out of a heart filled with assurance.

The final scene (portrayed in Gen. 49) presents a fitting climax, and demonstrates the power of God's grace. The whole family is gathered about the dying patriarch, and one by one he blesses them. All through his earlier and mid life, Jacob was occupied solely with himself; but at the end, he is occupied solely with others! In days gone by, he was mainly concerned with planning about things present; but now (see 49:1), he has thought for nothing but things future! One word here is deeply instructive: "I have waited for thy salvation, O Lord" (49:18). At the beginning of his life "waiting" was something quite foreign to his nature: instead of waiting for God to secure for him the promised birth right, he sought to obtain it for himself. And so it was, too, in the matter of his wages from Laban. But now the hardest lesson of all has been learned. Grace has now taught him how to wait. He who had begun a good work in Jacob performed and completed it. In the end grace triumphed. At eveningtide it was light. May God deepen His work of grace in the writer and reader so that we may "lay aside every weight, and the sin which doth so easily beset us, and run with patience the race that is set before us" (Heb. 12: 1).

38. JACOB'S PROPHECY

Genesis 49

We have at last reached the closing scene in Jacob's life. Here and there we have beheld the light of heaven shining on and through our patriarch, but only too often the clouds of earth have obscured it. The struggle between the flesh and the spirit in him was fierce and protracted, but as the end drew near the triumphs of grace, and the faith which overcomes the world, were more and more manifest.

Nowhere is this more evident than in the scene presented to us in Genesis 49. Long years before, God had promised to give the land of Palestine to Abraham and his descendants. This promise had been confirmed to Isaac, and renewed to Jacob. But, up to this time, there had been no visible signs that the promise was about to be made good. Abraham and Isaac had been but "strangers and pilgrims" in Canaan, owing none of it save a burying-ground for their dead, and this they had purchased. Jacob, too, had "dwelt in tabernacles (tents) with Abraham and Isaac." (Hebrews 11: 9.) And now Jacob is dying—dying not in the promised land, but many miles away from it. In a strange country, in Egypt, our partiarch prepares to leave this earthly scene; but despite the feebleness of nature, the vigor of his faith was strikingly manifested.

Jacob summoned to his bedside each of his twelve sons, and proceeded to utter one of the most striking predictions to be found in all the Old Testament. Like most prophecies, this one of our dying patriarch has, at least, a double fulfillment. In its ultimate accomplishment it looks forward to the fortunes of the Twelve Tribes in "the last days" (Genesis 49: 1); that is, it contemplates their several conditions and positions as they will be in the End-time, namely, during the Seventieth Week of Daniel and on into the millennium (cf. Jeremiah 23: 19, 29; Isaiah 2: 2 for the "last days" of Israel). Concerning the final fulfillment of Jacob's prophecy we cannot now write; instead, we shall note how strikingly the past history of the descendants of Jacob's twelve sons has corresponded with their father's dying utterance:

"Gather yourselves together, and hear, ye sons of Jacob; and hearken unto Israel your father. Reuben, thou art my first-born, my might, and the beginning of my strength, the excellency of dignity, and the excellency of power. Unstable as water, thou shalt not excel, because thou wentest up to thy father's bed, then defilest thou it; he went up to my couch." (Genesis 49:2-4.) Three things are here said of Reuben: First, as the first-born son of Jacob, the place of "excellency," the position of dignity, was his natural birthright. Second, this position of preëminency had been forfeited through his sin in defiling his father's bed, and Jacob here foretells that the tribe which is to descend from Reuben "Shalt not excel." Third, Jacob also predicted that this tribe should be "unstable as water," which is a figurative expression taken from the passing away of water which had dried up like a summer stream. We shall now refer to several passages in the Old Testament which treat of Reuben, showing how the fortunes of this tribe verified the words of the dying patriarch.

Let us turn first to 1 Chronicles v: 1, 2: "Now the sons of Reuben, the first-born of Israel (for he was the first-born); but, for as much as he defiled his father's bed his birthright was given unto the sons of Joseph, the son of Israel; and the genealogy is not to be reckoned after the birthright. For Judah prevailed *above* his brethren, and of him (viz., of Judah, instead of Reuben as it ought to-have been) came the Chief Ruler (*i. e.,* Christ); but the birthright was Joseph's." In this striking passage the "birthright" refers, of course, to the position of excellency, and this, as Jacob declared it should be, was taken away from Reuben and given to the sons of Joseph (they receiving the double or "first-born's" portion); and Judah, not Reuben, becoming the royal tribe from which Messiah sprang, and thus "prevailing" above his brethren. Verily, then, Reuben did not "excel."

Second, as we trace the fortunes of this tribe through the Old Testament it will be found that in nothing did they "excel." From this tribe came no judge, no king, and no prophet. This tribe (together with Gad) settled down on the wilderness side of the Jordan, saying, "Bring us not over Jordan." (Numbers 32:5.) From this same scripture it appears that the tribe of Reuben was, even then, but a cattle loving one—"now the children of Reuben and the children of Gad had a very great multitude of cattle; and when they saw the land of Jazer and the land of Gilead, that, behold, the place was a place for cattle ...... came and spoke unto Moses and Eleazar the priest saying.... the country which the Lord smote before the congregation of Israel, is a land for cattle, and thy servants have cattle. Wherefore, said they, if we have found grace in thy sight, let this land be given unto thy servants for a possession, and bring us not over Jordan." (Numbers 32: 1-5.) With this agrees Judges 5:15, 16: "For the divisions of Reuben there were great thoughts of heart. Why abodest thou among the sheepfolds, to hear the bleatings of the flocks. For the divisions of Reuben there were great searchings of heart." When the land was divided among the tribes in the days of Joshua, the portion allotted to Reuben served, again, to fulfill the prophecy of Jacob—it was the southernmost and smallest on the east of Jordan.

Third, this tribe was to be "unstable as water," it was to dry up like a stream in summer; it was, in other words, to enjoy no numerical superiority. In harmony with this was the prophecy of Moses concerning Reuben—"Let Reuben live, and not die; and (or "but") let his men be few." Note, that at the first numbering of the tribes, Reuben had 46,500 men able to go forth to war (Numbers 1:21), but when next they were numbered they showed a slight decrease—43,730. (Numbers 26: 7.) This is the more noteworthy because most of the other tribes registered an increase. Remark, too, that Reuben was among those who stood on Mt. Ebal to "curse," not among those who stood on Mt. Gerizim to "bless." (See Deuteronomy 27: 12, 13.) In 1 Chronicles 26: 31, 32, we read: "In the fortieth year of the reign of David they were sought for, and there were found among them mighty men of valor at Jazer of Gilead. And his brethren, men of valor, were two thousand and seven hundred chief fathers, whom king David made rulers over the Reubenites, the Gadites, and the half tribe of Manasseh, for every matter pertaining to God, and affairs of the king." It is also deeply significant to discover that when Jehovah commenced to inflict His judgments upon Israel we are told, "In those days the Lord began to cut Israel short; and Hazael smote them in all the coasts of Israel; from Jordan eastward, all the land of Gilead, the Gadites, and the Reubenites, and the Manassites, from Arser, which is by the River Arnon, even Gilead and Bashan." (2 Kings 10: 32, 33.) Thus it will be found throughout; at no point did Reuben "excel"—his dignity and glory completely dried up!

"Simeon and Levi are brethren; instruments of cruelty are in their habitations. O my Soul, come not thou into their secret; unto their assembly, mine honor, be not thou united; for in their anger they slew a man, and in their self-will they digged down a wall. Cursed be their anger, for it was fierce; and their wrath, for it was cruel; I will divide them in Jacob, and scatter them in Israel." (49: 5-7.) What a proof are these verses of the Divine Inspiration of the scriptures! Had Moses been left to himself he surely would have left out this portion of Jacob's prophecy, seeing that he was himself a descendant of the tribe of Levi!

Simeon and Levi are here linked together and are termed "instruments of cruelty." The historic reference is, no doubt, to Genesis 34: 25, where we read: "And it came to pass on the third day, when they were sore, that two of the sons of Jacob, Simeon and Levi, Dinah's brethren, took each man his sword, and came upon the city boldly, and slew all the males." It would seem from the fact that Simeon's name is here mentioned first that he was the leader in that wickedness. It is not unlikely that Simeon was also the one who took the lead in the conspiracy to get rid of Joseph, for Simeon was the one whom Joseph "bound" (Genesis 42: 24) ere he sent his brethern back to Jacob. It is highly interesting to notice how that the later references to this tribe correspond in character with what we know of their ancestor. For example: When Judah went up to secure his portion in Canaan, he called upon Simeon to help him (Judges 1: 3), as if summoning to his aid the men who possessed the old fierceness of their progenitor. "And Judah said unto Simeon his brother, Come up with me into my lot, that we may fight against the Canaanites; and I likewise will go with thee into thy lot—so Simeon went with him." And so again, we read in 1 Chronicles 4: 42, 43: "And some of them, even of the sons of Simeon, five hundred men, went to Mount Seir, having for their captains Pelatiah, and Neariah, and Rephaiah, and Uzziel, the sons of Ishi. And they smote the rest of the Amalekites that were escaped, and dwelt there unto this day."

Concerning Levi it is interesting to note that when Moses came down from the mount and saw Israel worshipping the calf, that when he said, "Who is on the Lord's side?" we read, "All the sons of Levi gathered themselves together unto him, and he said unto them, Thus saith the Lord God of Israel, Put every man his sword by his side, and go in and out from gate to gate throughout the camp, and slay every man his brother, and every man his companion, and every man his neighbor. And the Children of Levi did according to the word of Moses: and there fell of the people that day about three thousand men." (Exodus 32: 27, 28.) Beautiful is it, also, to learn how similar devotion to the Lord and boldness in acting for Him cancelled Jacob's "curse" and secured Jehovah's blessing. In Numbers 25: 6-13 we are told: "And, behold, one of the Children of Israel came and brought unto his brethren a Midianitish woman in the sight of Moses, and in the sight of all the congregation of the Children of Israel, who were weeping before the door of the tabernacle of the congregation. And when Phineas, the son of Eleazar, the son of Aaron the priest, saw it, he rose up from among the congregation, and took a javelin in his hand; and went after the man of Israel into the tent, and thrust both of them through, the man of Israel, and the woman through her belly. So the plague was stayed from the Children of Israel. And those that died in the plague were twenty and four thousand. And the Lord spoke unto Moses, saying, Phineas, the son of Eleazar, the son of Aaron the priest, hath turned My wrath away from the Children of Israel, while he was zealous for My sake among them, that I consumed not the Children of Israel in My jealousy. Wherefore say, behold, I give unto him my covenant of peace; and he shall have it, and his seed after him, even the covenant of an everlasting priesthood, because he was zealous for his God, and made an atonement for the Children of Israel." Thus the "curse" on Levi was revoked. Levi was first joined to Simeon in cruelty, but after, he was joined to the Lord in grace!

That which is most prominent, however, in Jacob's prophecy concerning the tribes of Simeon and Levi is that they were to be "divided" and "scattered" in Israel. (See 49: 7.) And most literally and remarkably was this fulfilled. When the land was divided in the days of Joshua, we learn that Simeon received not a separate territory in Canaan, but obtained his portion within the allotment of Judah (see Joshua 19: 1-8): thus the Simeonites were necessarily "scattered," being dispersed among the cities of

Judah. So it was with the Levites also; their portion was the forty-eight cities which were scattered throughout the inheritance of the other tribes. (See Numbers 35: 8; Joshua 14: 4, and Joshua 21.) Thus, while each of the other tribes had a separate portion which enabled them to be congregated together, the descendants of Simeon and Levi were "divided" and "scattered." Exactly as Jacob had, centuries before, declared they should be!

"Judah, thou art he whom thy brethren shall praise; thy hand shall be in the neck of thine enemies; thy father's children shall bow down before thee. Judah is a lion's whelp: from the prey, my son, thou art gone up: he stooped down, he couched as a lion, and as an old lion; who shall rouse him up? The sceptre shall not depart from Judah nor a law-giver from between his feet, until Shiloh come; and unto Him shall the gathering of the people be. Binding his foal unto the vine, and his ass's colt unto the choice vine; he washed his garments in wine, and his clothes in the blood of grapes: His eyes shall be red with wine, and his teeth white with milk." (49: 8-12.)

This part of Jacob's prophecy concerning Judah finds its ultimate fulfillment in Christ. With it should be coupled 1 Chronicles 5:2: "Judah prevailed above his brethren, and of him is the Chief Ruler," a, "Prince"; the Hebrew word here is "Nagid" and is the same term which is translated "Messiah the Prince" in Daniel 9: 24. It was from this tribe our Lord came. Returning now to the words of Jacob.

First, we are told of Judah: "Through art he whom thy brethren shall praise." The word here for "praise" is always used of praise or worship which is offered to God! Christ is the One who shall yet receive the praise and worship of His "brethren" according to the flesh, namely, Israel. Second, of Judah, Jacob said, "Thy hand shall be in the neck of thine enemies; thy father's children shall bow down before thee." (Genesis 49: 8.) So, again, Christ is the One who shall yet have dominion over Israel and subdue their enemies. This dominion of the tribe of Judah commenced in the days of David, who was the first king from that tribe; and it was during his reign that Judah's hand was "in the neck of" their "enemies." Third, the destinies of the tribe of Judah is here contemplated under the figure of a "lion," which at once reminds us of Revelation 5: 5, where the Lord Jesus is expressly denominated "The Lion of the Tribe of Judah."

In dealing with the destinies of the tribe of Judah under the figure of a "lion," it is to be observed that this tribe's history is contemplated under three distinct stages, according to the growth or age of the lion. First, we have "a lion's whelp," then "a lion," lastly "an old lion"—the gradual growth in power of this tribe being here set forth. We would suggest that this looks at the tribe of Judah first from the days of Joshua up to the time of Saul; then we have the full grown lion in the days of the fierce warrior David; lastly, from Solomon's reign and onwards we have the "old lion."

"The sceptre shall not depart from Judah; nor a lawgiver from between his feet, until Shiloh come; and unto Him shall the gathering of the people be." (49: 10.) This calls for a separate word. The Hebrew term for "sceptre" here is translated "tribe" in verses 16 and 28 of this same chapter—according to its usage in scripture it signifies the tribal-rod or staff of office which belonged to any tribe and was the ensign of authority. This part of Jacob's prophecy, then, intimated that the tribal-rod should not depart from Judah until a certain eminent Personage had come; in other words, that Judah should retain both its tribal distinctness and separate authority until Shiloh, the Messiah, had appeared. And most remarkably was this prophecy fulfilled. The separate Kingdom of Israel (the Ten Tribes) was destroyed at an early date, but Judah was still in the land when Messiah came.

It is further to be noted that Jacob declared of Judah that there should not depart from this tribe "a lawgiver until Shiloh." It is a striking fact that after Shiloh had come the legal authority vested in this tribe disappeared, as is evident from John 18:31: "Then said Pilate unto them, Take ye Him, and judge Him according to your law. The Jews therefore said unto him: It is not lawful for *us* to put any man to death." What a remarkable confession this was! It was an admission that they were no longer their own governors, but instead, under the dominion of a foreign power. He that has the power to condemn an offender to death is the governor or "lawgiver" of a country. It is "not lawful for us" said Caiaphas and his associates—you, the Roman governor, alone, can pass sentence of death on Jesus of Nazareth. By their own admission Genesis 49: 10 had received its fulfillment. No longer had they a "lawgiver" of their own stock! By their "words" they were "condemned." (Matthew 12: 37.) The "sceptre" had departed, the "lawgiver" had disappeared, therefore—Shiloh must have come.

"Unto Him shall the gathering of the people be" looks forward to Christ's second coming, as also do the words that follow: "Binding his foal unto the vine, and his ass's colt unto the choice vine; he washed his garments in wine, and his clothes in the blood of grapes. His eyes shall be red with wine, and his teeth white with milk." (Genesis 49: 11, 12.) The reference here seems to be a double one: first to the tribe of Judah, second to Christ Himself. Judah's portion in the land was the vine-growing district in the South. (See 2 Chronicles 26: 9, 10.) Note, too, in Song of Solomon 1: 14 that we read of "the vineyards of Engedi" and in Joshua 25: 62 we learn that "Engedi" was one of the cities of Judah; note further Joshua 15: 55 that "Carmel was also included in Judah's portion. The application of Genesis 49: 11, 12, to our Lord may be seen by comparing Isaiah 63: 1-3: "Who is this that cometh from Edom, with dyed garments from Bozrah? This that is glorious in His apparel, traveling in the greatness of His strength? I that speak in righteousness, mighty to save. Wherefore art Thou red in Thine apparel, and Thy garments like Him that treadeth in the winefat?—compare above 'he washed his garments in wine, and his clothes in the blood of grapes' —I have trodden the winepress alone; and of the people there was none with Me: for I will tread them in Mine anger, and trample them in My fury; and their blood shall be sprinkled upon my garments."

"Zebulun shall dwell at the haven of the sea; and he shall be for a haven of ships; and his border shall be unto Zidon." (Genesis 49: 13.) In blessing his children Jacob here passes from his fourth to his tenth son. Why should he do this? Everything in scripture is perfect. Not only is its every word Divinely inspired, but the very arrangement of its words also evidences the handiwork of the Holy Spirit. God is a God of order, and every diligent student discovers this everywhere in His word. When blessing his fourth son we found that the words of our dying patriarch manifestly looked forward to Christ Himself, who, according to the flesh, sprang from this tribe of Judah. Hence, because of the close connection of our Lord with the land of Zebulun during the days of His earthly sojourn, these two tribes are here placed in juxtaposition. Having spoken of the tribe of which our Lord was *born,* we have next mentioned the tribe in whose territory He *lived* for thirty years. This is, we believe, the main reason why the tenth son of Jacob is placed immediately after the fourth.

The part played by the tribe of Zebulun in the history of the nation of Israel was not a conspicuous one, but though referred to but rarely as a tribe, each time they do come before us it is in a highly honorable connection. First, we read of them in Judges 5, where Deborah celebrates in song Israel's victory over Jabin and Sisera, and recounts the parts taken by the different tribes. Of Zebulun and Naphtali she says, "*Zebulun* and Naphtali were a people that jeoparded their lives unto the death in the high places of the field." (Verses 18.) Again, in 1 Chronicles 12, where we have enumerated those who "Came to David to Hebron, to turn the kingdom of Saul to him" (verse 33), concerning Zebulun we read, "*Of Zebulun,* such as went forth to battle, expert in war, with all instruments of war, fifty thousand, which could keep rank, *they were not of double heart.*" And again, in this same chapter, "Moreover they that were nigh them, even unto Issachar *and Zebulun* and Naphtali, brought bread on asses, and on camels, and on mules, and on oxen, and meat, meal, cakes of raisins, and wine, and oil, and oxen, and sheep abundantly: for there was joy in Israel." (1 Chronicles 12: 40.)

Jacob's prophecy concerning the tribe, which was to spring from his tenth son, referred, mainly, to the *position* they were to occupy in the land of Canaan, and also to the *character* of the people themselves. Moses' prophecy concerning the twelve tribes, recorded in Deuteronomy 33, is very similar to that of Jacob's with respect to Zebulun: "And of Zebulun he said, Rejoice, Zebulun, in thy going out (*i. e.,* to sea); and, Issachar, in thy tents. They shall call the people unto *the* mountain (*i, e,* Zion); there they shall offer sacrifices of righteousness: for they shall suck of the abundance of *the seas,* and of treasures hid in the sand." (Verses 18, 19.)

The character of Zebulun as here outlined by Jacob is very different from that of Judah, who is pictured as dwelling, more or less, apart from the other tribes—as a lion "*gone up from* the prey;" very different, too, from Issachar, here referred to as an ass crouching down in lazy sloth. (See verses 14, 15.) Zebulun was to be a commercial and seafaring tribe. When Jacob said of Zebulun, "his border shall be unto Zidion," which was in Phœnica, he implied that it would take part in Phœnican commerce.

The portion which fell to the tribe of Zebulun (Joshua 19:10, 11), together with that of the tribe of Naphtali which joined theirs, became known as "Galilee of the Gentiles." (See Matthew 4: 15.) These Galileans were to be an energetic, enterprising people, who were to mingle freely with the nations. The prophecy of Moses concerning Zebulun, to which we have already referred, clearly establishes this fact (see Deuteronomy 33:18, 19), and, plainly looked forward to New Testament times, when the men of Galilee took such a prominent part as the first heralds of the Cross. Note that Moses said, "*Rejoice* Zebulun, in thy *going out.*" Is it not remarkable that no less than eleven out of the twelve apostles of Christ were men of *Galilee*—Judas alone being an exception! How beautiful are the next prophetic words of Moses in this connection: "They shall call the people unto the mountain: there they shall offer sacrifices of righteousness!" (Deuteronomy 33:19.)

One other word concerning Jacob's prophecy about Zebulun. Of this tribe he said, "He shall be *for a haven* of ships." Galilee was to provide a refuge, a harbor, a place where the storm-tossed ships might anchor at rest. And here it was that Joseph and Mary, with the Christ Child, found a "haven" after their return from Egypt! Here it was the Lord Jesus dwelt until the beginning of His public ministry. And note, too, John 12:1, "After these things Jesus walked in *Galilee*: for He would not walk in Jewry, because the Jews sought to kill Him." Galilee was still a "*haven*" to Him!

"Issachar is a strong ass couching down between two burdens: And he saw that rest was good, and the land that it was pleasant; and he bowed his shoulder to bear, and became a servant unto tribute." (Gen. 49:14, 15.) Upon these verses the writer has but little light. It is difficult to determine the precise force and significance of the several statements that Jacob made here concerning his fifth son; nor is it easy to trace the fulfilment of them in the record of the tribe which sprang from him. One thing is clear, however: to compare a man (or a tribe) to an "ass" is, today, a figure of reproach, but it was not so in Jacob's time. In Israel, the ass was not looked upon with contempt; instead, it was an honorable animal. Not only was it a useful beast of burden, but people of rank rode on them. (See Judg. 10:4; 12:14.) Until the days of Solomon Israel had no horses, being forbidden by Jehovah to rear them (see Deut. 17:16); but asses were as common and as useful among them as horses are now among us. The "ass" was a reminder to Israel that they were a peculiar (separated) people, whose trust was to be in the Lord and not in horses and chariots, which were the confidence of the other nations of antiquity.

"Issachar is termed by Jacob a "strong ass," and the fulfilment of this portion of Jacob's prophecy is clearly discovered in the subsequent history of this tribe. In Numbers 26, where we have recorded the second numbering of those among the tribes which were able to go forth to war, we find that only Judah and Dan out of the twelve tribes were numerically stronger than Issachar, and Dan had but one hundred fighting men more than Issachar. Again, in the days of the Kings, the tribe of Issachar had become stronger still, for while in Numbers 26:25, we read that the number of their men able to go forth to war were 64,300, in 1 Chronicles 7:5 we are told, "And the brethren among all the families of Issachar were valiant men of might, reckoned in all by the genealogies 87,000!"

39. JACOB'S PROPHECY, CONTINUED

Genesis 49

"Dan shall judge his people, as one of the tribes of Israel. Dan shall be a serpent by the way, an adder in the path, that biteth the horse's heels, so that his rider shall fall backward. I have waited for Thy salvation, O Lord." (Gen. 49:16-18.) With this prophecy of Jacob concerning the tribe of Dan should be compared that of Moses, recorded in Deuteronomy 33:22, "And of Dan he said, Dan is a lion's whelp: he shall leap from Bashan." It is to be seen that both predicted *evil* of that tribe, around which there seems to be a cloud of mystery.

The first thing that Scripture records of Dan is his low birth. (See Gen. 30:1-6.) Next, he is brought before us in Genesis 37:2, though he is not there directly mentioned by name. It is highly significant that of the four sons of Bilhah and Zilpah, *Dan* was the oldest, being at that time twenty years of age, and so, most likely, the *ringleader* in the "evil" which Joseph reported to their father. Next, in Genesis 46, reference is made to the children of Jacob's sons: the descendants of Reuben, Simeon, Levi, and the others, being specifically named in order. But when *Dan* is reached, the names of *his* sons are not given; instead, they are simply called by the tribal name—Hushim or Shuham. (See 46:23.) This is the more striking, because in Numbers 26 we meet with the same thing again: the children born to each of Jacob's twelve sons are carefully enumerated until Dan is reached, and then, as in Genesis 46, *his descendants are not named,* simply the tribal title being given. (See Num. 26:42.) This concealment of the names of Dan's children is the first indication of that silent "blotting out" of his name, which meets us in *the total omission* of this tribe from the genealogies recorded in 1 Chronicles 2 to 10, as well as in Revelation 7, where, again, no mention is made of any being "sealed" out of the tribe of Dan. There seems to have been an unwillingness on the part of the Holy Spirit to even mention *this tribe* by name. In cases where the names of all the tribes *are* given, Dan is generally far down, often last of all, in the list. For example, we read in Numbers 10:25, "And the standard of the camp of the children of Dan set forward, which was *the rearward of all the camps* throughout their hosts.'' Again, Dan was *the last* of the tribes to receive his inheritance when Joshua divided up the land—''This is the inheritance of the tribe of the children of Dan according to their families, these cities with their villages. When they had *made an end* of dividing the land for inheritance by their coasts, the children of Israel gave an inheritance to Joshua.'' (Josh. 19:47-49.) Note again that in 1 Chronicles 27:16-22, where all the tribes are referred to, Dan is mentioned *last!*

Putting together the several prophecies of Jacob and Moses we find two traits met in Dan—*treachery* ''a *serpent* by the way, an adder in the path''; and *cruelty:* ''Dan is *a lion's whelp;* he shall leap from Bashan.'' In Judges 18 the Holy Spirit has recorded at length how these predictions received their first fulfilment. The attack of this tribe on Laish was serpentile in its cunning and lionlike in its cruel execution. Then it was that Dan leaped from Bashan, and from the slopes of Mount Hermon (which was in the territory of this tribe) like a young lion and like an adder springing on its prey. From Judges 18:30 we learn that Dan was the first of the tribes to fall into Idolatry. Apparently they remained in this awful condition right until the days of Jeroboam, for we find that when this apostate king set up his two golden calves, saying, ''Behold thy gods, O Israel,'' he set up one in Bethel and ''the other put he *in Dan.*'' (1 Ki. 12:28, 29.) And, as late as the time of Jehu these two golden calves were still standing, and it is a significant and solemn fact that though there was a great reformation in his day, so that the prophets and worshippers of Baal were slain and the images were burned and the house of Baal was broken down, yet we are told, ''Howbeit, from the sins of Jeroboam the son of Nebat, who made Israel to sin, Jehu departed not from after them, to wit, the golden calves that were in Bethel, and that were in *Dan.*'' (2 Ki. 10:29.)

One other item in Jacob's prophecy concerning this tribe remains to be noticed—''Dan shall *judge* his people.'' This received a partial fulfilment in the days of Samson—though we doubt not that its final fulfilment awaits the time of the great tribulation. Joshua 19:41 informs us that among the towns allotted to this tribe were Zorah and Eshtaol. Compare with this Judges 13:2, which tells us that the parents of Samson belonged to the tribe of Dan and had their home in Zorah. How remarkably the prophecies of Jacob and Moses combined in the person of Samson (one of Israel's "judges") is apparent on the surface. Serpent-like methods and the lion's strength characterized each step in his strange career. How Samson "bit," as it were, "the horse's heels" in his death!

It is to be noted that after Jacob had completed his prophecy concerning Dan, and ere he took up the next tribe, that he said, "I have waited for Thy salvation, O Lord." (Gen. 49:18.) This is very striking and significant, coming in just where it does. Having spoken of Dan as "a *serpent* by the way," the Holy Spirit seems to have brought to his mind the words spoken by God to that old Serpent the Devil, recorded in Genesis 3:15. The eye of the dying patriarch looks beyond the "Serpent" to the one who shall yet "bruise his head," and therefore does he say, "I have waited for *Thy salvation,* O Lord." No doubt these very words will yet be appropriated in a coming day by the godly remnant among the Jews. If, as it has been generally held by prophetic students, both ancient and modern, both among Jews and Gentiles, that the Anti-Christ will spring from this tribe of Dan, the ancient prophecy of Jacob concerning the descendants of this son will then receive its final fulfilment. Then, in a supreme manner, will Dan (in the person of the Anti-Christ) *"judge"* and rule over "his people," *i. e.,* Israel; then, will *Dan* be a "serpent in the way" and "an adder in the path," then will he treacherously and cruelly "bite the horse's heels." And then, too, will that faithful company, who refuse to worship the Beast or receive his "mark," cry, "I have *waited* for Thy salvation, O Lord!"

"Gad, a troop shall overcome him: but he shall overcome at the last." (Gen. 49:19.) The Hebrew word for troop here signifies a marauding or plundering troop. The cognate to this word is rendered "companies" in 2 Kings 5:2—"And the Syrians had gone out by *companies,* and had brought away *captive* out of the land of Israel a little maid." The same word is translated "bands" in 2 Kings 24:2—"And the Lord sent against him *bands* of the Chaldees, and *bands* of the Syrians, and *bands* of the Moabites, and *bands* of the children of Ammon, and sent them against Judah to *destroy* it, according to the Word of the Lord, which He spake by His servants, the prophets." When, therefore, Jacob said of this tribe, "Gad, a troop shall overcome him, but he shall overcome at the last," the reference seems to be to alternate defeat and victory. This tribe was to be in a constant state of warfare, leading like the Bedouin Arabs a wandering, wild, and unsettled existence. One wonders whether the (slangy) expression "Gad about" may not have its origin in the character of this tribe."

We may notice, once more, how closely parallel with this prediction of Jacob is the prophecy of Moses concerning this tribe: "And of Gad he said, Blessed be he that enlargeth Gad: he dwelleth as a lion, and teareth the arm with the crown of the head. And he provided the first part for himself, because there, in a portion of the lawgiver, was he seated." (Deut. 33:20, 21.) The first part of this prophecy emphasizes the unsettled and warlike character of Gad. The second statement that Gad "provided the first part (of the inheritance) for himself," has reference to the fact that this tribe sought and obtained as their portion the land on the east side of the Jordan, and this *before* Canaan was divided among the tribes in the days of Joshua. This portion of Gad's became known as "the land of Gilead." (See Deut. 3:12-15.) Note, further, that Moses said, "Blessed be he that *enlargeth* Gad." The fulfilment of this may be seen by a reference to 1 Chronicles 5:16, where we read that the children of Gad dwelt in "all the suburbs of Sharon." Note that in Joshua 13:24-28 no mention is made of *Sharon:* their border was thus "enlarged!"

The position that Gad occupied was a precarious one. Being cut off from that of the other tribes, they were more or less isolated. They were open, constantly, to the attacks from the desert bands or troops, such as the Ammonites and Midianites, and consequently, they lived in a continual state of warfare. Jacob's words were being repeatedly fulfilled. Gad suffered severely from their lack of faith and enterprise in asking for the territory they did. Their choice was almost as bad as Lot's, and proved as disastrous, for they were among the first tribes that were carried into captivity. (See 1 Chron. 5:26.)

For particular illustrations of the fulfilment of Jacob's prophecy we may note the following: "And it came to pass in process of time, that the children of Ammon made war against Israel." Note now, the portion of Israel which they assailed: "And it was so, that when the children of Ammon made war against Israel, the elders of *Gilead* went to fetch Jephthah out of the land of Tob: and they said unto Jephthah, Come, and be our captain, that *we* may fight with the children of Ammon. . . . Then Jephthah went with the elders of *Gilead,* and the people made him captain over them: and Jephthah uttered all his words before the Lord in Mizpah. And Jephthah sent messengers unto the king of the children of Ammon, saying, What hast thou to do with me, that thou art come against me to fight in *my* land? (Judg. 11:4-6, 11, 12.) "Then Nahash the Ammonite came up, and encamped against *Jabesh-gilead:* and all the men of Jabesh said unto Nahash, Make a covenant with us, and we will serve thee." (1 Sam. 11:1.) But in the End-time Gad "shall overcome." It is to this, we believe, that Jeremiah 49:1-2, refers: "Concerning the Ammonites thus saith the Lord; hath Israel no sons? hath he no heir? why then doth their king inherit Gad, and his people dwell in his cities? Therefore, behold, the days come, saith the Lord, that I will cause an alarm of war to be heard in Rabbah of the Ammonites; and it shall be a desolate heap, and her daughters shall be burned with fire: *then* shall Israel be heir unto them that were his heirs, said the Lord." And again in Zephaniah 2:8-9, "I have heard the reproach of Moab, and the revilings of the children of Ammon, whereby they have reproached My people, and magnified themselves against their border. Therefore, as I live, saith the Lord of hosts, the God of Israel, Surely Moab shall be as Sodom, and the children of Ammon as Gomorrah, even the breeding of nettles and salt pits, and a perpetual desolation: the residue of My people shall spoil them, and the remnant of My people *shall possess them."*

"Out of Asher his bread shall be fat, and he shall yield royal dainties" (Gen. 49:20). Asher's descendants, in common with the tribes of Zebulun, Naphtali and Issachar, were settled in the northern part of Palestine, which was called by the general name of "Galilee of the Gentiles," which name was perfectly appropriate to Asher, for from first to last this was a half Gentile tribe. Asher's territory lay in the extreme north of Palestine between Mount Lebanon and the Mediterranean Sea, and included within its borders the celebrated cities of Tyre and Sidon (See Josh. 19:24-31). The portion of this tribe was better known by its Grecian name of Phœnicia, which means "land of the palms," so designated because of the luxuriant palms which abounded there. It was to this land, preëminently rich and beautiful, Jacob's prediction looked.

"Out of Asher his bread shall be fat, and *he shall yield ROYAL dainties.*" Let us turn now to a few Scriptures which furnish illustrations of the repeated fulfillment of Jacob's prophecy.

"And Hiram, king of Tyre, sent messengers to *David,* and cedar trees and carpenters and masons, and *they built David a house*" (2 Sam. 5:11). This city of Tyre was, as pointed out above, within the territory of the tribe of Asher (Josh. 19:29), and here we learn how the *king* of Tyre yielded or provided "royal dainties" by furnishing both material and workmen for building a house for king David.

We behold a repetition of this in the days of Solomon. In 1 Kings 5 we read: "And Hiram, king of Tyre, sent his servants unto Solomon, for he had heard that they had anointed him king in the room of his father: for Hiram was ever a lover of David. And Solomon sent to Hiram, saying, Thou knowest how that David, my father, could not build a house unto the name of the Lord his God, for the wars which were about him on every side, until the Lord put them under the soles of his feet. But now the Lord my God hath given me rest on every side, so that there is neither adversary nor evil occurrent. And, behold, I purpose to build a house unto the name of the Lord my God, as the Lord spake unto David, my father, saying, Thy son, whom I will set upon thy throne in thy room, he shall build a house unto my name. Now, therefore, command thou that they hew me cedar trees out of Lebanon; and my servants shall be with thy servants; and unto thee will I give hire for thy servants according to all that thou shalt appoint: for thou knowest that there is not among us any that can skill to hew timbers like unto the Sidonians. And it came to pass, when Hiram heard the words of Solomon, that he rejoiced greatly, and said, Blessed be the Lord this day, which hath given unto David a wise son over this great people. And Hiram sent to Solomon, saying, I have considered the things which thou sentest to me for: and I will do all thy desire concerning timber of cedar, and concerning timber of fir. My servants shall bring them down from Lebanon unto the sea, and I will convey them by sea in floats unto the place that thou shalt appoint me, and will cause them to be discharged there, and thou shalt receive them: and thou shalt accomplish my desire, in giving food for my household. *So Hiram gave Solomon cedar trees and fir trees according to all his desire*" (verses 1-10). Thus again do we see how Asher "yielded royal dainties."

Jacob also said: "Out of Asher his *bread* shall be fat." Is it not striking to discover that in the time of famine in the days of Elijah that God sent his prophet to the widow in Zarephath, saying: "Behold, I have commanded a widow woman *there* to *sustain* thee" (1 Ki. 17:9). Note Zarephath was in Sidon (see Lu. 4:26) and Sidon was in *Asher's* territory (Josh. 19:28).

In 2 Chronicles 30, we have another illustration, along a different line, of how Asher yielded "*royal dainties.*" It was at the time of a great religious revival in Israel. King Hezekiah "sent to all Israel and Judah, and wrote letters also to Ephraim and Manasseh, that they should come to the house of the Lord at Jerusalem, *to keep the passover* unto the Lord God of Israel" (verse 1). Then we are told, "So the posts passed from city to city, through the country of Ephraim and Manasseh, even unto Zebulun: *but they laughed them to scorn,* and mocked them" (verse 10). But in marked and blessed contrast from this we read: "Nevertheless, divers of *Asher* and Manasseh and of Zebulun *humbled themselves, and came to Jerusalem*" (verse 11).

The New Testament supplies us with two more illustrations. In Luke 2 we learn of how one who belonged to this Tribe of Asher yielded a most blessed "dainty" to Israel's new-born King, even the Lord Jesus. For when His parents brought the Child Jesus into the Temple, following the beautiful Song of Simeon, we read, "And there was one Anna, a prophetess, the daughter of Phanuel, of the Tribe of *Asher;* she was of a great age, and had lived with an husband seven years from her virginity. And she was a widow of about fourscore and four years, which departed not from the Temple, but served God with fastings and prayers night and day. And she coming in that instant *gave thanks likewise unto the Lord, and spake of Him* to all that looked for redemption in Jerusalem" (Lu. 2:36-38).

Finally, note in Acts 27 we are told that when the apostle Paul was being carried prisoner to Rome, that when the ship reached *Sidon* (which was in the borders of Asher) that "Julius courteously entreated Paul, and gave him liberty to go unto his friends to *refresh* himself" (verse 3). Thus, once more, do we read of "bread" out of Asher.

"Naphtali is a hind let loose: he giveth goodly words" (Gen. 49:21). The word Naphtali means "wrestling" (see Gen. 30:8). "Naphtali is a hind let loose"; it was as though Jacob said, Naphtali is as a deer caught in the toils of the hunters, hemmed in by them, but by his struggles she escapes from their snares. Naphtali would be a hind "let loose." This expression has a double meaning. In the Hebrew the word signifies, first, "sent" or "sent forth," just as a stag driven from its covert goes forth, scattering her pursuers. But the word also means "let loose" or "let go." It is the term used of Noah when he "sent forth" the raven and the dove from the ark; as also of the priest, when at the cleansing of the leper, he let go or let loose the living bird. The word expresses the joy of an animal which has been made captive and, in its recovered liberty, bounds forth in gladness, just as we have often seen a dog jumping for joy after it has been unchained. Jacob, then, pictures Naphtali rejoicing as a freed hind. Then he foretells the joy which the Tribe shall express after its escape—"goodly words" he shall give forth. After it regains its liberty, the Tribe shall sing a Song of Praise.

The striking fulfillment of this prediction by our dying patriarch is seen in the victory of Barak, the great hero of this Tribe (see Judg. 4:6), who, sent forth as a hind from its cover in the mountains of Galilee, came down Mount Tabor to face on foot the hosts of Sisera with his nine hundred chariots of iron. Barak, like a hind let loose, was at first timid of responding to Deborah's call. He had not dared to go forth with his little handful of men unless Deborah had sent for him and assured him of success. Read through Judges 4, and note the *hindlike swiftness* of his onslaught down the slopes of Tabor. It is significant that the name "Barak" means "lightning," and, like lightning he burst as a storm on the startled hosts of Sisera, which were scattered by the hand of God at his unexpected approach. (Note Judg. 4:14.) "So Barak went down from Mount Tabor, and ten thousand men *after* him," not "with him"—he running ahead of all!

The battle was not of Barak's choosing, rather was it forced upon him by Deborah. He was literally "sent forth" into the valley. (Note "sent" in Judges 5:15.) In the heights of Tabor, Barak and his men were beyond the reach of Sisera's cavalry and chariots. But down in the valley, on foot, they would be like a herd of defenseless deer, unarmed, without either spear or shield, for attack or defense. (See Judg 5:8.) In the defenselessness of Naphtali —deserted by their brethren (see 5:15-18)—hemmed in by the hosts of the Canaanites, they were indeed a picture of helplessness. Nevertheless, the hand of the oppressor was broken. God interposed, and Naphtali was *"set free,"* and the exuberance of their consequent joy found expression in the Song of Deborah and Barak recorded in Judges 5. *There* were the "goodly words" which Jacob had foretold. Thus Naphtali was a hind "let loose" in the *double* sense— "sent forth" by Deborah and "set free" from the yoke of the Canaanites by God!

But if this Tribe is interesting to us from its Old Testament association, it has far deeper interest for us from its New Testament connections. Zebulun and Naphtali were closely linked together, yet each had a separate interest. The land of Zebulun provided a "haven" of rest for the Lord Jesus during the first thirty years that He tabernacled among men; but it was in the bounds of Naphtali in the cities of Capernaum, Bethsaida, Chorazin, and other places, that He went about doing good and ministering the Word of Life. In His preaching of the Gospel to the poor were the "goodly words" of which Jacob spoke!

"Joseph is a fruitful bough, even a fruitful bough by a well; whose branches run over the wall: The archers have sorely grieved him, and shot at him, and hated him. But his bow abode in strength, and the arms of his hands were made strong by the hands of the mighty God of Jacob (from thence is the Shepherd, the Stone of Israel); even by the God of thy father, who shall help thee; and by the Almighty, who shall bless thee with blessings of heaven above, blessings of the deep that lieth under, blessings of the breasts and of the womb. The blessings of thy father have prevailed above the blessings of my progenitors unto the utmost bound of the everlasting hills: they shall be on the head of Joseph, and on the crown of the head of him that was separate from his brethren" (Gen. 49:22-26).

These words of Jacob concerning Joseph are to be divided into two parts: what is said in verses 22 to 24 is mainly retrospective; what is recorded in verses 25, 26 is prospective. This appears from the change of tense: in the first part the verbs are in the past tense, in the second part they are in the future. As Jacob reviews the past he mentions three things in connection with his favorite son. Verse 22 seems to view Joseph as a youth in his father's house, as an object of beauty, of tender care, and as well pleasing to his father's heart—all pictures under the beautiful figure of a "fruitful bough by a well." Next, Jacob refers to the bitter enmity and fierce hatred which were directed against him—the archers sorely grieved him; they shot at him their cruel arrows, they vented upon him their unreasonable spite. But through it all Joseph was Divinely sustained. The arms of the Eternal God were beneath him, and the Angel of the Lord encamped round about him. "His hands were made strong by the hands of the mighty God of Jacob."

Some have experienced difficulty with the wording of verse 24; even the translators do not appear to have been clear upon it. Inserting the word "is" in italics the verse as it stands in the Authorized Version reads as though it were a prediction concerning Christ. But many other plain Scriptures show that this is a mistake. The Messiah was not "from" the Tribe of Joseph, but came of the Tribe of Judah, just as Messianic prophecy declared He should. The little word "is" in italics should be omitted, and the verse punctuated thus—"His hands were made strong by the hands of the Mighty (One) of Jacob, from thence—the Shepherd, the Stone of Israel." It was "from *thence,*" *i. e.,* from the Shepherd and Stone of Israel, came all of Joseph's strength and blessing.

The prominent feature about this prophecy concerning Joseph is *fruitfulness,* and this received its fulfilment in the *double* Tribe which sprang from him—Ephraim and Manasseh, like two branches out of the parent stem. Joseph received a double portion in the land, viz., the firstborn's "birthright," this being transferred to him from Reuben. (See 1 Chron. 5:1, 2.) So, too, shall it be in the Millennium. Concerning the coming Kingdom, of which Ezekiel's closing chapters treat, we read: "Thus saith the Lord God, This shall be the border, whereby ye shall inherit the land according to the twelve tribes of Israel: *Joseph shall have two portions*" (Ez. 47:13). It is noteworthy that "Ephraim" means "*fruitfulness*," and of Manasseh Jacob had predicted, "Let them grow into a *multitude* in the midst of the earth." Finally, it should be pointed out that Joshua was from one of the tribes which sprang from Joseph (Num. 13:8), and in him Jacob's prophecy concerning his favorite son received its main fulfilment.

"Benjamin shall raven as a wolf: in the morning he shall devour the prey, and at night he shall divide the spoil" (Gen. 49:27). What a striking evidence is this of the complete setting aside of the natural man by God! Surely it is clear that had Jacob followed the inclinations of his heart he would not have said *this* of Benjamin, his youngest and dearly loved son! But this divine prediction was unmistakably fulfilled as the Scriptures which bear upon this tribe plainly show.

Benjamin is here likened to a "wolf," which is noted for its swiftness and *ferocity*. Benjamin was the fiercest and most warlike of the tribes. For illustrations, note the following passages; Judges 19, and mark verse 16; 2 Sam. 2:15, 16: "Then there arose and went over by number, twelve of Benjamin, which pertained to Ish-bosheth, the son of Saul, and twelve of the servants of David. And they caught every one his fellow by the head, and thrust his sword in his fellow's side; so they fell down together." (See also 1 Chron. 8:40; 12:2; 2 Chron. 17:17.)

The heroes of this tribe were marked by fierceness and wolf-like treachery. *Ehud* was of this tribe. (Read Judg. 3:15-22.) *King Saul* was a Benjaminite. (Read 1 Sam. 22:17-20.) Mark the *wolf* seizing the helpless sheep as recorded in 2 Samuel 4:1-6. *Saul of Tarsus,* who first persecuted the Church, was also of this Tribe (Rom. 11:1).

In closing our study of this remarkable prophecy from the dying Jacob, let us mark how everything good which he severally predicted of his sons finds its realization *in the Lord Jesus.*

1. The prophecy concerning Reuben (Gen. 44:3) reminds us of the Excellency and Dignity of Christ's person: He is the "Firstborn," in whom is "the excellency of dignity and the excellency of power."

2. The prophecy concerning Simeon and Levi (49:5-7) may well speak to us of Christ on the Cross: then it was

that "instruments of cruelty" were used against Him; Jacob says: "O my soul, come not thou into their secret"—he would have nothing to do with them: so on the Cross, Christ was forsaken by God and man; a "curse" is here pronounced by Jacob upon them, as Christ, on the Cross, was "made a Curse for us."

3. The prophecy concerning Simeon and *Levi* anticipated our Lord's *Priesthood,* for Levi became the priestly Tribe.

4. The prophecy concerning Judah (49:8-12) pictures our Lord's Kingship.

5. The prophecy concerning Zebulun (49:13) looks at Christ as the great Refuge and Haven of Rest.

6. The prophecy concerning Issachar (49:14, 15) prefigures His lowly Service.

7. The prophecy concerning Dan (49:16-18) views Him as the Judge.

8. The prophecy concerning Gad (49:19) announces His triumphant Resurrection.

9. The prophecy concerning Asher (49:20) looks at Him as the Bread of Life, the One who satisfies the hearts of His own.

10. The prophecy concerning Naphtali (49:21) regards His as God's perfect Prophet, giving forth "goodly words."

11. The prophecy concerning Joseph (49:22-26) forecasts His Millennial reign.

12. The prophecy concerning Benjamin (49:27) depicts Him as the terrible Warrior (Cf. Isa. 63:1-3).

40. JOSEPH AS A YOUTH

Genesis 37

In the first of our articles upon Jacob we called attention to the fact that each of the great Israelitish patriarchs illustrated some basic spiritual truth and that the chronological order of their lives agrees with the doctrinal order of truth. In Abraham we have illustrated the doctrine of *election,* for he was singled out by God from all the heathen and chosen to be the head of the Jewish nation. In Isaac we have foreshadowed the doctrine of *Divine sonship:* Abram's firstborn, Ishmael, represents the man born after the flesh, the old nature; but Isaac, born by the miraculous power of God, tells of the new man, the spiritual nature. In Jacob we see exemplified *the conflict* between the two natures in the believer, and also God's gracious *discipline* which issued, slowly but surely, in the triumph of the spirit over the flesh. Joseph, typically, speaks to us of *heirship* preceded by "suffering," and points forward to the time when the sons and heirs shall *reign* together with Christ. There is thus a beautiful moral order in the several leading truths illustrated and personified by these men. And it should be observed that here, as in everything which pertains to God's Word, its *orderliness* evidences its Divine Authorship; everything is in its proper place.

Joseph, then, speaks of *heirship* and, as another has beautifully expressed it, "And consistently with this, in Joseph, we get *suffering* before glories. * * * For while discipline attaches to us as children, sufferings go before us as heirs; and this gives us the distinction between Jacob and Joseph. It is discipline we see in Jacob, discipline leading him as a child, under the hand of the Father of his spirit, to a participation of God's holiness. It is sufferings, martyr-sufferings, sufferings for righteousness, we see in Joseph, marking his path to glories. And this is the crowning thing! and thus it comes as the closing thing, in this wondrous book of Genesis—after this manner perfect in its structure, as it is truthful in its records. One moral after another is studied, one secret after another is revealed, in the artless family scenes which constitute its materials, and in them we learn our calling, the sources and the issues of our history, from our election to our inheritance" (Mr. J. G. Bellett).

Joseph is the last of the saints which occupies a prominent position in Genesis. In all there are *seven*—Adam, Abel, Noah, Abraham, Isaac, Jacob, Joseph. More space is devoted to the last of these seven than to any of the others. There are several reasons for this which appear on the surface. In the first place, the history of Joseph is the chief link which connects Exodus with Genesis; the earlier chapters of Exodus being unintelligible without the last ten chapters of Genesis. It is Joseph's life which explains the remarkable development of the Hebrews from a mere handful of wandering shepherds to a numerous and settled colony in Egypt. But no doubt the chief reason why the life of Joseph is described with such fulness of detail is because almost everything in it typified something in connection with *Christ*. But more of this later.

"Joseph was the elder son of Rachel (30:24). Of his early life nothing is recorded. He could not have been more than five or six years old when his father left Mesopotamia. He was therefore the child of Jacob's later life, and escaped all the sad experiences associated with the earlier years at Haran. He comes before us in this chapter (Gen. 37) at the age of seventeen. His companions were his half-brothers, the grown-up sons of Bilhah and Zilpah. From all that we have hitherto seen of them they must have been utterly unfit companions for such a youth. Jacob's elder sons had, naturally, been affected by the life in Haran, by the jealousy at home, and by the scheming between Laban and Jacob. They had been brought up under the influence of the old Jacob, while Joseph had been the companion of the changed Jacob or 'Israel.' There are few people more unfitted for influence over younger brothers than elder brothers of bad character." (Dr. G. Thomas.)

"These are the generations of Jacob. Joseph being seventeen years old, was feeding the flock with his brethren; and the lad was with the sons of Bilhah, and with the sons of Zilpah, his father's wives: and Joseph brought unto his father their evil report. Now Israel loved Joseph more than all his children, because he was the son of his old age: and he made him a coat of many colors. And when his brethren saw that their father loved him more than all his brethren, they hated him, and could not speak peaceably unto him" (37:2-4).

There are perhaps few portions of Holy Writ with which we are more familiar than the one now before us. From earliest childhood many of us have listened to this beautiful but pathetic narrative. The aged patriarch, his favorite son, the coat of many colors, Joseph's dreams, the envious brothers, their wicked conduct—all so true to life—have been indelibly impressed upon our memories since we first learned them on our mother's knee, or from the lips of our Sunday School teacher. Many are the lessons which may be drawn, and pointed are the warnings which are found here. But we shall pass from these to something deeper and even more precious.

As we read thoughtfully the books of the Old Testament our study of them is but superficial if they fail to show us that in divers ways and by various means God was preparing the way for *the coming of His Son.* The central purpose in the Divine Incarnation, the great outstanding object in the life and death of the Lord Jesus, were prefigured beforehand, and ought to have been rendered familiar to the minds of men. Among the means thus used of God was the history of different persons through whom the life and character of Christ were to a remarkable degree made manifest beforehand. Thus Adam represented His Headship, Abel His Death, Noah His Work in providing a refuge for His people. Melchizedek pointed to Him as priest, Moses as prophet, David as King. But the fullest and most striking of all these typical personage was Joseph, for between his history and that of Christ we may trace fully a *hundred* points of analogy! Others before us have written upon this captivating theme, and from their writings we shall draw freely in the course of these papers on the typical significance of Joseph's history.*

In the verses quoted above from Genesis 37 there are seven points in which Joseph prefigured Christ, each of which is worthy of our attention, namely, the meaning of his name, the nature of his occupation, his opposition to evil, his father's love, his relation to his father's age, his coat of many colors, and the hatred of his brethren. Let us consider each of these in turn:

---

*We take this occasion to acknowledge our indebtedness to Dr. Haldeman and Mr. C. Knapp.

1. *The Meaning of his Name.* It is most significant that our patriarch had *two* names—Joseph, and Zaphnath-paaneah (41:45) which the rabbins translate "Revealer of secrets." This latter name was given to him by Pharaoh in acknowledgment of the Divine wisdom which was in him. Thus, Joseph may be said to be his *human* name and Zaphnath-paaneah his *Divine* name. So, also, the one whom Joseph foreshadowed has a double name—"Jesus" being His *human* name, "Christ" signifying "the Anointed" of *God,* or, again, we have his double name in "Son of Man" which speaks of His humanity, and "Son of God" which tells of His Deity. Let us note how the *meaning* of Joseph's names were typical in their significance.

"Joseph" means *adding* (see 30:24). The first Adam was the great *subtractor,* the last Adam is the great *Adder:* through the one, men became *lost;* by the other, all who believe are *saved.* Christ is the One who "adds" to Heaven's inhabitants. It was to this end that He came to this earth, tabernacled among men for more than thirty years, and then died on the Cross: "Verily, verily, I say unto you, except a corn of wheat fall into the ground and die, it abideth alone: but if it die, it bringeth forth much fruit" (Jno. 12:24). The ultimate result of His Death will be "much fruit," and at His return this will be gathered into the Heavenly garner (Jno. 14:3).

But Joseph's second name means "Revealer of secrets." This was a most appropriate name. Revealer of secrets Joseph ever was, not merely as an interpreter of dreams, but in every scene of his life, in every relation he sustained—when with his brethren in Potiphar's household, in prison, or before Pharaoh—his words and his works ever *tested* those with whom he had to do, making manifest their secret condition. How strikingly this foreshadowed Christ, of whom it was said in the days of His infancy, "Behold this Child is set for the fall and rising again of many in Israel; and for a sign which shall be spoken against * * * that the thoughts of many hearts *may be revealed*" (Lu. 2:34, 35).

In the incident now before us Joseph is seen as the Revealer of secrets in a double way. First, he revealed his father's heart, for he is here seen as the special object on which Jacob's affections were centered. Second, he revealed the hearts of his brethren by making manifest their wicked "hatred." In like manner, our blessed Saviour revealed the Father's heart, "No man hath seen God at any time; the only begotten Son, which is in the bosom of the Father, *He hath declared Him*" (Jno. 1:18). And in like manner, the Lord Jesus also revealed what was in the hearts of men. One of the most striking and prominent features presented in the four Gospels is the fact that everywhere He went the Lord Jesus *exposed* all. He made manifest the secret condition of all with whom He came into contact. He was truly "the *Light* of the world," shining in "a dark place"—detecting, displaying, uncovering, bringing to light the hidden things of darkness. Well, then, was Joseph named the one who *added,* and the one that *revealed.*

2. *By Occupation Joseph was a Shepherd,* "feeding the flock." This is one of the prominent lines which is found running through several of the Old Testament typical personages. Abel, Jacob, Joseph, Moses, David, were each of them "shepherds," and a close study of what is recorded of each one in this particular relation will reveal that each pointed forward to some separate and distinctive aspect of our Lord's Shepherdhood. No figure of Christ is more beautiful than this: our favorite Psalm (the twenty-third) presents Him in this character. One of our earliest conceptions of the Saviour, as children, was as the Good Shepherd. The figure suggests His watchful care, His unwearied devotion, His tender solicitude, His blessed patience, His protecting grace, His matchless love in giving His life for the sheep. Above, Joseph is seen "feeding the flock," pointing to the earthly ministry of Christ who, sent unto "the lost sheep of the House of Israel," spent Himself in tending the needs of others.

3. *His Opposition to Evil.* "And Joseph brought unto his father their evil report." It is truly pathetic to find how this action of Joseph has been made an occasion for debate, some arguing that in doing what he did Joseph acted wrongly; others defending him. But it is not as a tale bearer that Joseph is here viewed, rather is he seen as the *truth-speaker.* Not by cowardly silence would he be the accomplice of their evil-doing. And here too we may discern a clear foreshadowing of the Lord Jesus Christ. We will quote but one verse, but it is sufficient to establish the type: "The world cannot hate you; but Me it hateth, be-

cause *I testify of it* that the works thereof *are evil*" (Jno. 7:7).

4. *His Father's Love.* "Israel loved Joseph more than all his brethren." This is one of the lines which stands out most distinctly in this lovely Old Testament picture. How Jacob loved Joseph! His mark of special esteem in making for him the coat of many colors: his unconsolable grief when he believed that Joseph had been devoured by beasts; his taking of that long journey into Egypt that he might again look upon his favorite son ere death overtook him—all tell out the deep love of Jacob for Joseph. And how all this speaks to us of *the Father's love* for His only begotten Son! Through Solomon the Spirit of prophecy, speaking of the relation which existed between the Father and the Son in a past eternity, said, "The Lord possessed Me in the beginning of His way before His works of old;" and again, "Then I was by Him, as One brought up with Him, and I was daily *His delight,* rejoicing always before Him" (Prov. 8:22, 30). How sweetly was this illustrated by Jacob's love for Joseph! Again, when the Son of God became incarnate, and was about to begin His public ministry, the heavens were opened and the Voice of the Father was heard saying, "This is My *beloved Son,* in whom I am well pleased" (Mat. 3:17). So, also, when His public ministry neared its close, once more the Father's Voice was heard, upon the Mount of Transfiguration, saying, "This is My *beloved Son,* in whom I am well pleased; hear ye Him" (Mat. 17:5). The Son, too, affirmed the Father's love for Himself—"Therefore doth My Father *love me,* because I lay down My life, that I might take it again" (Jno. 10:17). And when the Son had finished the Work given Him to do, when He had laid down His life and had risen again from the dead, the Father displayed His love by removing Him from the scenes of His sufferings and shame, "Wherefore God also hath highly exalted Him, and given Him a name which is above every name" (Phil. 2:9). And not only did God highly exalt His blessed Son, but He also seated Him upon *His own* throne (Rev. 3:21), that during these centuries when the Church is being built *Christ might be near to the Father!*

5. *His Relation to his father's Age.* "He was the son of his old age." No line in this picture is without its own meaning—how could it be, when none other than the Spirit

of God drew it! Every word here is profoundly significant. We quote from the words of another: "Old age, translated into spiritual language and applied to God, signifies 'eternity.' Jesus Christ was the Son of God's eternity. From all eternity He was God's Son. He was not derived, He was eternally begotten; He is God of God, very God of very God, equal with, and of the same substance as, the Father." As the opening verse of John's Gospel declares, *"In the beginning* was the Word, and the Word was with God and the Word was God." And again, in His high-priestly prayer the Lord Jesus said, "And now, O Father, glorify thou Me with Thine own self with the glory which I had with Thee *before the world was"* (Jno. 17:5). The Lord Jesus Christ is no creature, He is Creator (Jno. 1:3); He is no mere emanation of Deity, He is the One in whom dwelleth "all the fulness of the Godhead bodily" (Col. 2:9). He is far more than a manifestation of God, He is Himself "God manifest in the flesh" (1 Tim. 3:16). He is not a person who had His beginning in time, but is Eternal in His being; as the true rendering of Micah 5:2 declares, the One who was born in Bethlehem of Judea was none other than He "whose goings forth have been from of old, *from the days of Eternity."* Christ then was, in the language of our type "the Son of (His Father's) old age"—the *eternal* Son of God.

6. *His Coat of Many Colors.* Thus far the interpreting of the type has been simple, but here, we encounter that which is not quite so easy. How gracious of God for providing us with help on this point! We are not left to our own imaginations to *guess* at the meaning of the many colored coat. No; guesswork is not only vain, but altogether needless in regard to God's blessed Word. Scripture is *its own interpreter.* In Judges 5:30, we read, "Have they not sped? have they not divided the prey; to every man a damsel or two; to Sisera a prey of *divers colors,* a prey of divers colors of needlework, of divers colors on both sides, *meet for* the necks of them that take the spoil?" Here we learn that such garments were to be worn as a *mark of distinction.* Again in 2 Samuel 13:18 we read, "And she had a garment of *divers colors* upon her: for with *such* robes were *the King's daughters* that were virgins apparelled." Here again we get the same thought: This was the attire of unmarried princesses; it was a mark of honor, singling out

the wearer as one of noble birth. This, no doubt, was Jacob's object to distinguish Joseph (born of Rachel) from his half brothers (born of the slave-wives).

How appropriate was this as an adumbration of Christ! He, too, was marked off from all His brethren according to the flesh, marked off as one of noble birth, marked off by outward signs of peculiar distinction and honor. It is blessed to behold what care and pains God took to manifest this coat of many colors, in connection with His blessed Son. The "virgin's" Babe was distinguished from all others born by the Angelic Song o'er Bethlehem's plains—none other was ever welcomed thus by the Heavenly hosts! So, too, the "star" that appeared to the wise men gave evidence of the Heavenly Origin of the new-born King. At His baptism we see again the many-colored coat: multitudes presented themselves to John at the river Jordan and were baptized of him; but when the Christ of God came up out of the waters, the Heavens were opened and the Spirit of God descended upon Him in the form of a dove, thus distinguishing Christ from all others! Behold again the coat of many colors in John 12. In John 13 the feet of the disciples (pointing to their walk) are defiled, and need to be washed with water (type of Word); but in the previous chapter (for in all things Christ must have the preëminence) we see the feet of our blessed Lord, not washed with water (for there was no defilement in Him), but *anointed with precious ointment,* the fragrance of which filled the house, telling that the walk of Him (as well as His blessed person) was a sweet smelling savor to the Father. Thus again was Christ distinguished from and elevated above all others. So, too, at the Cross, the distinguishing coat of many colors may be seen. In death, as everywhere, His uniqueness was manifested. He died as none other ever died or could: He "laid down His life." And the uniqueness of His death was divinely attested in the supernatural phenomena that accompanied it: the three hours darkness, the quaking of the earth, and the rending of the veil. The "*many* colors" of the coat also speak to us of Christ's varied glories and infinite perfections.

7. *The Hatred of his Brethren.* "They hated him and could not speak peaceably to him." It was Jacob's love which brought out the heart's enmity of these men. Joseph then, made manifest both his father's love and his breth-

ren's hatred. So when Christ came to the earth He did these two things. He revealed the Father's heart and He exposed man's enmity. And one of two things always followed: either men hated Him for exposing them, or they accepted such exposure and took refuge in the Grace which He revealed. When Christ exposed the hypocrisy of the Pharisees they hated Him; but when He exposed to the woman at the well her sinful life and condition, she welcomed it, and availed herself of God's grace. So it is now: those who hear the truth of God faithfully preached, the lost and guilty condition of the natural man fearlessly proclaimed, either they hate it, and seek to hide behind the filthy rags of their own self-righteousness, or they come out into the light, bow to God's verdict, and casting themselves in the dust before Him as Hell-deserving sinners, believe in the Saviour which the Gospel makes known. In which class are *you* found, dear reader? Are you, like the brethren of Joseph who hated the son of the father's love, "despising and rejecting" Christ? Friend, make no mistake here. You either *love* or you *hate* the Lord Jesus Christ! and it is written, "If any man love not the Lord Jesus Christ *let him be accursed*" (1 Cor. 16:22). O heed now this solemn admonition of God, "Kiss the Son, lest He be angry, and ye perish from the way, when His wrath is kindled but a little. Blessed are all they that *put their trust in Him*" (Ps. 2:12).

Before we turn to consider the special subject of this article we must first notice three or four points in the first eleven verses of Genesis 37 which, through lack of space, we omitted from our last.

"And Joseph dreamed a dream, and he told it his brethren: and they hated him yet the more. And he said unto them, Hear, I pray you, this dream which I have dreamed: For, behold, we were binding sheaves in the field, and, lo, my sheaf arose, and also stood upright; and, behold, your sheaves stood around about, and made obeisance to my sheaf. And his brethren said to him, Shalt thou indeed reign over us? or shalt thou indeed have dominion over us? And they hated him yet the more for his dreams, and for his words. And he dreamed yet another dream, and told it his brethren, and said, Behold, I have dreamed a dream more; and, behold, the sun and the moon and the eleven stars made obeisance to me. And he told it to his father, and to his brethren: and his father rebuked him, and said unto him, What is this dream that thou hast dreamed? Shall I and thy mother and thy brethren indeed come to bow down ourselves to thee to the earth? And his brethren envied him; but his father observed the saying" (verses 5-11). Continuing our numeration we may note:

8. *Joseph is hated because of his Words.* There are two lines which are, perhaps, made more prominent than others in this first typical picture: the *love* of Jacob for his son, and the *hatred* of the brethren. Three times over within the compass of these few verses reference is made to the "hatred" of Joseph's brethren. In verse 4 we read, "they *hated* him, and could not speak peaceably unto him." Again, in verse 5 we are told, "and they *hated him* yet the more." And again in verse 8: "And they *hated him* yet the more for his dreams and for his words." It will be seen from these references there was a twofold occasion for their wicked enmity. First, they hated Joseph's *person,* because of Jacob's special love for him; second, they hated him because of *"his words."* They hated him because of what he *was,* and also because of what he *said.* Thus it was, too, with the One whom Joseph typified.

As we turn to the four Gospels it will be found that those who were our Lord's brethren according to the flesh *hated Him* in this same twofold way. They hated Him because He was the beloved Son of the Father, and they also hated Him because of His teaching. As illustrations of the former we may note the following passages: "Therefore the Jews sought the more to kill Him, because He not only had broken the Sabbath, but said also that God was His Father, making Himself equal with God" (Jno. 5:18). "The Jews then murmured at Him, because He said, I am the Bread which came down from heaven" (Jno. 6:41). "I and My Father are one. *Then* the Jews took up stones again to stone Him" (Jno. 10:30, 31). Such was their wicked hostility against His person. And it was just the same, too, in regard to His *teaching:* "And all they in the synagogue when they *heard* these things, were filled with wrath, and rose up and thrust Him out of the city, and led Him unto the brow of the hill whereon their city was built, that they might cast Him down headlong" (Lu. 4:28, 29). "The world cannot hate you; but *Me* it hateth, *because I testify of it,* that the works thereof are evil" (Jno. 7:7). "But now ye seek to kill Me, a man that hath *told you the truth,* which I have heard of God'' (Jno. 8:40).

9. *Joseph was to enjoy a remarkable future.* These dreams of Joseph intimated that this favored son of Jacob was the subject of high destinies: they were Divine announcements of his future exaltation. There can be little doubt that Jacob and his sons perceived that these dreams were prophetic, otherwise the brethren would have regarded them as ''idle tales,'' instead of being angered by them. Note, too, that ''his father observed the saying'' (verse 11).

So, too, of the Antitype. A remarkable future was promised to the One who first appeared in lowliness and shame. Concerning the Child that was to be born unto Israel, the Son given, it was pre-announced: ''The government shall be upon His shoulder: and His name shall be called Wonderful, Counsellor, the mighty God, the everlasting Father, the Prince of Peace. Of the increase of His government and peace there shall be no end" (Isa. 9:6, 7). To his mother the angel declared, ''Behold, thou shalt conceive in thy womb, and bring forth a son, and shalt call His name Jesus. He shall be great, and shall be called the Son of the Highest: and the Lord God shall give unto Him the throne of His father David; and He shall reign over the House of Jacob for ever: and of His kingdom there shall be no end" (Lu. 1:31-33). That Joseph's Antitype was to enjoy a remarkable future was thus intimated beforehand.

10. *Joseph foretold his future Sovereignty.* It is worthy of notice that the two recorded dreams of Joseph contemplated a *double* sovereignty: the first dream concerned ''the field,'' which pointed to *the earthly* dominion of our Lord; but the second dream was occupied with the sun, the moon and the stars, and tells, in type, of *the Heavenly* dominion of Christ, for all power (or authority) has been given to Him in heaven and on earth.

Joseph's announcement of his future exaltation only served to fan the fires of enmity, and gave intensity to his brethren's hatred. And so it was with the Saviour. The more our Lord unfolded the glory of His person, the more He spoke of His future exaltation, the more did the Jews—His brethren according to the flesh—hate Him. The climax of this is to be seen in Matthew 26:64: ''Nevertheless, I say unto you, Hereafter shall ye see the Son of Man sitting on the right hand of power, and coming in the clouds of heaven." Here was the announcement of His future sovereignty, and mark the immediate effects of His words on those that heard Him: "*Then* the high priest rent his clothes, saying, He hath *spoken blasphemy.*"

11. *Joseph was envied by his brethren.* "When his brethren saw that their father loved him more than all his brethren, they hated him" (verse 4). In these words are found the key to what followed. That which was the prime cause of the brethren's hatred was envy: as verse 11 tells us, "And his brethren envied him." They were jealous of the partiality shown by Jacob to their half-brother. This is a sin which has characterized human nature all down the ages: the difference between envy and covetousness is this —we envy *persons,* we covet things.

Here, too the type holds good. Christ was "envied" by those who were His brethren, according to the flesh. This comes out in His parable of the Wicked Husbandman, "Having yet therefore one son, His well-beloved, He sent Him also last unto them, saying, They will reverence My Son. But those husbandmen said among themselves, This is the Heir; come, let us kill Him, and the inheritance shall be ours" (Mk. 12:6, 7). Again, "For this cause the people also met Him, for that they heard that He had done this miracle. The Pharisees *therefore* said among themselves, Perceive ye how *ye* prevail nothing? behold, the world is gone *after Him*" (Jno. 12:18, 19). How that utterance manifested the jealousy of their hearts! But even plainer is the testimony of Matthew 27:17, 18, for there the very word "envy" is found, "Therefore when they were gathered together, Pilate said unto them, Whom will ye that I release unto you? Barabbas, or Jesus which is called Christ? For he knew that *for envy* they had delivered Him." In our next we shall consider, Joseph betrayed by his brethren.

41. JOSEPH BETRAYED BY HIS BRETHREN

Genesis 37

"And his brethren went to feed their father's flock in Shechem. And Israel said unto Joseph, Do not thy brethren feed the flock in Shechem? Come, I will send thee unto them. And he said to him, Here am I" (37:12, 13).

12. *Joseph sent forth by his father.* The verses just quoted above introduce to us the second of these marvelous typical scenes in which Joseph shadows forth the Lord Jesus. Here the brethren of Joseph are seen *away from* their father. Jacob says to his beloved son, "Come, and I will send thee unto them." How this reveals the heart of Jacob to us. He was not indifferent to their welfare. Absent from the father's house as they were, Jacob is concerned for the welfare of these brethren of Joseph. He, therefore, proposes to send his well beloved son on an errand of mercy, seeking their good. And is it not beautiful to mark the *promptness* of Joseph's response! There was no hesitancy, no unwillingness, no proffering of excuses, but a blessed readiness to do his father's will, "Here am I."

One cannot read of what passed here between Jacob and Joseph without seeing that behind the historical narrative we are carried back to a point before time began, into the eternal counsels of the Godhead, and that we are permitted to learn something of what passed between the Father and the Son in the remote past. As the Lord God with Divine omniscience foresaw the fall of man, and the alienation of the race from Himself, out of the marvelous grace of His heart, He proposed that His beloved Son should go forth on a mission of mercy, seeking those who were away from the Father's House. Hence we read so often of the Son being *sent* by the Father, "Herein is love, not that we loved God, but that He loved us, and *sent His Son* to be the propitiation for our sins" (1 Jno. 4:10). And blessed it is to know that the Beloved of the Father came forth on His errand of love, freely, willingly, gladly. Like Joseph, He, too, promptly responded, "Here am I." As it is written of Him in Hebrew 10:7, "Then said I, Lo, I come (in the volume of the book it is written of Me) *to do Thy will,* O God."

13. *Joseph seeks the welfare of his brethren.* "And he said to him, Go, I pray thee, see whether it be well with thy brethren, and well with the flocks, and bring me word again" (37:14). Joseph could not have been ignorant of his brethren's "envy"; he must have known how they "hated" him; and in view of this, one had not been surprised to find him unwilling to depart on such a thankless errand. But with gracious magnanimity and filial fear he stood ready to depart on the proposed mission.

Two things are to be particularly observed here as bringing out the striking accuracy of this type: First, Joseph is sent forth with a definite object before him—to seek his brethren. When we turn to the Gospels we find the correspondence is perfect. When the Beloved of the Father visited this world, His earthly mission was restricted to His brethren according to the flesh. As we read in John 1:11, "He came unto His own, and His own received Him not": His "own" here refers to His own people, the Jews. Again, in Matt. 15:24, it is recorded that the Lord Jesus Himself expressly declared, "I am not sent but unto the lost sheep of the House of Israel." And again, in Rom. 15:8, we are told, "Now I say that Jesus Christ was a Minister of the Circumcision for the truth of God, to confirm the promises made unto the fathers."

In the second place, observe *the character* of Joseph's mission: *said* Jacob, "Go, I pray thee, see whether it be *well* with thy brethren." He was sent not to censure them, but to inquire after their welfare. So, again, it was with the Lord Jesus Christ. As we read in John 3:17, "For God sent not His Son into the world to condemn the world; but that the world through Him might be saved."

14. *Joseph was sent forth from the vale of Hebron:* "So he *sent* him out of the vale of Hebron, and he came to Shechem" (37:14). There is no line in this lovely picture, drawn by the Spirit of God, which is without its own distinctive significance. We quote here from the well chosen words of Mr. C. Knapp: "Hebron means fellowship or communion. The vale suggests quiet peacefulness and rest. It was intended, I believe, to point them forward (and point *us* back) to the fellowship of the Son with the Father in heaven's eternal calm and peace previous to His entrance, at His incarnation, into this scene of sin and toil and sorrow" (A Fruitful Bough).

The peaceful vale of Hebron, then, was the place where Joseph dwelt in happy fellowship with his father; there he was at home, known, loved, understood. But from this he was sent to a place characterized by strife and blood-shedding, unto those who appreciated him not, yea, to those who envied and hated him. Faintly but accurately this tells of the love-passing-knowledge which caused the Lord of Glory to leave His Home above and descend to a hostile realm where they hated Him without a cause.

15. *Joseph came to Shechem* (37:14). The word "Shechem" means "Shoulder," being taken from "the position of the place on the 'saddle' or 'shoulder' of the heights which divide the waters there that flow to the Mediterranean on the west and to the Jordan on the east" (Smith's Bible Dictionary). The meaning of this name conforms strictly to the Antitype. The "shoulder" speaks of burden-bearing and suggests the thought of service and subjection. The moral meaning of the term is Divinely defined for us in this very book of Genesis—"and bowed his shoulder to bear and become a servant unto tribute" (49:15). How striking it is to read, then, that on leaving his father in the vale of Hebron, Joseph came to Shechem. How marvelously this foreshadowed *the place* which the Lord of Glory took! Leaving His peaceful place on high, and coming down to this scene of sin and suffering. He took the *Servant's* place, the place of submission and subjection. As we read in Phil. 2:6, 7, "Who, being in the form of God, thought it not robbery to be equal with God: but made Himself of no reputation, and took upon Him the form *of a servant.*" And again in Gal. 4:4, "When the fulness of time was come, God sent forth His Son, made of a woman, *made under the law.*" Verily, "Shechem" was the place that the Beloved of the Father came to.

Moreover, is it not significant that Shechem has been mentioned before in the Genesis narrative—see 34:25-30—especially when we note what occurred there. Shechem was the place of sin and sorrow, of evil passions and blood-shedding. Little wonder that Jacob was anxious about his sons in *such* a place, and that he sent Joseph to them *there* to inquire after their welfare. And how what we read of in Gen. 34 well depicts in terse but solemn summary the history of this earth. How aptly and how accurately the scene there portrayed exhibited the character of the place into which the Lord Jesus came. The place which He took was that of the Servant; the scene into which He came was one of sin and strife and suffering.

16. *Joseph now became a Wanderer in the field.* "And a certain man found him, and, behold, he was wandering in the field: and the man asked him: saying, What seekest thou? And he said, I seek my brethren: tell me, I pray thee, where they feed their flocks" (37:15, 16). In His interpretation of the Parable of the Tares, the Lord Jesus said, "the field is *the world*" (Matt. 13:38). Like Joseph, the Beloved of the Father became a *Wanderer,* a homeless Stranger in this world. The foxes had holes, and the birds of the air had their nests, but the Son of man had not where to lay his head. What a touching word is that in John's Gospel, "And every man went unto his own house: Jesus went unto the Mount of Olives" (John 7:53; 8:1). Every other man had his own house to which he could go, but the Lord Jesus, the homeless Wanderer here, must retire to the bleak mountain side. O my soul, bow in wonderment before that matchless grace which causes thy Saviour who, though He was rich, yet He for our sakes became poor, that we through His poverty might be rich!

17. *Joseph seeks until he finds his brethren.* "And the man said, They are departed hence; for I heard them say, Let us go to Dothan. And Joseph went after his brethren and found them in Dotham" (37:17). When Joseph arrived at Shechem he found his brethren gone; they were not there. "Now is his chance to return to Hebron if his heart is not wholly in his mission. Here he has given him a good excuse for turning back and giving up the undertaking. But no; he has no thought of turning back, or giving up the work given him of his father to do" (Mr. K.). Thus it was with that blessed One whom Joseph foreshadowed. From start to finish we find Him prompted by unswerving devotion to His Father and unwearied love toward His lost sheep, continuing the painful search until He found them. No seeming failure in His mission, no lack of appreciation in those to whom He ministered, daunted Him. Man might despise and reject Him, those nearest might deem Him "beside Himself"; Peter might cry, "Spare Thyself," yet none of these things turned Him aside from going about His Father's business! A work had been given Him to do, and He would not rest till it was "finished."

"And Joseph went after his brethren." How these words gather up into a brief sentence the whole story recorded in the four Gospels! As the Redeemer went about from place to place, one end only was in view—He was going after His brethren. He enters the synagogue and reads from the prophet Isaiah, and with what object? That His brethren might be reached. He walks by the Sea of Galilee, seeking out those who should walk with Him for a season. He must needs go through Samaria we read; and why? Be cause there were some of His "brethren" in that place. Yes, the Son of man came to seek and to save that which was lost. And, my Christian reader, of what do these words remind *you,* "Joseph *went after* his brethren?" Ah, how patiently and untiringly that One of whom Joseph was but a type "went after" *you!* How many years His unwearied love pursued you; pursued you over the mountains of unbelief and across the precipices of sin! All praise to His marvelous grace.

"And found them in Dothan." Dr. Haldeman tells us that "Dothan" signifies "Law or Custom." "And it was there Jesus found His brethren, dwelling under the bondage of the Law, and slaves to mere religious formalism." Yes, the Law of Jehovah had degenerated into the "customs" of the Pharisees, "Laying aside the commandments of God, ye hold the traditions of men" (Mark 9:8), was our Lord's charge against them.

18. *Joseph conspired against.* "And when they saw him afar off, even before he came near unto them, they conspired against him to slay him" (37:18). The hatred of the brethren found opportunity in the love that sought them. It is striking to notice how that a conspiracy was formed against Joseph "before he drew near unto them." How this reminds us of what happened during the days of our Saviour's infancy. No sooner was He born into this world than the enmity of the carnal mind against God displayed itself! A horrible "conspiracy" was hatched by Herod in the attempt to slay the newly born Saviour. This was in the days when He was "afar off." Thirty years before He presented Himself publicly to the Jews. The same thing is found again and again during the days of His public ministry. "Then the Pharisees went out and held a council again Him, how they might destroy Him" (Matt. 12:14), may be cited as a sample.

19. *Joseph's words disbelieved.* "And they said one to another, Behold this dreamer cometh. Come now, therefore, and let us slay him, and cast him into some pit, and we will say, Some evil beast hath devoured him; and we shall see what will become of his dreams" (37:19, 20). The prophetic announcement of Joseph seemed unto his brethren as idle tales. They not only hated him, but they refused to believe what he had said. Their scepticism comes out plainly in the wicked proposal, "Let us slay him .... and we shall see what will become of his dreams." Thus it was with the Christ of God. After He had been nailed to the cross, "they that passed by reviled Him, wagging their heads, and saying, Thou that destroyed the temple and buildest it in three days, save Thyself. *If* Thou be the Son of God, come down from the cross. Likewise, also the chief priests mocking Him, with the scribes and elders, said, He saved others; Himself He cannot save. *If* He be the King of Israel, let Him now come down from the cross, *And we will* believe Him"—which was an admission that they *did not* believe. The Jews believed Him not. His teaching was nothing more to them than empty dreams. So, too, after His death and burial. "The chief priests and Pharisees came together unto Pilate, saying, Sir, we remember that that deceiver said, while He was yet alive, After three days I will rise again. Command therefore, that the sepulchre be made sure" (Matt. 27). When the stone was sealed and the watch was set, the sceptical Pharisees were but saying in effect, "We shall see what will become of His dreams."

And is it any different now in modern Christendom? How do men and women today treat the words of the Faithful and True Witness? Do those who listen to the Gospel give credence to what they hear? Do they set to their seal that God is true? Do they *really* believe as true the Lord's own words, "He that believeth not is condemned already" (John 3:18)? Ah, unsaved reader, dost thou believe *that,* that even now the condemnation of a Holy God is resting upon thee? You do not have to wait until the last great day; you do not have to wait until the judgment of the great white throne. No; God's condemnation rest upon thee now. Unspeakably solemn is this. And there is but one way of deliverance. There was but one way of escape for Noah and his family from the flood, and that was to seek refuge in the Ark. And there is but one way of escape from God's condemnation for you, and that is, to flee to Christ, who was Himself condemned in the stead of all who believe on Him. Again: He who was truth incarnate declared, "He that believeth not the Son shall not see life, but the wrath of God abideth on him" (John 3:36). O unsaved friend, if you *really* believed these words of Him who cannot lie you would not delay another moment. You would not dare to procrastinate any longer. Even now, you would cast yourself at His feet, just as you are, as a poor needy and guilty sinner, receiving Him by faith as your own Saviour. Treat not, we beseech you, these words of the Son of God as idle tales, but believe them to the saving of your soul.

20. *Joseph is insulted.* "And it came to pass, when Joseph was come unto his brethren, that they stripped Joseph out of his coat, his coat of many colors that was on him" (37:23). How this brings out the wicked hatred of these men for the one who had come seeking only their welfare. Like beasts of prey they immediately spring upon him. It was not enough to injure him; they must *insult* him too. They put him to an open shame by stripping him of his coat of many colors. And how solemnly this agrees with the Antitype. In a similar manner the Lord of Glory was dealt with. He, too, was insulted, and put to shame: "Then the soldiers of the governor took Jesus into the common hall, and gathered unto Him the whole band of soldiers. And they *stripped* Him" (Matt. 27:27, 28). The same horrible ignominy is witnessed again at the Cross: "Then the soldiers when they had crucified Jesus, *took His garments*" (John 19:23).

21. *Joseph is cast into a pit.* "And they took him, and cast him into a pit; and the pit was empty, there was no water in it" (37:24). We quote now from Dr. Haldeman: "The pit wherein is no water, is another name for Hades, the underworld, the abode of the disembodied dead: of all the dead before the resurrection of Christ. 'The pit wherein is no water' (Zech. 9:11). 'For as Jonah was three days and three nights in the whale's belly, so shall the Son of man be three days and three nights in the *heart* of the earth' (Matt. 12:40). It was here our Lord, as to His Soul, abode between death and resurrection."

22. *Joseph was taken out of the pit, alive, in his body.* "And they lifted up Joseph out of the pit" (37:28). "The actual order of the occurrence is that Joseph was first cast into the pit and then sold; but the moral order of the type is not deranged by the fact; it is in the light of the Antitypical history that we make the type to be verified, as well as to verify it. The lifting out of the pit is one of those Divine anticipations of the resurrection scattered all through the Old Testament from Genesis to Malachi" (Dr. H.).

23. *Joseph's brethren mingle Hypocrisy with their Hatred.* "And they sat down to eat bread. .... And Judah said unto his brethren, What profit is it if we slay our brother and conceal his blood? Come, and let us sell him to the Ishmaelites, and let not our hand be upon him; for he is our brother and our flesh" (37:27). First, notice the opening words of verse 25, "And they *sat down* to eat bread," and this, while Joseph was helpless in the pit! How this reminds us of Matt. 27:35, 36—"And they crucified Him. .... And *sitting down* they watched Him there!"

But mark now this *hypocrisy*: "Come, and let us sell him to the Ishmaelites, and let not *our hand* be upon him." The parallel to this is found in John 18: "Then led they Jesus from Caiaphas unto the hall of judgment; and it was early; and they themselves went not into the judgment hall, *lest they should be defiled*" (verse 28). Such deceptions will men practice upon themselves. And again, how remarkable, in this connection, are the words found in John 18:31: "Then said Pilate unto them, Take ye Him and judge Him according to your law. The Jews therefore said unto him, It is not lawful for us to put any man to death!"

24. *Joseph is sold.* "They drew and lifted up Joseph out of the pit, and sold Joseph to the Ishmaelites" (37:28). Is it not exceedingly striking to note that from among the twelve sons of Jacob *Judah* should be the one to make this horrible bargain, just as from the twelve apostles *Judas* (the Anglecized form of the Greek *equivalent*) was the one to sell the Lord!

25. *Joseph's blood-sprinkled coat is presented to his father.* "And they took Joseph's coat and killed a kid of

the goats, and dipped the coat in the blood; and they sent the coat of many colors, and they brought it to their father." "The anticipation of the type is selfevident. The blood of Jesus Christ as the blood of a scapegoat, a sin offering, was presented to the Father" (Dr. H.). In our next, D. V., we shall consider Joseph in Egypt.

42. JOSEPH IN EGYPT

Genesis 39, 40

Genesis 37 closes with an account of Jacob's sons selling their brother Joseph unto the Midianites, and they, in turn selling him into Egypt. This speaks, in type, of Christ being rejected by Israel, and delivered unto the Gentiles. From the time that the Jewish leaders delivered their Messiah into the hands of Pilate they have, as a nation, had no further dealings with Him; and God, too, has turned from them to the Gentiles. Hence it is that there is an important turn in our type at this stage. Joseph is now seen *in the hands of the Gentiles.* But before we are told what happened to Joseph in Egypt, the Holy Spirit traces for us, in typical outline, the history of the Jews, while the antitypical Joseph is *absent from the land.* This is found in Gen. 38.

It is remarkable that Gen. 38 records the history of *Judah,* for long before the Messiah was rejected *by the Jews,* Israel (the ten tribes) had ceased to have a separate history. Here, then, Judah foreshadows the history of the Jews since their rejection of Christ. "And Judah saw there a daughter of a certain Canaanite, whose name was Shuah; and he took her, and went in to her" (Gen. 38. 2). How striking this is! "Canaanite" signifies "the merchantman," and "Shuah" means "riches." How plainly the meaning of these names give us the leading characteristics of the Jews during the centuries from the Cross! No longer are they the settled husbandmen and quiet shephards as of old; but, instead, travelling merchants. And "riches" has been their great pursuit. Three sons were born to Judah by Shuah, and the "Numerical Bible" suggests as the meaning of their names: "Er"—*enmity;* "Onan"—*iniquity;* "Shelah"—*sprout.* Deeply significant, too, are these names. "Enmity" against Christ is what has marked the Jews all through the centuries of this Christian era. "Iniquity" surely fits this avaricious people, the average merchant of whom is noted for dishonesty, lying and cheating. While "sprout" well describes the feeble life of this nation, so marvellously preserved by God through innumerable trials and persecutions. The chapter terminates with the sordid story of Tamar, the closing portions of which obviously foreshadowing the end-time conditions of the Jews. In the time of her *travail* "twins were in her womb" (38:27). So in the tribulation period there shall be *two* companies in Israel. The first, appropriately named "Pharez," which means "breach," speaking of the majority of the nation who will break completely with God and receive and worship the Antichrist. The second, "Zerah," that had the "scarlet thread" upon his hand (38:30), pointing to the godly remnant who will be saved, as was Rahab of old by the "scarlet cord." But we must turn now to Gen. 39.

Genesis 39 is more than a continuation of what has been before us in Gen. 37, being separated, as it is, from that chapter by what is recorded in 38. Genesis in 39 is really *a new beginning* in the type, taking us back to the Incarnation, and tracing the experiences of the Lord Jesus from another angle. Continuing our enumeration (see previous article), we may observe:

26. *Joseph becomes a Servant.*

"And Joseph was brought down to Egypt; and Potiphar an officer of Pharaoh, captain of the guard, an Egyptian, brought him out of the hands of the Ishmaelites, which had brought him down thither (39:1). What a contrast from being the beloved son in his father's house to the degradation of slavery in Egypt! But this was as nothing compared with the voluntary self-humiliation of the Lord Jesus. He who was in the form of God, and thought it not robbery to be equal with God, made Himself of no reputation, and took upon Him the form of a servant (Phil. 2:6, 7). "Bond-slave" expresses the force of the original better than "servant." It is to this the prophetic language of Psalm 40 refers. There we hear the Lord Jesus saying, "Sacrifice and offering Thou didst not desire; *Mine ears hast Thou digged;* burnt offering and sin offering hast Thou not required. Then said I, lo, I come; in the volume of the book it is written of Me. I delight to do Thy will, O My God." These words carry us back to Exod. 21:5, 6: And if the servant shall plainly say, I love my master, my wife, and my children; I will not go out free. Then his master shall bring him unto the judges; he shall also bring him to the door, or unto the door post; and *his master shall bore his ear through with an awl,* and he shall serve him for ever." The Lord Jesus was the Speaker of that prophecy in Psalm

40, and the fulfiller of this type in Exod. 21. He was the One who took the Servant place, and voluntarily entered into the degradation of slavery. And it is this which Joseph here so strikingly typified.

27. *Joseph was a Prosperous Servant.*

"And the Lord was with Joseph, and *he was a prosperous man,* and he was in the house of his master the Egyptian. And his master saw that the Lord was with him, and that the Lord made all that he did to prosper in his hand" (39:2, 3). Observe, particularly, it is here said, the Lord made all that Joseph did "to *prosper* in his hand." How these words remind us of two prophetic scriptures which speak of the perfect Servant of Jehovah. The first is the opening Psalm, which brings before us the "Blessed Man," the Man who walked not in the counsel of the ungodly, nor stood in the way of sinners, nor sat in the seat of the scornful; the Man whose delight was in the Law of the Lord, and in whose Law He did meditate day and night; the Man of whom God said, "And He shall be like a tree planted by the rivers of water, that bringeth forth His fruit in His Season; His leaf also shall not wither; and whatsoever He doeth shall *prosper*" (Psa. 1:3). Manifestly, this spoke, specifically, of the Lord Jesus, in whom, alone, the terms of the opening verses of this Psalm were fully realized. The second scripture is found in that matchless fifty-third of Isaiah (every sentence of which referred to the Son of God incarnate, and to Him, expressly, as Jehovah's "*Servant,*" see 52:13), we read, "The pleasure of the Lord shall *prosper* in His hand." How marvellously accurate the type! Of Joseph it is recorded, "*The Lord* made all that he did to *prosper in his hand*" (Gen. 39:3). Of Christ it is said, "The pleasure of *the Lord shall prosper in His hand*" (Isa. 53:10).

28. *Joseph's master was well pleased with him.*

"And Joseph found grace in his sight, and he served him: and he made him overseer over his house, and all that he had he put into his hand" (39:4). How could it be otherwise? Joseph was entirely different from any other servant that Potiphar ever had. The fear of God was upon him; the Lord was with him, prospering him; and he served his master faithfully. So it was with the One whom Joseph foreshadowed. The Lord Jesus was entirely different from any other servant God ever had. The fear of the Lord was upon Him (see Isa. 11:2). And so faithfully did He serve God, He could say, "I do *always* those things that please Him" (John 8:29).

29. *Joseph, the servant, was made a blessing to others.*

"And it came to pass from the time that he had made him overseer in his house, and over all that he had, that the Lord blessed the Egyptian's house for Joseph's sake; and the blessing of the Lord was upon all that he had in the house and in the field" (34:5). So, too, the Father entrusted to the Son all the interests of the Godhead—the manifestation of the Divine character, the glorifying of God's name, and the vindication of His throne. And what has been the outcome of the Beloved of the Father taking the Servant place, and assuming and discharging these onerous responsibilities? Has not the Lord "blessed" the antitypical "Egyptian's house," for the sake of that One whom Joseph foreshadowed? Clearly, the "Egyptian's house" symbolized *the world,* and how bountifully has the world been blessed for Christ's sake!

30. *Joseph was a goodly person.*

"And Joseph was a goodly person, and well favored" (39:6). How carefully has the Holy Spirit here guarded the type! We must always distinguish between the person and the place which he occupies. Joseph had entered into the degradation of slavery. He was no longer at his own disposal, but subject to the will of another. He was no longer dwelling in his father's house in Canaan, but instead, was a bond slave in an Egyptian's house. Such was his *position.* But concerning his *person* we are told, "Joseph was a *goodly* person, and well favored." So, too, the Son of God took a lowly place, the place of humiliation and shame, the place of submission and servitude. Yet, how zealously did the Father see to it that the glory of His person was guarded! No sooner was He laid in the manger (the *place* He took), than God sent the angels to announce to the Bethlehem shepherds that the One born (the *person*) was none other than "Christ, the Lord." A little later, the wise men from the East prostrate themselves before the young child in worship. As soon as He comes forth to enter (the place of) His public ministry—serving others, instead of being served—God causes one to go before Him and testify that he was not worthy to stoop down and unloose the shoe-latchet of the (person) of the Lamb of God.

So, too, on the Cross, where, supremely, God's Servant was seen in the place of shame, God caused Him to be owned as "the Son of God" (Matt. 27:54)! Truly, was *He* a "goodly person, and well favored."

31. *Joseph was sorely tempted, yet sinned not.*

"And it came to pass after these things, that his master's wife cast her eyes upon Joseph; and she said, Lie with me. But he refused and said unto his master's wife, Behold, my master wotteth not what is with me in the house, and he hath committed all that he hath to my hand. There is none greater in this house than I; neither hath he kept back anything from me but thee, because thou art his wife; how then can I do this great wickedness, and sin against God? And it came to pass as she spake to Joseph day by day, that he hearkened not unto her, to lie by her, or to be with her. And it came to pass about this time, that Joseph went into the house to do his business; and there was none of the men of the house there within. And she caught him by his garment, saying, Lie with me: and he left his garment in her hand, and fled, and got him out" (39:7-12).

It is surely not without design that the Holy Spirit has placed in juxtaposition the account of the unchastity of Judah in Gen. 38 with the chastity of Joseph here in Gen. 39. And how significant that the *un*-faithfulness of the one is placed *before* the faithfulness of the other! Joseph's temptation foreshadowed the temptation of the Lord Jesus, the last Adam, and His faithfulness in refusing the evil solicitations of Satan, which was in marked contrast from the failure of the first Adam, before Him. The marvellous accuracy of our type may be further seen by observing that Joseph's temptation is here divided into *three* distinct parts (as was that of our Lord), see verses 7, 10, 12. So, again, it should be remarked, that Joseph was tempted not in Canaan, by his brethren, but in Egypt (symbol of the world), by the wife of a captain of Pharaoh's guard. And the temptation suffered by the Lord Jesus emanated, not from His brethren according to the flesh, but from Satan, "the prince of this world."

Beautiful is it to mark how Joseph resisted the repeated temptation—"How then can I do this great wickedness and sin against God?" This is the more striking if we link up this utterance of Joseph's with Psa. 105:19, "The *Word* of the Lord tried him." So it was by the same Word that the

Saviour repulsed the Enemy. But notice here one point in *contrast*: "And he (Joseph) left his garment in her hand, *and fled,* and got him out" (39:12). So, the Apostle Paul, writing to Timothy, enjoined him to "*Flee* youthful lusts" (2 Tim. 2:22). How different with the Perfect One! He said, "Get thee hence, Satan" (Matt. 4:10), and we read, "Then the Devil *leaveth* HIM." In all things *He has the* preëminence.

32. *Joseph was falsely accused.*

"And she laid up his garment by her, until his lord came home. And she spake unto him according to these words, saying, The Hebrew servant, which thou hast brought unto us, came in unto me to mock me. And it came to pass, as I lifted up my voice and cried, that he left his garment with me, and fled out" (39:16-18). There was no ground whatever for a *true* charge to be brought against Joseph, so an *unjust* one was preferred. So it was, too, with Him who was "holy, harmless, undefiled, separate from sinners." His enemies "the chief priests, and elders, and all the council, sought false witness against Jesus, to put Him to death. *But found none.*" Yet, at the last, "came two *false* witnesses" (Matt. 16:59, 60), who bore untruthful testimony against Him.

33. *Joseph attempted no defence.*

"And it came to pass, when his master heard the words of his wife, which she spake unto him, saying, After this manner did thy servant to me: that his wrath was kindled" (39:19), though notice, it does not add, "against Joseph." In Gen. 37, we beheld Joseph's passive submission to the wrong done him by his heartless brethren. So here, when falsely and foully accused by this Egyptian woman, he attempts no self-vindication; not a word of appeal is made; nor is there any murmuring against the cruel injustice done him, as he is cast into prison. There was no recrimination; nothing but a quiet enduring of the wrong. When Joseph was reviled, like the Saviour, he reviled not again. And how all this reminds us of what we read in Isa. 53:7, with its recorded fulfillment in the Gospels, "He was oppressed, and He was afflicted, *yet He opened not His mouth;* He is brought as a lamb to the slaughter, and as a sheep before her shearers is dumb, so He opened not His mouth!"

34. *Joseph was cast into prison.*

"And Joseph's master took him, and put him into the prison, a place where the king's prisoners were bound; and he was there in the prison" (39:20).

"Taking the garment that Joseph had left behind him in his flight, she used it as a proof of his guilt, and first to the servants, and then to her husband. She made out a case against the Hebrew slave. The way she spoke of her husband to the servants (verse 14) shows the true character of the woman, and perhaps also the terms of her married life; while the fact that Potiphar only placed Joseph in prison instead of commanding him to be put to death is another indication of the state of affairs. For appearance' sake Potiphar must take some action, but the precise action taken tells its own tale. He evidently did not credit her story" (Dr. G. Thomas).

Just as Joseph, though completely innocent, was unrighteously cast into prison, so our Lord was unjustly sentenced to death by one who owned repeatedly, "I find no fault in Him." And how striking is the parallel between the acts of Potiphar and Pilate. It is evident that Potiphar did not believe the accusation which his wife brought against Joseph—had he really done so, as has been pointed out, he would have ordered his Hebrew slave put to death. But to save appearances he had Joseph cast into prison. Now mark the close parallel in Pilate. He, too, it is evident, did not believe in the guilt of our Lord or why have been so reluctant to give his consent for Him to be crucified? He, too, knew the character of those who accused the Saviour. But, for the sake of appearances—as an officer of the Roman Empire, against the One who was charged with being a rebel against Cæsar, for political expediency—he passed sentence.

35. *Joseph thus suffered at the hands of the Gentiles.*

Not only was Joseph envied and hated by his own brethren, and sold by them into the hands of the Gentiles, but he was also treated unfairly by the Gentiles too, and unjustly cast into prison. So it was with his Antitype, "The kings of the earth stood up, and the rulers were gathered together against the Lord, and against His Christ. For of a truth against thy holy child Jesus, whom Thou hast anointed, both Herod and Pontius Pilate, *with the Gentiles,* and the people of Israel were gathered together'' (Acts 4: 26, 27).

36. *Joseph, the innocent one, suffered severely.*

In Stephen's speech we find a statement which bears this out. Said he, ''And the patriarchs, moved with envy, sold Joseph into Egypt,'' and then, referring to his experiences after he had become a slave, he adds, ''but God was with him, and delivered him out of *all his afflictions*'' (Acts 7: 9, 10). How much, we wonder, is covered by these words! What indignities, trials and pains, was he called on to suffer? In Psa. 105 there is another word more specific, ''He (God) sent a man before them, even Joseph, who was sold for a servant: *whose feet they hurt with fetters;* he was laid in iron'' (verses 17, 18). How these references remind us of that Blesed One, who was mocked and spat upon, scourged and crowned with thorns, and nailed to the cruel tree!

37. *Joseph won the respect of his jailor.*

''But the Lord was with Joseph, and showed him mercy, and gave him favor in the sight of the keeper of the prison'' (39:21). Is not the antitype of this found in the fact that the Roman centurion, the one who had charge of the Crucifixion of the Saviour, cried, ''Certainly this was a Righteous Man'' (Luke 23:47). Thus did God give His Son favor in the sight of this Roman who corresponded with Joseph's jailor.

38. *Joseph was numbered with transgressors.*

''And it came to pass that after these things, that the butler of the king of Egypt, and his baker had offended their lord the king of Egypt. And Pharaoh was wroth against two of his officers, against the chief of the butlers and against the chief of the bakers. And he put them in ward in the house of the captain of the guard, into the prison, the place where Joseph was bound'' (40:1-3). What a marvellous line is this in our typical picture. Joseph was *not alone* in the place of shame and suffering. Nor was the Lord Jesus as He hung on the heights of Calvary. And just as there were *two* malefactors crucified with Him, so *two* offenders were in the prison with Joseph! But the analogy extends ever further than this.

39. *Joseph was the means of blessing to one, but the pronouncer of judgment on the other.*

His fellow prisoners had each of them a dream, and in interpreting them, Joseph declared that the butler should be delivered from prison, but to the baker he said, "Within three days shall Pharaoh lift up thy head from off thee, *and shall hang thee on a tree,* and the birds shall eat thy flesh from off thee" (40:19). It is not without good reason that the Holy Spirit has seen fit to record the details of these dreams. Connected with the spared one, the butler, we read of "the cup" into which the grapes were pressed (49:10-12), suggesting to us the precious Blood of the Lamb, by which all who believe are delivered. Connected with the one who was not delivered, the baker, were baskets full of bakemeats (40:16, 17), suggesting human labors, the works of man's hands, which are powerless to deliver the sinner, or justify him before God: for all such there is only the "Curse," referred to here by the baker being "hanged on a tree" (cf. Gal. 3:13). So it was at the Cross: the one thief went to Paradise; the other to Perdition.

40. *Joseph evidenced his knowledge of the future.*

In interpreting their dreams, Joseph foretold the future destiny of the butler and the baker. But observe that in doing this he was careful to ascribe the glory to Another, saying, "Do not interpretations belong to God?" (40:8). So the One whom Joseph foreshadowed, again and again, made known what should come to pass in the future, yet did he say, "For I have not spoken of Myself; but the Father which sent Me, He gave Me a commandment, what I should say, and what I should speak" John 12:49).

41. *Joseph's predictions came true.*

"And it came to pass the third day, which was Pharaoh's birthday, that he made a feast unto all his servants; and he lifted up the head of the chief butler and of the chief baker among his servants. And he restored the chief butler unto his butlership again; and he gave the cup into Pharaoh's hand. But he hanged the chief baker: *as Joseph had interpreted to them*" (40:20-22). Just as Joseph had interpreted so it came to pass. So shall it be with every word of the Son of God, Heaven and earth shall pass away, but His words shall not pass away. And O, unsaved reader, just as the solemn announcement of Joseph concerning the baker was actually fulfilled, *so* shall these words of the Lord Jesus be found true—"he that believeth not shall be damned!"

42. *Joseph desired to be Remembered.*

Said Joseph to the butler, "But *think on me* when it shall be well with thee" (40:14). So, in connection with the Supper, the Saviour has said, "This do in remembrance of Me."

As we admire these lovely typical pictures, like the queen of Sheba, there is no more strength left in us, and we can only bow our heads and say, "How precious are Thy thoughts unto me, O God! How great is the sum of them!"

43. JOSEPH'S EXALTATION

Genesis 41

Our present chapter opens by presenting to us the king of Egypt dreaming two dreams, and awaking with his spirit troubled. The court magicians and wise men were summoned, and Pharaoh told them his dreams, but "there was none that could interpret them to Pharaoh." Then it was that the chief butler recalled his experience in prison. He remembers how *he* had a dream, and that a Hebrew slave had interpreted aright its significance. He recounts this now to the king, and Pharaoh sends at once for Joseph, who explains to him the meaning of his own dreams. There are several important truths which here receive a striking exemplification:

First, we are shown that "*The king's heart* is in the hand of *the Lord,* as the rivers of waters. *He* turneth it whithersoever He will" (Prov. 21:1). It was no accident that Pharaoh dreamed as he did, and when he did. God's time had come for Joseph to be delivered from prison and exalted to a position of high honor and responsibility, and these dreams were but the instrument employed by God to accomplish this end. Similarly, He used, long afterwards, the sleeplessness of another king to lead to the deliverance of Mordecai and his fellows. This truth has been expressed so forcefully and ably by C. H. M. in his "Notes on Genesis," we cannot refrain from quoting him:

"The most trivial and the most important, the most likely and the most unlikely circumstances are made to minister to the development of God's purposes. In chapter 39 Satan uses Potiphar's wife, and in chapter 40 he uses Pharaoh's chief butler. The former he used to put Joseph into the dungeon; and the latter he used to keep him there, through his ungrateful negligence; but all in vain. God was behind the scenes. His finger was guiding all the springs of the vast machine of circumstances, and when the due time was come, he brought forth the man of His purpose, and set his feet in a large room. Now, this is ever God's prerogative. *He is above all,* and can use all for the accomplishment of His grand and unsearchable designs. It is sweet to be able thus to trace our Father's hand and counsel in everything. Sweet to know that all sorts of agents are at His sovereign disposal; angels, men and devils—*all are under His omnipotent* hand, and all are made to carry out His purposes" (p. 307: italics are ours). How rarely one finds such faith-strengthening sentiments such as these set forth, plainly, by writers of today!

Second, we are shown in the early part of Genesis 41 how that *the wisdom of this world is foolishness with God.* As it is well known, Egypt stands in Scripture as a figure of this world. In Joseph's time, the land of the Pharaoh's was the center of learning and culture, the proud leader of the ancient civilizations. But the people were idolaters. They knew not God, and only in His light can we see light. Apart from Him, all is darkness, morally and spiritually. So we see it in the chapter before us. The magicians were impotent, the wise men displayed their ignorance, and Pharaoh was made to feel the powerlessness of all human resources and the worthlessness of all human wisdom.

Third, the *man of God* was the only one that had true wisdom and light. How true it is that "the *secret* of the Lord is with them that fear Him!" These dreams of Pharaoh had a prophetic significance: They respected the future of Egypt (typically, the world), and no Gentile, as such, had intelligence in the purpose of God respecting the earth. God was pleased to make known His counsels to a Gentile, as here, *a Jew* had to be called, each time, as interpreter. It was thus with Nebuchadnezzar. The wise men of Chaldea were as helpless as the magicians of Egypt; Daniel, alone, had understanding. So, too, with Belshazzar and all his companions—the aged prophet had to be called in to decipher the message upon the wall. Well would it be if leaders of the world today turned to the inspired writings of the Hebrew prophets of the things which must shortly come to pass.

Fourth: That "all things *work together for good* to them that love God, to them who are the called according to His purpose," is writ large across our lesson. And well for us if we take this to heart. But the trouble is, we grow so impatient under the process, while God is taking the tangled threads of our lives and *making them* "work together for good." We become so occupied with present circumstances that hope is no longer exercised, and the brighter and better future is blotted from our view. Let us bear in mind that Scripture declares, "*Better is the end of a* thing than the beginning thereof" (Ecc. 7:8). Be of good cheer, faint heart; sorrow may endure for a night, but *joy cometh in the morning.* So it was with Joseph. For a season he suffered wrongfully, but at the last God vindicated and rewarded him. Remember Joseph then, troubled reader, and "let patience have her perfect work." But we must turn from these moralizings and consider the typical bearings of our chapter. We continue our previous enumeration.

43. *Joseph, in due time, was delivered from prison.*

Joseph had been rejected by his brethren, and treated unjustly and cruelly by the Egyptians. Through no fault of his own he had been cast into prison. But God did not suffer him to end his days there. The place of shame and suffering was to be exchanged for one of high dignity and glory. The throne was to supplant the dungeon. And now that God's time for this had arrived, nothing could hinder the accomplishment of His purpose. So it was with our blessed Lord. Israel might despise and reject Him, wicked hands might take and crucify Him, the powers of darkness might rage against Him; His lifeless body might be taken down and laid in the tomb, the sepulchre sealed and a watch set, but *"it was not possible* that He should be holden of death" (Acts 2:24). No; on the third day, He rose again in triumph o'er the grave, leaving the cerements of death behind Him. How beautifully this was prefigured in the case of Joseph. "Then Pharaoh sent and called Joseph, and they brought him hastily out of the dungeon; and he shaved himself, *and changed his raiment,* and came in unto Pharaoh" (41:14). Compare John 20:6, 7!

44. *Joseph was delivered from prison by the hand of God.*

It is evident that, apart from Divine intervention, Joseph had been suffered to languish in the dungeon to the end of his days. It was only the coming in of God—Pharaoh's troubled spirit, the failure of the magicians' to interpret his dream, the butler's sudden recollection of the Hebrew interpreter—that brought about his release. Joseph himself recognized this, as is clear from his words to his brethren, at a later date: "And *God* sent me before you to preserve you a posterity in the earth, and to save your lives by a great deliverance. So now it was not you who sent me hither, *but God:* and *He hath made me* a father to Pharaoh, and Lord of all his house, and ruler throughout all the land of Egypt. Haste ye, and go up to my father, and say unto him, Thus saith thy son Joseph, *God hath made me* lord of all Egypt'' (45:7-9). So it was with the Saviour in being delivered from the prison of the tomb: ''Whom *God* hath raised up, having loosed the pains of death'' (Acts 2:24). ''This Jesus *hath God raised up*'' (Acts 2:32). Him *God* raised up the third day, and showed Him openly'' (Acts 10:40).*

45. *Joseph is seen now as the Revealer of secrets.*

Like the butler and baker before him, Pharaoh now recounted to Joseph the dreams which had so troubled his spirit, and which the ''wise men'' were unable to interpret. It is beautiful to mark the modesty of Joseph on this occasion, ''And Joseph answered Pharaoh, saying, It is not in me: *God* shall give Pharaoh an answer of peace" (41:16). So, in a much higher sense, the Lord Jesus said, ''I have given unto them the words which Thou gavest Me'' (Jno. 17:8). And again, ''As the Father hath taught Me, I speak these things" (Jno. 8:28). Once more, ''For I have not spoken of Myself: but the Father which sent Me, He gave Me a commandment, what I should say, and what I should speak'' (Jno. 12:49).

Having listened to the king's dream, Joseph said: ''God hath showed Pharaoh what He is about to do'' (41:25), and then he made known the meaning of the dreams. How close is the parallel between this and what we read of in the opening verse of the Apocalypse! Just as God made known to the Egyptians, *through Joseph,* what *He* was ''about to do,'' so has He now made known to us, *through Jesus Christ,* the things He will shortly do in this world. The parallel is perfect: said Joseph, ''What God is about to do He *showeth* unto Pharaoh'' (41:28), and the Apocalypse, we are told, is ''the revelation of Jesus Christ, which God gave unto Him *to show* unto His servants things which must shortly come to pass.''

46. *Joseph warned of a coming danger, and urged his hearers to make suitable provision to meet it.*

Joseph was no honied-mouthed ''optimist,'' who spake only smooth and pleasant things. He fearlessly told the truth. He shunned not to declare the whole counsel of God.

*There are other Scriptures which show that the Lord Jesus *raised Himself* (John 2:19; 10.17. 18, etc.). But, above, we have quoted those which emphasized the fulfillment of the type.

He declared that, following the season of Divine blessing and privilege, there would come a time of famine, a famine which should consume the land, and be "very grievous." And in view of this, he warned them to make ready and be prepared. So also was Christ the faithful and true Witness. He made known the fact that death does not end all, that there is a life to come. He warned those who trusted in their earthly possessions and who boasted of how they were going to enjoy them, that their souls would be "required" of them, and that at short notice. He lifted the veil which hides the unseen, and gave His hearers a view of the sufferings of the damned in Hell. He spake often of that place where their worm dieth not and the fire is not quenched, and where there is weeping and wailing and gnashing of teeth. He counselled men to make provision against the future. He bade men to prepare for that which lies ahead of all—a face to face meeting with God.

47. *Joseph appeared next as the Wonderful Counsellor.*

Having interpreted to Pharaoh the meaning of his dreams, Joseph then undertook to advise the king as to the wisest course to follow in order to meet the approaching emergency, and provide for the future. There were to be seven years of plenty, which was to be followed by seven years of famine. Joseph, therefore, counselled the king to store up the corn during the time of plenty, against the need which would arise when the season of scarcity should come upon them. Thus did Joseph manifest the wisdom given to him by God, and display his immeasurable superiority over all the wise men of Egypt. Again the analogy is perfect. Christ, too, has been exhibited as "the Wonderful Counsellor," the One sent by God with a message to tell men how to prepare for the future, and make sure their eternal interests. He is the One "in whom are hid all the treasures of wisdom and knowledge" (Col. 2:3).

48. *Joseph's counsel commended itself to Pharaoh and his officers.*

"And the thing was good in the eyes of Pharaoh and in the eyes of all his servants. And Pharaoh said unto his servants, Can we find such a one as this is, a man in whom the Spirit of God is? And Pharaoh said unto Joseph, Forasmuch as God hath showed thee all this, there is none so discreet and wise as thou art" (41:37-39). Pharaoh recognized that the wisdom manifested by this Hebrew slave had its source not in occult magic, but in the Spirit of God. Joseph had spoken with a discretion and wisdom far different from that possessed by the court philosophers, and this was freely owned by the king and his servants. So, too, the words of the Lord Jesus made a profound impression upon those who heard Him. "And it came to pass, when Jesus had ended these sayings, the people were *astonished at His doctrine.* For He taught them as One having authority, and not as the scribes" (Mat. 7:28, 29). "And when He was come into His own country, He taught them in their synagogues, insomuch that *they were astonished,* and said, Whence hath this man *this wisdom?*" (Mat. 13:54). Just as Pharaoh and his servants were struck by the wisdom in Joseph. So here, those who listened to the Lord Jesus marvelled at His wisdom. And just as Pharaoh confessed, "Can we find such a one as this is? . . . there is *none so discreet and wise,*" so the auditors of Christ acknowledged, "Never man spake like this Man" (Jno. 7:46)!

49. *Joseph is duly exalted, and set over all Egypt.*

"And Pharaoh said unto Joseph, Forasmuch as God hath showed thee all this, there is none so discreet and wise as thou art. Thou shalt be over my house, and according unto thy word shall all my people be ruled: only in the throne will I be greater than thou" (41:39, 40). What a blessed change this was: from shame to glory, from the dungeon to the place of rule, from being a slave in fetters to being elevated high above all, Pharaoh alone being excepted. This was a grand reward for his previous fidelity, and a fitting recognition of his worth. And how beautifully this speaks to us of the One whom Joseph foreshadowed! He was here in humiliation and shame, but He is here so no longer. God has highly exalted Him. He is "gone into heaven, and is on the right hand of God; angels and authorities and powers *being made subject unto Him*" (1 Pet. 3:22).

50. *Joseph was seated on the throne of another.*

How marvellously accurate is the type. Joseph was not seated upon his own throne; he was not in the place of rule over his brethren. Though he was placed over Pharaoh's house, and according to his word was all Egypt to be ruled yet, "in the Throne" Pharaoh was greater than Joseph. So we read in Revelation 3:21, that the ascended Christ has said, "to him that overcometh will I grant to sit with Me in My Throne, even as I also overcame, and am set down with My Father in His Throne."

"Today our Lord Jesus Christ shares the throne of the Father as Joseph shared the throne of Pharaoh. As Joseph ruled over Pharaoh's house with his word, so today our Lord Jesus Christ rules over the Father's household, the household of faith, the Church, by and through His Word. And today, while the Lord Jesus Christ is on the throne of His Father, He is not on His own throne. Read the passage just quoted in Revelation again, and it will be seen that our Lord Jesus Christ Himself makes a distinction between His own throne and the Father's throne, and promises reward to the overcomer, not on the Father's throne, but on His own; and we know, according to the promise of the angel made to Mary, and the covenant made to David, and the title He wears as the King of Israel, 'the Son of David, the Son of Abraham,' that His throne is at Jerusalem, 'the city of the great King.' On His Father's throne He sits today as the Rejected Man, the Rejected Jew" (Dr. Haldeman).

51. *Joseph was exalted to the throne because of his personal worth.*

"All this is typical of the present exaltation of Christ Jesus the Lord. He who was once the Crucified is now the Glorified. He whom men once put upon a gibbet, has been placed by God upon His throne. Joseph was given his place of exaltation in Egypt purely on the ground of his personal worth and actual service rendered by him to the country and kingdom of Egypt" (Mr. Knapp). And what a lovely parallel to this we find in Phil. 2—yet as far as our Lord *excelled* Joseph in personal worth and service, so far is His exaltation the higher—"Who, being in the form of God, thought it not robbery to be equal with God: But made Himself of no reputation, and took upon Him the form of a servant, and was made in the likeness of men. And being found in fashion as a man, He humbled Himself, and became obedient unto death, even the death of the cross. *Wherefore* God also hath highly exalted Him" (Phil. 2:6-9).

52. *Joseph was invested with such insignia as became his new position.*

"And Pharaoh took off his ring from his hand, and put it upon Joseph's hand, and arrayed him in vestures of fine linen, and put a gold chain about his neck" (40:42). And thus we read of the Antitype: "Him hath God exalted with His right hand *to be a Prince,* and a Saviour" (Acts 5:31). And again, "But we see Jesus, who was made a little lower than the angels for the suffering of death, *crowned with glory and honor*" (Heb. 2:9). Compare, too, the description of our glorified Lord as given in Revelation 1. There we behold Him, "clothed with a garment down to the foot, and girt about the breasts with a golden girdle" (5:13).

53. *Joseph's authority and glory are publicly owned.*

"And he made him to ride in the second chariot which he had; and they cried before him, Bow the knee; and he made him ruler over all the land of Egypt" (41:43). On the day of Pentecost, Peter said to the Jews who had condemned and crucified the Saviour, "Therefore let all the House of Israel know assuredly, that God hath made that same Jesus, whom ye have crucified, *both Lord and Christ*" (Acts 2:36). And it is the part of wisdom, dear reader, to recognize and own this. *Have you* recognized the exalted dignity of Christ, and by faith seen that the One who died on Calvary's Cross is now seated on the right hand of the Majesty on high? *Have you* submitted to His Lordship, so that you live now only to please Him? *Have you* "bowed the knee" before Him? If not, O, may Divine grace constrain you to do so without further delay, voluntarily and gladly, that you may not be among the great crowd who shall, in the coming Day, be *compelled* to do so; for God has sworn, "that at the Name of Jesus *every knee should bow,* of things in heaven and things in earth and things under the earth" (Phil. 2:10).

54. *Joseph received from Pharaoh a new name.*

"And Pharaoh called Joseph's name Zaphnath-paaneah" (41:45), which signifies, according to its Egyptian meaning, "the Saviour of the world." So, to quote once more from Phil. 2, we read, "Wherefore God also hath highly exalted Him, *and given Him the Name which is above every name . . . Jesus*" (Phil. 2:9, 10). This name He bore while on earth, but at that time it was held as pledge and promise, "Thou shalt call His name Jesus: for He shall save His people from their sins" (Mat. 1:21) said the angel. But He could not "save His people from their sins" until He had borne them in His own body on the tree, until He had risen from the dead, until He returned to heaven and sent forth the Holy Spirit *to apply* the benefits and virtues of His finished work. But when He ascended on high He became Saviour in fact. God exalted Him with His right hand *"to be* a Prince and *a Saviour"* (Acts 5: 31), and therefore did *God* Himself *then* give *to* His beloved Son the Name which is above every name, even the Name of *"Jesus,"* which means *the Saviour;* just as *after* the period of his shame was over, and Joseph had been exalted by Pharaoh, *he, then,* received the name which signifies "the Saviour of the world!"

Reader, have you an interest, a personal one, in the value and saving efficacy of that Name which is above every name? If not, receive Him now as your own Saviour. If by grace, you have, then bow before Him in adoration and praise.

44. JOSEPH THE SAVIOUR OF THE WORLD

Genesis 41

55. *Joseph has a wife given to him.*

"And Pharaoh called Joseph's name Zaphnath-paaneah (the Egyptian meaning of which is 'Saviour of the world'); and he gave him to wife Asenath, the daughter of Poti-pharah priest of On" (40:45). It is with some hesitation and much reluctance that at this point the writer finds himself differing from other students and commentators. Many whom we respect highly have regarded Asenath as here prefiguring the Church. Their principal reason for doing this is because Joseph's wife was a *Gentile.* But while allowing the force of this, we feel that it is more than counterbalanced by another point which makes against it. Believing that *everything* in this inspired narrative has a definite meaning and typical value, and that each verse has been put into its present place by the Holy Spirit, we are confronted with what is, to us, an insuperable difficulty if Asenath prefigures the Church, namely, the fact that in the very next verse which follows the mention of Pharaoh giving a wife to Joseph, we are told, "And Joseph was *thirty years old* when he stood before Pharaoh king of Egypt" (41:46). Had this statement followed immediately after 41:14, which records Joseph being brought out of prison to appear before Pharaoh, and *after* this we had been told Joseph received his wife, we should be obliged to regard Asenath as a type of the Church; but as it is, we believe the typical application must be sought elsewhere, as we shall now proceed to point out.

The Holy Spirit has here (we are assured, with definite design) made mention of Joseph having a wife *before* his "age" is referred to, and *before* his life's work began. That *the age* of Joseph at the time his real work started, pointed to the age of the Lord Jesus when *His* public ministry commenced, is too obvious to admit of dispute. The fact, then, that the Holy Spirit speaks of Joseph's wife *before* the mention of him being thirty years of age, suggests to the writer that the typical significance of Asenath must be sought at some point of time *before* the Lord Jesus entered upon His life's mission. And that, of course, takes us back to Old Testament times. And there, we *do* learn of Jehovah (the Lord Jesus) possessing a "wife," even Israel. From the various Scriptures which bring this out we select two verses from Jeremiah 3. There, God's prophet, when expostulating with His wayward people, said, "Turn, O backsliding children, said the Lord; for I am *married unto you*" (verse 14); "Surely *as a wife* treacherously departeth from her husband, *so* have ye dealt treacherously with Me, O house of Israel, saith the Lord" (verse 20).

But against this it will be objected, How could Asenath, the *Egyptian,* wife of Joseph, typify *Israel,* the wife of Jehovah? Formidable as this objection appears at first sight, it is, nevertheless, capable of easy solution. The difficulty disappears if we go back to the time when Israel first became Jehovah's wife. Upon this point the Scriptures are very explicit. In Ezekiel 16, where the prophet is outlining the sad history of Israel, and where he says, "How weak is thine heart, saith the Lord God, seeing thou doest all these things, the work of an imperious whorish woman; in that thou buildest thine eminent place in the head of every way, and makest thine high place in every street; and hast not been as a harlot, in that thou scornest hire. *But as a wife* that committeth adultery, which taketh strangers instead of her husband;" here, at the outset, the prophet declares, "Thus saith the Lord God unto Jerusalem, Thy birth and thy nativity *is of the land of Canaan;* thy father was an Amorite, and thy mother a Hittite" (Ezek. 16:3). Here, then, we learn the *origin* (the *moral* origin, no doubt) of Israel, and how fittingly did Asenath, the Gentile, prefigure Jehovah's wife at that time! It was not until *after* Israel was redeemed from Egypt's bondage and corruption that they became *separated* from all other nations. If further confirmation be necessary it is found in Jeremiah 2:2, "Go cry in the ears of Jerusalem, thus saith the Lord; I remember thee, the kindness of thy youth, the love of thine espousals, *when* thou wentest after Me in the wilderness, in a land that was not sown." Israel, then, became Jehovah's *in Egypt,* when redeemed by blood, and after by power.

The *issue* from Joseph's marriage appears to us to fit in with the interpretation suggested above much better than with the common application of the type of Asenath to the Church. "Unto Joseph were born two sons" (41:50), and does not this correspond with the history of Israel *after* she became Jehovah's wife? Was not *the issue* of that union the *two kingdoms* in the days of Rehoboam, and does not the meaning of the names of Joseph's two sons well describe the two kingdoms which, ultimately, issued from Israel? "Joseph called the name of the first born Manasseh" (41:51), which signifies "*Forgetting,*" and was it not *that* which, peculiarly, characterized the ten-tribed kingdom! "The name of the second called he Ephraim" (41:52), which means "*Fruitful,*" and such was Judah, from whom the Lord Jesus came!

56. *Joseph's marriage was arranged by Pharaoh.*

How perfectly this agrees with what we read of in Matthew 22:2! "The kingdom of heaven is like unto a certain king, *which made a marriage for* His Son." The fact that Asenath is mentioned *before* we are told that Joseph was thirty years old when he stood before Pharaoh and began his life's work (type of Christ as He began His public ministry), and that the birth and naming of his sons occurred *afterward,* suggests (as is so often the case, both in types and prophecies) that there is here a *double* foreshadowment. This Gentile wife of Joseph points backward, first, to Israel's condition *before* Jehovah separated her from all other peoples and took her unto Himself; and, second, the type seems to point forward to the time when the Lord shall resume His dealings with her, see Jeremiah 31:31-34; Ezekiel 16:62, 63; Hosea 2:19-23; Isaiah 54:5-8*). Then, too, shall the names of Joseph's two sons be found to possess a *double* significance, for God's will "*forget*" Israel's past, and Israel shall then, as never before, be found "*fruitful.*"

57. *Joseph was thirty years old when he began his life's work.*

"And Joseph was thirty years old when he stood before Pharaoh king of Egypt" (41:46). Every line in this wondrous picture has its own beauty and value. There is nothing here without profound significance. The Holy Spirit has a definite design in telling us what was Joseph's age when his public service began. He was thirty years old. How perfectly does type and antitype correspond! In Luke 3:23 we read, "And Jesus Himself began to be about *thirty*

*The spiritual and dispensational condition of Israel at the moment when God shall resume His dealings with His ancient people, is, again, aptly figured by a *Gentile,* for they are termed by Him now, and until then "Lo-ammi" (Hosea 1:9), which means *"Not My people."*

years of age." This was the age of the Lord Jesus when He commenced His public ministry, as it was Joseph's when he began *his* life's work.

58. *Joseph went forth on his mission from Pharaoh's presence.*

"And Joseph was thirty years old when he stood before Pharaoh king of Egypt. And Joseph went out from the presence of Pharaoh" (41:46). In this chapter Pharaoh—as the one who ruled Egypt, who delighted in the excellences of Joseph, who set Joseph over all his house, but who retained the position of supremacy as to the throne—prefigured God the Father. Viewed in this light, how blessed is the typical force of the last-made quotation. It was from Pharaoh's "presence" Joseph began his life's work! How marvellously this corresponds, again, with what we read in Luke 3! The words which immediately precede the mention of the Lord being thirty years old when His public service began, are the well-known utterance of the Father at the time of His baptism, "Thou art My beloved Son; in Thee I am well pleased" (Lu. 3:22). So little is told us about the Saviour before His active ministry began. The years spent at Nazareth, save for that one brief statement which covered the period of His boyhood, are passed over in silence. But as He came up out of the waters of baptism, the Father bore public testimony to the perfect life which His Son had lived here on earth, for, without doubt, the words, "In Thee I am well pleased," not only affirmed the excellency of Christ's person, but witnessed to the Father's approval of the thirty years which His incarnate Son had spent in obscurity. That which we desire to call attention to here is, just as Joseph went forth to his work from Pharaoh's "presence," so the Lord Jesus started out on His public service from the Father's presence, there manifested at the Jordan!

59. *Joseph's service was an active and itinerent one.*

"And Joseph went out from the presence of Pharaoh, and went throughout all the land of Egypt" (41:46). Joseph was no idler. He did not betray Pharaoh's confidence in him, but faithfully discharged his duty. He did not remain in the place of ease and comfort, but "went throughout all the land of Egypt." How well these words remind us of what we read in the Gospels concerning that One whom Joseph foreshadowed. Of Him we read, "And Jesus *went about all Galilee,* teaching in their synagogues, and preaching the gospel of the kingdom, and healing all manner of sickness" (Mat. 4:23). And again, "And Jesus went about *all the cities and villages*" (Mat. 9:35).

60. *Joseph's exaltation was followed by a season of plenty.*

"And in the seven plenteous years the earth brought forth by handfuls. And he gathered up all the food of the seven years, which were in the land of Egypt, and laid up the food in the cities: the food of the field, which was round about every city, laid he up in the same. And Joseph gathered corn as the sand of the sea, very much, until he left numbering; for it was without number" (41:47-49). Concerning the typical meaning of these verses we quote from Mr. Knapp: "These seven years of great abundance picture, if they do not typify, the present dispensation of grace in which it is our happy lot to live. 'Now is the accepted time; behold, now is the day of salvation' (2 Cor. 6:2). There were seven years, not of plenty merely, but of 'great plenty.' And during those years, we read 'the earth brought forth by handfuls.' It was a time of extraordinary abundance. And there was never a day like the one in which we live. Never before the present dispensation did God send His messengers out into all the world to proclaim to every sinner a free and a full salvation through faith in the name of His own exalted Son. There never was a time of such 'abundance,' such 'great plenty,' at any former period of God's dealings with the earth. And it is a remarkable fact, which I have not seen previously noted, that of all the distinct dispensations of time referred to in Scripture, the present is by far the longest. And oh, what a tale of grace this tells! God is indeed 'long suffering to usward, not willing that any should perish.'"

We doubt not that the saved of *this* dispensation are far in excess of any previous one. How few were saved during the centuries which passed from the days of Abel up to the Flood! How few appear to have been saved during the times of the patriarchs! How few among Israel, from the days of Joshua onwards, gave evidence of being born again! How few seem to have been saved during the public ministry of Christ—but a hundred and twenty were found in the upper room waiting for the Holy Spirit. How evident it is, then, that in contrast from all that has preceded, the earth is *now* bringing forth "in abundance"! It is the "*much* fruit" (Jno. 12:24) which our Lord declared should issue from His death.

61. *Joseph's exaltation was also followed by a period of famine.*

"And the seven years of plenteousness, that was in the land of Egypt, were ended. And the seven years of dearth began to come, according as Joseph had said; and the dearth was in all lands; but in all the land of Egypt there was bread" (41:53, 54). Just as the "seven years"—a *complete* period—pointed to the present interval of Grace, during which the great spiritual harvest is being garnered, so the "seven years" of famine (another *complete* period) look onward to that which shall follow the present dispensation. After the going forth of the Gospel of God's grace has accomplished its Divine purpose, and "*the fulness* of the Gentiles be come in" (Rom. 11:25), the Holy Spirit will depart out of the world, and there shall come that season which Scripture denominates "the great tribulation." Many are the passages which refer to that season. It is termed "the time of Jacob's trouble" (Jer. 30:7), for then will be the season of Israel's darkest hour. It was to this Daniel referred when he said, "There shall be a time of trouble, such as never was since there was a nation even to that same time" (Dan. 12:1). Concerning this same period the Lord Jesus spake, when He said, "For in those days shall be affliction, such as was not from the beginning of the creation which God created unto this time, neither shall be. And except that the Lord had shortened those days, no flesh should be saved" (Mk. 13:19, 20). It will be the time when Satan is cast down to the earth, when the Antichrist shall be here in full power, and when the storm of God's judgment shall burst upon the world. Morally and spiritually, it will be a time of "famine," and, like that which typified it in the days of Joseph, it shall be "very grievous" (Gen. 41:31). Moreover, the sphere encompassed by God's sore judgments in that day will be no local one, but just as we are told that the dearth of old was not confined to Egypt, but that "the famine was over the face of all the earth" (41:56), so in Revelation 3:10 we are told, the "Hour of Temptation" comes upon "*all the world,* to try them which dwell upon the earth." It was of this same period that

Amos prophesied, "Behold, the days come, saith the Lord God, that I will send *a famine* in the land, not a famine of bread, nor a thirst for water, but of hearing the words of the Lord. And they shall wander, from sea to sea, and from the north even to the east; they shall run to and fro to seek the Word of the Lord, and shall not find it" (Amos 8:11, 12). At present the world is enjoying the years of plenty, and how little it believes in the coming time of "famine," now so near at hand! Be warned then, dear reader, and "Seek ye the Lord while He may be found, call ye upon Him while He is near" (Isa. 55:6); for, if you are left on earth for the coming Day of Wrath, it shall be said, "*the harvest is past,* the summer is ended, and we are not saved" (Jer. 8:20).

62. *Joseph is now seen dispensing bread to a perishing world.*

"And when all the land of Egypt was famished, the people cried to Pharaoh for bread: and Pharaoh said unto all the Egyptians, Go unto Joseph; what he saith to you, do" (41:55). "It was a wonderful thing that the despised and rejected Jew should be the passport to the favor of Pharaoh; a wonderful thing that the rejected Jew should be exalted into the place of a Saviour for a famine-smitten world; it was a wonderful thing that this rejected Jew should be the *only* Saviour for that starving world. Equally true and wonderful is it today that Jesus the rejected Jew is the passport to the favor of God; that He is 'the Way, the Truth, and the Life,' and that 'no man cometh unto the Father but by Him'; wonderful that this rejected Christ should be exalted into a Saviour for a famine-smitten world; wonderful that this rejected Christ is the *alone* Saviour for a starving world.

"Joseph was sent by his father to his brethren that he might be a blessing unto them, and they refused; then God turned their sin so that while it should remain as a judgment to them, it might become a blessing to others. In sending His Son to fulfill the promises made to the fathers, God would have brought covenant and numberless blessings to Israel; they refused, and God has made use of their blindness and sin to turn salvation to others. He has made the very sin and blindness of the people to be the occasion of grace and mercy to the whole world. 'Through their fall salvation is come unto the Gentiles' (Rom. 11:11)."—Dr. H.

63. *Joseph alone dispensed the Bread of Life.*

It is beautiful to observe here how Pharaoh directed all who cried to him for bread to go unto Joseph: "And when all the land of Egypt was famished, the people cried to Pharaoh for bread: and Pharaoh said unto all the Egyptians: *Go unto Joseph;* what *he* saith to you, do" (41:55). May we not say this was the Gospel for Egypt, the good news that Joseph was the appointed Saviour, the glad tidings that whosoever was hungry might go to Joseph and obtain relief. How perfectly this foreshadowed the present Gospel of God's grace! When a guilty and convicted sinner, with a great hunger in his soul, cries unto God, what is His response? Why, does He not refer all such to the person of His blessed Son! Only in Christ is salvation to be found, for "neither is there salvation in any other: for there is none other Name under heaven, given among men whereby we must be saved" (Acts 4:12). Just as of old Pharaoh said to the Egyptians, "Go unto Joseph: what *he* saith to you, do," so, upon the Mount of Transfiguration the Father said to the disciples of Christ, "This is My beloved Son, in whom I am well pleased; hear ye *him*" (Mat. 17:5), and this is what He is still saying to men.

64. *Joseph became a Saviour to all peoples.*

"And all countries came into Egypt to Joseph for to buy corn; because that the famine was so sore in all lands" (41:57). Joseph was raised up by God to meet a world-wide need. The "dearth" was in "all lands" (41:54). But God, through Joseph, made ample provision to supply the wants of all. There was nothing provincial about the bounties which Joseph dispensed, he readily gave to each alike, no matter whether it was the Egyptians, his own brothers, or strangers from distant lands, all were fed. And how blessed to know this is equally true of the Antitype! God's Saviour for sinners is no provincial one. He is for both Jew and Gentile, rich and poor, educated and illiterate, old and young, men and women—all, alike, may find in Him that which can satisfy their deepest need, the Gospel is for every creature, and its terms are, "*Whosoever believeth* in Him shall not perish, but have everlasting life." And just as peoples from "all countries came to Joseph," so those who will sing the new song in heaven shall proclaim, "Worthy art Thou to take the book, and to open the seals thereof; for Thou wast slain, and didst purchase unto God with Thy blood *men of every tribe,* and tongue, and people and nation" (Rev. 5:9).

65. *Joseph had illimitable resources to meet the need of all.*

"And Joseph gathered corn as the sand of the sea, very much, until he left numbering; for it was without number" (41:49). How abundant was God's provision! He provided with no niggardly hand. There was to be amply sufficient for every one that applied for the alleviation of his need. And how this reminds us of those blessed expressions which we meet with so frequently in the Epistles! There we read of "the riches of His grace" (Eph. 1:7), yea, "the exceeding riches of His grace" (Eph. 2:7). There we read of God being "rich in mercy" (Eph. 2:4), and, again, of His "abundant mercy" (1 Pet. 1:3). There we read of "the unsearchable riches of Christ" (Eph. 3:8), for "in Him dwelleth all the fullness of the Godhead bodily" (Col. 2:9). And again we are told, "The same Lord over all is rich unto all that call upon Him" (Rom. 10:12).

Thank God, the Saviour He has provided for us is possessed of illimitable resources. There is no shortness or strainness in Him. There is *infinite* value in that precious blood which He shed upon the Cross to make an atonement for sin. There is *infinite* pity in His heart toward sinners. There is *infinite* readiness and willingness on His part to receive *all* who will come to Him. There is *infinite* power in His arm to deliver and keep that which is committed unto Him. There is no sinner so depraved that Christ's blood cannot cleanse him. There is no sinner so bound by the fetters of Satan that Christ cannot free him. There is no sinner so weary and despondent that Christ cannot satisfy him. The promise of the Saviour Himself is, "Come unto Me, *all* ye that labor and are heavy laden, and I will give you rest" (Mat. 11:28). O, sin-sick soul, put Him to the test for yourself, and see. Come to Christ just as you are, in all your wretchedness and need, and He will gladly receive you, blot cut all your iniquities, and put a new song into your mouth. May God, in His grace, cause some despondent ones to prove for themselves the infinite sufficiency of His Son.

45. JOSEPH AND HIS BRETHREN DISPENSATIONALLY CONSIDERED

Since we left Gen. 37-38 nothing more has been heard of the family of Jacob. Joseph is the one upon whom the Holy Spirit has concentrated attention. In Gen. 37 we saw how Joseph was sent by his father on an errand of mercy to his brethren, inquiring after their welfare; that Joseph came unto them and they received him not; that, instead, they envied and hated him, and sold him into the hands of the Gentiles. Then, we have followed his career in Egypt, and have seen how that the Egyptians, too, treated him badly, casting him into the place of shame and humiliation. Also, we have seen how God vindicated His faithful servant, bringing him out of prison-house and making him governor of all Egypt. Finally, we have learned how that Joseph's exaltation was followed by a season of plenty, when the earth brought forth abundantly, and how this in turn, was followed by a grievous famine, when Joseph came before us as the dispenser of bread to a perishing humanity. But during all this time *the brethren* of Joseph faded from view, but now, in the time of famine they come to the front again.

All of this is deeply significant, and perfect in its typical application. Joseph foreshadowed the Beloved of the Father, sent to His brethren according to the flesh, seeking their welfare. But they despised and rejected Him. They sold Him, and delivered Him up to the Gentiles. The Gentiles unjustly condemned Him to death, and following the crucifixion, His body was placed in the prison of the tomb. In due time God delivered Him, and exalted Him to His own right hand. Following the ascension, Christ has been presented as the Saviour of the world, the Bread of Life for a perishing humanity. During this dispensation the Jew is set aside: it is out from the Gentiles God is now taking a people for His name. But soon this dispensation shall have run its appointed course and then shall come the tribulation period when, following the removal of the Holy Spirit from the earth, there shall be a grievous time of spiritual famine. It is during this tribulation period that God shall resume His dealings with the Jews—the brethren of Christ according to the flesh. Hence, true to the antitype, Joseph's brethren figure prominently in the closing chapters of Genesis. Continuing our previous enumeration we shall now follow the experiences of the brethren from the time they rejected Joseph.

66. *Joseph's brethren are driven out of their own land.*

In Gen. 37 the sons of Jacob are seen delivering up Joseph into the hands of the Gentiles, and nothing more is heard of them till we come to Gen. 42. And what do we read concerning them there? This: "Now when Jacob saw that there was corn in Egypt, Jacob said unto his sons, Why do ye look one upon another? And he said, Behold, I have heard that there is corn in Egypt: get you down thither, and buy for us from thence; that we may live, and not die. And Joseph's ten brethren went down to buy corn in Egypt. And the sons of Israel came to buy corn among those that came: for the famine was in the land of Canaan" (42:1-3, 5). Canaan was smitten by the scourge of God. It was eaten up by a famine. Jacob and his family were in danger of dying, and the pangs of hunger drove the brethren of Joseph out of their land, and compelled them to journey down to Egypt—symbol of the world. This was a prophecy in action, a prophecy that received its tragic fulfillment two thousand years later. Just as a few years after his brethren had rejected Joseph, they were forced by a famine (sent from God) to leave their land and go down to Egypt, so a few years after the Jews had rejected Christ and delivered Him up to the Gentiles, God's judgment descended upon them, and the Romans drove them from their land, and dispersed them throughout the world.

67. *Joseph was unknown and unrecognized by his brethren.*

"And Joseph was the governor over the land, and he it was that sold to all the people of the land. And Joseph's brethren came, and bowed down themselves before him with their faces to the earth. And Joseph knew his brethren, but they knew not him" (42:6, 8). Joseph had been exalted over all the house of Pharaoh, but Jacob knew it not. All these years he thought that Joseph was dead. And now his family is suffering from the famine, the scourge of

God, and his sons, driven out of Canaan by the pangs of hunger, and going down to Egypt, they know not the one who was now governor of the land. So it has been with Jacob's descendants ever since the time they rejected their Messiah. They received not the love of the truth, and for this cause God has sent them strong delusion that they should believe a lie. They know not that God raised the Lord Jesus: they believe He is dead, and through all the long centuries of the Christian era a veil has been over their hearts, and the beginning of the tribulation period will find them still ignorant of the exaltation and glory of the Lord Jesus Christ.

68. *Joseph, however, saw and knew his brethren.*

"And Joseph saw his brethren, and he knew them" (42:7). Yes, Joseph "saw" his brethren, his eye was upon them, even though they knew him not. So the eye of the Lord Jesus has been upon the Jews all through the long night of their rejection. Hear His words (as Jehovah) through Jeremiah the prophet, "*For mine eyes are upon all their ways:* they are not hid from My face, neither is their iniquity hid from Mine 'Eyes' " (16:17). So, too, through Hosea, He said, "I know Ephraim, and Israel is not hid from Me" (5:3).

69. *Joseph punished his brethren.*

"And Joseph saw his brethren, and he knew them, but made himself strange unto them, and spake roughly unto them........and he put them all together into ward three days" (42:7, 17). We quote here from the impressive words of Dr. Haldeman: "Joseph was the cause of their troubles now. Joseph was punishing them for their past dealing with himself. The secret of all Judah's suffering during the past centuries is to be found in the fact that the rejected Messiah has been dealing 'roughly' with them. He has been punishing them, making use of their wilfulness and the cupidity of the nations, but, all the same, punishing them. 'My God will cast them away, because they do not hearken unto Him: and they shall be wanderers among the nations' (Hosea 9:17). 'For I say unto you, Ye shall not see Me henceforth, till ye shall say, Blessed is He that cometh in the name of the Lord.' (Matt. 23:38, 39) 'That upon you may come all the righteous blood shed upon the earth, from the blood of righteous Abel unto the blood of Zecharias, son of Barachias, whom ye slew between the temple and the altar. Verily I say unto you, All these things shall come upon this generation (nation)' (Matt. 23:35, 36). Nothing can account for the unparalleled suffering of this people, but the judgment and discipline of the Lord."

70. *Joseph made known to them a way of deliverance through Substitution.*

"And he put them all together into ward three days. And Joseph said unto them the third day, this do, and live, for I fear God. If ye be true men, let one of your brethren be bound in the house of your prison; go ye, carry corn for the famine of your houses.... And he took from them Simeon, and bound him before their eyes" (42:17-19, 24). Once more we quote from Dr. Haldeman's splendid article on Joseph:

"On the third day he caused Simeon to be bound in the place of his brethren, and declared that by this means they might all be delivered, in the third day era, that is to say, on the resurrection side of the grave. On the day of Pentecost, the apostle Peter presented our Lord Jesus Christ as the risen one whom God had exalted to be a Prince and a Saviour unto Israel, declaring that if the latter should repent of their evil and sin toward Him whom He had sent to be Messiah and King, He would accept His death as the substitution for the judgment due them; that He would save them and send His Son again to be both Messiah and Saviour."

71. *Joseph made provision for his brethren while they were in a strange land.*

"Then Joseph commanded to fill their sacks with corn, and to restore every man's money into his sack, and to give them provision for the way; and thus did he unto them" (42:25). Although they knew not Joseph, and although he spoke roughly unto his brethren and punished them by casting them into prison, nevertheless, his judgments were tempered with mercy. Joseph would not suffer his brethren to perish by the way. They were here in a strange land, and he ministered unto their need. So it has been throughout this dispensation. Side by side with the fact that the

Jews have been severely punished by God, so that they have suffered as no other nation, has been their miraculous preservation. God has sustained them during all the long centuries that they have been absent from their own land. God has provided for them by the way, as Joseph did for his erring brethren. Thus has God fulfilled His promises of old. "For I am with thee, saith the Lord, to save thee: though I make a full end of all nations whither I have scattered thee, yet will I not make a full end of thee; but I will correct thee in measure, and I will not leave thee altogether unpunished" (Jer. 30:11). And again; "Thus saith the Lord God; although I have cast them far off among the heathen, and although I have scattered them among the countries, yet will I be to them as a little sanctuary in the countries where they shall come" (Ezek. 11:16).

72. *Joseph was made known to his brethren at the second time.*

This was emphasized by Stephen in his parting message to Israel; "And at *the second time* Joseph was made known to his brethren" (Acts 7:13). At their first visit, though Joseph knew his brethren, they knew not him. It was on the occasion of their second visit to Egypt that Joseph revealed himself to them. How marvelously accurate the type! The first time the Lord Jesus was seen by His brethren after the flesh, they knew Him not, but when they see Him the second time He shall be known by them.

It is significant that the Holy Spirit has singled out this highly important point, and has repeated it, again and again, in other types. It was thus with *Moses* and Israel. "And it came to pass in those days, when Moses was grown, that he went out *unto his brethren,* and looked on their burdens; and he spied an Egyptian smiting a Hebrew, one of his brethren. And he looked this way and that way, and when he saw that, there was no man, he slew the Egyptian, and hid him in the sand" (Ex. 2:11, 12). And how did his brethren appreciate his intervention on their behalf? They despised him; they said, "Who made thee a prince and a judge over us" (Ex. 2:14). They said, in effect, as Israel said of Christ, "We will not have this Man to reign over us" (Luke 19:14). But *the second time* (after a long interval, during which Moses was hid from them) that he appeared unto them, they accepted him as their Leader.

It was thus with *Joshua* and Israel. The first time that Joshua appeared before the Nation was as one of the two "spies" who brought to them a favorable report of the land, and counselled his brethren to go up and possess it. But Israel rejected his message (Num. 13). It was not until long after when Joshua came before the people, publicly, for the *second* time, that they accepted him as their Leader, and were conducted by him into their inheritance.

The same principle is illustrated, again, in the history of *David.* David was sent by his father seeking the welfare of *his brethren;* "And Jesse said unto David his son, take now for thy brethren an ephah of this parched corn, and these ten loaves, and run to the camp to thy brethren. And carry these ten cheeses unto the captain of their thousand, and look how thy brethren fare, and take their pledge" (1 Sam. 17:17-18). But when he reached them, they resented his kindness, and their "anger was kindled against David" (See 1 Sam. 17:28), and it was not until years later that they, together with all Israel, owned him as their King.

Each of these was a type of the Lord Jesus. The first time *He* appeared to Israel they received Him not; but at His second advent they shall accept Him as their Leader and King.

73. *Joseph's brethren confess their Guilt in the sight of God.*

"And Judah said, What shall we say unto my lord? What shall we speak? or how shall we clear ourselves? *God hath found out the iniquity of thy servants"* (44:16). There are several striking verses in the prophets which throw light upon the antitypical significance of this point. "And ye shall know that I am the Lord, when I shall bring you into the land of Israel, into the country for the which I lifted up Mine hand to give it to your fathers. And there shall ye remember your ways, and all your doings, wherein ye have been defiled; *and ye shall loathe yourselves* in your own sight for all your evils that ye have committed" (Ezek. 20:42, 43). And again, "I will go and return to My place, till *they acknowledge their offence,* and seek My face; in their affliction they will seek me early" (Hosea 5:15). So it was with Joseph; he did not reveal himself to his brethren until they had acknowledged their "iniquity." And so will Israel have to turn to God in real and deep penitence before He sends His Son back to them (see Acts 3:19, 20).

74. *Joseph's brethren were also, at first, troubled in his presence.*

"And Joseph said unto his brethren, I am Joseph; doth my father yet live? And his brethren could not answer him, for they were *troubled* at his presence" (45:3). How perfectly does antitype correspond with type! When Israel shall first gaze upon their rejected Messiah, we are told, "And they shall look upon Me whom they have pierced, and they shall *mourn* for Him, as one mourneth for his only son, and shall be in bitterness for him as one that is in bitterness for his first born" (Zech. 12:10). As Israel shall learn then the awfulness of their sin in rejecting and crucifying their Messiah, they shall be "troubled" indeed.

75. *Joseph acted toward his brethren in marvelous grace.*

"And Joseph said unto his brethren, Come near to me, I pray you. And they came near, And he said, I am Joseph your brother, whom ye sold into Egypt. Now therefore be not grieved, nor angry with yourselves, that ye sold me hither; for God did send me before you to preserve life...... Moreover he kissed all his brethren, and wept upon them, and after that his brethren talked with him" (45:4, 5, 15). So shall it be when Israel is reconciled to Christ; "In that day there shall be a fountain opened to the house of David and to the inhabitants of Jerusalem for sin and for uncleanness" (Zech. 13:1). Then shall Christ say to Israel, "For a small moment have I forsaken thee, but with great mercies will I gather thee. In a little wrath I hid My face from thee for a moment; but with everlasting kindness will I have mercy on thee, saith the Lord thy Redeemer" (Is. 54:7, 8).

76. *Joseph was revealed as a Man of Compassion.*

"And there stood no man with him, while Joseph made himself known unto his brethren, And he *wept aloud*" (45:1-2). Seven times over we read of Joseph weeping. He wept when he listened to his brethren confessing their guilt (42:24). He wept when he beheld Benjamin (43:30). He wept when he made himself known to his brethren (45:

1-2). He wept when his brethren were reconciled to him (45:15). He wept over his father Jacob (46:29). He wept at the death of his father (50:1). And he wept when, later, his brethren questioned his love for them (50:15-17). How all this reminds us of the tenderheartedness of the Lord Jesus Christ, of whom we read so often, He was "moved with compassion," and twice that He "wept"—once at the graveside of Lazarus, and later over Jerusalem.

77. *Joseph revealed himself to Judah and his brethren, before he was made known to the rest of Jacob's household.*

So, too, we are told in Zech. 12:7, "The Lord also shall save the tents of Judah first."

78. *Joseph then sends for Jacob.*

"In Scripture, Judah stands for Judah and Benjamin considered together. You will note that it is Judah and Benjamin who are made prominent in the revelation of Joseph. Jacob in prophetic language signifies the Ten Tribes. Sending for Jacob and his household, in typical language, is sending for the Ten Tribes of Israel. Precisely as the type brings Judah before the self-disclosed Joseph, and then Jacob is brought into the land in the presence of Joseph, so the scriptures clearly teach us that after the Lord comes to repentant Judah and is received by them at Jerusalem, He will send for the remaining household of Jacob, for the lost and wandering tribes of Israel, to come into the land to own and greet him. 'And they shall bring all your brethren for an offering unto the Lord, out of all nations' (Is. 66:20)"—*Dr. Haldeman.*

79. *Joseph's brethren go forth to proclaim his glory.*

"Haste ye, and go up to my father, and say unto him, thus saith thy son Joseph, God hath made me *lord of all Egypt;* come down unto me, tarry not...... And ye shall tell my father of *all my glory* in Egypt" (45:9, 13). In like manner, after Israel has been reconciled to Christ, they shall go forth to tell of the glories of their King: "And I will send those that escape of them unto the nations, to Tarshish, Pul and Lud, that draw the bow, to Tubal and Javan, to the isles afar off, that have not heard My fame, neither have seen My glory, and they shall *declare My glory* among the Gentiles" (Is. 66:19). And again: "And the remnant of Jacob shall be in the midst of many people as a dew from the Lord, as the showers upon the grass, that tarrieth not for man'' (Micah. 5:7).

80. *Joseph makes ready his chariot and goes forth to meet Jacob.*

''And Joseph made ready his chariot, and went up to meet Jacob his father'' (46:29). Says Dr. Haldeman, ''This is really the epiphany of Joseph. He reveals himself in splendor and Kingliness to his people. He meets Judah in Goshen first and then meets his father, the household of Jacob. This is a representation of the truth as we have already seen it. It is the coming of Christ in His glory to meet Judah first, and then all Israel. Our attention is specially drawn to his appearing to the people in chariots of glory. So of the greater Joseph we read, 'For, behold, the Lord will come with fire, and *with His chariots* like a whirlwind' (Is. 66:15).''

81. *Joseph settles his brethren in a land of their own.*

''And Israel dwelt in the land of Egypt, in the country of Goshen; and they had possessions therein, and grew, and multiplied exceedingly'' (47:27). Goshen was the best part of the land of Egypt (symbol of the world). As Pharaoh had said, ''The land of Egypt is before thee, in *the best of the land* make thy father and brethren to dwell; in the land of Goshen let them dwell'' (47:6). So Palestine, when restored to its pristine beauty and fertility, shall be ''the best land'' in all the earth; and there, in the Millennium, shall Israel have ''possessions'' and ''multiply exceedingly.''

82. *Joseph's brethren prostrate themselves before him as the Representative of God.*

''And his brethren also went and fell before his face; and they said, Behold we be thy servants. And Joseph said unto them, Fear not; for (am) I in the place of God?'' (50:18, 19). The prophetic dream of Joseph is realized. The brethren own Joseph's supremacy, and take the place of servants before him. So in the coming Day, all Israel shall fall down before the Lord Jesus Christ, and say, ''Lo, this is our God; we have waited for Him, and He will save us; this is the Lord; we have waited for Him, we will be glad and rejoice in His salvation'' (Is. 25:9).

We close at the point from which we started. Joseph

signifies "Addition," and Addition is Increase, and "increase" is the very word used by the Holy Spirit to describe the dominant characteristic of the Kingdom of Him whom Joseph so wondrously foreshadowed. "Of the *increase* of His government and peace there shall be no end, upon the throne of David, and upon His Kingdom, to order it and to establish it with judgment and with justice from henceforth even for ever" (Is. 9:7).

46. JOSEPH AND HIS BRETHREN EVANGELICALLY CONSIDERED

We have grouped together again the last nine chapters of Genesis, which treat principally of Joseph and his brethren, and have singled out from them the most prominent and significant of their typical teachings. In our last article, we contemplated the *dispensational* bearings of the type, and this is, no doubt, its primary application. But there is also a secondary one, one which we may term the *evangelical,* and it is this we shall now consider. Joseph here strikingly prefigures Christ as the Saviour of sinners, while his brethren accurately portray the natural condition of the ungodly, and in the experiences through which they passed as their reconciliation with Joseph was finally effected, we have a lovely Gospel representation of the unsaved being brought from death unto life. Continuing our previous enumeration, note.

83. *Joseph's brethren dwelt in a land wherein was no corn.*

They dwelt in Canaan, and we are told, "the famine was in the land of Canaan" (42:5). There was nothing there to sustain them. To continue where they were meant death, therefore did Jacob bid his sons go down to Egypt and buy from there "that we may live, and not die" (42:2). Such is the condition which obtains in the place where the ungodly dwell. Alienated from the life of God, they are living in a world which is smitten with a Spiritual famine, in a world which furnishes no food for the Soul. The experience of every unregenerate person is that of the Prodigal Son—there is nothing for him but the husks which the swine feed upon.

84. *Joseph's brethren wished to pay for what they received.*

"And Joseph's ten brethren went down to *buy* corn in Egypt" (42:3). It is striking to observe the prominence of this feature here. The word "buy" occurs no less than five times in the first ten verses of this chapter. Clearly, they had no other thought of securing the needed food than by *purchasing* it. Such is ever the conception of the natural man. His own mind never rises to the level of receiving a *gift* from God. He supposes that he must earn God's approval, win God's favor, and merit God's acceptance of him. It was thus with Naaman, when he went to the prophet of God, to be healed of his leprosy. This was the Prodigal's conception—"make me as one of thy *hired* servants," that is, as one who *worked* for what he received. So it was here with Joseph's brethren. And so it is still with every natural man.

85. *Joseph's brethren assume a self-righteous attitude as they come before the lord of Egypt.*

When they appeared before Joseph he tested them. He "spoke *roughly* unto them" (42:7). He said, "Ye are spies; to see the nakedness of the land ye are come" (42:9). And what was their response? They answered him, "Nay, my lord, but to buy food are thy servants come. We are all one man's sons; *we* are *true* men; thy servants are no spies" (42:10, 11). It is thus when God begins His work with the sinner. He wounds before He heals, He wounds in order that He *may* heal. By His Spirit He speaks "roughly." He sends forth the arrow of conviction. He speaks that which *condemns* the natural man. And what is the sinner's first response? He resents this "rough" speaking. He repudiates the accusations brought against him. He denies that he is totally depraved and "dead in trespasses and sins." He attempts to vindicate himself. He is self-righteous. He boasts that *he* is a "*true* man"!

86. *Joseph's brethren were cast into prison for three days.*

"And he put them all together into ward three days" (42:17). This was not unjust, nor was it harsh treatment. It was exactly what they deserved. Joseph was putting these men into their proper place, the place of shame and condemnation. It is thus God deals with the lost. The sinner must be made to realize what is his just due. He must be taught that he deserves nothing but punishment. He must be shown that the place of condemnation and shame is where he, by right, belongs. He must be abased before he can be exalted.

87. *Joseph's brethren were now smitten in their Conscience.*

"And they said one to another, We are verily *guilty* concerning our brother, in that we saw the anguish of his soul, when he besought us, and we would not hear; therefore is this *distress* come upon us" (42:21). Notice they said this "one to another," not yet were their consciences active in the presence of *God!* The analogy holds good in the experience of the unregenerate. As God's work goes forward in the soul, conscience becomes active, there is deep "distress," and there is an acknowledgment of sin, but at this stage the awakened and troubled one has not yet come to the point where he will take the place of a *lost* sinner *before God.*

88. *Joseph makes it known that deliverance is by Grace.*

"Then Joseph commanded to fill their sacks with corn, and *to restore every man's money* into his sack, and to give them provision for the way: and thus did he unto them" (42:25). What a lovely touch to the picture is this! The Bread of Life cannot be purchased. It must be accepted as a free gift, if it is received at all. The terms of the Gospel are "*without* money, and *without* price." And how beautifully was this shown forth here, when Joseph, as the type of Christ, orders the money to be restored to those who came to "buy the corn." Clearly, this was a foreshadowing of the blessed truth, "By *grace* are ye saved, through faith; and that not of yourselves: it is the gift of God: not of works, lest any man should boast" (Eph. 2:8, 9).

89. *Joseph's brethren now enjoy a brief respite.*

"And they laded their asses with the corn, and departed thence" (42:26). They had been brought out of prison, the desired corn was obtained, and they were returning home. Their minds were now at rest, and we may well conclude that their recently disturbed consciences were quiet again. But not yet had they been brought into their true rest. Not yet had they been reconciled to Joseph. Only temporary relief had been obtained after all. Deeper exercises lie before them. And how strikingly this prefigures the experiences of the awakened sinner! After the first season of conviction is over, after one has first learned that salvation is by grace and not by works, there generally follows a season of relief, a temporary and false peace is enjoyed, before the sinner is truly and savingly brought into the presence of Christ.

90. *Joseph's brethren soon had their superficial peace disturbed.*

"And as one of them opened his sack to give his ass provender in the inn, he espied his money; for, behold, it was in his sack's mouth. And he said unto his brethren, My money is restored, and lo, it is even in my sack: and *their heart failed them,* and they were afraid, saying one to another, What is this that God hath done unto us?" (42:27, 28). How true to life again! The type is easily interpreted. God will not allow the awakened soul to rest until it rests upon Christ alone. And, so, He causes the experiences of the way to dispel the false peace. What do we read of next? "And the famine was sore in the land. And it came to pass, when they had eaten up the corn which they had brought out of Egypt, their father said unto them, Go again, buy us a little food" (43:1, 2). And again, the analogy is easily traced. The hunger of the Soul becomes more acute in the one with whom the Spirit of God is dealing; the sense of need is deepened; the "famine" conditions of this poor world are felt more keenly. And there is no relief to be obtained until, once more, he comes into the presence of the true Governor of Egypt.

91. *Joseph's brethren continued to manifest a legal spirit.*

"And their father Israel said unto them, If it must be so now, do this; take of the best fruits in the land in your vessels, and carry down the man a present, a little balm, and a little honey, spices and myrrh, nuts and almonds.... And the men took that present, *and they took double money* in their hand, and Benjamin, and rose up, and went down to Egypt, and stood before Joseph" (43:11, 15). How like the soul that has begun to be exercised before God! Uneasy in conscience, and discerning more and more the vanity of the world, the sinner *redoubles his efforts to please God.* He turns over a new leaf and seeks harder than ever to win God's approval. How little these men knew Joseph —what did he, as Governor over all Egypt, want with their presents! And how little, as yet, the newly awakened soul, knows Christ! Joseph said, "These men shall dine with me at noon" (43:16). So, too, *Christ* is the One who has spread the feast. The word of the Gospel is, "Come for all things are now ready" (Luke 14:17). Christ is the *Provider;* the poor sinner is but the receiver.

92. *Joseph's brethren are now made happy again.*

"And they sat before him, the firstborn according to his birthright, and the youngest according to his youth: and the men marvelled one at another. And he took and sent messes unto them from before him: but Benjamin's mess was five times so much as any of theirs. And they drank, *and were merry* with him" (43:33, 34). Ah, what is man! Not yet had sin been told out. Not yet had a right relationship been established. Nevertheless, they could be "merry." A superficial observer would have concluded that all was now well. It reminds us of the stony ground in the parable of the Sower—he "heareth the Word, and anon *with joy* receiveth it; yet *hath he not root in himself*" (Matt. 13:20, 21). It is greatly to be feared that there are many such to-day. God's saving work goes much deeper than producing evanescent emotions.

93. *Joseph is determined to bring his brethren out into the light.*

"And he commanded the steward of his house, saying, Fill the men's sacks with food as much as they can carry, and put every man's money in his sack's mouth. And put my cup in the sack's mouth of the youngest, and his corn money. And he did according to the word that Joseph had spoken" (44:1, 2). There could be no settled or real fellowship between Joseph and his brethren until the wrong had been righted. There could be no communion of heart until full confession of guilt had been made. And this is the goal God has in view. He desires to bring us into fellowship with Himself. But He is *holy,* and sin must be confessed and put away, before we can be reconciled to Him.

94. *Joseph's brethren, at last, take their true place before God.*

They had been in the presence of Joseph, though they knew him not; they had been "merry" before him, and they were now going on their way light-heartedly. Joseph, then, sent his "steward" after them, saying, "Up, follow after the men; and when thou dost overtake them, say unto them, Wherefore have ye rewarded evil for good?"

(44:4). In like manner, the Lord sends His Holy Spirit to follow up His work in the heart of the awakened soul. The "steward" brought back the brethren into the presence of Joseph once more. Thus, too, does the Holy Spirit bring the convicted sinner back into the presence of God. And mark the sequel here: "And Judah said, What shall we say unto my lord? what shall we speak? *or how shall we clear ourselves? GOD hath found out the iniquity of thy servants*" (44:16). How blessed is this! What a change from their earlier attitude before him, when they affirmed they were "*true* men"! Now, they give up all attempt to clear themselves, and take the place of *guilty* ones before Joseph, acknowledging that God had "found out" their "*iniquity.*" This is the goal Joseph has had before him all the way through. And this is the design of the Spirit's work in the sinner. Not till he ceases to vindicate himself, not till he comes out into the light, not till he owns he is *guilty*, and *unable* to "clear himself," can he be blest. Once the sinner acknowledges before God that he is undone, lost, it will not be long till Christ is revealed to him as the One who can fully meet his deep, deep need. So it was with Joseph and his brethren.

95. *Joseph made himself known to his brethren.*

"Then Joseph could not refrain himself before all them that stood by him, and he cried, Cause every man to go out from me. And there stood no man with him, while Joseph made himself known unto his brethren" (45:1). How blessed to note the opening word here—"*Then.*" Now that his brethren had acknowledged their guilt, there was no delay. That which had hindered Joseph from revealing himself sooner was now gone.

Notice, particularly, that as Joseph made himself known unto his brethren he cried, "Cause *every man* to go out from me." Thus it is when Christ reveals Himself to the self-confessed and needy sinner. None must come between the needy soul and the Redeemer. Away, then, ye priests, who pose as mediators. Away, ye ritualists who would interpose your ordinances as conditions of salvation. Away, all ye human interferers, who would get the poor sinner occupied with any but Christ alone. Let "*every man* go out."

96. *Joseph invites his brethren to come near to him.*

"And Joseph said unto his brethren, Come near to me, I pray you. And they came near" (45:4). Unspeakably blessed is this. There is no aloofness here. All distance is done away with. So, too, in marvelous grace, the Saviour bids the poor trembling sinner "Come near" unto Himself. Joseph did more. He proclaimed in their ears a wondrous message; he said, "God hath sent me before you to preserve you a posterity in the earth, and *to save your lives by a great deliverance*" (45:7).

"It is a *great* salvation, mark. It is not the limited, partial, mean salvation that some men would make it out to be—saving only those who help to save themselves, or saving them for a time, and allowing them to lapse and be lost again. Oh no, thank God, it is a salvation worthy of Himself, and such a salvation as only could result from that finished, faultless work of Christ on the Cross. And what but a great salvation could avail for sinners such as we? We are all of us great sinners; our guilt was great, our need was great, and nothing but a great salvation could be of any use to us. I hope you have it, friend. Don't neglect it. 'How shall we escape,' the Spirit asks, 'if we neglect so great salvation?' (Heb. 2:3)" (Mr. Knapp).

97. *Joseph tells his brethren of full provision made for them.*

He said, "And thou shalt dwell in the land of Goshen, and thou shalt be near unto me, thou, and thy children, and thy children's children, and thy flocks, and thy herds, and all that thou hast. And there will I nourish thee; for yet there are five years of famine; lest thou, and thy household, and all that thou hast come to poverty" (45:10, 11). How this tells out, in type, what is in the heart of our blessed Saviour! He desires His redeemed to be near to Himself! He is to be no Stranger to them now. Moreover, He promises to sustain them—"there will I nourish thee" said Joseph, and the promise to all who believe is, "My God shall supply all your need according to His riches in glory by Christ Jesus" (Phil. 4:19).

98. *Joseph gives proof that he is fully reconciled to his brethren.*

"Moreover, he kissed all his brethren, and wept upon them, and after that his brethren talked with him" (45:15).

The "kiss" betokened the fact they were forgiven. It speaks, too, of love. Thus was the Prodigal greeted after he returned from the far country and owned himself as a sinner. Notice, it was Joseph who kissed them, and not the brethren who kissed Joseph. So, also, it was the Father who kissed the Prodigal. God always takes the initiative, at every point. How blessed, too, the words which follow, "and after that his brethren *talked with him.*" Their fears were all gone now. Reconciled to Joseph, they could now enjoy his fellowship and converse with him. So it is with the saved sinner and his Saviour.

99. *Joseph's joy was shared by others.*

"And the fame thereof, was heard in Pharaoh's house, saying, Joseph's brethren are come, and it pleased Pharaoh well, and his servants" (45:16). "This is the Old Testament fifteenth of Luke. Sinners are received and reconciled; the lost is found; it is, as it were, 'life from the dead' with souls. 'And there is joy in the presence of God.' God and the angels, like Pharaoh and his servants, rejoice when sinners are brought to repentance. There is joy all around. Joseph rejoices; his brethren rejoice; Pharaoh rejoices; his servants rejoice" (Mr. Knapp).

100. *Joseph's brethren now go forth seeking others.*

Joseph gave to his brethren an honorable commission. He had said to them, "Haste ye, and go up to my father, and say unto him, Thus saith thy son Joseph, God hath made me lord of all Egypt: come down unto me, tarry not...... And ye shall tell my father of all my glory in Egypt, and of all that ye have seen; and ye shall haste and bring down my father hither" (45:9, 13). So, too, in marvelous grace, the Lord commissions those whom He saves. He bids them go forth seeking others who know Him not. Joseph bade his brethren tell Jacob that he was alive, that God had made him "lord of all Egypt," and they were to tell of his "glory." In like manner, believers are sent forth to tell of a Saviour that is alive for evermore; of a Saviour whom God hath made "both Lord and Christ"; of a Saviour, who has been crowned with "glory and honor." Notice that twice over Joseph bade his brethren to make "haste" in their going forth (vv. 9, 13). So with us: there is to be no tardiness. The King's business "requireth haste." The time is short, and precious souls are perishing all around.

101. *Joseph gives his brethren a word of admonition as they go forth.*

"So he sent his brethren away, and they departed and he said unto them, *See that ye fall not out by the way*" (45:24). And how much *we* need this word of exhortation. The flesh is still in us. The Devil seeks to stir up a spirit of rivalry and jealousy. But says the apostle, "The servant of the Lord must not strive; but be gentle unto all" (2 Tim. 2:24). If each of us were to heed this, there would be no "falling out by the way"!

We leave the reader to trace out for himself the typical application of the sequel. Joseph's brethren were faithful to the commission given them. They did not invent a message of their own as they approached Jacob. They had no need to do so. Joseph had told them what to say; their business was to *repeat* the words of Egypt's "governor." And God owned their message. The end for which it was designed was achieved. Jacob and his household—seventy souls in all—went down to Egypt and were royally received by Joseph. So, too, we do not have to invent our message. We are sent forth to "preach the Word," and as we are faithful to our calling, God will reward us, for He has promised that *His* Word "shall not return unto Him void." Let us be encouraged then by this example of the first Old Testament evangelists, and go forth into a famine-stricken world telling of One who is mighty to save, leaving the measure of our success to the sovereign will of Him who alone giveth the increase. Thus shall we have a share in discharging our honorable commission of giving the Gospel to every creature, thus shall we glorify God, and thus shall we be bringing nearer that glad Day when the One whom Joseph foreshadowed shall return to this earth, and, taking the government upon His shoulder, shall reign in righteousness and peace.

Moody Press, a ministry of the Moody Bible Institute, is designed for education, evangelization and edification. If we may assist you in knowing more about Christ and the Christian life, please write us without obligation to: Moody Press, c/o MLM, Chicago, Illinois 60610.